Introduction to Landscape Design

Introduction to Landscape Design

John L. Motloch

Department of Landscape Architecture
Texas A&M University

 VAN NOSTRAND REINHOLD
New York

To Cindy for her untiring
psychological support and to Pam
for her understanding

Copyright © 1991 by Van Nostrand Reinhold

Library of Congress Catalog Number 90-32585
ISBN 0-442-23688-3

Printed in the United States of America.

Van Nostrand Reinhold
115 Fifth Avenue
New York, New York 10003

Chapman and Hall
2-6 Boundary Row
London SE1 8HN, England

Thomas Nelson Australia
102 Dodds Street
South Melbourne 3205
Victoria, Australia

Nelson Canada
1120 Birchmount Road
Scarborough, Ontario M1K 5G4, Canada

16 15 14 13 12 11 10 9 8 7 6 5 4 3 2

Library of Congress Cataloging-in-Publication Data

Motloch, John.
    Introduction to landscape design / John L. Motloch.
        p.   cm.
    Contents: Includes bibliographical references.
    ISBN 0-442-23688-3
    1. Landscape architecture.   I. Title.
SB472.M68 1990
712—dc20   90-32585
                                                    CIP

Contents

Preface

Man is a singular creature. He has a set of gifts which makes him unique among the animals: so that, unlike them, he is not a figure in the landscape. He is a shaper of the landscape. In body and in mind he is the explorer of nature, the ubiquitous animal, who did not find but has made his home in every continent (Bronowski, 1973).

There is a reawakening in our society. It is a rediscovery of the interactive relationship between people and the environment. I hope that this text will contribute to the reawakening. It is intended for those who are embarking on what will be a lifelong devotion to shaping the landscape. It seeks to help the landscape designer become what Erich Jantsch has referred to as an "appreciative system" which realizes humans as a "unique device for relating to a reality in whose shaping. . . . (he or she) is actively and creatively participating" (Jantsch 1975). As such, it defines design as more than just an artistic endeavor, but rather the synergism of art and science for the creative management of ecological and human systems.

This text consists of three parts. Part 1 presents the concept of landscape with an overview of the forces that must synergize to create and manage landscapes. It introduces the systems that will be explored in the remainder of the text. Chapter 1 enumerates and explores various perceptions of landscape and interpretations of meaning. It develops an appreciation that meaning is not fixed in the landscape, but rather is the synergism of setting with the individual's consciousness. Chapter 2 explores underlying issues that affect landscape perception, developing a context within which to interpret the present landscape condition and to predict the future. It does not present a history of landscape design, but rather introduces recurring paradigms of thought and value systems. Examples from history show the ebb and flow of specific paradigms as drivers of landscape decision-making. Chapter 3 introduces design thinking. It discusses the groundwork laid by our primary and secondary public education systems and the formal landscape design education that occurs in most universities.

Part 2 is an in-depth exploration of the forces, influences, and issues that should be considered as the landscape designer manages, plans, and designs the landscape. Chapter 4 describes the ecological (geological and biological) processes that influence and give meaning to landscape form and that function to interrelate ecological and built form. It establishes interrelationships between force, material, and time. Chapter 5 reviews the material palette of landscape design, including landform, water, plants, construction materials, and technology. It explores the technical issues that must be considered with each material and technology. Chapter 6 explores sensual perception, focusing on visual and spatial perception. Chapter 7 explores the often overlooked temporal aspects of design and the interrelationships of temporal and spatial perception. Chapter 8 explores elements and principles of visual arts as they apply to landscape design. Chapter 9 explores classical notions of euclidean geometry as a mechanism for ordering the landscape, and the tendency of Western cultures to encode and decode meaning through euclidean geometry. It also explores the evolving geometries of nature. Chapter 10 explores movement as a mechanism for interrelating space and time and for temporally organizing spatial experience. It includes perceptual and technical issues and the design implications of pedestrian and automotive circulation. It offers suggestions concerning the design implications of rail, air, and water transportation systems. Chapter 11 explores spatial perception and sense of place and investigates design and spatial development that enrich this sense. Chapter 12 reviews issues relevant to understanding the relationships between buildings and their sites. It presents architecture as poetry and as the integration of systems that are structural and infrastructural.

Part 3 recalls the introductory chapters of the book and the influences to which the landscape designer must respond. It explores design paradigms and develops the case for the redefinition of landscape design as "design for health," including the health of systems that are ecological and human, while embracing both physiological and psychological health. Chapter 13 discusses landscape design in a traditional sense as ecologically and culturally responsive problem-solving. Chapter 14 explores changing cultural and professional paradigms, and changing perceptions of the role and societal value of landscape architecture. It explores new landscape management and design processes that are emerging from these new paradigms. Chapter 15 explores the themes that human health and wellness are dependent on a healthy ecological environment and that ecological health is dependent on development that is sustainable. It explores management and design processes that promote sustainability. Chapter 16 explores the concept of place as introduced in Chapter 11. It develops this concept as the synergism of landscape setting and the individual that perceives that setting. It explores landscape design as the management of placeness for human psychological health.

This text is broad in scope, as any publication presenting an overview of landscape design must be. Presentations of most issues are brief, given the limitations of space and time; and even the more in-depth chapters are little more than overviews. However, the value of this text is in the interrelatedness of its parts to develop an appreciation for design as the creative response to multiple influences. I hope that individual chapters may encourage the reader to explore topical areas more deeply. With this in mind, references and suggested readings are provided at the end of each chapter to assist the reader who wishes to explore these topics in more detail. A glossary of terms follows at the end of the book.

This book is a critical analysis. My intent is not to criticize particular groups but rather to explore the expressions of certain attitudes and perceptions in the designed environment and the inherent opportunities and constraints they impose.

ACKNOWLEDGMENTS

After years of teaching landscape design and being frustrated by the absence of a text appropriate to my teaching approach, I began thinking seriously about putting one together. With the encouragement of Lane L. Marshall, I began in 1986 to organize my readings and class notes into a comprehensive volume. I wish to thank Lane for issuing the challenge to write this text as a manual for introductory landscape architecture students and for assistance in seeing the project to fruition. His valuable suggestions, criticism, and support are greatly appreciated.

I am grateful to Ian L. McHarg and the late Narendra Junega for introducing me to landscape and architecture as process and to design as creative response. Pliny Fisk and Hadley Smith provided insight in systems thinking and challenging thought. I thank Michael Murphy for the years of dialogue concerning sustainable approaches to design and Bruce Hull for asking appropriate questions concerning environmental perception and placemaking. The excellent rendering for the cover was done by Ali A. Chowdrury. Finally, I thank Michael M. McCarthy for the vision to see design, first and foremost, as an issue of health.

Many students at Texas A&M University made important contributions through the years, including John Holloway, Gwen Jordaan, Melinda Jones, and Kevin Conner, who developed many of the sketches and provided feedback, criticism, and proofreading.

I especially thank Abbe Saenz, Rechelle Volek, Laurie Marshall, Carmen Espitia, and Lisa Grimaldo for struggling through the years with my scribbles in the margins and for typing and proofing.

Finally, I thank Harlow C. Landphair for helping me to discover that even a nonverbal thinker prone to mental contortions and verbal gymnastics can write an introductory text.

Introduction

This text begins with a definition of terms, because in many cases conventional terms are used in a nonconventional sense in response to world views that are changing, new perceptions occurring in our culture, and the realization that some historic definitions no longer fit our working ones, or our evolving world views.

LANDSCAPE

In defining the term *landscape,* this text takes a different stance from other recent books, including John Stilgoe's *Common Landscape of America.* These earlier books reserved the term landscape only for those lands modified for permanent human occupation and defined landscape as the "anti-thesis of wilderness." This text acknowledges the historic accuracy of these restrictive definitions and the origin of the term landscape as the German *landschaft,* meaning a small collection of buildings as a human concentration (both physically and in spirit) in a circle of pasture or cultivated space surrounded by wilderness. However, it contends that the anthropomorphic basis of this earlier definition and its segregation of people and nature do not reflect current theories of the interrelated character of reality and the oneness of people and nature, or the current working definitions of the profession of landscape architecture. On the contrary, and in its contemporary sense, landscape is herein used as an inclusive term, embracing both wilderness and urbanness. Wilderness is natural landscape, suburbia is suburban landscape, and the inner city is urban landscape.

DESIGN

Design is the creative process of responding to conditions while concentrating meaning. *Landscape design* is the creation of evocative, meaningful, and sustainable landscapes. The *designed landscape* is a totality that evolves over time in response to a wide range of diverse influences. These formative influences impart order and give form and meaning to the landscape. The character of the built landscape, its form, material, scale, texture, and spirit are responses to these form-giving influences.

To the degree that design resolves these various and often competing forces, it becomes one with context and functions as an integral part of the landscape. To the degree it fails to do so, it creates incongruities, disruptive changes, and other unwanted problems, and impedes ecological relationships and human relationships. Landscape design, therefore, can first be seen as the innovative resolution of ecological, technological, and cultural forces. These forces themselves are constantly changing, however, and any new element introduced by the designer changes the landscape. Good landscape design, therefore, by integrating with changing ecological and human forces, is an integral part of a dynamic evolving cultural landscape.

Integration of designed elements with their contexts does not, as some may claim, stifle creativity. Rather, the creative response to multiple influences, and the generation of locally relevant aesthetics, is perhaps the highest art form and the most complex form of creativity. It results in highly innovative integrations of constantly changing landscapes, technologies, and cultures. It usually precludes universal applications of form, or borrowed forms that may have had relevancy to the ecological, technological, and cultural forces from which they evolved, but that have little relevancy in the context of current influences.

The creation of relevant, meaningful, and dynamically built landscapes that satisfy ecological, technological, and cultural needs and aspirations through appropriate responses to the spirit of a place and the spirit of its people requires the concentrated effort of an informed and sensitive designer. Such knowledge and sensitivity are developed through observations, experimentation, and critical self-evaluation. Therefore, it is imperative that the landscape designer, as shaper of the built landscape, understand the behavior and interrelationship of ecological, technological, and cultural forces.

1

Design paradigms are world views held by the designer. These views affect design decisions and the character of the designed landscape. Various paradigms and their landscape implications are discussed in this text.

LANDSCAPE DESIGN

Landscape design is the conscious process of managing, planning, and physically changing the landscape. It involves the physical management of the landscape and the design of places. *Places* are the mental constructs that occur in the viewer's mind, through the synergism of specific settings, previous experience, and the individual's mental state. Places are discussed in more detail in later chapters, and at length in Chapter 16.

Landscape architecture is a profession whose primary societal role is the synergism of art and science for the management, planning, and design of the entire physical and cultural landscape, including its vestal wilderness and its growing urbanness. This text recognizes that the profession is changing, and develops the case for a redefined societal role for landscape architecture as promoting human as well as ecological health and well-being. In so doing, it develops the case for landscape *sustainability,* that is, the ability of a landscape to be sustained without resource depletion or degradation (Chapter 15). It also speaks for *place-making,* the design of strong positive *placeness* (Chapter 16), which is the ability of a place to evoke strong desirable mental images and to be remembered over extended periods of time.

FORCES

If we are to design meaningful and relevant landscapes, we must first understand the forces that influence form. We must also be sensitive to the meanings that these forces impart. Amos Rapoport, in *House, Form and Culture* (1969), suggested that in preindustrial cultures there are three major considerations or types of forces. These include (1) *physical forces* and conditions such as site, climate, materials, and so on; (2) *cultural perceptions and aspirations* and the world view that provides the philosophical underpinnings of the culture, and that influences basic attitudes concerning the meaning of humankind, human-nature relationships, social interaction, economics, time, and so on; and (3) the *resources and technologies* available to modify conditions so as to realize cultural aspirations. In industrial cultures, and postindustrial ones such as ours, a fourth major force comes into being, the professional *designer* as landscape form-giver.

Together, to varying degrees, these forces give form

to landscape elements and, over extended periods of time, to the ecological and cultural landscape. In fact, these landscapes can be understood as the accumulated litter left behind by these forces. They can also be seen as the base and the context into which future decisions must be integrated. The landscape can therefore be seen as living-history, alive-present, and embryonic-future.

To the degree that decisions evolve holistically with their context, the landscape is a meaningful, relevant, efficient whole. To the degree that they fail to be integrated, the meanings are confused and irrelevant, and the landscape more inefficient.

RESOURCES

The degree to which each of the above forces affects form depends on the intensity of the force and the resources available to address that force. Landscape ecology has shown us that in times of limited resource late-successional ecosystems that maximize their efficiency are most competitive. This is true in the natural and the designed environment. In both cases, as resources become more scarce (limited materials or technology, paucity of energy, or lack of economic resource), systems must become more responsive to context if they are to remain competitive. When resources are scarce, design becomes the integrative response to place, material, technology, and culture, rather than the overt personal expression of the designer. In these situations, strongly regional expressions will usually evolve in response to local physical and cultural characteristics. This was the case in the medieval city. It is also true in vernacular architecture and generally in third world countries today, where the architectural tradition is a rich regional vocabulary finely tuned to context. Conversely, in times of resource plenty, such as the last thirty years in America, the surplus of resource can be used to overcome constraints, and forms can become more expressive of cultural perceptions and personal design theories. This usually results in decreased efficiency and a loss of regional expression. Unfortunately, America's long history of inefficient use of resources has ill prepared us to compete in the present and future condition of resource scarcity and highly degraded environment. Our dilemma is that our historic and current actions are creating a present and future condition in which we will be progressively less competitive.

One might well ask why this is so, and why we are not sensitive to our changing resource base. To understand why, we must consider that systems are self-educating and self-perpetuating. Having spent years designing inefficiency into the system (and having been successful), we are educated to believe that inefficient design is appropriate. However, inefficiency is only a viable alternative as long as there is surplus in the system. Although this surplus vanished long ago, we have continued to perceive it to exist. Therefore, through recent years, we have embarked on a path of irresponsibility concerning human-environment relations. We are feeling the impact of these inappropriate decisions today and will continue to feel it for years to come. During the past decade, and in an effort to respond to economic constraints, we have aggressively set about removing the regulations that were established in the 1970s, which were intended to maintain system carrying capacity and long-term productivity. We have degraded our ecological and human health and well-being. This will inevitably result in decreased productivity. We fiddle while Rome burns and continue to pursue our inappropriate decision-making at the expense of the resource potential of our children and grandchildren.

LOOKING FORWARD

In November of 1980 William A. Behnke, then President of the American Society of Landscape Architects (ASLA), appointed a task force on "Landscape Architecture into the 21st Century," chaired by Lane L. Marshall. As Marshall later stated in *Action by Design* (1983), the task force concluded that "developing countries were running out of their own nonrenewable energy and raw material sources (and that) importation of these materials was fast becoming exorbitantly expensive. Finally the availability of cheap labor was dwindling rapidly in the developing countries."

As our culture realizes the impact of resource scarcity (energy, material, and economic resources), landscape designers, including architects and landscape architects, will be expected to do more with fewer resources. A failure to do so will result in decreased quality of life and a high degree of stress. The designer who can design efficient systems through holistic response to multiple interactive influences will be in demand in the future. With this in mind we will begin by exploring the perspective from which we make landscape decisions.

REFERENCES

Jantsch, Erich. 1975. *Design for Evolution*. New York: Braziller.

Marshall, Lane. 1983. *Action by Design: Facilitating Design Decisions into the 21st Century*. Washington, DC: American Society of Landscape Architects.

Stilgoe, John R. 1982. *Common Landscape of America, 1500–1845*. New Haven: Yale University Press.

Part 1

Concepts and Overview

1

Landscape Meanings

Landscapes are point-in-time expressions of a myriad of influences that are ecological, technological, and cultural. *Settings* are particular locations, designed or nondesigned, that are generated by these influences, and experienced by people. The *individual,* for physiological survival and security, and for psychological enrichment, has developed processes for encoding and decoding *meaning* in settings. The individual ascribes meaning to the perceptual characteristics of the setting *(perceptual meaning),* and also draws associations *(associational meaning)* from these settings by relating them to previous direct and indirect experiences.

The manner in which designed form responds to the specifics of the landscape, its materials, and its processes will affect the meaning conveyed by that landscape. *Holistic* designs will synergize these various influences, serve as dynamic places, function in many different manners, and convey a range of meanings to different users. It was to such design that Christopher Alexander alluded when he wrote "A City Is Not a Tree" (1965). The environmental design in his discussion was an architecture, the individual components of which were integrated into systems that became progressively more interactive through design. Places were designed to be experienced in different ways, by different people at different times. As new elements were added to the system, the whole became richer. The environmental design of which Alexander spoke was the coming together of multiple and often competing influences into synthesized wholes that enriched experience and intensified meaning. The design became part of the place and its activities. In short, it became alive.

METHOD OF STUDY

In *Peasant, Society and Culture* (1956), Robert Redfield draws a distinction between classic and folk culture, that is, the learned and popular tradition. This relationship was said to exist in many disciplines including music, religion, and others. In *House Form and Culture* (1969), Amos Rapoport considers these distinctions as they relate to physical design in the landscape. He defines the grand tradition of architecture to be the creation of monuments "built to impress the populace with the power of the patron, or the peer group of designers and cognoscenti with the cleverness of the designer and good taste of the patron." He defines the folk tradition, on the other hand, to be

> the direct and unselfconscious translation into physical form of a culture, its needs and values, as well as the desires, dreams and passions of a people. It is the world view writ small, the "ideal" environment of a people expressed in buildings and settlements, with no designer, artist, or architect with an axe to grind.

Within the folk tradition, Rapoport distinguishes between primitive and vernacular buildings. Primitive buildings are, simply stated, the buildings produced by societies identified by anthropologists as primitive based on their technological and economic levels. In such primitive societies, according to Redfield, knowledge, limited though it may be, is shared by all. The populace are generalists. In terms of building, the common people have, as a part of their cultural heritage, the knowledge to build their own dwellings.

In the vernacular process, the building is built by trades people, but the building type, form, and materials are known by everyone. It is part of the cultural body of knowledge. In the vernacular tradition, the building type is consistent, that is, it follows the cultural tradition. The individual building, however, is usually a subtle variation on the traditional theme, adjusted to specific conditions such as family size, site, microclimate, and so on.

House, Form, and Culture was a seminal work in the study of the built landscape, because it chose not to study monuments. As Rapoport said,

> The physical environment of man, especially the built environment, has not been, and still is not, controlled by the designer. This environment is the result of vernacular (or folk, or popular) architecture, and it has been largely ignored in architectural history and theory.... In addition, the high style buildings usually must be seen in relation to, and in the context of, the vernacular matrix, and are in fact incomprehensible outside that context, especially as it existed at the time they were designed and built.

The foregoing extract identifies one major deficiency of modern architectural education, that it has often studied past high-styled buildings as form, and tried to learn from these forms, rather than studying the forces that generated high-styled and popular architecture, interpreting form as an expression of these forces and searching for relevant meaning. It has studied architecture as object, not as process.

Rapoport was not alone in his concern for these issues. Others of the period, such as Christian Norberg-Schulz *(Genius Loci: Towards a Phenomenology of Architecture,* 1980), Adolph Rudofsky *(Architecture Without Architects,* 1964), Robert Venturi *(Learning From Las Vegas,* 1964), and Tom Wolfe *(From Bauhaus to Our House,* 1981), were struggling with the lack of relevant meaning in modern, and in the case of the later works, in postmodern architecture. However, the ideas promulgated by these men were not generally embraced by the architectural community. The more widely published designers were not those exploring holistic and cultural meanings, but rather those pursuing design theories, movements, and styles such as modernism (expression of an industrialized culture), postmodernism (visual topological explorations), and the more recent deconstructivism (dismantling conventional mental constructs whereby the populace decodes meaning).

The challenge to address the vernacular (represented by these rebels in design education) has continued to grow in professional acceptance and lay popularity. Its proponents contend that cultural expressions such as the strip development or Disneyland are not inherently bad. On the contrary, they contend that these places accurately portray the values, dreams, and aspirations of major portions of our heterogeneous culture. However, vernacular expressions are often discounted by designers because they clash with classical notions of design and form, as taught in universities (Chapters 2, 3, and 9). Perhaps by recognizing the cultural value of common places, and the meanings that nondesigners ascribe to landscapes, we can use our design knowledge to create locally relevant aesthetics that convey greater cultural meaning to a wider population. This will result in a rich, evocative landscape, which functions as a living, integral part of our culture, and which synergizes designed and nondesigned elements for maximum landscape meaning.

MEANINGS

With a rudimentary understanding of the forces that influence form, and the belief that design should respond to these forces, how does one begin to discover the forces that are in effect at a certain place and time, and to understand the meaning of forms as expressions of these forces? In other words, how do we interpret the landscape? What do we interpret, and how do we make landscape decisions?

In the introduction to *The Interpretation of Ordinary Landscapes* (1979), D. W. Meinig states that "environment sustains us as creatures; landscape displays us as culture"; and "landscape is defined by our vision and interpreted by our minds." Landscapes that are inhabited by humans are records of, and transmit meaning about, the culture. According to Mae Theilgard Watts (Meinig 1979), we can "read that landscape" as we might read a book. Any culture can read its autobiography to discover itself.

The largest portion of the landscape consists of the common elements that Amos Rapoport referred to as the folk tradition. The smaller portion is the preconsciously conceived, professionally designed elements that Rapoport called the "grand tradition." Together, the common and the grand express two sides of "who we are"; our innate self and our overt self. They communicate, as Pierce F. Lewis ("Axioms for Reading the Landscape") said, "our tastes, our values, our aspirations, and even our fears in tangible, visible form" (Meinig). The fact that the vast majority of this landscape is unself-conscious, that we seldom think about it, results in a landscape that more honestly reflects the underlying forces to which it responds.

Landscapes are usually quite difficult to read for two reasons. First, they are confusing, often contradictory, as they evolve in response to competing, often contrasting influences, and forces that change over time. Second, as we discuss in Chapters 3 and 14, we have also been educated to focus on singular and grand issues, not to perceive the gestalt of landscape, and not to explore the messy and uncontrolled world around us.

AXIOMS FOR READING THE LANDSCAPE

To design more responsively in any culture, we can begin by reading that culture's autobiography—its landscape. In so doing, it is helpful to keep in mind Pierce F. Lewis's published "Axioms for Reading the Landscape," which are, as he said, "essential ideas underlying the reading of America's cultural landscape." These axioms, published in *The Interpretation of Ordinary Landscapes* (Meinig), are summarized as follows, with some added comments concerning the implications of the axioms to landscape interpretation, design, and design education.

1. The Axiom of Landscape as Clue to Culture

This axiom asserts that the commonplace elements in the landscape provide insight as to "the kind of people we are." There are several corollaries to this axiom. The corollary of cultural change says that the landscape represents a large investment and that major changes to the landscape only occur in response to major cultural changes. The regional corollary says that if one region looks significantly different from another that the region varies not only ecologically, but culturally as well. The corollary of convergence contends that as landscapes begin to look more similar, that their cultures are in fact converging. The corollary of diffusion says that landscapes will change through imitation, and that the degree of communication affects the rate of diffusion. Finally, the corollary of taste says that different cultures possess different biases as to what they like/dislike, promote/prohibit, and so on.

As we read the cultural landscape, we should keep in mind whether we are looking at an example of the vernacular tradition or the grand one. The first will tell us more about the actual culture and common life; the latter more about the culture's grand aspirations, as viewed through the eyes of the design intelligentsia.

2. The Axiom of Cultural Unity and Landscape Equality

This axiom says that all items in the human landscape convey meaning and that most items convey about the same amount of meaning.

According to this axiom, the vernacular building communicates about as much concerning the culture as does the architectural monument of the grand tradition. In areas dominated by vernacular expressions, the primary communication will be that of the common person. In areas dominated by elements of the grand tradition of design, the main communication will be that of the design intelligencia.

3. The Axiom of Common Things

The lack of scholarly writing about common elements of the landscape is addressed here. However, the corollary is that there exists a wealth of nonacademic literature, such as the writings of Tom Wolfe and Adolph Rudofsky, trade journals, commercial advertisements, travel literature, and books written by persons studying cultural geography, environmental psychology, or landscape meaning.

In terms of landscape design and design education, the bulk of landscape design texts and professional journals communicate the grand tradition of design. To discover the vernacular tradition, and the issues that affect decision-making by people other than the professional designer, we must often search for other sources of information.

4. The Historic Axiom

This axiom addresses the significance of a knowledge of history when reading the landscape. On the one hand, our behavior is conditioned by the past, and understanding past decisions can prevent us from "reinventing the wheel" as we respond to ongoing processes. On the other hand, many artifacts are relics of conditions that have since changed, and a knowledge of history will prevent misinterpreting these as expressions of active forces. A knowledge of history helps us "read" the artifact.

This axiom has two corollaries. The corollary of historic lumpiness asserts that major cultural change occurs in sudden leaps; and that the landscape changes little between these leaps. The mechanical (or technological) corollary asserts that leaps of cultural change are usually associated with changes in technology or communication, and that a knowledge of the level of technology and communication is essential for one to interpret an element, or the entire landscape.

As we apply the historic axiom to reading the landscape, we should keep in mind that we are reading physical elements not as abstract forms, but as expressions of conditions and influences. We should also be aware that we are presently in a period of unprecedented cultural and technological change; accordingly, our landscapes are changing at an unparalleled rate.

5. The Geographic (or Ecologic) Axiom

To understand the meaning of elements of a cultural landscape, we must study these elements in relation to their geographic or locational context. Our interpretation of the elements should be as much a response to their relation to context, as it is to the physical characteristics of the elements themselves.

Today, this axiom seems to be lost to a great number of practitioners of the grand tradition of architecture. It has been replaced with the notion that the designer's "overriding concept" gives meaning to the design. This trend has progressed to the point that a great number of projects that receive professional acclaim are communicated during the design phases as an "uncompromised" expression of the building, on a plane of green grass that recedes to infinity, where it meets a blue sky. However, once constructed, the building is perceived in its context. While the element in the drawing may be the element that is eventually built, the contextual relationships are dramatically different, as are the perception and interpretation of the element and the designed landscape.

6. The Axiom of Environmental Control

According to this axiom, cultural landscapes relate intimately to the physical environment, and an understanding of natural systems is essential if one is to read the cultural landscape accurately. Since any landscape is a point-in-time expression of forces, this axiom implies that an understanding of the ecological forces that have created a region is essential to understanding the meaning of that landscape.

This axiom speaks for a regional attitude toward landscape design, and an appreciation for regionalism in design education. The regionalism being suggested here is not, as is often implied in architecture today, the "reference" to an established or relic tradition by some design detail or "abstracted form," but rather a systemic and integrative response to the multiplicity of forces that interact to create a given landscape. This axiom speaks for regional design traditions that evolve from, and integrate with, regional forces.

7. The Axiom of Landscape Obscurity

While landscapes carry many meanings, they do not convey these messages in a pure and objective manner. Rather, they are somewhat nebulous and schizophrenic. Each statement is subject to many interpretations; and each is communicated in dialogue with a multiplicity of other statements. Discovering appropriate meanings requires that the landscape designer ask the right questions and remain sensitive to the multiplicity of landscape expressions.

The landscape designer should be sensitive to the obscure, dialectic character of the landscape, and the fact that people generally prefer open-ended landscapes (Chapter 16) that carry multiple meanings, and that allow the viewer to complete their message. We should also be aware of the human tendency to reduce complex entities to singular statements, and the reduced landscape meaning and reduced desirability that results from this tendency. We should seek to design open-ended landscapes that communicate multiple meanings as discussed in Christopher Alexander's "A City Is Not a Tree."

With the preceding axioms, one has some basic tools to interpret the landscape. As one makes these interpretations, it is essential to realize, as axiom 7 shows, that the process is not passive. Landscape elements that convey many meanings through obscure expressions are subject to various interpretations. If the landscape is, as Meinig stated, "interpreted by our minds," then the "reader" of the landscape is integral to its meaning. Restated, the same landscape means different things to different people.

LANDSCAPE INTERPRETATIONS

In "The Beholding Eye: Ten Versions of the Same Scene," Meinig (1979) explored "observer bias." He stated that "any landscape is composed not only of what lies before our eyes, but also what lies within our heads." He suggested an exercise where a diverse group of people are taken to a view that includes both city and countryside, and are asked to describe the landscape, and to identify its elements, composition, and meaning. In this seminal article, Meinig then exposed different biases that affect landscape interpretation, by discussing ten different perceptions of the viewed landscape. Meinig's ten versions of the same scene present an excellent overview of the range of landscape interpretations that people are prone to perceive. These ten views are listed below, with comments and a visual image for each viewpoint. These images should not be seen as physical settings that express only this meaning, but rather as the tendency of a viewer to perceive this type of image, often with only the slightest cue from the setting, and in the face of the other stronger cues that encourage the observer to see the landscape from different viewpoints.

1. Landscape as Nature

This view holds nature to be dominant and human beings to be subordinate. This is a nostalgic, romantic

Figure 1-1. Landscape as nature.

view that reached its apex in the Romantic movement of the eighteenth century. Nature is seen as pristine (a wilderness) without the presence of people (Figure 1-1). This is the conservationist's view, which holds the natural landscape to be essential, and to be an entity that should be preserved at all costs, for its own sake. Proponents believe that decisions that leave the landscape in an unmodified pristine state are desired, good, and appropriate decisions. For holders of this view, all human works and all human gestures in the landscape are weak and feeble efforts that dim in comparison to the majesty, power, and magnificence of the natural landscape. The purity, power, and dominance of the natural landscape are the vanguards of this view. Humans are relegated to a secondary, inconsequential position, and considered the negative influence in a natural landscape of perfection.

Proponents of this view are prone to remove people from the scene, or at least to remove any visible human expression. They see the cultural landscape as an imposed, unreal landscape, and as an aberration.

The undisturbed landscape, even though in many cases a relic feature no longer expressive of formative influences, is still considered the real and appropriate one. This view is held even when, in many cases, the natural landscape being envisioned has been physically absent for centuries, and if recreated would not be self-sustaining in the context of present forces. In fact, present forces themselves can be seen in this view as inappropriate.

This viewpoint separates humankind and nature. It tends, in many cases, to be a reactionary stance, and often comes to prominence in periods of landscape degradation, and as a response to wholesale human destruction of the environment. Philosophically, it establishes a confrontational relationship between nature and people, with people as aggressors and despoilers of a legitimate, pure, and pristine natural landscape.

Proponents are often politically active at a grassroots level. They promote legislation that preserves the landscape and limits people's ability to impact the environment. They work actively to create parks and wildlife areas, and to codify ordinances and standards that place constraints on the ability of planners, designers, developers, and others to impact the environment. The environmental impact statement is one of the primary vehicles used by these people to encourage human decisions that will not adversely affect the physical and ecological environment.

Designers who strongly embrace this role perceive their primary societal value to be that of "conserving nature," nurturing and protecting the environment. Many of these landscape design professionals work in public service for city, state, or federal governments. Others work with grass-roots environmental groups, others in environmentally oriented private practice offices. Still others teach in landscape architecture or related academic programs.

2. Landscape as Habitat

In this view, the landscape is a home for humankind. Holders of this viewpoint envision people working with the land, altering it to increase its productivity and redefining it as a resource. This point of reference is best summarized as people domesticating the earth.

By this view nature is the benign provider, and people interact with nature, accept its basic organization, structure, and behavior, and modify nature so as to convert its basic materials into resources that sustain and enhance quality of life. In this view people manipulate the landscape, but are motivated by a desire to harmonize, to steward, to cultivate, and to manage the landscape so as to maintain its bounty (Figure 1-2).

Figure 1-2. Landscape as habitat.

This is the view of the interrelatedness of people and their environment. It reached its zenith in this country after the American Revolution, when people embraced the traditional structure and spatial arrangement of the agrarian landscape. Wilderness and cityscape were judged against this ideal, and were found to be lacking. Landscape as habitat takes its basic cues from the landscape, with human gesture responsive to condition, and development patterns integrating with natural ones. It sees human gestures as physical expressions of ecological roots, modified in a manner that enhances nature's benefit to people. In this view, humankind is one with an environment that is consciously modified for human benefit. Every landscape is therefore both an expression of nature, and that of culture.

According to this paradigm, decisions that function to maximize the human potential are deemed appropriate. Quality of life is seen to be integrally linked to a healthy habitat, and this view promotes the maintenance of a high-quality, healthy environment. Decisions that prove to degrade the environment are soon abandoned, and nature heals its wounds.

Perhaps the most well-known proponent of this viewpoint was Buckminister Fuller (Chapter 3). His "world games" sessions for exploring the carrying capacity of "spaceship earth," and maximizing its ability to sustain cultures, greatly increased our understanding of the world from this viewpoint.

Landscape as habitat is a synergistic view of humans integrating with, and becoming a part of, a managed nature. This view tends to be dominant in vernacular and low-technology third-world cultures that are directly dependent on the land for basic sustenance. These cultures modify the environment to redefine its materials as resources, but in so doing have little ability or desire to change nature in a profound manner. They are involved in a dialectic interchange with the landscape, and realize to use nature, they must obey it. The underlying assumption is that nature is a kind and gentle provider that, if respected and nurtured, will sustain life and provide a healthy, meaningful habitat. People who hold this view see their primary societal role as facilitators, to help nature sustain humankind.

In third-world and low-technology cultures, the perception of landscape as habitat is often a necessity for survival. However, this view has also endured in some first-word, high-technology countries. In both cases, the landscapes evolved by this view have two positive characteristics. First, they tend to be characterized by a high degree of harmony. Human gestures integrate

Figure 1-3. Landscape as artifact.

with ecological expressions, and there is a sense of synergism of people and environment. These environments are highly preferred by a broad range of peoples, and cultural landscapes that have evolved under this paradigm are often seen to have a strong sense of place (Chapter 16). Americans and others travel great distances, often at considerable expense, to visit the quaint hamlet, remote village, or unique neighborhood that has evolved from this world view.

The second benefit of these landscapes is that they tend to be efficient and self-sustaining (Chapter 15). Since human gestures are integrated with ecological ones, natural forces do not set about to destroy these human expressions, but rather reinforce their function (Chapter 4) and facilitate their maintenance.

3. Landscape as Artifact

This is an anthropomorphic view that sees the landscape as an entity created by people (Figure 1-3). The holder of this view sees human gestures everywhere, and perceives the natural landscape as little more than the stage on which the cultural drama is played and recorded.

From this viewpoint, nature no longer exists. The entirety of the landscape is human-created. The soil,

for example, is not seen as a human-modified biologically active medium, but rather as an entity "created" by the complex human activities of clearing, tilling, fertilizing, mulching, planting, irrigating, supplementing, enhancing, and so on. Waterways are not seen as streams that are integral parts of a hydrologic system, but rather as engineered infrastructural conduits. The ultimate expression of this view is "made-land," whereby the coastal marshes of our seaboards have been anthropomorphically filled and re-created as major metropolitan areas (including, for example, most of the land area of Boston, Massachusetts). Another example of this anthropomorphic view is the building itself: a human artifact, complete with a human-created climate and atmosphere.

According to the landscape-as-artifact viewpoint, people have conquered nature and reshaped it to their purposes, and as an expression of self. They no longer need, or desire, to respond to natural patterns, for these patterns are irrelevant in the presence of an all-dominating technology. Human beings can and should re-create a better landscape, free from the constraints of natural patterns. In this view, humankind is ecologically dominant and superior to nature, and is the quintessential form-giver. The landscape is redefined and reordered in the human image. This anthropomorphic order is not an integrative one, but rather an overt individualistic one.

Like the other views, the landscape as artifact is a mental construct that has recurred at various times in history. However, until recently, because of a limiting technology, its expression has been a rather localized phenomenon. In the garden, for example, people could anthropomorphically re-create nature; but this restructuring could not be extended to the global scale. We have recently achieved the ability to apply this view on a much larger scale, thanks to a rapidly escalating technology. With this increased potential to re-create the landscape, we have also come to perceive humans as the technological re-creator of the global condition. This view is driving the engineer to re-shape the landscape physically, and the biotechnologist to redefine life forms and life processes.

The landscape-as-artifact viewpoint addresses the human desire for self-expression. However, when combined with our massive technology, it has had profound environmental ramifications. The application of this technology to the wholesale re-creation of the physical condition, without an appreciation for integrating with natural processes, has resulted in widespread pollution and natural system degradation. This degradation includes groundwater and surface water quality and quantity problems, loss of topsoil and soil productivity, ozone depletion, and an almost infinite number of other environmental problems (Chapter 14). The landscape as artifact is a short-term ego-driven viewpoint. It generally disregards the problems created by its implementation.

4. Landscape as System

This holistic view has the landscape as a system consisting of interdependent subsystems. Elements of the landscape are seen as expressions of, and cues for understanding, underlying processes. This is a relatively new and rapidly expanding and evolving viewpoint. It began as a reaction to a reductive newtonian science, and a propensity to take complex systems apart and to study their pieces, rather than understanding the whole. The landscape as system viewpoint has grown rapidly since the emergence in the 1930s and growing acceptance of the new science of relativity as the preferred view of reality. This new scientific viewpoint is holistic and integrative, and holds meaning to be accrued not primarily from elements, but from the interrelationship of these elements with one another, with their behavior as systems, and with the processes that have created them. Landscape as system also holds that elements holistically express the various systems of which they are part.

In this mindset humans and nature are expressions of a single systemic oneness. The landscape system and its subsystems are the relevant entity to be understood and managed for environmental and human well-being. The health and well-being of the system are considered to be essential to ecological and human health and wellness, and human wellness to be expressive of a healthy environmental system.

From this viewpoint, elements are not things, but integrations of systems. For example, a building is an event within a spatial continuum. It expresses itself as mass from without, and as space from within. It is an integral and integrated part of a spatial system that is experienced over time, as the viewer moves through the landscape. At the same time, the building can be an integral element of an open climatic system (Figure 1-4), with energy freely exchanged with the landscape. In this sense, the building and site can be designed for maximum energy exchange.

The landscape as system holds actions not in isolation, but rather in the context of their primary, secondary, tertiary, and quaternary reactions. Human behavior and design decisions are considered in their internal and external systemic contexts, and decisions are evaluated in terms of their reactions and their implications to the health and productivity of the landscape as system. Implications to various landscape subsystems are also considered. Good landscape decisions are those that promote management of landscape systems and maintain or enhance their carrying capacity, health, and productivity.

This viewpoint's popularity has grown with our increased cultural awareness of the major system breakdowns that have resulted from our recent history of anthropocentric behavior. In contrast to the landscape as artifact view, landscape as system tends to promote cultural landscapes that integrate in form and function with landscape forces. These are highly sustainable landscapes (Chapter 15) that maximize the long-term health and productivity of the physical and cultural landscape.

Designers who hold this viewpoint pursue a "systems management" approach to design: they see landscape design as, first and foremost, the management of systems. They see design response to systems not as a lack of creativity, but rather as the creative response to systemic behavior, and a much more synergistic act than merely expressing one's ego independent of context. People who hold this viewpoint tend to function in various capacities. Many work in private professional firms, as landscape architects or planners. Others work for city, state, or federal governments as resource managers. They promote an understanding of the systems within which design decisions are made, and develop decision-making processes that result in the effective manage-

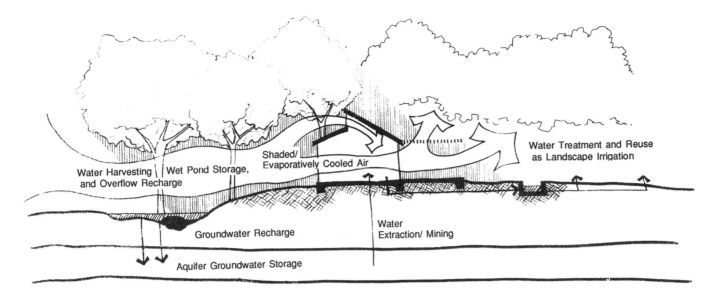

Figure 1-4. Landscape as system.

ment of ecological and human systems. They are active in systems assessment, systems-sensitive planning and design, ecological and human system impact assessment and mitigation, the development of systems-based performance type ordinances and development controls, and other means of integrating the decisions of many people over long periods of time to the effective management of ecological and human systems (Chapter 14). Also, many teach in schools of regional or urban planning and design, landscape architecture, and architecture.

5. Landscape as Problem

In this view the landscape is seen as a situation needing correction. This view tends to be applied to both natural and human-made elements of the landscape. Ozone depletion, polluted air, urban crime, abandoned housing, spoiled beaches, contaminated estuaries, soiled streams, eroded lands, urban blight and sprawl, congestion, and dilapidated buildings are seen as physical evidence of this problematic landscape. In this view a pervasive and ubiquitous presence of ecological, physiological, and psychological illness are the essence of the landscape (Figure 1-5).

This mindset can include an appreciation for the preceding four views, that is, a reverence for nature, an appreciation of landscape as habitat, a sensitivity to landscape as artifact, and a response to landscape as system. However, it differs from the four in its underlying premise that all is in disarray. A compelling case was made for this point of view by Rachel Carson in *Silent Spring* (1982), and more recently in the film *Koyaanisqatsi*, which is a Hopi word that loosely trans-

Figure 1-5. Landscape as problem. (From *Design with Nature*, Ian L. McHarg)

lates to "life out of balance." Like the landscape as system, this is a growing view, owing to the recent, rapid rise in technology, and our exponentially increasing ability to degrade the landscape and thereby change it from a resource to a problem.

Expressions of this view of the world range in intensity from a shrill cry of alarm, to a more optimistic view taken by many landscape designers. These designers take a problem-solving approach (Chapter 13), that every landscape is seen as a design "problem." Sometimes these are severe problems needing immediate correction; at other times they are merely challenges to create a better world. In this later sense, this view shares ground with the landscape as artifact.

This view is promoted by design education that addresses landscape design as problem-solving, including problems that are functional, infrastructural, behavioral, or aesthetic. It renders nonsensical the divergent opinion that "in this case, nothing should be done"! This mindset dominated most schools of architecture and landscape architecture in the 1970s and continues in some today.

From the viewpoint of landscape as problem, the landscape designer sees the task at hand as the application of professional skills, scientific knowledge, and aesthetic sensitivity to the correction of environmental ills. Unlike the landscape-as-artifact view, the landscape-as-problem view does not hold the value of the landscape to be in human expression, but rather in the landscape problems that the expression represents. This view can be a short-term one, focusing on the existing situation as the problem, and paying little attention to the secondary, tertiary, and quaternary problems that may result from human intervention. It can, conversely, focus on long-term problem-solving.

When proponents take a long-term perspective, a landscape-as-problem view tends to promote landscapes that have few problems. However, when the perspective is a short-term one, the design action to solve the immediate problem often causes reactions that are even more problematic than the original condition. In addition, as we saw in the 1970s, this viewpoint can create boring landscapes, characterized by a placelessness (Chapter 16) that fails to provide the enrichment necessary to sustain the human spirit and promote psychological health.

6. Landscape as Wealth

This view is based on the perception that people "own" land. In this view the primary value of land is its economic worth, and all other measures of the landscape are secondary to its investment potential. Land is a commodity whose value is determined in the marketplace, in units of currency (Figure 1-6). This is the view of the real estate appraiser, and is epitomized by the concept of "highest and best use," which is itself an economic measure of land. In its own way, this is an integrative view, for various influences are

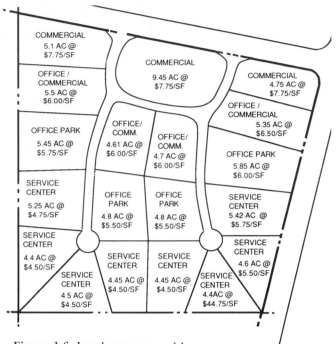

Figure 1-6. Landscape as wealth.

integrated in the marketplace to establish land value. This view comprehensively incorporates many influences, and is constantly updated in response to new conditions.

This view is an abstract and geographic one. Landscape is not seen as a physical entity, but rather translated into some economic unit such as square footage of commercial space, or number of single-family residences. As such its proponents factor in not only the physical characteristics of the land but also market influences, external conditions that influence value, and the intrinsic potential of the land to accommodate the support systems that are necessary to service the site and promote development. Advocates need at least a working knowledge of, and appreciation for, the landscape and support systems as economic inputs. Accessibility is often more important than the physical characteristics of the landscape, and the availability and capacity of support systems including sanitary and storm sewerage and electrical service must be considered. The sense of the place and perceptual context are important economic influences. The people who reside or associate in the place are important, for where the rich and poor congregate affects perceptions of status and therefore the economic value of the landscape. In this view, image is a valued economic resource.

Believers in landscape as wealth factor in economic opportunities and constraints that are intrinsic to the landscape and improvements that can be introduced to change the status quo, so as to affect value. Therefore, they include both landscape as present wealth, and landscape as future wealth. They are futures oriented, as the economic value of landscape is, to a large degree, a prediction of its future condition, use, and value.

In a very real sense, landscape as wealth drives the design of the twentieth-century American landscape. This view is strongly seated in our capitalistic ideology. We are also a materialistic culture (Chapter 2), and money is our primary unit of measure. We have opted for a short-term economic perspective, and landscape as wealth has therefore had a profound impact on the efficiency and sustainability of our landscapes. This perspective has enabled us to exploit the environment and grow rapidly, and it has served us well during the period of resource abundance created by the exploitation of fossil fuels. It will serve us poorly during the period of resource scarcity, which we have recently entered (Chapter 15).

The perception of landscape as wealth has also had a profound effect on development. The pattern of development has been primarily a response to the impact of image and accessibility on property values, rather than to the intrinsic carrying capacity of the landscape.

7. Landscape as Ideology

In this view, the landscape is seen as a symbol of the values, ideals, aspirations, hopes, and dreams of a culture (Figure 1-7). The person who holds this view is concerned with the encoding and decoding of meanings concerning the collective consciousness of the culture, its underlying philosophies, and its self-perception. For these people, the landscape represents not only the physical expression but also the hopes and dreams of that culture. As such, it is rich in associations, and takes on the personality of those who have created it. This view sees the landscape as the embodiment of values, and asserts that if we are to change the landscape, we must first change the cultural philosophy that has created that landscape.

This mindset maximizes the cultural meaning of the landscape. In homogeneous, slowly changing cultures, and when complete landscapes are created to convey a single ideology, this view can result in landscapes that have a strong and integrated sense. Conversely, in heterogeneous societies and ones that change very rapidly, such as contemporary America, this view generates a cultural landscape that is spontaneous and

Figure 1-7. Landscape as ideology.

stimulating. In these highly diverse societies, it can also result in a landscape whose elements relate poorly to one another, and that lacks the relatedness necessary to establish a strong sense. It can, therefore, create a landscape that is overly stimulating, chaotic, and psychologically unhealthy (Chapter 16).

8. Landscape as History

The landscape in this view is the complex documentation of the history of activities of nature and man, in a particular location. It is seen as a cumulative record, documented chronologically. Elements in the landscape have meaning in context to the chronology, the events leading to the creation of the elements, and the subsequent changes these elements heralded. In this view of landscape, everything is positioned in time and sequence. Settlement patterns, urban form, architectural style, site detail, and other design characteristics are seen as means for dating elements, and for contributing to the chronology (Figure 1-8).

In this view the landscape is layers of history. Sometimes these layers are separated in space, as when an entire community is settled during one time period. More commonly, they are interwoven in space, and the landscape becomes a rich historic mosaic. A major

emphasis of the historical view of the landscape is to decipher this landscape tapestry and develop the mental construct of landscape as living history. To do so, the landscape historian decodes the environment, that is, reads and interprets cues, and extrapolates from these cues to reconstruct history. Over time, the historian develops a sensitivity to which cues normally survive for long periods (such as settlement and urban patterns), and those that are more ephemeral (such as landscape plantings).

The landscape in this view is seen as the record of physical gestures of many generations and peoples, and the record of ecological processes, structured in time. Proponents seek to decipher this record, but usually find it to be an incomplete document. As the landscape historian deciphers the record, organizational patterns, materials, forms, and details tell something about the culture, subculture, and individuals, and about the natural forces that created the landscape. To understand the landscape and correctly interpret its elements, the landscape historian views these data in their historic context, and in relation to their linkages with the past and future.

Like the landscape-as-system viewpoint, landscape as history addresses ecological and human processes. However, whereas landscape as system seeks to un-

Figure 1-8. Landscape as history.

Figure 1-9. Landscape as place.

derstand the landscape as processes that build inter-active systems, this view considers processes structured in time to explain and interpret changes to physical elements as landscape gestures, and thereby to build a more complete historical record.

From the landscape-as-history perspective, gestures in the landscape are viewed in relation to the cultures and individuals that created them, rather than to present-day culture and individuals. Yet, the aggregate of these gestures, that is, the contemporary landscape, is the context within which the historic element is displayed and interpreted, and within which the current drama of life is performed. Therefore, the current landscape affects our perception of history, and the landscape as history affects our current perception and behavior. In this interactive manner, the landscape becomes a living history.

This viewpoint allows us to develop a better understanding of who we are, by giving us an understanding of how we came to be. It reinforces our collective consciousness as a culture by focusing on our shared history. However, in our heterogeneous, rapidly changing culture, this view can result in an overly stimulating landscape whose elements lack a visual relatedness to one another, and can therefore be alienating. Also, if focused only backward, this view does not address the relevancy of the individual element

to current and future conditions. Conversely, if looking to the present as living history and the future as history yet to express itself, this view shares ground with the landscape-as-system mindset, and becomes an integral part of daily life.

9. Landscape as Place

Landscape in this view is a sensual experience. This is a phenomenological view that does not focus on landscape elements, but rather embraces all elements to establish a sensual gestalt. It is largely a visual and spatial interpretation, but incorporates all sensory inputs including sounds, smells, and tactile characteristics. It focuses on the psychological feel, flavor, and ambience of the place, the richness of the mental constructs and associations that it evokes, and its ability to be remembered over time (Figure 1-9).

Holders of this view take pleasure in the immense variety, uniqueness, and individuality of places. They move beyond the generalized understanding of an area, and seek to discover the uniqueness of the place. They contend that all places have their own special sense, and resultant value. This view can be a powerful one, stimulating great numbers of people to travel around the world to experience a special city like Venice, or a region like the Alps.

Adherents to this view believe that the individual and the environment are inextricably bound in one-ness, and that the sensing of healthy places is an essential dimension of human health and wellness. This viewpoint has been influenced by the philosopher Heidegger (1977) and the architect Norberg-Schulz (1980). The making of place, as human expression and concentration of meaning, is seen to be one of the major efforts of human existence. Chapter 16 pursues this topic in detail and explores design as psychological health and placemaking.

This view is often held by the geographer who is concerned with the characteristics of places, and who analyzes how places are organized, structured, and spatially arranged to create the perceived landscape. This view also has value to the environmental psychologist, who seeks to understand the relationships between places and human consciousness. Place is also a basic unit of analysis of the area of study known as environmental perception.

The landscape as place is communicated in many ways. For example, writers have eloquently used words to convey ambience. Evocative photographic images have been produced by Ansel Adams and others, and many painters have moved beyond reproduction to intensify the communication of placeness. Geographers have developed cognitive mapping techniques to communicate the mental construct of place, and aerial and locational maps to communicate the spatial arrangement of special places in the landscape.

Landscape as place focuses on the phenomena of place, not on individual elements. The landscapes generated by this view downplay the designer's ego and concentrate on landscape character. They tend to produce visually coherent, exciting, and sensually rewarding environments. These landscapes therefore share characteristics with ones generated by the landscape-as-system view. Individual gestures integrate with context. They tend not to be conceptually pure abstract expressions, but rather complex expressions that arbitrate among a multitude of contextual influences.

In previous slowly changing low-technology cultures, the landscapes that emerged usually had an integrated, strongly systemic sense, because of the limited choices available. With our rapidly changing heterogeneous culture and powerful technology, however, achieving a coherent sense now requires a strong landscape-as-place emphasis and aggressive management of placeness.

10. Landscape as Aesthetic

This view places primary emphasis on the artistic quality of landscape features (Figure 1-10). Other views of the landscape that address its meaning or relationship to culture, use, or economics are not factored into this view. Rather, the focus is on the landscape as visual scene.

In contrast to the landscape as place, in which landscapes are seen experientially, landscape as aesthetic takes a detached, abstract approach. It interprets visual forms on the basis of some language of art, for example, as line, form, color, texture, rhythm, proportion, balance, symmetry, harmony, tension, unity, variety, and so on (Chapter 8). This view may synergize with other ones such as landscape as history, or landscape as place. However, these considerations are seen as secondary to the primary message: the landscape as a vehicle for communicating aesthetic relationships.

This is a cerebral view of the landscape, that holds truth and beauty not to be in function or experience, but as some aesthetic ideal. The intended human involvement with this landscape is not experiential, but rather contemplative. In this point of view the landscape is seen as object, and the "scene" is detached

Figure 1-10. Landscape as aesthetic.

from human behavior. Landscapes are endowed with high viewing value. Whether landscapes function properly or have high cultural meaning is of little importance in this viewpoint.

These ten views are, of course, not a complete list of observer biases. They do, however, provide a comprehensive overview, and they reveal the complexity of landscape interpretation. This complexity becomes more evident as we realize that these views do not exist in isolation. The observer usually espouses and is influenced by more than one bias simultaneously. The individual's interpretation of landscape is usually a complex synergism of many of these (and other) views.

REFERENCES

Alexander, Christopher. 1965. A City Is Not a Tree. *Architectural Forum* 122, April (58–62), May (58–62).

Carson, Rachel. 1982. *Silent Spring.* Boston: Houghton Mifflin.

Heidegger, Martin. 1977. *Basic Writings from Being and Time (1927) to the Task of Thinking (1964).* David Farrell Krell, editor. New York: Harper & Row.

Koyaanisqatsi. An IRE presentation, produced and directed by Godfrey Reggio.

McHarg, Ian. 1969. *Design with Nature.* Garden City, NY: American Museum of Natural History: Natural History Press.

Meinig, D. W., ed. 1979. *The Interpretation of Ordinary Landscapes.* New York: Oxford University Press.

Norberg-Schulz, Christian. 1980. *Genius Loci: Towards A Phenomenology of Architecture.* New York: Rizzoli.

Rapoport, Amos. 1969. *House Form and Culture.* Englewood Cliffs, NJ: Prentice-Hall.

Redfield, Robert. 1956. *Peasant Society and Culture: An Anthropological Approach to Civilization.* Chicago: University of Chicago Press.

Rudofsky, Bernard. 1964. *Architecture Without Architects: A Short Introduction to Non-Pedigreed Architecture.* Garden City, NY: Doubleday.

Venturi, Robert. 1972. *Learning from Las Vegas.* Cambridge, MA: MIT Press.

Watts, M. T. 1975. *Reading the Landscape of America.* New York: Macmillan.

Wolfe, Tom. 1981. *From Bauhaus to Our House.* New York: Farrar, Straus & Giroux.

SUGGESTED READINGS

Alexander, Christopher. 1977. *A Pattern Language: Towns, Buildings, Construction.* New York: Oxford University Press.

———. 1979. *The Timeless Way of Building.* New York: Oxford University Press.

Eckbo, Garrett. 1969. *The Landscape We See.* New York: McGraw-Hill.

Marshall, Lane. 1983. *Action by Design: Facilitating Design Decisions into the 21st Century.* Washington, DC: American Society of Landscape Architects.

Meinig, D. W. Environmental Appreciation: Localities as a Humane Art. *The Humanities Review.*

Simonds, John. 1978. *Earthscape: A Manual of Environmental Planning.* New York: McGraw-Hill.

2

People, Attitudes, and Perceptions

As we begin to study people, attitudes, and perceptions and their relation to the landscape, three main questions emerge. The first is what issues to consider. Most landscape history texts, for example, look at issues such as environmental context, social history, and the philosophical underpinnings (or paradigm) of the culture. Authors usually interpret these issues to explain the art forms, architecture, and landscape that these cultures developed. An excellent example of this format, and one of the finest books on landscape history, is *The Landscapes of Man*, by Geoffrey and Susan Jellicoe (1975).

The second question is how to organize and communicate the analysis of people, attitudes, and perceptions. The most common method is chronological, by historic epoch, and by periods within these epochs. The third question is how to use this information.

This chapter is a response to these questions, in three sections. The first section is an analysis of the primary issues that affect attitudes and therefore the manner in which people express themselves through landscape gesture. The second is an analysis of the major tendencies in attitudes, perceptions, and expressions that have recurred through history, in many different environmental and social contexts. These are presented as the interplay of attitudes rather than a chronology. The third section is a discussion of the landscape implications of the foregoing theories and design traditions.

In this chapter we will discuss peoples, attitudes, and perceptions at the cultural, not the individual, level. We do not address the differences between the lay person and the professional landscape designer. These significant differences are discussed in Part 3.

THE BASIS OF ATTITUDES

A huge number of issues affect people's attitudes and perceptions of the world around them. We have chosen to address a few major ones, to lend insight into how attitudes and perceptions develop. These include world views, human beings and their environment, social relationships, time, units of measure, art and science, and science and technology.

World Views

World views (also referred to as paradigms) are largely responsible for the way we perceive the landscape, and the differences in landscape meaning discussed in Chapter 1. In fact, the history of civilization can be understood as the ebb and flow of different world views. An understanding of the range of world views can provide valuable information for interpreting the cultural landscape.

There are perhaps as many world views or paradigms as there are people, but these views fall into categories. The range of these categories can be seen from the following representative views.

One commonly occurring view is that of *harmonious interrelatedness*. This view accepts, as truth and beauty, the interconnectedness and interdependency of all that is observed in nature. This is a systemic view that embraces interaction as its organizational force, and the complex webs of social and ecological relations as its organizational patterns.

A very different viewpoint is that of *multiple-window thinking*. People who hold this view embrace the world as viewed through their own "window," or area of expertise. They adhere to the belief that if they see the world through their window, and take care of their area of responsibility, that someone else will look through other windows, and take care of those areas. Running the ship is seen as another window, and the underlying assumption is that someone is serving as navigator. This viewpoint is promoted by our Cartesian mindset (Chapter 14), and by our educational system (Chapter 3), which prepares people to deal with the world as viewed from the perspective of a specific academic discipline or subject.

Somewhat related to this viewpoint is the belief that the complex world around us can best be understood through a *positivist mindset.* Positivism reduces complex entities to their simplest elemental parts, and studies those parts to develop an understanding of the whole. The assumption is that the sum of the parts does in fact constitute the whole. This view reduces complexity and restructures the world in a manner that is more controllable, predictable, and replicable. It is the rational view of reality upon which newtonian science is built. It is also the dominant mechanistic view around which present Western culture is structured.

Human Beings and Their Environment

Perceptions of the relationship between people and their environment range from one of people as being dominated by, and therefore subservient to, nature, to one of people as being dominant over, and therefore, master of nature. In the former, human beings serve nature; in the latter, nature serves human needs.

One view that dates to ancient times, and that endures today, sees every place in the landscape as having its own spirit. This view, in which each *genius loci,* or "spirit of place" has its own intrinsic value was addressed by Lynn White, Jr. (1967), in *The Historical Roots of the Ecological Crisis:* "in antiquity, every tree, every spring, ever stream, every hill had its own genius loci, its guardian spirit . . . Before one cut a tree, mined a mountain, or dammed a brook, it was important to placate the spirit in charge of that particular situation, and keep it placated." This is also the paradigm around which the poignant documentary *Koyaanisqatsi* is based.

In this "Genius Loci" viewpoint the human spirit is integrally bound to the spirit of place, and human health and well-being are inextricably tied to the health and well-being of the landscape. Heidegger's (1977) concept of "dwelling" embraces this viewpoint; and Norberg-Schulz's *Genius Loci: Towards a Phenomenology of Architecture* (1980) applies this concept to architecture.

This view of the world is closely related to the *landscape ecology* view, wherein all elements of the landscape are interwoven into a complex interactive whole, consisting of many overlapping niches. In this view, the whole and all of its parts are integrated in function and behavior, and the entirety is integrated with its context. All parts and the whole are changing in a dynamic equilibrium, and humankind is but one of these many parts. In this view people are an integral part of the dynamic of nature, and of its processes. Their gestures reinforce the nature of the landscape, and intensify its interrelatedness.

The *anthropocentric* view, on the other hand, has humans as the center of the universe, dominant over nature; and nature exists to serve human needs. The environment has value only in its ability to serve; it exists to be exploited for people's use and benefit.

In the words of Ian McHarg (1969):

> man exclusively is divine and given dominion over all things, indeed that God is made in the image of man. . . . man . . . seeks not unity with nature but conquest. . . . the world consists solely as a dialogue among men, or men and God, while nature is a faint decorative backdrop to the human play. If nature receives attention, then it is only for the purpose of conquest, or even better, exploitation—for the latter not only accomplishes the first objective, but provides a financial reward for the conqueror.

Social Relationships

One of the primary issues around which cultures are built is the relationship among people. At one pole of social interaction is an emphasis on *individualism.* According to this view, the individual is self-providing and communal obligations are minimal. According to this view, the individual has the right to make any decisions that do not limit the rights of others. The health and well-being of the individual is a personal obligation; and the health and well-being of each individual is seen apart from that of others. This viewpoint as practiced in America has generated an ever-widening gap between the affluent and the poor, a measure of the wide range of individual successes. This view promotes individualistic, overt expressions and a visually complex cultural landscape.

The alternative view, *communalism,* focuses on social interrelatedness and perceived obligations between the individual and others within a society. This view gives the collective body of the community great power in determining what types of behavior and decision-making are appropriate for the individual. According to this view, individuals are psychologically fused with others in the culture, that is, there is a social consciousness. Individual health and well-being are perceived as being inextricably linked with the health and well-being of others and the health and wellness of the society. According to this view, the high rate of crime, increased urban stress, and the great increase in heart disease and strokes that characterize many contemporary societies are all indications that the health and well-being of even the affluent individual are integrally tied to the poor health of others and to the society at large. In this view the collective consciousness and community expression takes precedent over individual considerations and expressions.

Cultures also vary in their desired degree of isolation, ranging from a desire for *publicness* to one for *privateness*. For example, a society that perceives an interdependence of individuals will express itself with a multiplicity of public cues to communicate and encourage interaction. Private areas will link to public space with few perceptual cues to discourage movement between the two. Conversely, the community that values privacy will set up a whole series of cues that serve as deterrents or social filters. In contemporary American communities, for example, sidewalks are designed as cues to support a high degree of privacy. They communicate appropriate behavior and serve as psychological barriers: the public is encouraged to use the street-related walk; the walk to the house is more private than public; the front porch is considered part of the private residence.

Generally, these interpersonal dynamics change with the degree of familiarity among individuals, the specifics of a location, perceived territories, time of day, and many other variables.

Time

Time is perhaps the least understood influence on people's attitudes and perceptions. Short-term thinkers see the relevant time period as the near one, and make decisions that maximize short-term benefits. Long-term thinkers see the longer time period as relevant, and select for behavior that maximizes long-term effectiveness. Short-term thinkers tend to exploit resources for immediate benefit; long-term thinkers place a portion of energies back into the system to sustain that system and maximize its carrying capacity.

Time also affects our attitudes, perceptions, and behavior in other ways. For example, some cultures are based on a belief in fundamental *universal rhythms* or fluctuations between two polar extremes on some continuum. These cultures often espouse paradigms that embody both ends of the continuum, and decisions usually reflect the interplay of these extremes. Perhaps the best known example is the Eastern concept of Yin and Yang; where people are one aspect of nature. In these universal rhythmic paradigms, past, present, and future are often linked to physical expressions that synergize these polar extremes. In this

view, the rhythmic cyclical perception of time is reinforced by the diurnal progression of day and night, seasonal rhythms, and longer natural rhythms such as those of animal populations, draughts, etc.

Other cultures perceive *linear time*. Rather than seeing time as a rhythm, they see it moving forward. This attitude toward time is somewhat removed from the fluctuations of the physical world, and tends to separate past, present, and future, and to see them as conceptually different entities to be addressed discretely.

Cultures also differ in their perception of the *relation of time and space*. For example, prior to the advent of perspective, in the fifteenth century, space and time were integrally linked. To communicate form, the artist would present multiple images from different locations in space and time. Often the ideal image of the whole, as in the Egyptian figure, was the aggregate of the ideal images of each of its parts (with the torso shown from the front and the head and feet shown in profile, from the side). Thus the image itself would incorporate differences in space and time. On the other hand, perspective communicates form as viewed from a location fixed in space and time; and optical tricks such as foreshortening replace time as the primary means of building a mental construct of space.

As we discuss in later chapters, the perceived relationship between time and space differs substantially within the design professions. Architects, who work basically with static materials, often embrace the separation of time and space. Landscape architects, whose design palette consists to a large extent of materials that change over time, usually demonstrate a more integrated relationship between space and time.

Unit of Measure

The unit of measure by which the individual evaluates the world is critical to landscape perception and behavior. Some people see the *carrying capacity* of the system as the relevant unit, and employ long-term decision-making to maximize carrying capacity. Others, as George Bush in his description of a "kinder and gentler world," see love and friendship as the measure. This is an inner *spiritual* unit of measure. Still others see *energy* as the unit of measure, and make their decisions based on the energetics of a given situation. Others see any limiting *resource* as the appropriate unit.

In contemporary American society, *economics* has come to be our primary unit of measure. This point of view assigns an economic value to every resource, and decisions are based on an economic evaluation of alternatives. Time is also critical in this economic analysis, as short-term economics and long-term economics often yield two very different types of decisions: short-term economics often results in system decay that ultimately undermines long-term economic return.

Regardless of the unit of measure, time is an essential consideration. Whether the measure is ecological carrying capacity, energy flows, or economics, long-term decisions are usually quite different from short-term ones, as are the outcomes of these decisions.

Art and Science

In our culture, we perceive art and science as discrete entities. Many civilizations do not abstract the aesthetic characteristics of an entity from its technical aspects. However, in the period of reductionism introduced by Cartesian philosophy and Newtonian science, the Western world has seen art and science as conceptually different. This view is now giving way to the new science of relativity that speaks for a synergism of art and science, as interrelated expressions of an underlying oneness. This topic, and its implications for design, are discussed at length in Chapter 14.

Science and Technology

About 1850, according to Lynn White, Jr. (1967), there emerged a widespread cultural perception, the "Baconian creed that scientific knowledge means technical power over nature." Prior to that time, this attitude would not have occurred because of the underlying social differences associated with science and technology. Science was aristocratic, technology was lower class. The Baconian creed was an outgrowth of the democratic revolutions that were occurring. With the new democratic social underpinnings, a merging of science and technology became possible. This merging led to rapid technological growth and development, and dramatically increased our ability to manage or, conversely, to degrade the physical environment.

RECURRING TRADITIONS OF EXPRESSION

In exploring traditions of landscape expressions, this section takes an atypical temporal viewpoint. It contends that the most appropriate way to explore attitudes is to view history not in the normal chronological ordering of time moving forward, but rather from a cyclical point of view. We focus here on fundamental traditions in history and the rhythmic ebb and flow of these traditions as cultural expressions. The history of civilization is seen as the interplay of these traditions concerning: land ethics;

Western and Eastern attitudes; pantheism and theism; description and prescription; consumption and stewardship; primitive, vernacular, and grand expressions; early successional and late successional strategies; and different cultural value systems.

Land Ethics

Individual (or cultural) attitudes concerning the relationship of people and their environment lead to perceptions concerning resource. As attitudes change, so do perceptions of resource. In *Living in the Environment* (1975), G. Tyler Miller, Jr., categorized these differing perceptions of resource into four land use ethics: the economic ethic, the preservationist ethic, the balanced multiple-use ethic, and the ecological ethic. These four land ethics are presented here as perceptual tendencies that have greatly affected the history of different civilizations, and the cultural landscapes they have generated.

Economic Ethic

In this ethic, the land is viewed as an economic resource. This is the ethic of the pioneer who perceives the land to be hostile and foreboding. It seeks to clear the land and to make its resources available for use. It is often operative when the level of technology is low and the environment is harsh. It also predominates in technologically advanced societies, which perceive the human role to be the establishment of dominion over the earth, and resource to be that which provides short-term economic gain. The economic ethic has been expressed in the recent political effort to improve short-term economics by the dissolution of many environmental and energy regulations.

Preservation Ethic

At the other end of the spectrum lies the *preservation ethic*, which promotes the maintenance of land in a nondisturbed state. Such land would serve as a living ecological laboratory, with its uses limited to nondestructive ones. It would be preserved for future generations. Since many natural resources would not be harvested within this ethic, members of the economic ethic would regard it as being wasteful of resources.

Balanced Multiple-Use Ethic

According to Miller, this ethic is espoused by scientific conservationists. These people believe that certain lands should be used for a variety of purposes but managed so as to conserve them for future generations. The essence of this view is a balance between use and management. As the level of use and subsequent tendency to degradation increase, so too must the level of management to mitigate deleterious effects.

Ecological or Sustainable Earth Ethic

In this ethic there is a need to balance human needs with those of other life-forms, with the central intent being the maintenance of the carrying capacity of the system.

In any culture, the prevailing ethic concerning land use speaks forcefully to the attitudes and perceptions of the people. It also substantially affects the quality of the human condition.

Western and Eastern Attitudes

The Western view of reality is one of fixed absolutes. The Eastern world view is much more dynamic and is based on continuums and the interplay of opposing forces. In the Eastern view, reality is not absolute; rather, all manifestations of reality are generated by the dynamic interplay of opposing forces, such as the Yin and the Yang.

According to landscape architect Ian L. McHarg, these different paradigms have resulted in significantly different attitudes about the relationship of humans to their environment, and profoundly different implications for the health and well-being of both people and environment. In discussing Western and Eastern thought, McHarg said:

> The first . . . is man-oriented. The cosmos is but a pyramid erected to support man at its pinnacle . . . The opposing view, identified with the Orient, postulates a unitary and all encompassing nature within which man exists, man in nature.
>
> These opposing views are the central duality, man and nature, West and East, white and black, brains and testicles, Classicism and Romanticism . . . anthropomorphism and naturalism. The Western tradition vaunts the individual and the man-brain, and denigrates nature, animal, non-brain. In the Orient nature is omnipotent, revered, and man is but an aspect of nature. It would be as unwise to deny the affirmative aspects of either view as to diminish their negative effects. Yet today, the duality demands urgent attention. The adequacy of the western view of man and nature deserves to be questioned. Further, one must ask if these two views are mutually exclusive.
>
> The inheritors of the Judaic-Christian-Humanist tradition have received their injunction from Genesis, a man-oriented universe, man exclusively made in the image of God, given dominion over all life and non-life, enjoined to subdue the earth . . . From its origin in

Judaism, extension in Classicism, reinforcement in Christianity, inflation in the Renaissance and absorption in the nineteenth and twentieth centuries, the anthropomorphic-anthropocentric view has become the tacit view of man versus nature.

Today, of course, Eastern cultures are rapidly becoming westernized. Conversely, the naturalist view is growing in the West. This view was described by McHarg as follows:

> The Naturalist tradition in the West . . . may be described as holding that . . . all systems are subject to common laws yet having unlimited potential; that in this world man is simply an inhabitant, free to develop his own potential. This view questions anthropocentrism and anthropomorphism; it does not diminish either man's uniqueness or his potential, only his claim to primacy and exclusive divinity.

The Western and the Eastern view differ in another profound though related way. The Christian view of "man created in the image of God, and only on this earth for a short time," results in a Western goal-oriented attitude and a short-term value system. The Eastern attitude of "oneness with context" leads to the Zen of experiencing life as an ongoing dialogue, an innate desire to maximize the quality of the environment, and a long-term value system.

Pantheism and Theism

Pantheism is a doctrine that equates gods with the forces and laws of the universe. It is based on a oneness of people and nature. Spirit exists in every living thing, and there is a oneness in spirit in all living things. Humans are thereby integrated in spirit with the landscape. In pagan cultures, this translated into a reverence for the gods of living things as a prerequisite for successful hunts, good harvests, and survival in combat.

Theism, on the other hand, is the belief in a single God that is the creator of all that exists, including humans and the earth. As a doctrine, it denies the oneness in spirit of humans and nature. It redefines God as the master of the earth. In theism, people are perceived to be less dependent on nature, and therefore less familiar with the wilderness. Where wilderness was the home of the pantheist, for the theist it is the place beyond human control. In a world controlled by an all-powerful God, this wilderness beyond control is often seen as a loathsome, frightening, wicked place. Nature ceases to be the "dwelling" place for humans (Heidegger).

Description and Prescription

Cultural, environmental, and technological forces influence built form. The impact of these forces depends on their intensity, the resources available to mitigate them, and the approach the culture takes in addressing these forces. On the one hand, cultural expressions can *describe* force. Conversely, cultures can seek to *prescribe* forms irrespective of these forces.

In times of limited available resources (material, technological, economic, or energetic), cultural systems must become more efficient and therefore design becomes more responsive to conditions. In these cases, cultural expressions evolve that are descriptive of their context. Such was the case in the medieval period. As a result of a decentralization of power and a degradation in available material, technological, and cultural resources, attitudes became more gestaltic. Form described a myriad of influences, occurring simultaneously in time and space. The result was an architecture, as in Assisi, Italy (Figure 2-1), that integrated with these forces and described them through form. This architecture was also efficient in its function.

Conversely, in periods of resource abundance, cultural expressions can become more prescriptive. This was the case in ancient Rome and during the Renaissance. These were periods of abundance of usable resources, and this abundance allowed the cultures to redefine the world around them. During these periods, the surplus of resource, especially economic and cultural resources, was used to overcome the specifics of conditions, and to impose into the landscape a new order based on euclidean geometry and classical attitudes concerning form. The imposed order was primarily visual, and sought not to integrate with nature, but rather to imprint on nature a new order. McHarg defined this order as

> A rigid symmetrical pattern ... imposed relentlessly upon a reluctant landscape. If this pattern was, as is claimed, some image of a perfect paradisiac order, it was a human image which derived nothing from the manifest order and expression of wild nature. It was rather, I suggest, an image of flexed muscles, a cock's crow of power, and an arrogant presumption of human dominance over nature.

Many people have seen history as an interplay between description and prescription. Some have referred to the history of "organic" civilizations alternating with "critical" ones; others have spoken of the history of "integrating" civilizations alternating with "differentiating" ones. These two polar extremes in mindset, describing existing conditions or asserting new order, are of great significance to landscape de-

Figure 2-1 Integration of forces.

sign and to this text. As stated before, written history has tended to record the prescriptive classical periods of history, and to dismiss the descriptive periods and to apply to them condescending labels such as the dark ages. It has skimmed over the portions of history that were more integrative and descriptive in approach.

Consumption and Stewardship

Cultures have also differed in their approaches to resource utilization and management. On the one hand, in the consumptive tradition people have sought to extract maximum short-term human benefit from the landscape, thereby consuming or otherwise degrading it. On the other hand, the stewardship tradition has sought to nurture the landscape and sustain its bounty.

The consumptive tradition has been expressed through exploitative approaches to farming, ranching, timber and mineral extraction, and manufacturing. Nonrenewable resources and maximum short-term gain have been the focus, and little attention has been paid to long-term system health or sustainability (Chapter 15). Conversely, the stewardship tradition has been expressed through an ecologically sensitive approach to these and other activities, with a focus on the use of renewable resources and the long-term health and sustainability of the landscape.

The stewardship tradition has tended to dominate in low-technology cultures and in times of resource scarcity. The consumptive tradition has tended to dominate in high-technology cultures and in times of resource abundance.

Primitive, Vernacular, and Grand Traditions

Differing attitudes and perceptions and differing resource bases lead to different approaches toward architecture and land design, and different traditions of expression. Many people summarize these into the three primary groupings of the primitive, vernacular, and grand approaches to human expressions in the landscape.

Primitive societies are those that are characterized by a relatively low level of technology and develop-

ment. There is little specialization of roles within the society, so that while the level of technology is low, the knowledge of that technology is shared by all. For example, in the primitive approach, the individual usually builds the residence. In these societies architectural and cultural landscape expressions are extremely consistent, as the cultures tend to be homogeneous and tradition oriented. Over time, forms are subtly adjusted to satisfy cultural, physical, and maintenance needs, and the culture develops an expressive tradition that integrates place, culture, and form. The hogans of the Navajo tribe of the south-

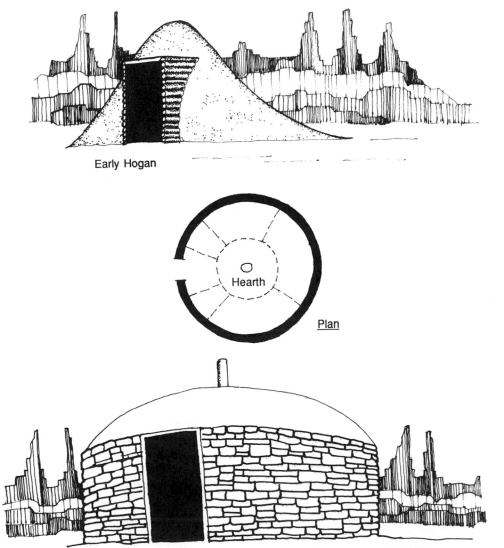

Early Hogan

Hearth

Plan

stone and earth hogan

Figure 2-2. Primitive architecture. (Adapted from A. Bowen, "Historical Responses to Cooling Needs in Shelter and Settlement," *Passive Cooling Conference Proceedings,* American Solar Energy Society, Miami Beach, Florida, 1981)

western United States is an architectural form representative of the primitive approach to human gesture in the landscape (Figure 2-2).

The vernacular approach, and the building tradition it generates, is described in many different ways. Some define this tradition as the architecture that is built by a tradesperson, but in concert with the resident, so that the dweller is an integral part of the formative process (Figure 2-3). Others define it as the unconsciously designed "low" architecture that evolves as the cultural counterpart to the designed "high" or grand tradition of architecture. In either case, the form, the model, and the materials and construction of the vernacular are norms, and do not change for any specific building. Rather, the model is adjusted in response to family requirements, site, microclimate, and so forth, as the work proceeds. Characteristics of a vernacular tradition, according to Rapoport, include the "lack of theoretical or aesthetic pretensions, working with the site and microclimate, respect for other people and their houses and hence for the total environment, human-made as well as natural, and working within an idiom with variations within a given order" (Rapoport 1969).

The urban fabrics that evolve from vernacular attitudes and comprise vernacular traditions (as the travel posters of Greece indicate) are open-ended and dynamic. In the vernacular Greek town, the Italian hilltown, and the medieval village, the individual element is perceived as secondary to the relationships that exist between the elements; the tradition is synergistic.

The grand tradition of architecture includes its monumental and overt buildings (Figure 2-4). This tradition is the "stock in trade" of the professional designer, who seeks to communicate the uniqueness of people. It is the "high" art that is generally taught in schools of architecture. It communicates an anthropocentric (human as center) and anthropomorphic (human as form-giver) mindset. It promotes an imposed order, that is, the designer's idea as the "overriding design statement," and classical notions of order.

Early Successional and Late Successional Strategies

The history of civilization is a record of cultures that have either opted to maximize and live for the present or to focus on the future. As we see in Chapters 7 and 15, early successional systems are those that adopt short-term effectiveness as their competitive strategy. Late successional ones are those that embrace a long-term strategy. Whether a civilization perceives the short term or the long term as the relevant

Figure 2-3. Vernacular architecture.

Figure 2-4. Grand tradition of architecture.

time period will affect the long-term viability of that civilization, and the character of the cultural landscape it evolves.

Cultural systems that have opted for short-term decision-making have been very successful in periods of resource abundance, because they have used the surplus to grow rapidly. This is the basic strategy (in nature) of early successional ecosystems; and we therefore refer herein to short-term thinking as an early successional cultural strategy. On the other hand, in times of resource scarcity, successful and efficient cultures have placed their emphasis on maintaining the long-term health and productivity of the system. This is the late successional ecological strategy; and we refer to long-term thinking as a late successional cultural strategy.

In most cases, the rise and fall of civilizations can be traced to the appropriateness of the competitive strategy of the culture in the context of resource availability. For example, the success of the American culture over the last two centuries can be understood as an effective early successional strategy in a time of resource abundance. Whether we are competitive in the future will be determined by whether we can make the transition to a late successional culture, in response to our rapidly degrading global ecology and resource base.

Value Systems

According to Sorokin, in *Social and Cultural Dynamics* (1937–41), the history of civilizations has been characterized by a fairly regular fluctuation of value systems, and these changes have precipitated shifts in paradigms and physical expressions. Sorokin analyzed Western civilization as the fluctuation among three value systems, which he referred to as the sensate, the ideational, and the idealistic. In the *sensate value system,* as one polar extreme, matter is reality, sensory perception is truth and knowledge, and spiritual phenomena are merely expressions of a material reality. In the *ideational value system,* as the other polar extreme, reality lies beyond the material world, in the spiritual one, and knowledge exists in the inner consciousness. It is an espousal of ideal values, ethics, and truths. This value system is expressed in Western societies through the Judeo-Christian concept of God, and platonic ideals; and in Eastern cultures through Taoism, Zen Buddhism, and Hinduism.

Intermediate between these two polar extremes, serving as a transition between them, and expressed as a synergism of the two is the *idealistic value system.* According to this view, reality expresses itself both materially and spiritually. Periods of history characterized by this view, including the Golden Age of Greece (fourth century B.C.) and the Renaissance (fifteenth century A.D.), are often unique periods in which materialistic and spiritual truth and beauty are merged; and a synergism is achieved among philosophy, art, and science and place, people, and technology.

LANDSCAPE IMPLICATIONS

All life forms modify their environment. The degree to which they do so relates to many issues. It is affected by human attitudes and constructs of reality, and perceptions of resource that grow from these attitudes. It also relates to people's physical ability to modify the environment. The manner in which people modify their environment in turn has implica-

tions for human and ecological health; and our recent actions have created a human and ecological health crisis. Toffler (*The Third Wave,* 1980), Capra (*The Turning Point,* 1982), and others have recently painted a picture of our world in crisis. This crisis has many roots.

World-View Roots

Each world view has its landscape ramifications. This fact is stated succinctly in the introduction to *Landscape Architecture,* by Tobey (1973). In this introduction, Tobey recalls a contest that was held in 1962 by the *Tennessee Conservationist.* In this contest, a photo of an abandoned dilapidated farmhouse was shown in an abandoned field, and the reader was offered a prize for the best 100-word description. An American Indian took the prize with the following:

> Picture show white man crazy. Cut down tree. Make big tepee. Plow hill. Water wash. Wind blow soil. Grass gone. Door gone. Windows gone. Whole place gone. Buck gone. Squaw gone. Papoose too. No chuckaway (food). No pigs, no corn. No plow. No hay. No pony.
> Indian no plow land. Great spirit make grass. Buffalo eat grass. Indian eat buffalo. Hide make tepee; make moccasin. Indian no make terrace. All time eat. No hunt job. No hitchhike. No ask relief. No shoot pig. No build dam. No give dam. Indian waste nothing. Indian not work. White man crazy.

This description, showing the different environmental impact associated with two different world views, is included here not as an indication of a preference for the primitive life-style; but rather to indicate that with an increased technology and life-style also goes a responsibility to increase our management of the environment. Otherwise, the environment will be degraded and its health and productivity reduced.

Human–Environment Roots

According to Lynn White, Jr., in "The Historical Roots of the Ecological Crisis" (1967), the ecological crisis of the 1960s was deeply ingrained in our attitudes about time and about human-environmental relationships. Of course, the crisis of the 1960s was a short-term pulse in a long-term trend of global degradation.

Many people, including McHarg in *Design with Nature* (1969), see the conceptual roots of our world crisis to be linked with our perceptions of the origins of humans, of which there are two primary (though certainly many other) theories. One is that humans were created at a certain point in time and generally apart from the evolution of the landscape as system. The other is that humans evolved in concert with other organisms, and with an environment that was itself evolving. These two different views can have profound implications for the landscape. The first can allow the perception that humans and nature are discrete entities, and that their health and well-being are not inextricably bound. The second makes it extremely difficult to separate the health and well-being of humans and nature.

This was expressed by Lynn White, Jr., in "The Historical Roots of the Ecological Crisis," when he stated:

> By destroying pagan animism, Christianity made it possible to exploit nature in a mood of indifference to the feelings of natural objects .... Especially in its Western form, Christianity is the most anthropocentric religion the world has seen ... [It], in absolute contrast to ancient paganism and Asia's religions (except, perhaps, Zoroastrianism), not only established a dualism of man and nature but also insisted that it is God's will that man exploit nature for his proper ends.

Social Roots

Our world society is today characterized by much homelessness, crime, stress, and a high incidence of what is referred to as "diseases of civilization," including heart disease, cancer, and strokes. These are all indications of a psychologically unhealthy culture. A large part of this unhealthiness is attributable to the fact that the designed urban environment does not address user psychological needs. This, in turn, speaks for the necessity to design healthy environments as one takes a holistic view of human health.

Temporal Roots

The rise and fall of civilizations can be seen as the ebb and flow of successional traditions, with the successful strategy interdependent with resource availability. The successional tradition being employed also affects the quality of the environment. For example, recent economic history is quite clear. Since the industrial revolution and the greater exploitation of the earth made possible by the development of fossil fuels, Western cultures, and particularly the American one, using short-term decision-making and early successional cultural strategies, has been very successful. The American culture has "wasted" little time feeding back to the environmental system so as to manage its long-term viability. However, as we have grown to the limits of this resource base, the competitive edge has shifted from short-term to long-term thinking. Recently, in a matter of three years, we saw the United States move from the position of the world's greatest creditor nation, to become its largest debtor nation. We are maintaining our short-term decision-making at the expense of reduced system productivity for our children and grandchildren.

Art and Science

Cartesian philosophy and newtonian science have caused a schism between art and science. They have placed in opposition intuitive and rational thinking. They have pitted logic against feeling. This rift has contributed in no small way to the psychological ills of contemporary society. The synergism of art and science, heralded by the new science of relativity, has the potential to lead us into a new period of enlightenment that synergizes the rationality and materialism of the recent past with a new spiritualism and sensitivity to the world around us.

Science and Technology

About 140 years ago a democratic revolution occurred that allowed the synergism of science and technology, and their application to the task of establishing dominion over nature. Since this confluence, the ability of the human race to change the world has accelerated at an unprecedented pace. Unfortunately, our ability to change the environment has not been accompanied by the necessary application of science and technology to environmental management, and environmental quality has therefore been severely degraded. At present, we have the scientific and technological capability to manage the ecological and human condition effectively, if we choose to do so.

Economic Roots

Contemporary society has accepted economics as the universal unit of measure. A major implication of economic decision-making is the ecological impact of applying the deficit spending concept of economics to physical and environmental decision-making.

As shown in Figure 2-5, when a new resource base is developed, systems grow until they reach, exceed, and then settle back into a steady-state carrying capacity. However, the economic concept of deficit spending allows growth to continue far beyond the steady-state condition, and "finances" that growth with deficit spending. The end result is reduced carrying capacity, and an ecological system in degradation (Figure 2-6). This ecological breakdown will ultimately result in economic collapse. Many people would look at the tremendous national debt we are accumulating,

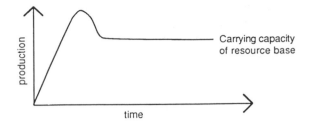

Figure 2-5. Carrying capacity.

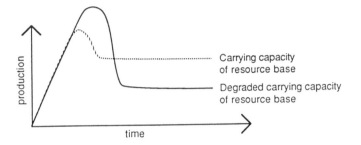

Figure 2-6. Deficit spending and environmental degradation.

current runaway inflation in many parts of the world, massive unemployment, and the maldistribution of income and wealth as indications of an economic system in disarray.

LANDSCAPE DESIGN IN THE TWENTY-FIRST CENTURY

According to Capra in *The Turning Point,* and if we analyze modern history in the context of Sorokin's model, we can understand the rise of Christianity in the Middle Ages as an ideational period leading to the aesthetic fulfillment of art, philosophy, science, and technology in the European Renaissance. The spiritual truth of this period slowly gave way to a sensate period of materialism in the seventeenth to nineteenth centuries, including the Enlightenment, the modern philosophy heralded by René Descartes, newtonian science, and the industrial revolution. This age of materialism has generated our current cultural world view and many of the problems of our culture. It further suggests that the crises that we face are indications that we have arrived at one of the true transition periods in history, and that the crises will increase in severity until that transition is achieved.

This recent past has also prepared the stage for a new period of enlightenment. This period of cultural transition can lead to a true synergism of art and science, of technology and philosophy, of materialism and spiritualism, and of humans and their environment. To prepare for this great transition, it is imper-ative that we reexamine the premises and values of our culture. As landscape designers, we can begin this analysis by looking at education in general as a mechanism for becoming acculturated to a world view, and by considering design education in particular.

REFERENCES

Bowen, Arthur. 1981. Historical Response to Cooling Needs in Shelter and Settlement. *International Solar Energy Passive Cooling Conference.* Delaware: American Section of the International Solar Energy Society.

Capra, Fritjof. 1981. *The Turning Point: Science, Society, and the Rising Culture.* New York: Simon & Schuster.

Heidegger, Martin. 1977. *Basic Writings from Being and Time (1927) to the Task of Thinking (1964).* David Farrell Krell, editor. New York: Harper & Row.

Jellicoe, Geoffrey, and Jellicoe, Susan. 1975. *The Landscape of Man: Shaping the Environment from Prehistory to the Present Day.* New York: Viking Press.

Koyaanisqatsi. 1983. An IRE presentation, produced and directed by Godfrey Reggio.

McHarg, Ian. 1963. Man and Environment. *The Urban Condition.* Leonard J. Duhl, M.D., editor. New York: Basic Books.

———. 1969. *Design with Nature.* Garden City, NY: American Museum of Natural History, Natural History Press.

Miller, G. Tyler, Jr. 1975. *Living in the Environment: Concepts, Problems, and Alternatives.* Belmont, CA: Wadsworth.

Norberg-Schulz, Christian. 1980. *Genius Loci: Towards a Phenomenology of Architecture.* New York: Rizzoli.

Rapoport, Amos. 1969. *House Form and Culture.* Englewood Cliffs, NJ: Prentice-Hall.

Sorokin, Pitirim. 1937–41. *Social and Cultural Dynamics.* Vol. 1: Fluctuation of Forms of Art; vol. 2: Fluctuation of Systems of Truth, Ethics and Law; vol. 3: Fluctuation of Social Relationships, War and Revolution; vol. 4: Basic Problems, Principles, and Methods. New York, Cincinnati: American.

Tobey, George. 1973. *History of Landscape Architecture: The Relationship of People to Environment.* New York: American Elsevier.

Toffler, Alvin. 1980. *The Third Wave.* New York: Morrow.

White, Lynn, Jr. 1967. The Historical Roots of the Ecological Crisis. *Science* 10:1203–1207.

SUGGESTED READINGS

Altman, Irwin. 1975. *The Environment and Social Behavior: Privacy, Personal Space, Territory, Crowding.* Lawrences, Wrightsman, ed. Monterey, CA: Brooks/Cole.

Tuan, Yi-Fu. 1974. *Topophilia: A Study of Environmental Perception, Attitudes, and Values.* Englewood Cliffs, NJ: Prentice-Hall.

3

Education and Design Thinking

Human beings start out as butterflies and end up in cocoons.

Source Unknown

THINKING AND EDUCATION

Most learning is based on making connections that relate the new to the familiar. Education, then, is the development of the skills necessary to integrate new information into existing patterns or to build, from the information, new patterns. With this in mind, the following paradox by Marilyn Ferguson in *The Aquarian Conspiracy* (1980) is presented.

> Our culture's great learning disability [is] an education system which emphasizes being "right" at the expense of being open . . . taught us young how to be still, look backwards, look to authority, construct certainties. . . . This is the poignant paradox: a plastic brain (of tremendous potential) capable of being trained into self-limiting behavior . . . the child who may have come to school intact, with the budding courage to risk and explore, finds stress enough to permanently diminish that adventure. . . . whereas the young need some sort of initiation into the uncertain world, we give them the bones of culture's graveyards . . . . where they need to find meaning, the schools ask memorization, discipline is divorced from intuition, pattern from parts.

The result of this approach is dismal. We continue to invest heavily in education but our students languish behind those of countries that spend much less. Americans score near the bottom in achievement tests in both math and science as compared to many other industrial nations. Many people consider the condition of the American education system to be a national crisis.

Formal Education

Educational institutions in this country convey and extend bodies of information, but often thwart the student's innate desire to think independently and to explore. They flood the mind with data while creating obstacles to the development of skills for exploring alternatives, developing insights, interpreting data, and synthesizing meaningful responses. By contrast, the education system should be developing the student's ability to explore the unknown and to search for meaning. It should also be presenting a range of world views and paradigms; developing understanding of the nature of reality, underlying forces, and value systems; and exploring the implications of implementing alternative value systems. It should be building an awareness of the relationships between world views and health; humans and environment; space and time; energy, economics, environment, and humans; art and science; science and technology; and other critical relationships. It should be exploring alternative mindsets and attitudes about decision-making. It should be encouraging students to feel, to become more "in tune" with, and aware of, their inner consciousness.

For better or for worse, formal education in this country has assumed many of the educative roles formerly residing in the parent. However, the primary roles of the parent have historically included the cultivation of self-reliance in the child and the promotion of desired value systems. As surrogate parent, the role of the educator should include developing the student's ability to self-educate, and to make conscious decisions concerning value systems. However, the self-directed student has often been seen as a problem, and public schools have avoided addressing values as part of thinking and learning. In an effort to explore alternatives, let us now take a short detour though self-education, through the eyes of a truly self-directed individual, by paraphrasing an account of his education (Aulaire 1985).

Self-Education

Buckminster Fuller, one of the geniuses of this century, contended that self-education was "the only real education." This philosophy was expressed in Bucky's life as he, like a surprising number of truly creative people, was largely self-taught. However, when discussing his mental prowess, Bucky would deny his genius, but state rather that "some of us are just less damaged than others." This is a sore indictment of our educational system, but is a justified statement about a system so different from that of many geniuses who have taught themselves to use information to fuel insight. Perhaps it would be beneficial to look at the education of Mr. Fuller.

Like every male in the Fuller family since 1760, Bucky had enrolled at Harvard. Unlike the others who graduated, however, he soon realized that Harvard did not want to teach what he felt he needed to learn. He withdrew his tuition and used it to treat the entire chorus line of the Ziegfeld Follies to an expensive dinner. He was duly expelled. The next ten years were a series of highs and lows as he became at times fascinated with synergism—wholes that exceeded the sum of their parts—and at other times frustrated with a culture in which he did not fit. After a series of emotional, personal, and business failures, alcoholism, and attempted suicide, Bucky experienced what he called his "private vision" and realized, as he later said, that "You have no right to eliminate yourself. You do not belong to you. You belong to the universe." So began his "second life," a single-minded journey, a trip to discover what he called "the principles of the universe."

The trip began with an intense saturation period. For one full year, Bucky read physics, mathematics, engineering, architecture, philosophy, and poetry (for twenty-two hours a day). He spoke to no one, not even, he later claimed, his wife. On emerging from this period of saturation he spoke endlessly to anyone who would listen. He spoke in convoluted terms in a language of synergism, in streams of consciousness, and verbal structures as integrated as the systems of which he spoke. Underlying the complexity of his exposure, however, were the burning desire and developed ability to attain insight, to see the essence of a situation. This ability he eloquently displayed, for example, when his second daughter Allegra pointed to a burning log and asked "What is fire?" Fuller answered, "fire is the sun unwinding from the tree's log. When the log-fire pop-sparks, it is letting go a sunny day of long-ago, and doing it in a hurry." This expressed oneness (of past and present, rationality and feeling, analysis and sensitivity, science and poetry) to discover and communicate the essence of a situation in his own inimitable way was the product of his self-educative process.

When Bucky became immersed in his self-educative process, he embarked on a lifelong journey. This journey cultivated one of the "least damaged," most thoughtful, expansive, and insightful minds of the twentieth century. Rather than train himself to deal with a narrow "window onto the world," he educated himself to see relationships, to make connections: to be creative. He became a synthetic thinker and feeler; an effective navigator of what he referred to as this "spaceship earth"; and the holder of more than 170 patents; the inventor, in 1935, of a car designed to carry eleven people, to cruise at 120 miles per hour and to get 35 miles per gallon; the inventor of the geodesic dome; the holder of dozens of honorary degrees and a Nobel Prize nomination; and at age 87, the recipient of this nation's highest civilian honor, the Medal of Freedom. Bucky was an effectively educated person.

Buckminster Fuller was truly "learned" because he was able to make connections and see relationships. It was this insight that allowed him to significantly advance the level of knowledge of the laws of the universe, and human potential. While others aspired to learn existing knowledge or generate new data, Bucky would use this knowledge to discover new relationships, new potentials, new realities, and to develop new ideas. By so doing he developed his abilities of insight. When experiments "failed," he saw these not as failures, but as "models to stimulate the imagination."

Educational Models

Why does our education system discourage expansive thinking? It does so because it is based on an inappropriate model. Our education system was formed by a society long past, a culture that had little knowledge of how the mind worked, or of systems and their functioning. It was formed in a time of reductionist thinking, of Cartesian philosophy, where, according to René Descartes, complexities could be understood by reducing them to simple components, and then analyzing these parts. Functioning wholes were seen as the sum of their parts. However, current thought in the sciences speaks to a different reality. Physicist Fritjof Capra states in *The Turning Point* that "systems are integrated wholes whose properties cannot be reduced to those of smaller units." This attitude is founded in the belief that the whole is more than the sum of its parts—Bucky's synergism, today most commonly referred to as holism. This type of thinking, similar to system thinking, further asserts that the relationship between units is more important than the units themselves. Unfortunately, our educational system is based on the Cartesian, not the holistic, model. It is based on objects and disciplines, not on synergisms and integrated decisions. Paraphrasing Howard Odum (1981), "what is needed is a course, perhaps at the sixth grade level, that addresses the interrelationship of ecology, energy, economics and man." Although far too limited as a single course, the notion of curricula based on the interrelationships among these four major influences rather than the segmented approach to academic subjects, is certainly appropriate.

An education system based on the Cartesian model was perhaps acceptable in the past. The world changed slowly and the student learned what was needed in a given field or specific window onto the world. Today, however, change is rapid. Today's students are the first generation of what Alvin Toffler referred to as the third wave in his book of the same name. This generation will be the first asked to make appropriate holistic responses for an electronic-age world, radically different from the preceding industry-based one. These responses will include appropriate landscape design decisions for a changing world. The student today must be ready to find new meaning and relevant relationships in the radically changed cultural context, and to use this understanding to create new, dynamic, relevant systems and landscapes.

MECHANICS OF THE MIND

In preparing for this challenge, a basic understanding of the mechanics of the mind would be helpful, but the human mind belies such analysis. Since the nineteenth century, we have recognized that different parts of the brain specialize in different tasks. We have recently discovered that when one part of the brain is damaged, another part can often accept its tasks. We also believe that the mental pathways and processing of information within the brain vary among cultures. We are also discovering that differences in language structure may affect the mechanics of image processing in the mind. Language may play a part, for example, in the evolution of a Japanese culture in harmony with its surroundings, which turns everyday routines into art forms—as opposed to our Western culture's competitive relationship with our surroundings, and our goal-oriented attitudes and separation of routine life and art. The relationship between decision-making and language makes the current work in semiotics and alternative languages of design particularly significant.

Despite the complexity of the mind, there are several generalizations and observations that can be helpful as we pursue more open and creative thinking. The first is that as humans evolved, so did the brain, and as new brain (limbic and cortical) evolved, old brain (pre-cortical) remained. The two brains now function somewhat differently. The most recently evolved cortical brain, the seat of reasoning and logic, is often referred to as the left hemisphere (in which right-handed or rational thinking occurs). The older limbic brain, the site of intuition and feeling, remains as right hemispheric thought (in which left-handed intuitive thinking and feeling occur). There are also those who contend that deep within the limbic brain resides a reptilian brain, the residual lizard at the base of our spine, which functions to maintain basic survival. According to this three-brain theory, the reptilian brain serves as a filter. It uses mechanisms such as the *fight or flight syndrome,* our innate need for prospect and refuge (Chapter 16) and our tendency to consider only safe alternatives.

While the processing of stimuli through the neurophysiological pathways of the brain remains a mystery, we do know that if we change the stimuli, we can alter the pathway of information processing or the pattern in the mind. This subject, and its implication for design, are discussed at length by Edward DeBono in the book *Lateral Thinking* (1973). DeBono also addresses techniques for rerouting design thinking, that is, for recircuiting design thought.

FEELING

Our educational system is the product of our past and continuing sensate value system. This value system sees rational thought as truth and knowledge, and discourages intuitive thought. It teaches us to discount or override our feelings.

We are beginning to place higher value on intuition and insight. Even in the hard sciences, the bastions of rational thought and scientific method, many leaders are speaking for the value and necessity of intuitive thought. In this new paradigm, rational thought and scientific method, while being seen as means for proving specific pieces of the story, are usually *not* seen as the primary means by which the story is evolved. Rather, the intuitive leap is seen as the main process by which we move toward truth and beauty.

Where rational thought seeks to be objective, intuition is subjective. Reality is also subjective, and subjective reality directs our behavior. Our primary means of interpreting nature, the world around us, and the designed environment is emotional. Our design behavior is emotional as well.

There is a growing awareness of, and appreciation for, intuitive thought in this new view of reality, and in emerging cultural paradigms, as we discuss in Chapter 14. This respect for intuition is consistent with the new relativistic science that sees reality not in a materialistic, rational sense but in a phenomenological sense: as the interrelationship of an event and an instrument that records that event. In this sense the physical world is but a stage on which reality is constructed, and true reality lies as the synergism of the physical world and human consciousness. Reality is subjective, intuitive, and emotional.

The growing perception of the value of intuition is an indication that our civilization is moving from a sensate value system to an ideational one in which reality has a spiritual sense, or to an idealistic one that synergizes rational and intuitive thought. Either case speaks for a growing sensitivity to the landscape as experience. Each also speaks to design processes that include both rational right-handed thinking (generally referred to in design schools as problem-solving) and left-handed thinking (landscape as art, landscape as meaning, and landscape as a language of design expression).

WHOLE-BRAIN KNOWING

In the recent past, the use of both brains, *whole-brain knowing*, was considered mystical, and the province of the mentally elite: the Zen master, the philosopher, or the genius. American culture, on the other hand, had a passion for logic, prescriptions, order, and sequence. According to Ferguson, however, the human brain has little use for logic of this kind:

> It is a computer of incredible power and subtlety, but far more analog than digital. It works not by precision, but probabalistically, by great numbers of often rough or vague approximations . . . quick perception of truth without conscious attention or reasoning . . . knowledge from within.

This instinctive knowing, so comfortable to the brain, has been the object of attack by our formal education system. Intuitive knowing has been distrusted because it could not be proven—because it was non-rational. As survivors in our Cartesian-newtonian education system, we have learned to quiet the limbic mind, to equate thinking with thinking rationally, and

to distrust our feelings. In the process, we have become less sensitive, less feeling individuals.

We have been conditioned to think logically. However, to be able to have insight and then realize the potential of this insight requires ambidextrous thinking. In the first sense we need to think intuitively, subjectively, sensually, and with feeling, allowing a multiplicity of influences to saturate the mind, and promoting the emergence of new patterns and relationships. We also need to think logically and deductively to determine the workability, desirability, or appropriateness of a solution. This requires that we use both types of thinking, and that we be able to turn off the rational brain at times, and revel in the chaos. At other times, it requires that we tune out the chaos and think rationally. True education develops the ability to think in both modes.

DESIGN THINKING

The responsive, creative landscape designer must be an ambidextrous thinker. Such a person, capable of dealing effectively with both intuition and logic, is said to be "centered," and to think more holistically and integratively. To help the student become more centered, more creative, better at perceiving relationships, and more insightful is one of the primary tasks of design education. We begin this task by looking at design thinking; conceptual blocks to creativity; problem-solving (right-handed thinking); and design languages, meaning, and semiotics.

Conceptual Blockbusting

As stated above, the design student has spent more than a decade in a formal education system that has taught self-limiting behavior. In the process, a number of conceptual roadblocks have been constructed within the mind, as behavioral filters. These function as subliminal survival mechanisms to promote what the student has been taught to see as appropriate behavior. A part of design education is dismantling these conceptual blocks to creativity.

To become more centered and creative, the landscape designer needs to be knowledgeable about thinking forms, blocks to fluency and flexibility in thinking, and techniques that can be effective in dismantling these blocks. These are discussed by James L. Adams in *Conceptual Blockbusting* (1979). In terms of thinking forms, Adams identifies three primary types: visual, verbal, and mathematical. His book allows the reader to discover which type(s) of thinking is (are) subconsciously used and avoided, to discover how flexibly one thinks, and to improve thinking effectiveness. All young designers are encouraged to read this delightful book.

In *Conceptual Blockbusting*, the reader discovers that some situations are understood most easily by visual thinking, while others are difficult to understand visually but lend themselves to verbal or mathematical solutions. Each form of thinking is effective for certain types of situations. For example, landform manipulation causes many landscape designers trouble because it involves both the visualization of existing and designed landform (visual thinking) and the computation of slopes and elevations (mathematical thinking). An individual's tendency to avoid thinking in either mode can make the task much more difficult. As in most cases, the key to successful landform manipulation is the use of appropriate thinking forms.

In a given situation, the flexible thinker quickly and intuitively explores various forms of thinking and selects the most feasible form, and the search is probably an unconscious one. However, the educative process can develop the ability to think flexibly, so that if the selected form proves nonproductive, the thinker can then explore alternative thinking forms. Without such flexibility, unfortunately, the thinker can flounder.

Problem-Solving

According to Adams, blocks to creative thinking are "mental walls that block the problem-solver from correctly perceiving a problem or conceiving its solution." We all experience these blocks. According to Adams, there are four major types of blocks: perceptual blocks, emotional blocks, cultural and environmental blocks, and intellectual and expressive blocks. *Perceptual blocks* prevent the designer from clearly perceiving either the problem or the information necessary to solve the problem. One type of perceptual block is *stereotyping*, that is, placing inappropriately narrow boundaries on conceptualization. Such boundaries prematurely limit the range of alternatives being considered by the designer. To dissuade stereotyping in the academic design studio, projects are often written in connotatively poor language, for example, the student is asked to design a human container rather than a chair. The intent is that the designed container will respond more to specifics of the situation (materials, user, and so on) and that the task at hand will not be confused by the introduction of irrelevant stereotypical information such as chair arms, four legs, and the like.

Another perceptual block identified by Adams is the *inability to isolate a problem*. If it cannot be isolated and defined, the problem cannot be solved. The problem can also be *defined too narrowly*. The textbook example was the attempt to invent a machine sensitive enough to pick tomatoes, thereby automating this labor-intensive industry. After years wasted on a problem too narrowly defined, the problem was redefined more broadly, and a tougher skinned tomato was developed and harvested using conventional equipment. An *inability to see the problem from different perspectives* results in solving only parts of the problem, or even in creating more problems than those solved. This block relates to our tendency to see the world through narrow windows and our inability to look through other windows. Role playing, in which different people identify and articulate specific roles, is an effective and stimulating technique commonly used in the design studio, to develop the ability to overcome this block.

According to Adams, another perceptual block, *familiarity*, occurs when, because of the multiplicity of stimuli, the mind becomes saturated and filters out the commonplace as assumed information. For example, it is because of its familiarity that we cannot, if asked, place the appropriate letters with their corresponding numbers on a telephone dial. It is also why crab-walking through a space helps us "see" it better (the perspective changes, and the place becomes less familiar and therefore more noticeable).

Failure to use all our sensory stimuli is also a perceptual block, as we find if we move blindfolded through a familiar area, suddenly "hearing" what was previously ignored, and thereby perceiving the place differently. Generally, we emphasize the visual to the exclusion of other sensory stimuli. However, the perception of place can be much richer if all our senses contribute to, and intensify, the experience.

Emotional blocks are, according to Adams, perhaps the most inhibitive of all thinking blocks. Humans have an instinctive urge to create, as expressed in the excellent movie *Why Man Creates* (1968). However, Freud revealed the other sides of self that can serve as blocks: the ego or socially aware self, and the superego or moralistic self. The ego rejects (often prematurely) ideas that it feels cannot be implemented; the superego rejects on the basis of self-image. Together, the ego and superego introduce an insidious set of emotional blocks. *Fear of failure* is often the most devastating mental block. However, in terms of learning, a fear of risk-taking results in a greatly compromised learning experience. A closely related block in academia is an *overemphasis on grades*. This block becomes quite destructive when grades are marginal and the student becomes more concerned with the grade than with exploration. Under these circumstances, the student often avoids taking risks. Learning (and the grade) often suffer. *Being overly concerned with the opin-*

ion of others can result in trying to please rather than trying to learn. While feedback is important, it must be internalized, and must become a part of the synergistic process in which the designer remains true to self and design direction while also responding to feedback. A *lack of appetite for chaos* is a distrust of left-handed thinking that can result in premature judgment. Complex problems, on the other hand, often require a gestation period of tolerated chaos, so that the subconscious mind can intuitively weigh variables to discover relevant patterns. Elimination of this period can result in poorly conceived solutions.

Closely related to an intolerance for chaos is a tendency to judge rather than generate ideas. An idea generated but not judged can incubate and cultivate other ideas. *Premature judging* removes the idea, as well as its seeding tendency. Lack of curiosity results in too little conceptualizing. Lack of access to one's imagination, or an undeveloped ability to form and manipulate vivid images and a failure to distinguish between reality and fantasy, although less common, are equally devastating emotional blocks.

Adams also discussed cultural or environmental blocks, caused by the cultural or physical context. *Cultural blocks* are those that are established to implement rules of social conduct, and to eliminate inappropriate behavior. Types of behavior that are often unfortunately labeled as inappropriate for adults include fantasy, reflection, playfulness, humor, intuition, feeling, pleasure, qualitative judgment, and a desire for change. There are also many cultural taboos, which society imparts or which the designer may fear that society will impose. Such taboos discourage consideration of many alternatives that would otherwise be considered.

Environmental blocks are created by the immediate physical and human context. These include stressful interpersonal dynamics like distrust, lack of communication, and lack of earned rewards. They also include physical disruptions like noise, glare, and so on.

Intellectual and expressive blocks, according to Adams, include the selection of inappropriate thought processes or ineffective communication of ideas. *Intellectual blocks* include the use of an ineffective thinking form, the inability to move freely between forms, and the generation of incorrect data. *Expressive blocks* are the result of inadequate graphic or verbal communication skills, or an inability to apply these skills.

Any of the preceding blocks can function as impediments to effective decision-making. Removing or avoiding these blocks facilitates the consideration of appropriate stimuli as well as the thought processes conducive to creative conceptualization, which allow the emergence of rich and relevant patterns in the mind's eye.

Design Languages

Problem-solving is but one aspect of design. To a large extent, this was the view that dominated in modern architecture, which in the 1960s and early 1970s promoted the notion that "form follows function." During this period there was a strong desire to avoid subjective meanings and to reduce design to a single functional statement.

In the late 1970s and in the 1980s designers (especially architects) reacted strongly against modernism. This reaction came for many reasons, including the tendency of modern architecture to reduce the meaning of the building to functional terms, and to take its shapes from other disciplines such as machine technology or cubist aesthetics. It also came from the perceived inability of modern architecture to develop a coherent visual language. As a part of this break, design theories such as postmodernism have largely abandoned problem-solving as a design approach. Rather they have embraced the concepts of design languages, typologies of form, and meanings. This text takes the position that both viewpoints are relevant. Problem-solving aspects and rational concerns are essential, and are discussed throughout this text. On the other hand, language and meaning are the essence of civilization.

Landscape Semiotics

Semiotics is the science of language and logic. It is concerned with the creation of a vocabulary of symbols and the use of these symbols to communicate meaning. We have discussed the issues that affect the way people encode and decode meaning. Each of these issues is a window onto the world and affects the language we use to design and interpret meaning in the landscape. In Chapter 16 we look very specifically at the process of ascribing meaning to place.

Seminal works in the development of landscape semiotics are Christopher Alexander's two tandem books *A Timeless Way of Building* (1979), and *A Pattern Language* (1977). The first presents the concept of a language of human expression and discusses how to recognize symbols and how to encode and decode meaning. The second develops some of the vocabulary of symbols for this language. While certainly not the first, nor even the most recent work in semiotics, these two books remain some of the best; for they do not discuss a language of buildings or site developments, but rather a language of patterns and genera of places that have recurred throughout history and in various cultures. It is not a prescriptive language, but rather a descriptive, issue-responsive one. Alexander addresses the context within which an element of the vocabulary, such as an alcove, emerges but that allows that element to be expressed in a manner that addresses place-specific issues. The language does not focus on the building or the site, but on places and patterns of expression that recur at various scales and in various contexts.

One of the main questions of landscape semiotics is the broad range of possible meanings of the land-scape, and how this complexity is addressed through design. There have been two basic responses to this question. The initial response in the reaction against modernism was to embrace an eclectic language. This approach was probably best represented by Christopher Alexander and by Robert Venturi's *Learning from Las Vegas* (1972), which stresses signs with conventional meaning understood by the populace. This approach allowed the attribution of different meanings to the same physical gesture. It relished complexity and pluralistic meanings, and did not seek to prescribe the appropriate solution, nor to limit the language structure.

More recently, the emphasis has shifted to form, and to grammatical issues in the language of design. These grammatical issues prescribe acceptable rules. This approach is concerned with the forms themselves and the linguistic structures or rules by which those forms are generated. The best example of this later approach is the work of Peter Eisenman, which is based on Noam Chomsky's *Cartesian Linguistics: A Chapter in the History of Rational Thought* (1966).

Landscape Design Thinking

This search for a language of design, for design meaning, for the forms, symbols, or typologies that generate those forms, and for the structure of the language is a worthy pursuit for the landscape designer. And when we take a Cartesian approach (as we have in the past) and look at the element to be designed, we generate some highly creative gestures. However, as we discuss in Chapter 16, the jury is not yet in as to whether this approach can be successful at synergizing the myriad of expressions into meaningful coherent places and managing our complex world for urban placeness and psychological health.

In the classical and Renaissance worlds, society was relatively homogeneous. It changed slowly, allowing the architectural vocabulary and syntax to become established, and the architectural types to become symbols with relatively fixed meanings. On the other hand, modern architecture, occurring in a rapidly changing heterogeneous culture and changing technology, was never able to achieve this meaning. Taking a different approach, postmodern architecture has been trying to fix the symbol and the meaning, when

the condition itself is not fixed. Whether semiotics can provide for psychological health and well-being will depend on whether it can effectively reconcile design intent, the nature of complex systems, environmental perception, and user psychological needs.

Relevant landscape design thinking, and appropriate design education embrace the search for language and meaning. It does not, however, seek to reduce meaning to a singularity, or to prescribe a fixed vocabulary in a changing condition. Rather it embraces the complexity and pluralism of reality. It solves problems while concentrating meanings and embracing pluralistic interpretations. It responds to, and expresses, a range of influences. Part 3 of the text explores desired changes in paradigms, professional roles, design processes, and design intentions to make landscape design more relevant. Before we explore these issues however, we must develop further our understanding of the influences to which landscape design must respond. This is the objective of Part 2.

REFERENCES

Adams, James. 1979. *Conceptual Blockbusting: A Guide to Better Ideas.* New York: Norton.

Alexander, Christopher. 1977. *A Pattern Language: Towns, Buildings, Construction.* New York: Oxford University Press.

———. 1979. *The Timeless Way of Building.* New York: Oxford University Press.

Aulaire, E., and Aulaire, O. 1985. The Man Who Saw the Future. *Reader's Digest* January: 123–127.

Capra, Fritjof. 1982. *The Turning Point: Science, Society, and the Rising Culture.* New York: Simon & Schuster.

Chomsky, Noam. 1966. *Cartesian Linguistics: A Chapter in the History of Rationalist Thought.* New York: Harper & Row.

DeBono, Edward. 1973. *Lateral Thinking: Creativity Step by Step.* New York: Harper Colophon Books. Harper & Row.

Ferguson, Marilyn. 1980. *The Aquarian Conspiracy: Personal and Social Transformation In the 1980's.* Los Angeles: J. P. Tarcher. New York: St. Martin's Press.

Odum, Howard. 1981. Paper read at the Florida Conference on Energy. Gainesville, FL.

Toffler, Alvin. 1980. *The Third Wave.* New York: Morrow.

Venturi, Robert. 1972. *Learning from Las Vegas.* Cambridge, MA: MIT Press.

Why Man Creates. 1968 Videorecording. Directed by Saul Bass; produced by Saul Bass and Assoc.; conceived and written by Saul Bass and Mayo Simon. Presented by Kaiser Aluminum and Chemical Corporation. Santa Monica, CA: Pyramid Film and Video.

SUGGESTED READINGS

Buffington, Perry. 1984. Understanding Creativity. *Sky Magazine* (Delta Airlines Inflight Magazine). June 1984.

Hanks, Kurt. 1977. *Design Yourself.* Los Altos, CA: William Kaufmann.

Koberg, Don, and Bagnall, Jim. 1974. *The Universal Traveler: A Soft-Systems Guide to Creativity, Problem-Solving, and the Process of Design,* rev. ed. Los Altos, CA: William Kaufmann.

Marshall, Lane. 1981. *Landscape Architecture into the 21st Century: A Special Task Force Report from the American Society of Landscape Architects.* New York: American Society of Landscape Architects.

Ornstein, Robert E. 1972. *The Psychology of Consciousness.* New York: Viking Press.

Sibatani, Atuhiro. 1980. The Japanese Brain. *Science 80.* December.

Part 2

Design Influences

4

Landscape Process

Landscapes are point-in-time expressions of ongoing processes. Some of these processes are ecological, some cultural; but all operate to change the landscape over time. *Places* are specific locations in the landscape. The degree to which designed form responds to the specifics of a place, its physical conditions, and its processes helps determine the appropriateness of the form. It also affects efficiency and the resources that must be allocated to maintain the form over time. Landscapes are, in a positive sense, the environmental litter left behind by a multitude of forces.

ECOLOGICAL FORCES

Landscapes evolve over time in response to ecological forces, which can be grouped into three categories: geologic processes including tectonic, hydrologic, glacial, wind, and weathering processes; soil-forming processes; and biological processes. These processes interact to form an ecological system, or an ecosystem. Change is the essence of these systems, and by means of succession, these processes, operating through time, create our rich and varied landscapes.

LANDSCAPE FORM AND PATTERN RECOGNITION

A given landscape is read both as form and as pattern. The specific forms and their distribution or *pattern* give the informed designer clues to the nature and intensity of forces operative in the landscape. These clues include whether the forces are current and active or no longer in effect. *Pattern recognition* is the ability of the designer to read the landscape and understand its elements and forces.

Evocative form and pattern are given throughout the following sections. These examples are often identified as young or old, or as early or late successional expressions. Such terms refer to relative, not absolute, time. A young or early successional pattern is one in the early stages of a predictable sequence of form evolution. An old or late successional pattern is in the later stages of an evolutionary form sequence.

GEOLOGIC PROCESSES

Geologic processes are predictable sequences of events, powered by geologic forces. They are, according to Press and Siever in *Earth* (1974), the activities through which "rock materials pass from a sedimentary form, through diastrophism and deformation of sedimentary rock, through metamorphism and eventual melting and magma formation, through vulcanism and plutonism to igneous rock formation, and through erosion to form more sediments."

In less technical terms, and greatly simplified, geologic processes are those by which rocks are formed, differentiated, eroded, and deposited to be reformed again into rocks. They involve tectonic forces—the forces powered from within the earth by radioactive decay (according to the theory of plate tectonics). They also include erosional and weathering forces.

Any given landscape can be seen first as a point-in-time expression of the interplay of two sets of geologic processes. On the one hand, tectonic forces (powered by radioactive decay within the earth) uplift the land and build new form. Relating these forms to basic design vocabulary, one could say that the forms of the uplifted landscape are *positive (mass-generated) forms* (Figure 4-1). In this case, the mass expresses the generative forces from below.

Figure 4-1. Uplifted landscape.

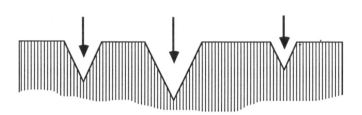

Figure 4-2. Erosional landscape.

On the other hand, erosional forces (wind, rain, and ice flows) and weathering forces (physical and chemical decay) reduce or soften the uplifted form and eventually create erosional landforms. In basic design terms, the eroded landscape is dominated by *negative (space-generated) forms* (Figure 4-2). These forms most vividly communicate the erosional forces from above.

Tectonics

Tectonic forces, powered from within the earth, function to move the geological plates of the earth, and in so doing create regions of tectonic activity. In some regions, the earth's crust is being destroyed; in others it is being twisted, contorted, or broken; in still others new crust is being created. The new material being formed varies with the chemical nature of the melt—its pressure, temperature, and movement—and with the climate within which it cools. The range of landscape patterns and physical forms therefore varies tremendously.

Landforms that evoke tectonic forces purely, without the ravaging influences of erosion and weathering, are referred to as *young* tectonic forms. For example, the angular landforms so familiar in Chinese art, and the ragged thrusting forms of the Himalayas in India are young tectonic landforms (Figure 4-3). The much softer rounded forms of the Alleghenies in Pennsylvania are *old* tectonic forms. In these older ranges the mountains that formed millennia ago have eroded over the years to a less angular, softer form (Figure 4-4).

Hydrolics

The hydrologic cycle—the movement of water from the ocean to the atmosphere, through rain, across the surface as runoff, through the land as soil water and groundwater, and back to the sea—is a major erosional force.

Landforms are modified by both groundwater and surface water relationships. Groundwater modifies land form primarily through dissolution of the substrate, by dissolving the geologic base. As water dissolves soluble geologic materials, a cavernous underground landscape can develop. As this system of caverns becomes extensive and approaches the surface, structural failure and collapse can occur. The resulting surface expression is referred to as a sinkhole (Figure 4-5). Over time, the landscape that develops on the surface in these regions underlain by soluble geologies can become characterized by many sinkholes and vanishing and reappearing streams (as water enters and exits underground caverns). This type of landscape is referred to as *Karstic*, after the Karst region of Yugoslavia. Spelunkers, sightseers, and sometimes swimmers who frequent Karstic landscapes take advantage of the ability of water to dissolve the limestone of the region, and to create sometime dramatic landscapes (Figures 4-6 and 4-7).

The landform expressions of groundwater are generally limited to Karstic or other collapse type landscapes in areas of soluble geologies. However, the landform expressions of surface flow are more varied and ubiquitous. In most landscapes, the surface flow of water is the primary agent of erosion. In fact, there are few regions where surface flow does not express itself literally in the form of the land.

The degree to which water erodes the land is based on the volume of water, its rate of flow, and the material over which it flows. As rain falls on the ground, it soaks into the surface. When the rate of rainfall

Figure 4-3. Young mountains.

Figure 4-4. Old mountains.

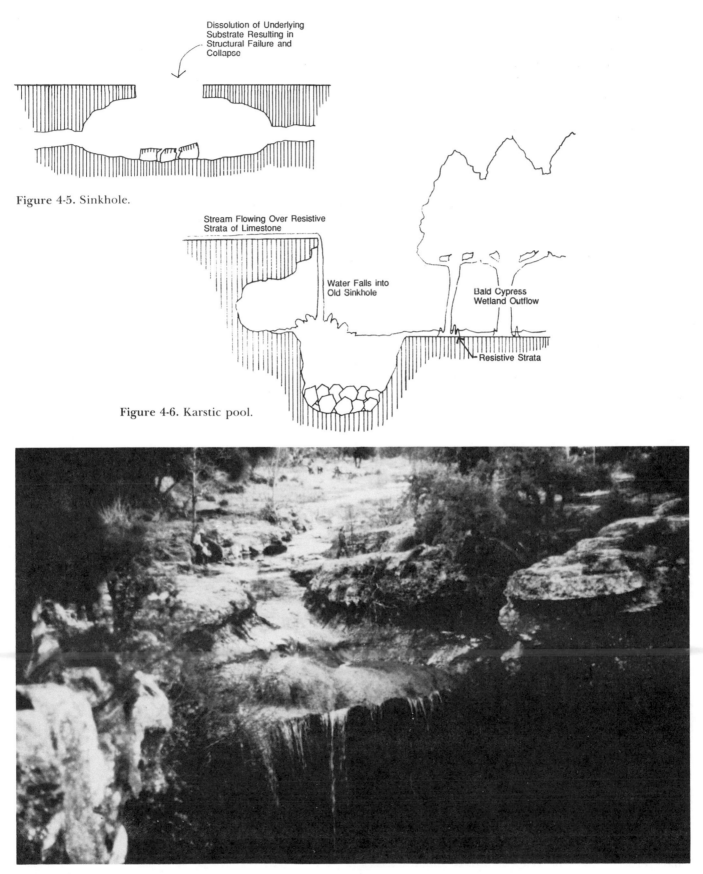

Dissolution of Underlying
Substrate Resulting in
Structural Failure and
Collapse

Figure 4-5. Sinkhole.

Stream Flowing Over Resistive
Strata of Limestone

Water Falls into
Old Sinkhole

Bald Cypress
Wetland Outflow

Resistive Strata

Figure 4-6. Karstic pool.

Figure 4-7. Sinkhole. (Hamilton's Pool, Central Texas Hill Country)

exceeds the infiltration rate, runoff occurs. This runoff begins as a sheet of water. Because of skin friction its velocity is slow and it has little erosive force. It soon begins to collect into rivulets and then these rivulets combine to form streams. As they do so, the volume, velocity, and erosive force of the water increase.

The ground surface and its vegetative cover have a limited ability to resist the water's erosive force. As the force exceeds that ability, erosion occurs. The stream begins to erode through the surface at the point of greatest concentration of water, usually near the stream outflow. The stream then erodes in three directions, downward, headward, and laterally (Figure 4-8). The young stream, over time, matures (ages) into a dendritic (treelike) pattern, as viewed from above. The upper reaches of this dendritic pattern are char-

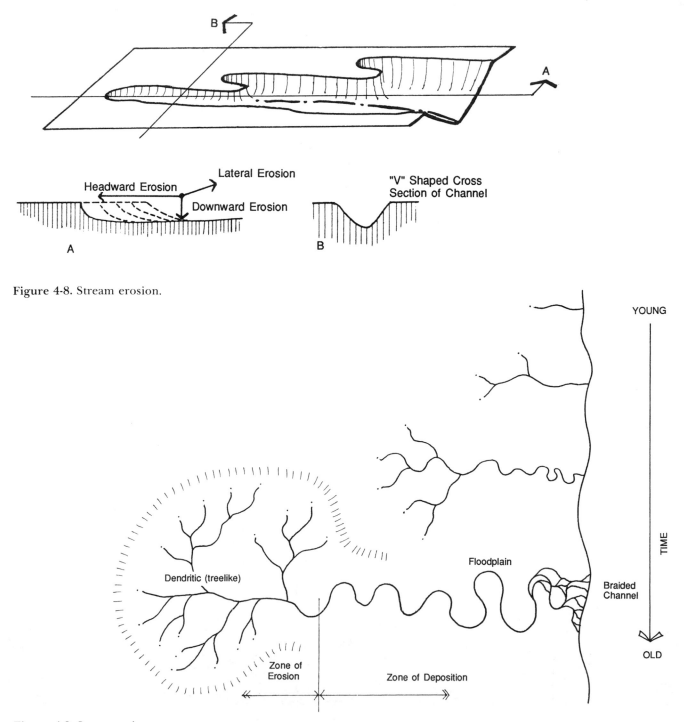

Figure 4-8. Stream erosion.

Figure 4-9. Stream aging.

acterized by relatively steep slopes, high velocities, and straight channels; the lower reaches by flat slopes, reduced velocities, and a meandering channel (Figure 4-9).

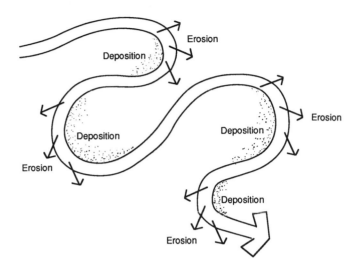

Figure 4-10. Direction of stream erosion.

The ability of water to transport sediments is affected by its velocity. In the steep headwater areas, the rapidly moving water is highly erosive. In the lower flatter reaches, the slower water is unable to continue carrying its sediment load. It deposits this material on the land, and in times of flooding, creates a fertile floodplain. In times of normal stream flow, the slow-moving water flows in a stream that meanders through this floodplain. On the outside of the bends of the meander, the water accelerates and erodes; on the inside it slows and deposits. Though this process, the meander changes its shape over time (Figure 4-10).

In the lowest reaches of very mature old streams, near their outflow and base elevation, the land is very nearly level. The velocity slows to an almost stagnant condition, the stream clogs with sediment, and a braided channel develops (Figure 4.9).

The stream-aging pattern of Figure 4-9 is an idealized one. Usually, because of variations in subsurface conditions, the stream pattern evolves somewhat differently from this ideal. Figure 4-11 shows some of the more common variations to the idealized pattern and

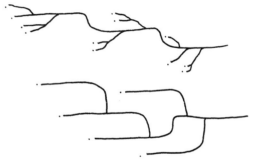

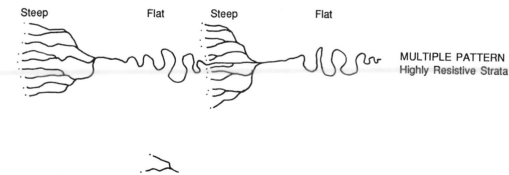

LINEAR PATTERN
Folded Substrate

BLOCKY PATTERN
Underlying Fracture Pattern

MULTIPLE PATTERN
Highly Resistive Strata

INCOMPLETE PATTERN
Karstic Condition

Figure 4-11. Variation in stream pattern.

underlying geologic conditions that can influence evolution into these modified patterns. Of course, the educated eye uses these and other pattern variations as cues to landscape materials and processes that may not be observed directly.

Glaciers

Glaciers are masses of surface snow and ice that persist throughout the year and that flow under their own weight. They are tremendously heavy, they scrape massive amounts of bedrock, and they dislodge and push boulders to their fronts and sides as they flow.

Some of the forms associated with glacial flows are striated scoured landforms, characteristic "U" shaped valley cross-sections, linear strips of boulders (called moraines) alongside and at the end of valleys, hanging valleys and associated waterfalls (Figure 4-12), and drumloidal shapes (Figure 4-13). These forms are often indicators of prior glacial processes. When present, they can provide the designer critical information concerning whether the patterns being viewed are indicative of current processes or relic features from

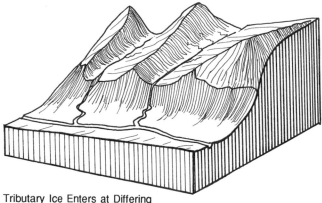

Tributary Ice Enters at Differing
Levels Depending Primarily on Depth
of Ice Flow and Subsequent Depth of Scouring

Figure 4-12. Hanging valleys and waterfalls.

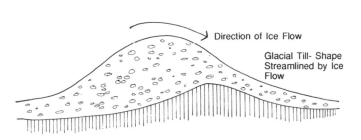

Figure 4-13. Drumlin.

Direction of Ice Flow

Glacial Till- Shape
Streamlined by Ice
Flow

millions of years past. This is significant because when designing in the context of forms that express active processes, the designer must respond to physical form and material, *as well as* the activities that are creating the form. For relic form, the designer responds to form and material but must design for processes that are different from those expressed by the relic form.

Wind

Wind, although less powerful than water, can still effectively erode, transport, and deposit sediment. However, wind has little erosive ability of its own. To erode, it must suspend particles in the airflow. The requirements for wind erosion are therefore a readily available supply of sediment, wind with an adequately sustained velocity, and a dry climate to allow the particles to be easily freed from the surface and to remain suspended in the air. Regions of low wind speed and high humidity experience little wind erosion; regions of high wind speed and low humidity can be characterized by wind-eroded landscapes.

To achieve wind erosion, particles must first become part of the airstream. However, near the ground (within 1 millimeter), surface friction results in a stagnant layer of air. Clay particles that lie flat against the ground are highly resistive to wind erosion; sand particles that protrude into the airstream are subjected to its forces. Although sand particles are too heavy to be carried by the wind, they can be bounced. On impact, they knock other larger (and more numerous) particles into the airstream. By this process, called *saltation* (which also happens to pebbles in a stream of water), a layer of sand particles is transported. This layer is an extremely effective erosional agent (Figure 4-14).

Smaller, silt-sized particles are less abrasive than sand particles, but they are also less heavy. While they are not as effective as erosional agents, large amounts can be transported over great heights and distances

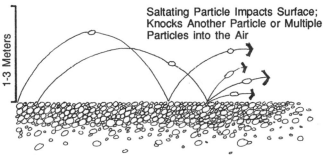

Saltating Particle Impacts Surface;
Knocks Another Particle or Multiple
Particles into the Air

1-3 Meters

Figure 4-14. Saltation transport of sand by wind.

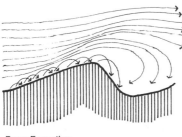

Dune Formation

Saltating Grains Land on Slip
Face; Accumulation Slips to Form
Foreset Bed; Compression of
Air Over Dune Increases Velocity
and Determines Maximum Height

Figure 4-15. Dunes. (Dune formation section adapted from F. Press and R. Siever, *Earth*)

by the wind. In the dust bowl of the 1930s, for example, entire houses were buried by the deposition of airborne sediments. Often this material, called *loess*, has been subsequently eroded into unique steep-walled landscapes.

While wind erosion sculpts rocks into angles, blocks, cracks, and vents, the depositional form of windborne sand, the dune (Figure 4-15), is a soft undulating form, often articulated with sharp crestlines. The form expresses not only the flow of air, but also the amounts of available sand and the form of underlying rocks. The resulting dunes, though seemingly disorganized, are holistically ordered, and are usually rhythmic, sensual landscapes, evocative of wind (eolian) forces.

Weathering

Weathering is the primary mechanism of erosion. It consists of mechanical weathering or decay and chemical weathering. These two forms of weathering support and reinforce each other. The greater the mechanical decay or fracturing, the more surface area available for chemical decay. In addition, chemically weakened material is more susceptible to mechanical decay.

Mechanical weathering includes the erosional activities that have been discussed above. It also includes temperature- or plant-induced breakage. Temperature causes mechanical weathering in two primary ways. It heats and cools rocks, and because of differential rates of expansion (of different minerals) induces stresses that lead to breakage. Water then enters crevices in the rocks. This water expands on freezing and crumbles layers of the rock. Plant roots penetrate fissures that have filled with soil, and through their growth processes, force these cracks to expand and the rocks to break. Mechanical weathering tends to dominate in dry climates characterized by temperature extremes.

Chemical weathering occurs primarily as minerals that were formed underground, often under intense heat and pressure, chemically decompose at the earth's surface conditions. The rate of chemical decay depends on climate, tectonics, rock composition, and time. It often accelerates greatly under the chemically enriched air of the urban environment. Chemical weathering tends to dominate in humid climates.

Mechanical and chemical weathering work together to generate the dissolved substances carried in our water, and in our air. They are also the first steps in the formation of soils that are essential to supporting life on the surface of the earth.

SOIL-FORMING PROCESSES

The thin layer of soil that covers the terrestrial portions of the earth controls the existence and distribution of life on its surface. Without this thin layer of soil, land plants and animals as we know them would not exist; and the rise and fall of civilizations can be correlated with the development and loss of their soil resource. It is therefore a matter of concern that we are currently losing the soil base on which the productivity of America and the spaceship earth are based.

The process by which soil is formed consists of mechanical and chemical weathering, and of abiotic (nonliving) and biotic (living) activities. In the initial phases of soil formation, differential expansion and contraction (because of temperature changes) cause fissures to develop in rocks. Then, water enters these fissures and, on freezing, causes breakage. Chemical constituents in the water contribute to chemical decay. Within the bits of crumbled rock, lichen (a symbiotic relationship of algae and fungus) begins to grow. The powdered rock accelerates chemical decay and through plant growth and death, begins to accumulate the organic matter essential for the soil to sustain life. As the organic content of the soil rises, pioneering plants (such as Junipers), capable of sustaining themselves in the hostile environment, invade. These pioneering plants increase the rate of mechanical weathering (through root action) and chemical decay. As the layer of powdered rock grows, and the amount of living and dead organic matter increases, it becomes a biologically active and productive soil.

BIOLOGIC PROCESSES

The spaceship earth is powered by energy, which can be understood as the capacity to do work. Tectonic processes are powered by thermonuclear energy as the core of the earth decays radioactively. Surface processes are powered primarily by solar energy which is available in its raw state, solar radiation, and in its stored states—wood, coal, lignite, and petroleum. For practical purposes, the energy of fusion and fission are still not commonly available.

In order to use energy to achieve work, we must change its state. According to the laws of thermodynamics, when we do so, energy is neither created nor destroyed, for the total amount of energy in the system is constant. However, there is a natural tendency toward innate uniformity. For example, if we erase a blackboard, and blow the dust from the eraser, the chalk dust does not re-form the words that were erased from the blackboard, but rather distributes itself as a relatively uniform distribution on the floor. To reorder the dust into words on the blackboard would require the expenditure of energy to gather and replace the particles of dust as desired. Conversely, as highly ordered material degrades, usable energy is released. This universal tendency toward disorder is called *entropy.*

As we change energy from a more complex, concentrated state to a less concentrated one, there is a decrease in the amount of energy bound, and an increase in the amount released and therefore available to do work.

Biological systems function to increase order, organization, and complexity, and therefore to increase the amount of energy stored for later reuse. In this sense, they are *negentropic (negative entropy).* They capture a low-grade energy, solar radiation, and through the process of photosynthesis, concentrate it in chemical bonds to form more highly organized complex forms called plant protein. Other life forms eat these plant proteins, and through the process of respiration, convert their low-grade chemical bonds into higher-grade animal proteins. In each case, this energy is processed through complex movements of minerals such as oxygen, nitrogen, carbon, trace elements, and water. Each of these is essential to the pro-

cess, and therefore any one can become an ecologically limiting material.

The nonliving (abiotic) and living (biotic) components together form an *ecosystem (ecological system).* Within the system, parts relate holistically. Ecosystems evolve over time toward greater order, diversity, complexity, and stability, and toward a more efficient utilization of the energy resource. We refer to this organizational sequence as succession. Early successional ecosystems (Figure 4-16) are characterized by a minimum diversity of components, each generally tolerant of a relatively wide range of habitats (ecological conditions). There is little differentiation of roles in the system, and little organization or specificity in pattern. Early successional ecosystems have, as their ecological survival strategies, the toleration and exploitation of harsh environments and their ability to migrate quickly into an area. However, they are relatively inefficient in energy utilization, lack the ability to compete effectively over long periods of time for limited energy resources, and are therefore relatively short-lived.

Late successional ecosystems (Figure 4-16) are highly ordered. This order tends to be holistic, responding to a myriad of environmental variables, including solar radiation, temperature, air humidity, soil humidity, soil acidity, available nutrients, and so on. It is also a probabalistic, not a predictive, order, that is, the myriad of influences interact to increase or decrease the probability that a specific form or material will occur, but without the ability to predict exactly where or how it will occur.

There is a high degree of organization and diversity in late successional ecosystems. Individual species serve very specific roles in these systems; and they are fine tuned to their ecological condition. As such, they

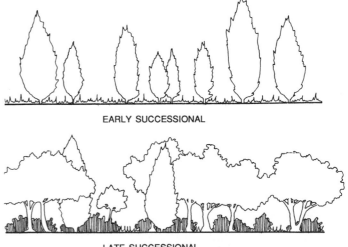

EARLY SUCCESSIONAL

LATE SUCCESSIONAL

Figure 4-16. Early and late successional ecosystems.

function more efficiently in obtaining usable energy from the system, and have an ecological advantage over time and when resources are limited. They tend to be dominant until some disturbance changes the environmental conditions, thereby upsetting the fine-tuned relationship between organism and environment. The success of late successional organisms is closely tied to their condition, and these organisms are relatively intolerant to environmental modifications.

FORM AS EXPRESSION OF FORCE, MATERIAL, AND TIME

The natural form of a place can be seen as the interrelationship among the preceding (and other) ecological forces, the materials of the place, and time. Certain materials are highly resistant to specific forces of nature; others are quite susceptible to these same forces. For example, Cleopatra's Needle, a granite obelisk had survived for more than thirty-five centuries in the hot, dry climate of Egypt. Then it was placed in the Metropolitan Museum of Art in New York City. In the subsequent few decades, it has weathered more than it had in the preceding 3500 years. This occurred because granite is particularly susceptible to the wet, chemically polluted air of New York City.

When ecological forces are strong, landscape patterns and physical form express these forces in a reasonably "pure" manner. This tends to be the case in humid climates, and those characterized by temperature extremes. On the other hand, when forces are weaker or the materials particularly resistant, patterns and forms express the character of the material and modify the pure pattern that the forces try to create. The pattern becomes the synergism of force and material. The degree to which form expresses material is more pronounced in mild and dry climates.

Natural form also expresses time. With increases in time, form that initially expresses material evolves to express the interplay of materials and force, or to be more expressive of force. It should be kept in mind, however, that highly resistant materials or weak forces (as in mild, dry climates) extend the time frame, allowing forms to remain young in their expression over long periods of time. These landscapes are very slow to heal, once they are disturbed. Conversely, strong forces and weak materials compress the time frame, and result in rapidly healing landscapes.

As stated earlier, when discussing the age of a form—young or old, early or late successional—we are using these terms in a relative, not an absolute sense. As the preceding example shows, certain materials can remain ecologically young for great periods of time.

Granite mountains or a human artifact granite obelisk can remain largely unmodified for long periods of time in the hot, dry climate of Egypt, for example, but will age rapidly under humid, acid conditions.

REGIONAL LANDSCAPES

Ecological forces operating over time create regional landscapes, that is, regionally differing sets of expressions. For example, the historical sequence of ecological forces that have generated the aged glacial landscapes of the far Northeastern states have developed landscapes quite different from those generated by the arid continental climatic conditions of west Texas.

Each landscape is an integrated set of expressions, which holistically responds to a multiplicity of influences. As systems, they function differently, one from another; as visual resource they express themselves quite differently; but each has its unique spirit of place, or Genius Loci.

SPIRIT OF PLACE

According to Christian Norberg-Schulz, in *Genius Loci: Towards a Phenomenology of Architecture* (1980), a *place* in "the true sense of the word . . . [is] a space that has a distinct character." If this is so, then *placeness* can be understood as the characteristics that allow a specific location to make an impression in the mind, an image that endures long after the eye has moved on to other settings. *Placelessness* occurs when a location lacks the ability to endure in the mind.

Norberg-Schulz goes on to address the role of the designer of built form. He states:

> Since ancient times the genius loci, or 'spirit of place' has been recognized as the concrete reality man has to face and come to terms with in his daily life. Architecture means to visualize the genius loci, and the task of the architect is to create meaningful places . . . [where] he can orient himself within and identify himself with an environment.

With this approach, we can see the introduction of *new* built form as a concentration of the genius loci of the place, and an introduction of new placeness.

Some places are truly special. For instance, the hill country of central Texas is a unique region. On a smaller scale, Amalfi, Italy, is a city of singular placeness. Virtually every city has its own unique and memorable neighborhoods. Still smaller in scale, each community has its special public, interpersonal, and personal scaled places that conjure rich images in the mind's eye. However, by placing these rare examples on proverbial pedestals, we risk losing sight of the fact that every location has some unique characteristics of expression. The role of the creative and responsive designer is to perceive the elements in a given place that contribute to its character, and to generate form in light of that uniqueness. It is also to identify elements that destroy placeness and to eliminate these elements or to ameliorate their impact. In so doing, the designer is managing the sense of place.

In *Maintaining the Spirit of Place* (1983), Harry Launce Garnham identified ingredients contributing to spirit to include

> Aspects of the existing natural environment such as land form and topography, vegetation, climate and the presence of water; cultural expressions such as bridges, forts, or hilltop churches which are a reaction to landscape, social history, physical location, human activities, and place as a cultural artifact (a place's meaning beyond its physical expression such as Yorktown, Virginia, due to its historical significance); and the sensory experience, primarily visual, which results from the interaction of culture with the existing landscape.

The loss of spirit of place results from an inability to perceive or respond to this spirit as an interactive synthesis of these ingredients. Cities today are suffering from this loss, the condition we call placelessness.

Christopher Alexander, in *A Pattern Language* (1977) and its companion book, *A Timeless Way of Building* (1979), explores an alternative architecture, one that "lives" as an interactive relationship between natural form, human-made form and the life patterns of its inhabitants. His examples, not surprisingly, come primarily from vernacular traditions of building, not from the grand tradition. Most of our examples today come from strip developments and small forgotten towns, not, unfortunately, from the pages of architectural or landscape architectural magazines.

PLACE AS SYSTEM
AND INFRASTRUCTURE

Landscapes and places can be viewed sensually for their spirit; they can also be seen functionally as a set of interrelating ecological and human systems. The systems introduced by people are powered by human physical needs and technological growth.

In order to provide health, safety, and welfare and to promote technological growth and an improved quality of life, landscape planners and designers introduce systems that support a desired life-style. These systems, referred to as infrastructure, are introduced so that ecological systems can better serve concentrations of people in industrial and post-industrial societies.

Infrastructural systems make ecological resources available for human use, and address the integration of ecological and human needs. They provide potable water, electricity, natural gas, and communication services to a place, while facilitating the removal of storm water, refuse, and human wastes. They also facilitate the movement of people and goods. Their form is an expression of materials and technology and a response to site ecological systems and their pattern expressions. Infrastructural systems are static in nature; they grow over time, not in an organic or biological sense, but in increments. They grow as extensions to existing systems, or as new subsystems. To a large extent, sense of place is dependent upon the degree to which infrastructural systems integrate with other human and natural systems.

REFERENCES

Alexander, Christopher. 1977. *A Pattern Language: Towns, Buildings, Construction.* New York: Oxford University Press.

———. 1979. *The Timeless Way of Building.* New York: Oxford University Press.

Garnham, Harry. 1983. *Maintaining the Spirit of Place: A Process for the Preservation of Town Character.* Mesa, AZ: PDA.

Landphair, Harlow, and Motloch, John. 1985. *Site Reconnaissance and Engineering: An Introduction for Architects, Landscape Architects and Planners.* New York: Elsevier.

Norberg-Schulz, Christian. 1980. *Genius Loci: Towards a Phenomenology of Architecture.* New York: Rizzoli.

Press, Frank, and Siever, Raymond. 1974. *Earth.* San Francisco: W. H. Freeman.

SUGGESTED READINGS

Garner, H. F. 1974. *The Origin of Landscapes; a Synthesis of Geomorphology.* New York: Oxford University Press.

Keeton, William. 1980. *Biological Science,* 3d ed. New York: Norton.

Longwell, C., and Flint, R. 1969. *Physical Geology.* New York: Wiley.

McHarg, Ian. 1969. *Design with Nature.* Garden City, NY: American Museum of Natural History: Natural History Press.

5

Resources and Technology

Ecological forces operating over time have created regional landscape expressions. As systems, each expression functions differently; each is also a unique visual resource that makes available to the designer a basic palette of land design materials. This palette of materials combines with those generated by man, or those brought in from other regions. These materials, along with the technological capabilities of the society, determine design potential.

This chapter explores the basic palette of land design resources, including materials and technology. It begins by exploring landform and its implication for infrastructure and proceeds to review water, plants, and the range of construction materials. It closes with a discussion of structural concepts and a review of the basic litany of structural systems.

LAND AND LANDFORM

Land is the solid part of the surface to the earth; its three-dimensional relief is called topography or landform. This form develops as ecological, cultural, and technological forces operate, over time, on the earth's surface. The severity of the forces, the resistance of the surface, and the relative time those forces operate determine that form.

Regional Landform

Each physiographic region has its own set of ecological forces and materials. Over time, these determine the physical character of that region, including its vocabulary of landform. For example, the hill country physiographic subregion of central Texas has a history of tectonics, deposition, and subsequent erosion (primarily by water). The resultant geologies of interbedded limestones of differing resistivities, being subjected to water erosion, explain this region's expressive terraced landform (Figure 5-1). As one moves geographically to the east, the geologic materials change from limestone to clayey alluvium, and the landforms change substantially (Figure 5-2). In a similar manner, as ecological forces change, so too does the regional landform.

Communication

Landform communication, in most design situations, involves understanding and utilizing two-dimensional graphic techniques to represent three-dimensional form at a reduced scale. It can therefore be quite dif-

Figure 5-1. Hill country terraced landform.

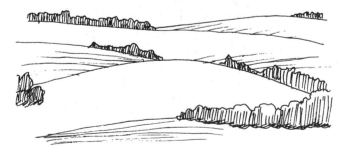

Figure 5-2. Blackland prairie rolling landform.

ficult, at first. However, when one begins by identifying key upper and lower spot elevations and ridge and valley lines, and then proceeds to use basic plan "signatures" of various landforms, reading and drawing landforms become quite easy.

Landform in Plan

Hachures are perhaps the most visually powerful manner of communicating landform in the two-dimensional plan drawing. Hachures are lines drawn parallel to the lines of steepest slope, connecting consecutive lines of elevation (Figure 5-3). While hachure lines are usually evenly spaced, this spacing can change to reflect the amount of sunlight that falls on the surface (a combination of the slope angle and direction, and the angle and direction of the sun), thereby giving a greater three-dimensional effect.

The most common way of representing landform on a two-dimensional surface is the contour plan. Contour lines are lines of equal elevation (Figure 5-4). Consecutive lines on the plan have a consistent vertical separation, referred to as the contour interval.

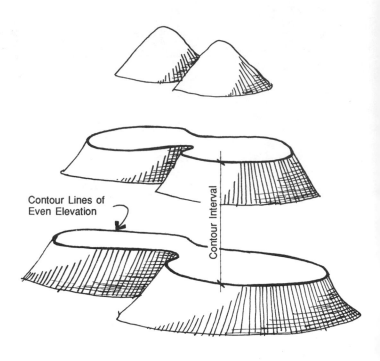

Figure 5-4. Contour lines.

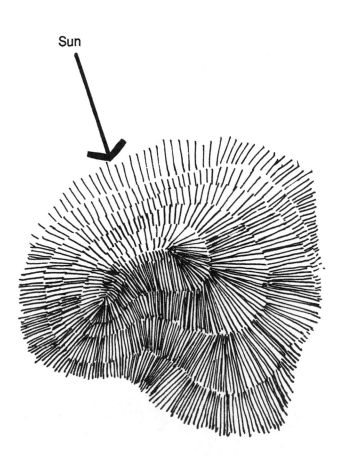

Figure 5-3. Hachures.

To understand a contour or topographic map, one must have an understanding of typical landforms and their contour signatures. Once these signatures are fixed in the mind, then the viewer can look at the two-dimensional signature and perceive the form. Figure 5-5 shows the two most basic signatures, ridges and valleys, as they might appear in a contour plan. In *Landscape Architecture Construction*, Dr. Harlow C. Landphair and Fred Klatt (1979) present a range of contour signatures and the forms they represent. The young landscape designer should become adept at using this full range of signatures to interpret contour maps and to understand the landform they represent.

Landform in Section or Profile

Landforms can also be represented two-dimensionally by looking at their vertical configuration. The drawing that allows us to do so is called a section when it shows only existing or proposed form, and a profile when it overlays both existing and proposed conditions. Figure 5-6 shows a contour plan and a section through that plan.

Sections and profiles are usually scaled drawings. The horizontal and vertical scales are the same when the section is intended to communicate the true characteristics of the form. In other cases, the vertical scale is larger than the horizontal (for example, horizontal scale 1 inch = 40 feet, vertical scale 1 inch = 10 feet).

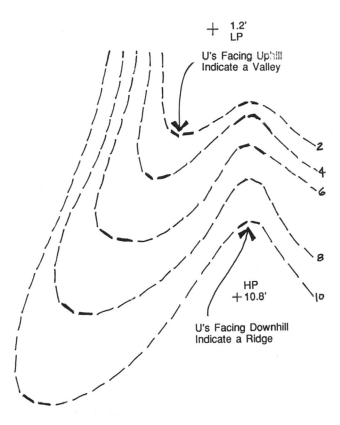

+ 1.2'
  LP

U's Facing Uphill
Indicate a Valley

HP
+ 10.8'

U's Facing Downhill
Indicate a Ridge

Figure 5-5. Ridge and valley signature.

This is usually done when accurate vertical measurements are needed, for example, when computing volumes of material being cut from, or added to, the existing landform.

Landform Manipulation

When representing landform manipulation, existing contour lines should be indicated with dashed freehand lines, proposed contours with solid lines. Existing contour lines are shown their entire length, but proposed contours are only drawn where they deviate from the existing condition (Figure 5-7).

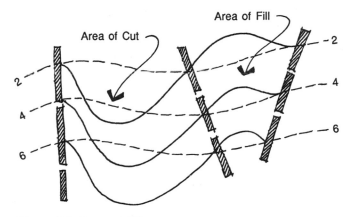

Area of Cut

Area of Fill

Figure 5-7. Cut and fill.

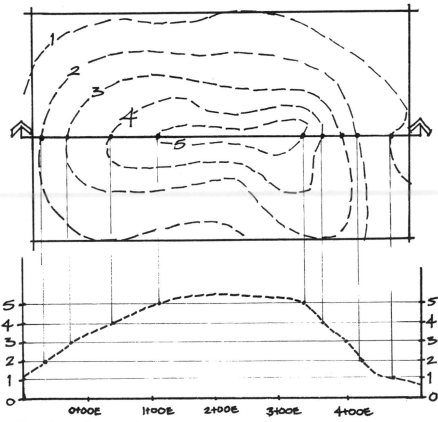

Figure 5-6. Landform in section.

Grading is the general term used to refer to modifications to the existing landform. Grading is performed to achieve drainage, to cause water to flow away from buildings or site-use areas, to create certain visual effects, and for a wide range of other reasons. Resculpting the land is an integral part of the design process, and forms do not work if they do not work in the third dimension as well as they work in plan.

Areas where the proposed contours are lower than the existing ones must have surface materials removed. These are referred to as areas of cut. Areas where proposed contours are higher in elevation than existing conditions require the importation of fill material (Figure 5-7). Usually, both areas of cut and fill occur in a reshaped site. In most cases, it is economically advantageous to balance the amounts of cut and fill so that no material is brought onto, or removed from, the site in order to achieve regrading.

Slope

The amount of incline of a surface is referred to as its slope, and slopes are quantified according to two systems. The ratio method of slope description defines slope steepness as a ratio or horizontal dimension to vertical elevation difference (3:1, 2:1, 1:1). By convention, the second number is always the vertical difference reduced to a factor of 1, as shown in Figure 5-8.

The percentage method describes slopes as a percentage, determined by dividing the difference in vertical elevation by the horizontal distance, and then converting this decimal to a percentage (Figure 5-8).

Design

There are numerous landform considerations in design. Some of the relevant concerns are landform as line and enclosure, slope considerations, drainage characteristics, and comfort issues.

Landform as Line

The perceptual effects of landform are highly affected by the type or character of line these forms impart to the landscape. For example, an angular line usually imparts a feeling of energy, power, and boldness. On the other hand, a sinuous line evokes a sense of calmness, passivity, and restfulness (Figure 5-9).

The designer can modify site landform in a very "architectonic" manner, or conversely in a more "naturalistic" one (Figure 5-10). Architectonic landforms utilize the quality of line (straight lines with sharp angles) that are usually associated with architecture. Therefore the forms feel very structured or contrived. Such landform can easily give the feeling of oneness with architectural elements of the site, and can intensify their power as the entire scene becomes, in a sense, architectural.

Naturalistic landforms utilize the evolving lines of nature and can soften the feeling of a place. If they establish themselves as a system that interacts with the architectonic forms of the buildings, then the dynamic interplay of opposites, the compliment through contrast, can be quite powerful. On the other hand, if they fail to attain their own integrity, these forms can become overpowered by the architecture of the place.

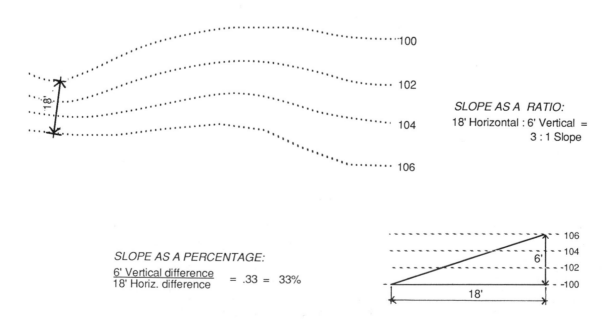

Figure 5-8. Slope.

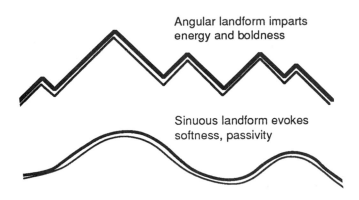

Figure 5-9. Angular vs. sinuous form.

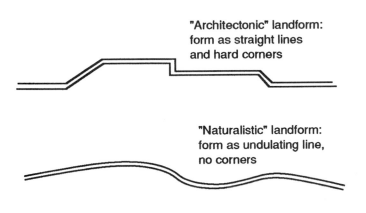

Figure 5-10. Architectonic vs. naturalistic form.

Landform as Enclosure

Landform can contribute to spatial character. Flat, level landscapes give the feeling of expansiveness. To achieve spatial articulation in these landscapes, the designer must either reshape the land, or supplement the landform with plant material, area walls, or some other elements that block or screen the vision. Conversely, landforms that fill a portion of the vertical plane have the ability to enclose space. The degree of enclosure imparted by these forms correlates to the amount of the vertical cone of vision that is occupied by the landform (Figure 5-11). Thus enclosure is a factor of the height of the form and the position of the observer.

As ridgelines rise above the eye, the landform blocks the vision, that is, it closes the view. The space enclosed that can be viewed is called the *viewshed.* As the spacing of the forms that create the visual edge increases, the viewshed enlarges, and the landscape becomes more expansive (Figure 5-12). It is said to have a larger scale and a coarser grain. As the dimension decreases, the space becomes smaller, more psychologically sheltered, and more private in its feeling. Such landforms create spaces that are smaller and more personally scaled and are said to be finer grained.

Ridgelines and promontories are zones of little enclosure. They are quite expansive. They offer long panoramic views and are themselves highly visible from distant areas. Valleys, on the other hand, afford reduced viewsheds, but have a feeling of centrality as views from the surrounding slopes are focused downward into the valley.

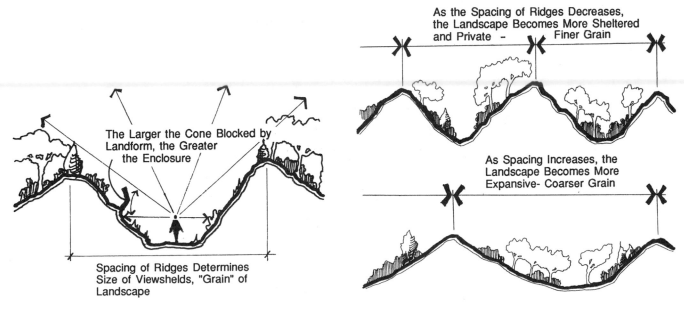

Figure 5-11. Grain and enclosure.

Figure 5-12. Landscape grain.

While ridgelines offer expansive distant views and are highly visible from great distances, they do not usually afford views into the valleys (Figure 5-13). There is, however, a zone along the upper slopes that is much less visible from the distance and which affords views into the valleys. This zone is the area where military leaders have historically placed their troops to see the enemy in the valley without themselves being seen from afar. Thus, this zone came to be called the military crest of the ridge (Figure 5-13). It offers unique opportunities to the designer as it allows nice valley views while allowing buildings to visually blend into the landform if viewed from distant locations. Therefore, while development on the ridgeline has a severe visual impact, this impact can be reduced if development is located at the military crest.

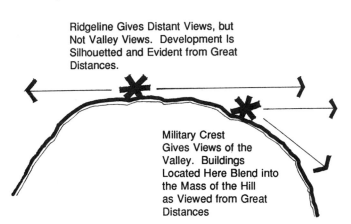

Figure 5-13. Ridgelines and military crests.

Site and Design Slopes

As site slopes increase, so too does their impact to design. For example, Figure 5-14 shows the relative areas of impact as one creates a flat surface (on which to place a building) and then modifies the landform so that water will flow around (rather than through) the building, without creating excessively steep, erosive slopes. While the actual dimensions of the regraded area would vary with allowable design slopes, it is evident that existing site slopes are a major development concern.

Site material and use also have slope implications. There is a range of minimum and maximum allowable slopes, as well as a range of desired slopes, associated with each material/use combination. Numerous desk references and books of "standards" have exhaustive lists of these design slopes.

Landform, Drainage, and Infrastructure

Ridges are topographic divides that break the landscape into a series of drainage areas called *watersheds*. All the water that falls on one side of the ridge sheds to one drainageway, on the other side to a different one (Figure 5-15). By charting the ridgelines and the path of surface water flow (perpendicular to the contour lines) on this figure, one can easily see that the area divides itself by ridgelines into a series of watersheds and subwatersheds. Water flows away from ridges and concentrates its flow in swale lines.

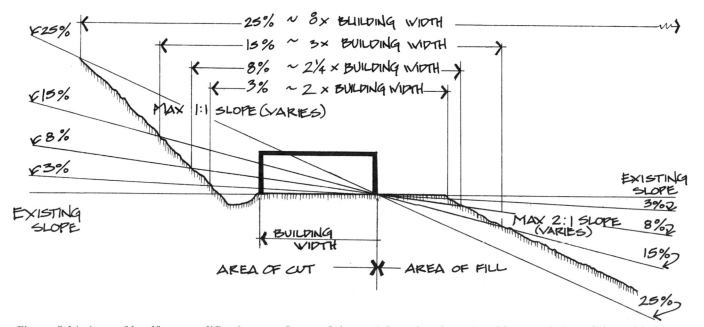

Figure 5-14. Area of landform modification as a factor of slope. (Adapted and reprinted by permission of the publisher from Landphair, H. C., and Motloch, J. L., *Site Reconnaissance and Engineering,* Fig. 1.9. Copyright 1985 by Elsevier Science Publishing Co., Inc.)

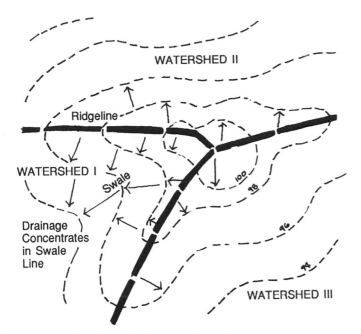

Figure 5-15. Watershed and surface flow.

Watersheds are important units for environmental management and land use planning. In management terms, since the area of a watershed is all the area that drains to a given point in a drainageway, and water quantity and quality is an important environmental variable to manage, then the watershed is often the most reasonable and effective management unit. In addition, in most landscapes, water is the primary ecological and erosional force. Managing this force, and the resultant stream erosion and soil loss, is best achieved through watershed management.

Land use planning includes the determination of land use locations and densities. In order for land to serve a human use, however, specific uses must usu-

ally be supported by several forms of *infrastructure,* or support systems. These systems include ones for circulation, power, potable water, stormwater and waste water transport, and communications.

Infrastructural systems consist of two basic types: gravity-flow systems, and pressure-flow systems. Gravity-flow systems, including storm and sanitary sewerage systems, are tied directly to topography. These utilities are powered by gravity and therefore depend on topographic difference for their motive force. They are the most constraining support systems. Their form should relate closely to landform, and they usually, therefore, affect substantially the developed form. For example, the limit of growth for most cities is the area that can be served by their gravity-flow wastewater collection and treatment system.

Pressure-flow systems, including potable water, electricity, natural gas, communication, and transportation networks, are freed from the constraints of topography, except for constraints imposed by gravity-flow systems that integrate with these pressure-flow ones. Therefore, they have a far lesser impact upon built form.

Watershed divides, or ridgelines, are natural boundaries for gravity-flow systems (Figure 5-16). Development will usually only leap across these divides after collection and treatment facilities are built in the new watershed. Topographic lows, or drainageways, are also boundaries of development. Since sanitary sewerage collection and treatment facilities are usually located near the drainageway, but above the area subject to flooding, areas across the drainageway from the collection and treatment facility cannot gravity-flow to the facility. In order to be serviced, these areas must rely upon some pressure-induced flow or some means of lifting the effluent that is being transported. Whenever lifting or pressure-forcing is

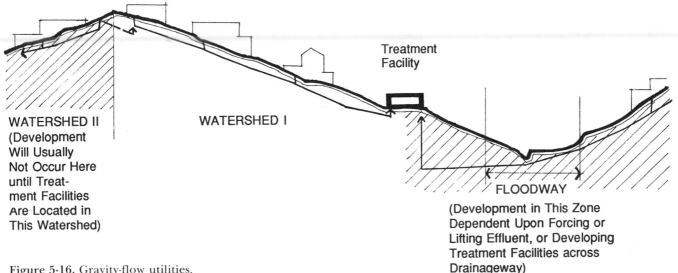

Figure 5-16. Gravity-flow utilities.

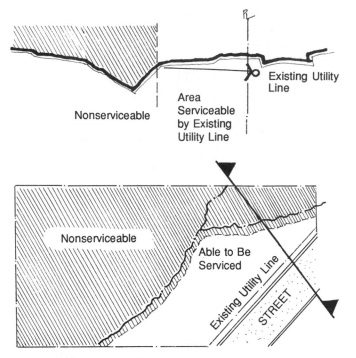

Figure 5-17. Topographic site development constraints.

not economically viable, the drainageway serves as a growth boundary.

There are site scale corollaries to the preceding statements. Ridgelines or swale lines can serve as boundaries to the land area that is economically serviceable by utilities (Figure 5-17). In this case, these natural edges can render the isolated areas unsuitable for development.

At the site scale, the designer is also concerned with causing surface water to flow around, rather than through, buildings and site-use areas. This is usually achieved by creating subtle swales or drainageways from the high side of the building or use area to the low side, collecting upslope water in these swales, allowing the swales to transport the water around the area, and then respreading the water so that it sheet-flows across the site downslope from the building or use area. Conceptually, this is shown in Figure 5-18. Grading a site so as to affect site drainage is a major design concern. It must be considered early, as well as throughout the design process, as it has significant implications to development form.

Landform and Comfort

Comfort is the sensation that results from a preferred combination of temperature, radiated energy, humidity, and windspeed. The human body perceives this condition as physiologically pleasant. Comfort is largely determined by the climate. At the regional scale this is termed macroclimate; at the land plan-

ning scale it is called mezzoclimate or topoclimate; and at the site scale it is referred to as microclimate. The shape of the land has a significant effect on local climatic conditions and on comfort, primarily through its affect on seasonal incoming solar radiation (insolation) and airflow.

Slope-Aspect or Slope-Orientation. The slope and direction of the land surface, referred to as slope-aspect or slope-orientation, along with the vertical angle and planar direction of the sun's rays, determine the relative amount of incoming solar radiation that is incident on the ground surface at any given time. As indicated in Figure 5-19, slope-aspect functions to distribute a given amount of the sun's energy into a relatively smaller or larger area, based on this relationship.

The summer sun rises in the Northeast, sets in the Northwest, and is near vertical at midday in southern

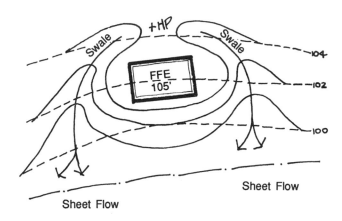

Figure 5-18. Conceptual grading around building or use area.

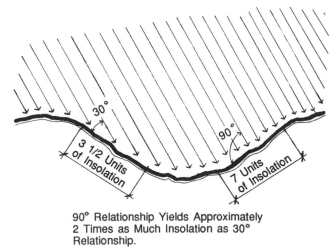

90° Relationship Yields Approximately 2 Times as Much Insolation as 30° Relationship.

Figure 5-19. Slope-aspect and incident radiation.

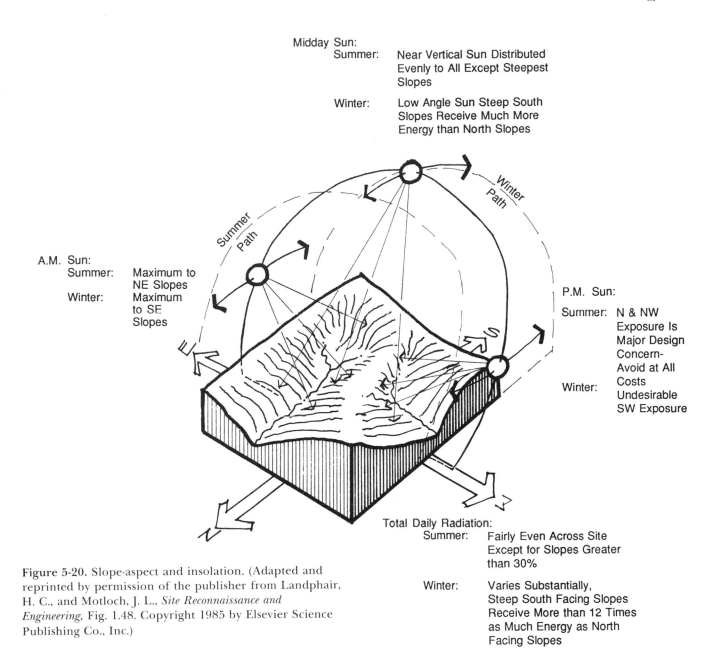

Midday Sun:
Summer: Near Vertical Sun Distributed Evenly to All Except Steepest Slopes

Winter: Low Angle Sun Steep South Slopes Receive Much More Energy than North Slopes

A.M. Sun:
Summer: Maximum to NE Slopes
Winter: Maximum to SE Slopes

P.M. Sun:
Summer: N & NW Exposure Is Major Design Concern-Avoid at All Costs
Winter: Undesirable SW Exposure

Total Daily Radiation:
Summer: Fairly Even Across Site Except for Slopes Greater than 30%

Winter: Varies Substantially, Steep South Facing Slopes Receive More than 12 Times as Much Energy as North Facing Slopes

Figure 5-20. Slope-aspect and insolation. (Adapted and reprinted by permission of the publisher from Landphair, H. C., and Motloch, J. L., *Site Reconnaissance and Engineering*, Fig. 1.48. Copyright 1985 by Elsevier Science Publishing Co., Inc.)

latitudes of the United States. In these same latitudes, the winter sun, on the other hand, rises and sets slightly south of east and west respectively, and remains low in the sky throughout the day. As Figure 5-20 indicates, slope-aspect determines the time of day that summer solar energy is delivered to site slopes. This information is useful when considering building and site-uses that are time specific. For example, the designer should try to avoid locating activities in areas subject to large amounts of afternoon summer sun, as this is the most problematic energy (coming as it does when the site is already overheated).

In the winter, solar radiation is generally seen as desirable. The designer would actively seek sunny ar-

eas in which to locate use areas. As Figure 5-20 indicates, slope-aspect not only affects the time of day that winter solar energy falls upon a site, but also the total amount of insolation that the surface collects throughout the day. The designer in this case would search not only for the places that collected the most total daily radiation, but also those that collected it at the appropriate time of the day.

The introduction of vertical elements radically compounds the differences, due to slope-aspect, in the amounts of solar radiation that enter site-use areas (Figure 5-21). On slopes that turn their backs to the sun, vertical elements usually function to further exclude solar energy from site-use areas. On slopes that

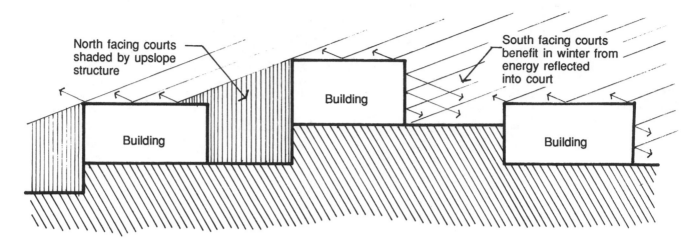

North facing courts
shaded by upslope
structure

South facing courts
benefit in winter from
energy reflected
into court

Building

Building

Building

Figure 5-21. Slope-aspect and vertical site elements.

face the sun, these same elements will usually function to bounce or reflect more energy into these areas, resulting in heat-sinks.

The relative value that the designer places on each season's solar opportunities and constraints depends on a number of factors. Primary, however, is the relative severity of the two seasons. For example, in south Texas summer is the most severe season. Emphasis is placed on responding to the summer condition. In Maine, the winter is more severe, and is therefore the primary design climate.

Ventilation. Topographic relief functions as a barrier to, and deflector of, airflow. As wind blows along the surface, its velocity is affected by the shape of that surface.

In most locations in the United States, wind direction changes by season. In the winter, the coldest winds (in most locales) generally come from the north or northwest. The coolest summer breezes usually come from the south, southeast, or southwest. In southeast Texas, for example, the coldest winter winds come from the north-northwest, the warmer summer breezes from the southeast. Winter winds are highly variable in direction. The summer breezes, however, are much more directionally consistent, as they blow off the Gulf of Mexico. Both the seasonal direction of the ventilation and the consistency of the direction are of value to the landscape designer.

When ridgelines and valleys orient along the direction of seasonal airflow, the valleys will usually be well-ventilated. When the same shaped valleys align perpendicular to the direction of airflow, however, the wind usually blows over, rather than through, the valley (Figure 5-22). The valley, in this case, is said to be in the wind shadow; the landform shields the valley from the wind. This condition would generally be seen

as an advantage in the winter, but a disadvantage in the summer when the ventilation is needed (so that the human body might evaporatively cool itself more efficiently).

As landforms penetrate into the airflow, seasonal wind directions also determine windward and leeward slopes. Ridgelines and windward slopes are subjected to slightly (10 to 20 percent) accelerated winds, as are the windward portions of side slopes. Portions of the landform shadowed from the wind by the form itself would generally have a reduced air velocity (Figure 5-23).

The designer can resculpt the site to funnel the desirable summer breezes into use areas, while protecting these same areas from undesirable winter winds (Figure 5-24).

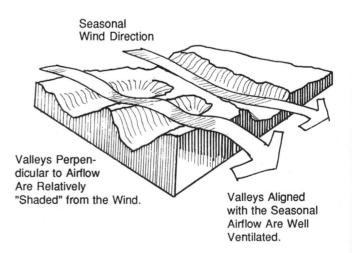

Seasonal
Wind Direction

Valleys Perpendicular to Airflow
Are Relatively
"Shaded" from the Wind.

Valleys Aligned
with the Seasonal
Airflow Are Well
Ventilated.

Figure 5-22. Ventilation and valley alignment.

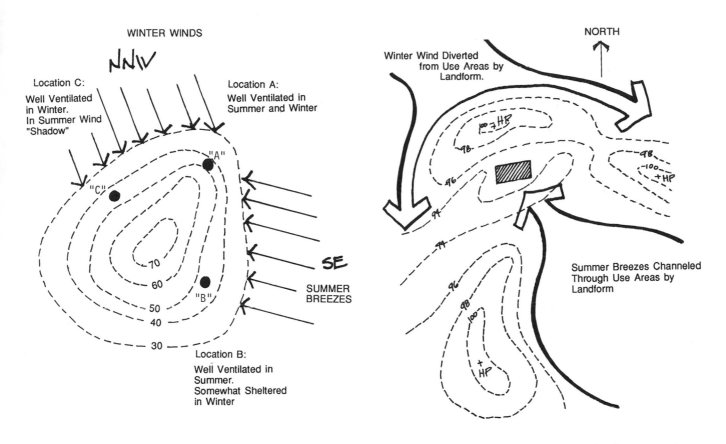

Figure 5-23. Ventilation around a knoll.

Figure 5-24. Resculpting the building site for seasonal airflow.

Landform Summary

Landform is a very important part of the landscape architect's design palette. It conveys a sense of region and place. It determines surface drainage and highly impacts and usually delimits the area served by gravity-flow cultural support systems. It also helps determine basic human comfort. The ability to understand and manipulate landform as a part of design process is an essential skill of the landscape designer.

WATER

Water is essential to human well-being and to life itself. It also has a unique power to stimulate the mind and to captivate attention. Therefore water is an essential element of the landscape architect's palette. It is also perhaps the site designer's most versatile tool.

This section explores water in several ways. It begins by addressing water as a system or process. It then interprets it as a resource, in a natural sense and in development. It concludes with an exploration of the relationship between water and design.

Water as Process

Water is the medium within which life processes occur. Without water, life as we know it could not exist. Perhaps this explains our innate fascination with water.

Water is a limited resource. It exists in various reservoirs on, above, and below the surface of the earth (Figure 5-25). It forms a process called the water cycle. In this cycle, water in the ocean evaporates and is brought landward by winds, then eventually falls again as rain, hail, sleet, or snow. A portion of the water is stored in a frozen form in glaciers; another major portion enters the soil and becomes available to plants. Some of this water moves deeper into geological strata, eventually becoming groundwater stored in the aquifer. A portion of the soil water evaporates from the surface; some is evapo-transpired by plants. What remains on the surface flows through a series of conditions including surface flow, and flow through rivulets, streams, rivers, lakes, braided streams, fresh water marshes, and brackish estuaries, until it finally returns to the ocean.

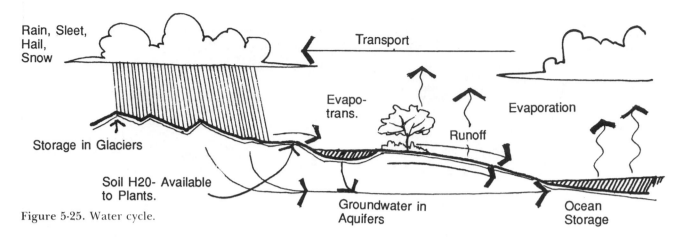

Rain, Sleet, Hail, Snow

Transport

Evapo-trans.

Evaporation

Runoff

Storage in Glaciers

Soil H20- Available to Plants.

Groundwater in Aquifers

Ocean Storage

Figure 5-25. Water cycle.

The various elements of the water cycle are highly integrated. For example, in some areas (such as those underlaid by fractured stone geologies) there is relatively free flow between ground and surface waters. Pollution that occurs on the surface is quickly carried into the groundwater reservoir. In addition, as development causes larger amounts of water to flow in lakes and streams, less enters the groundwater reservoir. Its level falls, and the groundwater reservoir becomes depleted.

Hydrologic elements are integrated not only with each other, but with associated ecological systems. Plant materials are totally dependent on water. The type of vegetation and its distribution correlates with water availability and quality. Through flooding, water replenishes the land with fertile soils and builds our most productive agricultural areas. Agricultural patterns, therefore, correlate with hydrologic ones; through irrigation, they impact those patterns.

Water as Resource

Much as the worth of a bank is determined by the number of dollars it has on hand and the strength of the currency, so too does the worth of the water resource depend on its quantity and quality. Our ability to manage this bank is the largest ecological challenge facing society over the next twenty years.

As in any integrated system, to manage any part, we must manage the whole. We must manage water on the regional level working with all components of the water cycle. Locally, the watershed is the logical unit for managing its surface component.

When managing the water bank we must control, among other things, flooding and the effects of draught, erosion and sedimentation, and pollutants. To the degree that decision-making incorporates management of these variables, we promulgate a water resource ethic. This ethic is an integral component of a larger, more encompassing management attitude commonly called a land ethic.

Surface Water

Water provides sustenance for humans. We use it for irrigation and industry, climate control, recreation, and frequently transportation. Historically the satisfaction of many of our needs was dependent on surface waters. We therefore located cities along waterways. We subsequently faced periodic flooding and found it necessary to control flooding through the building of dams and reservoirs. In so doing, we stopped the river's ability to replenish the land.

More responsive development, on the other hand, would recognize the ability of the water resource to serve human needs. The pattern and nature of development would respond to this ability, locating development outside the prime agricultural lands of the flood plain and allowing periodic flooding to occur and replenish the landscape.

Drainage Pattern

The pattern of drainage within the watershed has evolved in response to the surface flow of water. This pattern has, over time, attained an equilibrium with site forces. This equilibrium is one of the major opportunities for a site to do work for humans. Changes to the equilibrium impact this ability, and therefore should be avoided.

In order to fully utilize the water resource, development should avoid reshaping the land in the area of the drainage way (Figure 5-26). The banks should remain undisturbed when possible, with their surface matting of intertwined roots intact. The form and surface cover should be retained so that they can continue to resist the forces of surface flow.

It should be kept in mind, however, that the form and surface condition of the waterway have developed in response to the historic rate of surface flow. Development, however, usually replaces permeable ground conditions such as woodland or meadow with impervious ones such as concrete and buildings. This

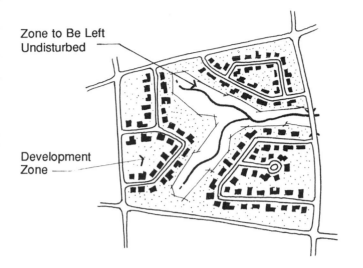

Zone to Be Left
Undisturbed

Development
Zone

Figure 5-26. Preservation of existing drainageways.

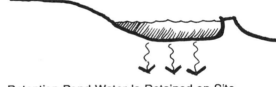

Detention Pond-Water Is Detained on Site
Outflow Is Metered at Predevelopment Rates

Retention Pond-Water Is Retained on Site,
and Caused to Infiltrate to the Groundwater
Reservoir

Figure 5-27. Detention and retention structures.

causes a significant increase in water volume (and usually velocity as well), upsets the equilibrium, and causes disruptive changes to occur. To avoid these unwanted changes, the designer can introduce retention or detention reservoirs sized to accommodate the increases in water volume generated through development and to reduce its velocity as well (Figure 5-27).

Retention structures collect storm runoff and store it until it can infiltrate and thereby be retained permanently on site. *Detention structures* also collect development generated stormwater but merely detain it, metering outflow of water from the reservoir at the predevelopment rate. They allow the total amount of runoff, but not its rate, to increase as development occurs. Development usually increases erosion and downstream sedimentation and degrades water quality. *Sedimentation structures* collect the sediment and

contaminant-rich runoff, usually the first one-half inch of runoff and filter it, usually through sand, to capture sediment and sediment-borne contaminants.

Groundwater

As discussed above, both retention and detention structures are helpful in managing the surface flow of water. Retention structures have the added benefit of augmenting recharge to the groundwater reservoir. As such they are important groundwater management tools, used to maintain the existing quantity of water in underground aquifers. This requires that the designer or user ensure that infiltration at least equals the amount of water discharged. Additional waters should be infiltrated to equal the amount removed for irrigation or industrial/process use or prevented by development from entering the groundwater reservoir. The quality of water infiltrated after development must also be no less than that supplied prior to development.

Wetlands

Stream banks, lakeshores, and wetlands are rich habitats that provide shelter and food for birds and animals. They are invaluable to ecological systems. Their continuity (and that of their valuable vegetative communities), is dependent upon existing hydrologic relationships. Development should not adversely affect these valued habitats.

Recreation

Water is an unparalleled recreational resource. It provides for fishing, swimming, and boating as well as associated activities such as camping and hiking. Development should allow public access to this resource and maintain it in adequate quantity and with a quality conducive to health, safety, and welfare.

Comfort

In the overheated condition, and particularly when the air is dry, evaporative cooling can be effectively used to improve site comfort. In these conditions, locating development downwind from water sources, such as ponds (Figure 5-28), pools (Figure 5-29), irrigated lawns or water sprays (Figure 5-30), can substantially reduce air temperatures. In addition, lush vegetation can shade use-areas as well as provide cooling through the evapotranspiration of water from plant surfaces.

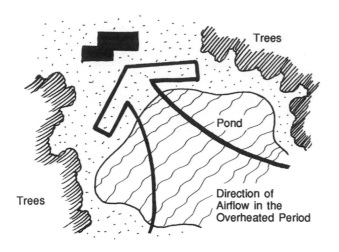

Figure 5-28. Site ponds and cooling.

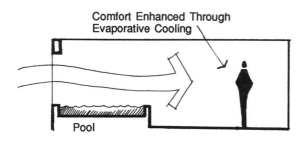

Figure 5-29. Pools and evaporative cooling.

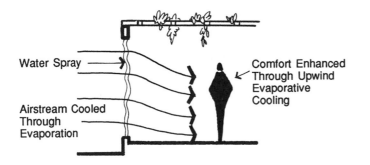

Figure 5-30. Water sprays and evaporative cooling.

Sensual Value

Water has a singular power to stimulate the mind. It performs its magic primarily through sight and sound. Essential to life in the landscape, it serves as the focus to which the mind concentrates meanings. It also reflects the landscape it nourishes, consolidating more meaning.

Through the sounds of water, meanings are intensified. The lapping wave, the gurgling brook, the thunder of waterfalls, the splash of trout, and the crash of surf, all intensify the image in the mind.

The sight and sound of water, as well as its smell and the way it feels to our skin, serve as stimuli to enrich the sensation of place. They are therefore invaluable resources to the landscape designer, the maker of place.

Land Values and Land Use

For the above reasons and others, water is a valued resource. Its value is reflected economically. Water in the environment commands a price; proximity to water is a marketable commodity.

A good indication of the resource value of water is the competition among land uses that occurs at the water's edge. This edge is valued for parks, recreation, housing, hotels, resorts, restaurants, shops, and other uses. Each of the uses has a degree of compatibility with the water's edge. For each use or combination of uses there is also a carrying capacity beyond which the system will suffer significant degradation. Development along the water's edge involves resolving competition among uses and reconciling desired development with system needs, so as to maintain this valued resource.

The value of wetlands is also recognized through land-use regulations. Generally, only water-dependent uses are allowed in wetland areas, and all development impacts to wetlands must be mitigated by recreating (often in multiples of what was destroyed) new wetland.

Water as Design

According to Norman Booth (1983):

> Water by itself has no distinct design properties other than that it is a liquid ... all the visible characteristics of water are directly dependent on exterior factors (plasticity, motion, sound, reflectivity, slope, container size, shape and roughness, temperature, wind and light) that bear on and reflect it. Water must depend on its environmental context for its particular qualities. Change the forces in the environmental setting and you also alter the characteristics of water in that setting.

To a large degree our perception of water is a visual one. With this and the above quote in mind, we will begin discussing the relationship between water and design by addressing its visual characteristics. We will then explore other sensual aspects of water as they relate to design, and consider water as movement, allusion, and symbol. We will look at specific types of water features including pools and ponds, channels, cascades and waterfalls, and water jets. We will close with some comments concerning water in its frozen state.

Elements of Visual Design

The particular characters of line, form, color, and texture displayed by water contribute to the mental images it evokes.

Line. The edge of the water, that is, the character of its outline, has a major impact upon the images it evokes in the mind of the beholder. A soft-textured line can evoke unbridled nature; a highly controlled sinuous line (Figure 5.31) can allude to a controlled or symbolic nature; a rectilinear line can refer to architecture; and an angular line can infer energy. The edge can be obscured with aquatic material giving a sense of mystery, or be crisp and decisively bulkheaded, leaving little to the imagination.

Water can also express its surface as line. Examples include the rhythmic line of waves that move across the surface under the influence of wind and the lines that pulse outward when something impacts the surface. By shaping the edge over which water falls, the water can become a rhythmic vertical line, accentuating the vertical direction and implying connections between the earth and sky (Figure 5.32).

Form. Water features can be linear, accentuating water movement and flow characteristics. They can be compact in form and convey a sense of centrality and arrival. Their form can be a complex combination of differing characters, thereby pulling together disparate elements (Figure 5.33); or conversely they can be consistent and convey a more unified sense (Figure 5.34).

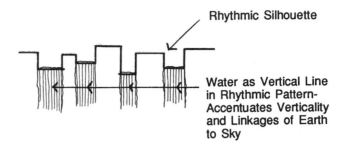

Figure 5-32. Water as rhythmic/directional line.

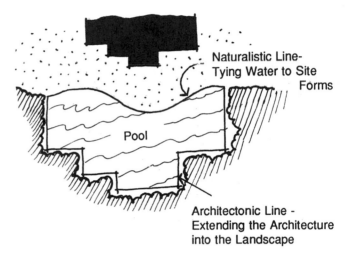

Figure 5-33. Water as complex form.

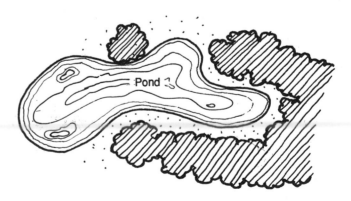

Figure 5-34. Water as simple form.

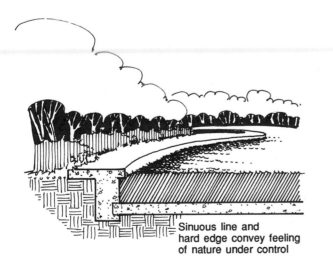

Figure 5-31. Controlled nature at the water's edge.

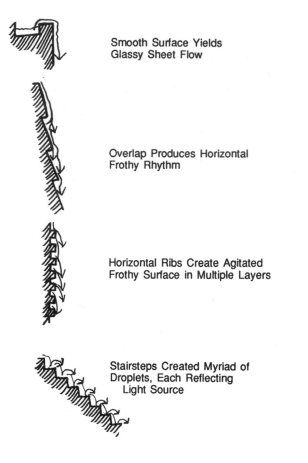

Smooth Surface Yields
Glassy Sheet Flow

Overlap Produces Horizontal
Frothy Rhythm

Horizontal Ribs Create Agitated
Frothy Surface in Multiple Layers

Stairsteps Created Myriad of
Droplets, Each Reflecting
Light Source

Figure 5-35. Visual effects of vertical wall textures.

Color. Good quality water has little color. Color is imparted by the reflections carried upon its surface, by its diffusing character, and by the color of its container. White-colored and mirrored containers express the transparent nature of water. They also create the illusion of shallowness. Light blue containers impart a clarity, cleanliness, and purity to the water. Dark blue and black containers maximize reflections and give the illusion of shadowy depths. The water within these dark containers seems especially wet.

Texture. When water is moving, its surface texture is determined by that of its container and by its depth and flow characteristics. Protrusions into the flow cause turbulence, which increases surface texture. Constrictions to flow also increase turbulence and texture. As the layer of water becomes thin, even minor differences in container alignment can cause surface textures. As Figure 5-35 indicates, when a thin sheet of water moves down a nearly vertical surface, minor ripples in the surface can impart interesting textures and aeration to the water. A stair-stepped container can convert a smooth sheet of water to a choreography of droplets, each reflecting the sun, and together creating a frolicking cascade of light.

Sensual Quality

It is hard to imagine a place in which sensual quality would not be enhanced by water. This enrichment can be through concentration of character (a brook bubbling through a meadow); conversely, it can be through counterpoint (an oasis in the desert).

Design Processes. Processes by which one addresses sensual quality in the design of effective water elements have three points in common. They begin by deciding design intent, including functional aspects, desired mood, and aesthetic and sensual character. They proceed to identify appropriate water effects to achieve the desired character, mood, and function. Finally, they shape the container and the environmental context to achieve these effects.

Design intent and water effect vary with context. For example, Figure 5-36 shows a fountain intended to enhance street character from one side, while providing visual amenity, screening, and evaporative cooling to the dining court. It also masks street noise from the court. The street side is a visual statement producing little sound or other nonvisual stimuli. The court side is a series of falls producing enough white sound to mask street noise. It also produces aeration to enhance evaporation and its cooling effect. By its proximity to foot traffic, it encourages the passerby to stop and touch the water. It transforms the dining area.

Water as Movement

Still (unmoving) water is reflective, both visually and psychologically. It invites contemplation. It is serene but fragile. The slightest breeze begins to dissolve its visual effect. It has little power to mask disruptive sounds.

Moving water, on the other hand, can be subtle or dynamic. It can move almost imperceptibly or can rush like a torrent. It can make scarcely audible gurgling sounds, or loud splattering ones. It can convey brute force and can mask the loudest of urban noises.

Water as Allusion and Symbol

Water can also serve as allusion and symbol. Moving water alludes to instability, movement toward a state of equilibrium, and unresolved gravity. Still water conveys stability, resolution, and peacefulness.

Natural landscapes hold a power and an interest. However, they do not often belong, in their literal sense, in the city. The architectonic interpretation of mountain stream, river, flood plain, and braided stream can make reference to this natural environ-

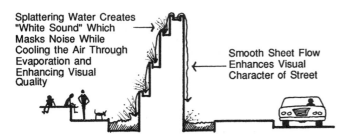

Figure 5-36. Multipurpose water wall and cascade.

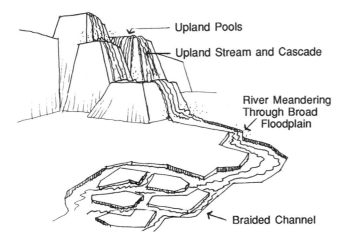

Figure 5-37. Symbolic stream.

ment with forms compatible with the urban context (Figure 5-37). It can serve as symbol to concentrate the meanings of the natural condition and to transpose these to the urban context.

Water as Ethic

The landscape designer communicates an ethic through design. The use of great volumes and velocities of water to overpower the observer symbolizes an anthropomorphic view of the world: man as conqueror and controller of nature. A small volume of water extended through an elaborate series of sensual experiences conveys an appreciation of the scarcity and value of water. This latter ethic is expressed by the Islamic tradition and its near deification of water.

Pools and Ponds

Pools and ponds are bodies of still water. Pools are architectonic (Figure 5-33); ponds are naturalistic (Figure 5-34).

Pools. Pools function primarily as reflecting surfaces. To do so effectively, they must have adequate depth and their containers should be dark in color. The re-

flecting surface (the water level) should be very close to grade (Figure 5-38). There must be something of visual interest to reflect, and there must be the proper sightlines to see the subject in the reflecting surface from the desired observation point. Disruptive glare should not occur. Finally, the pool must be of a proper size for reflections based on design intent, object size, and viewer location.

Ponds. Ponds are bodies of still water with naturalistic line quality, often reinforced by naturalized plantings. They are usually located at the lowest elevation of the landform to reinforce their equilibrium with gravity. They contribute markedly to the pastoral and bucolic mood of a place.

Channels

Channels are conduits that contain flowing water. They are linear in form and function to convey movement and to decentralize meanings. The sensual effect of a channel depends upon the volume of water, its rate of flow, and the channel size, shape, and steepness. Slick channels produce smooth flows, rough ones create turbulence. Obstructions in the channel divert flow; they are impacted by the water and in turn increase turbulence and downstream scouring until an equilibrium is achieved (Figure 5-39). Constrictions to flow increase both velocity and turbulence. As turbulence increases, so does the level of sound generated.

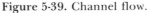

Figure 5-38. Reflecting pool.

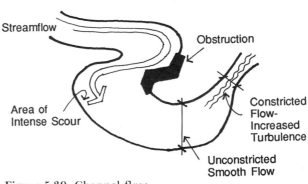

Figure 5-39. Channel flow.

Cascades and Waterfalls

Cascades and waterfalls involve falling water. The effect of falling water (which varies with the volume of water and rate of flow, the condition of the edge over which the water falls, the height and nature of the fall, and the surface terminating the fall), has almost unlimited possibilities. As the volume of water increases, flow tends to become more regular, and the effects of other variations (such as the character of the edge) become less visually pronounced.

Rate of flow also affects the inertia of the water and the manner in which it breaks when there is no underlying support. The smoother the edge over which the water falls, the more sheet-like the cascade; the rougher the edge, the greater is water turbulence and aeration. As volume, velocity, and coarseness of edge combine, the transparent sheet of water gives way to a frothing blanket. Slow-moving water flowing over a rounded edge clings to a vertical wall surface. In this case, and with certain container materials such as concrete, the water changes the wall color and character substantially. Conversely, subtle changes in edge condition can cause the flow to break free of the wall and the wall surface to remain (when controlled correctly) dry. Protrusions into the flow can cause the water to splatter. As it does so, each drop of water has the potential to reflect light, and the water becomes quite agitated, as discussed earlier in Figure 5-35. The greater the volume of water and distance of fall, the more intense the impact at its terminus. If the water impacts a hard surface such as concrete, the noise is a loud, harsh splat. If it falls instead into a pool of water, the sound is deeper in tone and more muted.

Water Jets

Relatively large volumes of water forced through small apertures result in high velocities of flow. This flow is capable of temporarily overcoming the force of gravity. The result is a vertical stream of water, flowing thin and fast, then slowing and falling back on itself.

Water jets serve to draw attention to specific points; they punctuate the landscape. They can be very effective in reinforcing points that have special meaning for other reasons. Sometimes they occur at the intersection of sightlines (Figure 5-40); at other times they serve as sculpture to reinforce the spaces which enclose them. Jets usually function as points of energy in bucolic settings. Through contrast they reinforce the pastoral character. They seldom occur in energetic contexts, as they would simultaneously lose their visual impact while competing with the setting.

There are four basic types of water jets. The *single-orifice jet* produces a relatively transparent stream of water. The *aerated jet* entrains air into the flow, giving the water an opaque and sparkling quality. It greatly enhances the visual prominence of the stream. The *spray jet* forces water through many fine apertures, creating a fine mist. Sprays are hard to control in windy conditions but are very effective in providing evaporative cooling. *Formed multijets* combine many individual jets to create sculptured composite water forms, such as rings, goblets, and morning glories.

Frozen Water

Water which appears dark and transparent as a liquid becomes light and opaque on freezing. On freezing, reflecting pools can become recreational resources for ice skating, if properly designed for this use.

Fountains, if left running when temperatures drop, can create wonderlands of ice, which become even more phantasmagoric as the ice begins to melt and as the forms come to life. Of course, operating fountains in these conditions can create maintenance and safety problems unless designed with this use in mind and closely monitored.

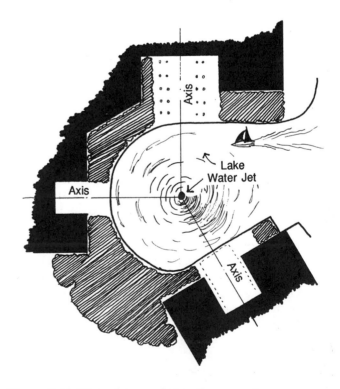

Figure 5-40. Water jet as point and punctuation.

PLANTS

All life forms on the face of the earth, including humans, receive from the sun the energy they need to power life processes. However, few life forms are capable of capturing and directly using the sun's energy. Without the lacy shroud of vegetation that covers portions of the land and water surface, the sun's energy would not be able to support life as we know it.

Plants, through the process of photosynthesis, capture large amounts of solar energy and concentrate a portion of this energy into chemical bonds. By so doing, they make it available to more advanced life forms. Plants are the crucial first step in the food chain, cycling nutrients through ecosystems and using solar energy to achieve work.

In addition to capturing large amounts of energy and making it available as food stuffs, green plants provide other ecological benefits. They remove carbon dioxide from the air and, as a by-product of photosynthesis, give off oxygen. Their roots force rocks apart, forming the beginnings of soil. Root action also aerates existing soils. Dead leaves, twigs, and roots contribute organic material to the soil, increasing both structure and fertility. They create a matting of roots and organic matter that functions to retain soil moisture. They also create varied microclimates, affording protection from wind and sun.

Plant Materials as Process

Plant materials are the result of biological processes operating within the specifics of place and time. They are dependent on the materials of the environment. In response to these materials the community of plants changes over time.

There are numerous environmental conditions necessary for growth. There must be sunlight, water, nutrients, and appropriate temperatures. Schimper (1903) summarized plant needs by first acknowledging the necessity for sunlight. He then asserted that *basic life form,* (desert, short grass prairie, tall grass prairie, savannah, or forest) was determined by available water (Figure 5-41). The *species* that could survive in an area, he stated, were determined by temperature. Actual *plant materials on-site* were ultimately determined by resident soils. These soils, of course, determine plant material by affecting the amount of water, nutrients, and soil gases available to the plants.

The character and amount of available sunlight, nutrients, gases, and water holistically define a habitat. To the degree that a habitat fulfills biological needs, an organism will thrive. As any element becomes inappropriate in character or amount, it becomes a factor that limits growth. Therefore, one can appreciate the strong interrelationship of environment and plant material.

Environments change over time. As they change, so does the plant community they support. However, in a classic chicken and egg phenomenon, the plant community also changes its environment. The plants and the habitat change together in relationship with each other, in a state of dynamic equilibrium. The composition of each is always changing, but at any point in time, there is an integrated relationship (to some degree) between plant and environment.

The degree of integration of plant and environment changes over time in a process known as *succession.* Conceptually, succession refers to the natural tendency of biological systems to change over time in response to available energy and resources. In so doing, plant associations change over time to have a more integrated relationship with their habitat. Given time, ecological systems (ecosystems) evolve from a relatively nondifferentiated physical environment inhabited by an undiversified, randomly ordered, inefficient biological community, to a highly differentiated environment with a great deal of biological diversity, order, and efficiency.

Early successional plants are pioneers; they colonize harsh environments where there is an energy abundance or lack of competition. Their ecological survival strategies include rapid movement into disturbed areas and an ability to tolerate a wide range of environmental conditions.

The ecological role of early successional communities includes the betterment of their environment. As communities, they are characterized by low diversity (only a few species), relative random distribution (Figure 5-42), and high net (seed) productivity. They are characterized as well by low overall efficiency (biomass production-energy processing). They are instrumental in upgrading the soil and in changing both

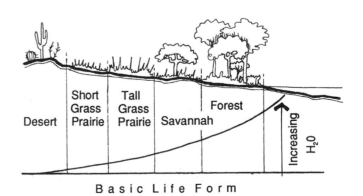

Figure 5-41. Basic life form and available water.

soil and air microclimates. They generally serve, over time, to increase the amount of organization, order, diversity, stability, and complexity in the system. They also increase the environment's ability to process energy, produce oxygen, and so forth. Since their ecological niche (habitat and role) involves harsh environments and changing the status quo, another of their ecological functions is to write their own demise. Early successional ecosystems are relatively short lived; they create the environmental conditions that make themselves obsolete.

Late successional plants depend upon efficiency as an ecological survival strategy. They maximize production, not of seed, but of biomass (energy processed). As communities, they have a high degree of diversity (many different species), order (in relation to environmental variables) (Figure 5-43), and stability over time. Organized as they are in response to environmental processes, they speak specifically to other variables of the site. They are good *indicators* of site conditions.

Succession as a process yields two results. First, as plant communities and environments change together over time, they evolve so as to have interrelated forms. Where the landform collects water, one can expect to find plants that enjoy "getting their feet wet." Where light is eliminated or highly screened, shade-loving plants reside. Second, because of differences in temperature, landform, slope-aspect, available sun, available water, etc., the ecological community of plants differs on a regional basis. Plant communities, responding to differences in locales, become identifiable regional expressions (Figure 5-44).

Plant Materials as Resource

Plant materials are valued natural resources. They capture solar energy and make it available to food chains; they also produce oxygen. They even purify water and make it available to the air through evapotranspiration.

Planning Resource. Beyond their value as global resources, plants serve useful purposes in planning and design. In planning, they are usually considered the most significant visual component of the landscape. Managing the sense of a region involves the maintenance of its plant materials and vegetative patterns.

The interfaces of two or more ecological zones, called *ecotones*, are vegetative corridors highly valued as wildlife habitats and movement systems. Preservation of these zones is essential to wildlife management.

Design Resource. At the project design scale, vegetation provides many sensual benefits. It gives enclosure and defines and articulates space. It can screen, enframe, or serve as backdrop for elements in the environment. It can contribute color to the landscape. It

Figure 5-42. Early successional community.

Figure 5-44. Desert plant community.

Figure 5-43. Late successional community.

can provide shelter from fierce winds, or through delicate movement, accentuate even the softest breeze. The following section explores its design potential.

As indicated in Figure 5-45, plant materials can also influence microclimates and human comfort in many ways. They transpire water that can cool the air through evaporation. When this occurs, small amounts of airflow will be induced. Foliage mass can divert airflow away from, or into, use areas and can provide shading. Each of these characteristics, and many others, can be either beneficial or detrimental, depending on climatic and seasonal conditions. These variables, in the hands of the knowledgeable and responsive designer, will allow plant materials on-site to become a major comfort resource.

Land Value. Significant vegetation usually contributes substantially to the economic worth of land. There are legally recognized economic formulas for evaluating the worth of these resources. These formulas usually consider the size, species, condition, and environmental location of the plant material, and then apply weighing factors applicable to the region.

The worth of plant material varies with its context and with its cultural significance. The same tree, for instance, would be worth several times its open field value if it were instead growing in the city. It would of course be worth even more if it carried special cultural or historic meaning. For example, the treaty oak under which a major historical agreement was reached would carry singular worth.

Plant Material as Design

In most every site design situation, the perception of place is tempered greatly by the community of plants. In most cases, plant material is the environmental variable that most strongly evokes images in the observer's mind. On even the most disturbed sites, there is usually a vegetative context that affects perception.

To a very large degree, the sensual perception of plant material is visual. Also, in most cases, plant material determines the visual character of a site more so than any other material of the site designer's palette. Therefore, it is imperative that the landscape designer understand plants as visual design materials. This section is intended to promote this understanding and begins by exploring plant materials as visual elements. It then discusses other sensual and temporal issues of planting design. It explores plant materials and movement and then discusses plants as environmental indicators. It looks briefly at some maintenance issues and closes with a review of the relationship between plants and site design. By so doing, it displays an appreciation for the range of issues relevant to planting design.

Visual Issues

As stated above, the perception of plant material is primarily a visual one. In discussing plant material we should therefore consider plant material in relation to the elements of visual design, plant strata and plant size, and spatial issues.

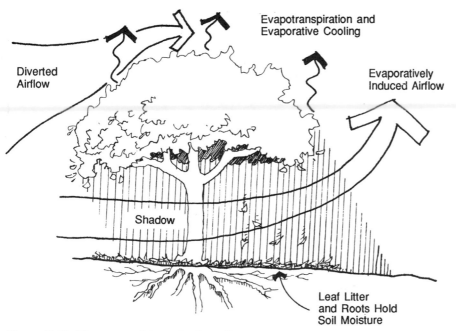

Figure 5-45. Plant materials and microclimate.

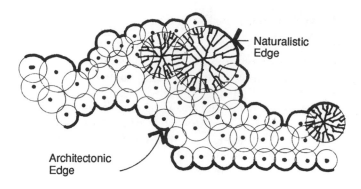

Figure 5-46. Edge of planted mass as "line."

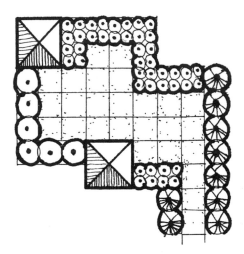

Figure 5-47. Plant material as line to link elements.

Elements of Visual Design. The character of line, form, color, and texture that is exhibited by plant material, is instrumental in determining sense of place.

Line. Shapes have outlines. The character of these edges can range from the sinuous evolving lines of nature, to the regularly spaced, straight, and geometric lines of architecture (Figure 5-46). The character, be it naturalistic or architectonic, contributes to the basic feeling of the place.

Plant materials can be organized as linear masses. Tight linear organizations usually speak to the presence of humans. Birds sit on telephone lines or fences constructed by people and they defecate, thereby sowing by their feces, linear plantings. The site designer creates allees to direct movement and to draw the eye. Rows of trees are planted along streets to reinforce their linear character and to unify disparate architectural elements that occur at their edges. Plants are also used as lines to extend architecture into the site and to visually link adjacent structures (Figure 5-47).

Form. When discussing plant material and form, we must discuss both the form of the individual plant, and that of groupings of plants.

Plant form is a combination of the overall plant shape and habit of growth (Figure 5-48). Each shape has its own unique characteristics and design potentials as follows:

1. Fastigiate plants accentuate the vertical. They usually act as focal points in design compositions.
2. Columnar forms are similar to fastigiate ones, but with rounder tops. They serve similar design purposes.
3. Round plants, the most common form, usually comprise the bulk of plants in a design composition. They are nondirectional, serve as context for more directional forms, and usually provide unity to planting compositions.
4. Spreading forms reinforce the horizontal direction. They can be effective in extending architectural forms into the site.
5. Pyramidal forms have a formal architectonic character. They lend rigidity and permanence to compositions.
6. Weeping plants generally occur in wet areas. Their form can be effective if they are silhouetted against, or allowed to cascade over, architectural forms.
7. Picturesque forms are irregular or contorted. They usually are caused by dynamic natural forces; through their form they express these forces. They are evocative specimens in the planted landscape. Picturesque forms can also evolve in an *understory* or an *edge* condition where plant materials reach for the limited light.

Aggregate form refers to the interrelationship of numbers of plants, and aggregate form changes with plant succession. Early successional communities are generally characterized by relatively random distributions of plant materials. They are organized as points in space (Figure 5-49). Late successional communities are organized as masses, in response to environmental variables. Shrub materials seeking light, for example, express themselves as somewhat linear masses arching out from underneath the linear sunlit edge of the wooded canopy (Figure 5-50).

The naturalistic mass is loosely organized by environmental criteria. The architectural counterpart, the bosque, is organized on a grid (Figure 5-51). It reads as a rectilinear mass from a distance; up close, it creates formal space articulated by a column grid of tree trunks. It feels very architectural.

Color. Color is quite effective in setting the mood of a

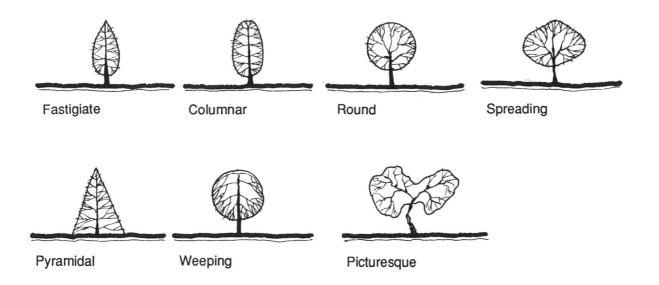

Figure 5-48. Plant form. (Redrawn from *Basic Elements of Landscape Architectural Design*, Booth, N. K., Figure 2.40, p. 94. Copyright © 1983, reissued 1990 by Waveland Press, Inc., Prospect Heights, Illinois)

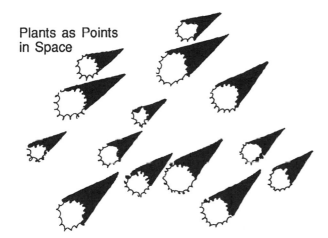

Figure 5-49. Early successional plant distribution.

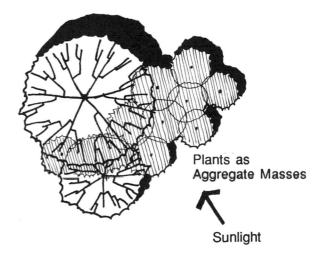

Figure 5-50. Late successional plant distribution.

place. Light green foliage creates an airy feeling, thus spring deciduous landscapes, lighter in color, seem more lively. Bright colors seem more cheerful, dark colors are more somber. Color in plant material is supplied by flowers, fruit, foliage, bark, twigs, and branches. Flower color can be quite varied and dynamic. However, it occurs as bursts and is usually not long lived. During most of the year, flower color is not an issue.

Fruit color can provide a nice contrast to foliage. It can complement leaf color and therefore enhance the visual quality of the plant in leaf. However, it is most dramatic when fruit linger after leaves have fallen.

Normal foliage varies in value from light to dark

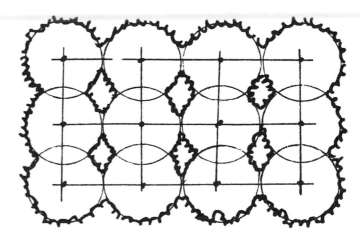

Figure 5-51. Bosque.

and in hue from yellow-green to blue-green to bronze, rust, and purple. Fall color has an even greater range of hues and is more dramatic. Like flower color, however, it is short lived.

Bark, twigs, and branches can themselves display interesting color. They are subtle compared to leaf, fruit, and flower color and are therefore most effective in the winter condition.

In design, color combines with line, form, and texture to display plant material. If a plant is selected to stand out in texture, form, size, or line, its character as accent is enhanced by a color that contrasts with its context.

The designer can plant masses that exhibit a subtle range of foliage color. This will create visual interest and eliminate blandness. In doing so, the designer should realize that colors are somewhat regional and site specific, and should avoid foreign or artificial-looking color schemes, unless the intent is to contrast regional expressions.

Texture. Texture refers to visual grain, that is, the coarseness or smoothness of the perceived surface. It is influenced by leaf size and edge character, by twig and branch size, by articulation of bark, by growth habit, and by viewing distance.

Coarse-textured plants are characterized by large leaves, massive branching, few twigs, and a loose habit of growth. They are dominant plants when used in a composition with medium- or fine-textured materials. Their dominance makes them useful as focal points. When so used, they should be displayed against fine-textured backgrounds. Coarse-texture plants tend to advance toward the viewer and to make the spaces within which they exist seem smaller. Therefore, they should not be used in small or tight spaces.

Most plants are of medium texture. Their role in planting is usually that of neutral mass, and as the backdrop within which fine or coarse materials are displayed as accents.

Fine-textured plants have many small leaves that are close together. They usually have a dense and full growth habit with many thin branches and fine twigs. They are most effectively viewed at very close range. They do not threaten or overpower small spaces. In fact they often make these spaces seem larger (as the small texture makes the plants seem to recede, tricking the viewer to perceive the space deeper than reality). Fine-textured plants seem very soft and delicate. When used as backdrop, they increase the impact of coarse-textured accent plants.

Perceived texture changes with the location of the viewer. When viewed up close, plant texture is determined by twig, leaf, and bark characteristics. Viewed from afar, growth habit and branching pattern are the relevant characteristics. Therefore, a plant can be seen as coarse textured when viewed up close, and medium textured when viewed from a distance, or vice versa.

Plant Strata and Size. Strata refers to the various horizontal layers that comprise a plant community, including canopy tree, understory tree, shrub, and ground cover (Figure 5-52). Size usually refers to the height to the top of the plant. In discussing size and strata, we will look at large and intermediate (canopy) trees, small and flowering (understory) trees, large shrubs, intermediate shrubs, small shrubs, and ground covers.

Large and Intermediate Trees. According to most plant lists, large trees are those generally taller than 40 feet; intermediate trees grow to 30 or 40 feet. Together, large and intermediate trees form the vegetated canopy. From outside they create mass; from within they create canopied space. Their trunks imply but do not enclose space (Figure 5-53). Their spaces have ceilings but no walls, only columns. They remain fairly open at eye level.

The overhead canopy changes the character of sunlight from hard and glaring to soft and dappled. This

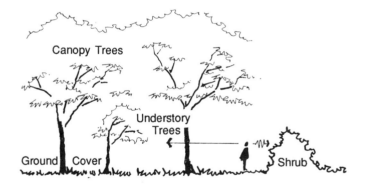

Figure 5-52. Plant strata.

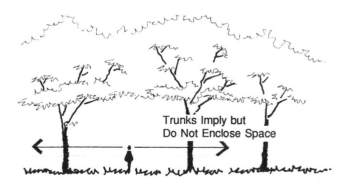

Figure 5-53. Trees and enclosure.

dappled quality of light is an important sensual aspect of being in the woods. When the canopy of large and intermediate trees is fairly continuous, a break in the canopy takes on the character of an outdoor room, open to the sky (Figure 5-54). The hard direct sunshine penetrating the space contributes to its dynamism.

Large and intermediate trees are effective modifiers of microclimate. They provide shade from high and mid angle sun (Figure 5-55). Also, if closed at their edge by lower branching material, or if great in depth (in the direction of airflow), they will substantially reduce ventilation. On the other hand, if the edge is open and the mass relatively shallow, they can accelerate airflow as the wind is compressed and forced below their canopy.

In planting design, large and intermediate trees can provide mass and contribute large scale (Figure 5-56). If planted to extend the lines or rhythm of architecture into exterior space, tree trunks can give an architectural character to the site (Figure 5-57).

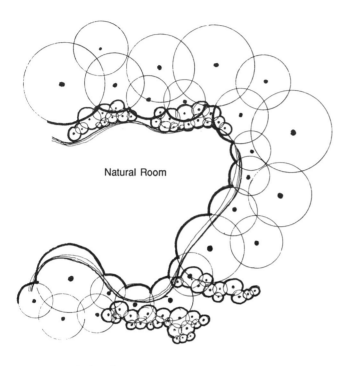

Natural Room

Figure 5-54. Outdoor room.

Figure 5-56. Large and intermediate trees provide bulk to plant mass.

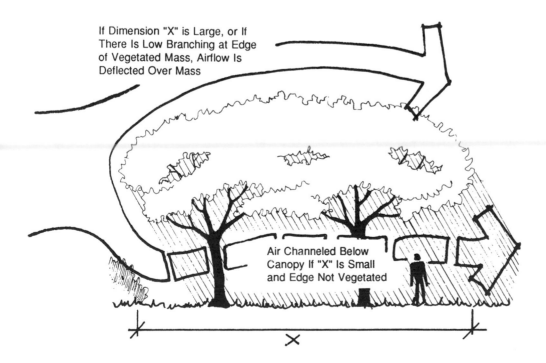

If Dimension "X" is Large, or If There Is Low Branching at Edge of Vegetated Mass, Airflow Is Deflected Over Mass

Air Channeled Below Canopy If "X" Is Small and Edge Not Vegetated

X

Figure 5-55. Large trees and microclimate.

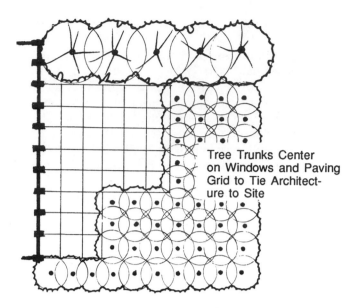

Figure 5-57. Tree trunks as landscape "columns."

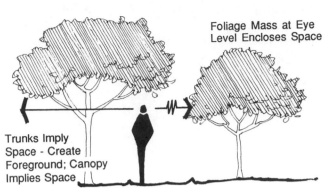

Figure 5-58. Small trees and spatial enclosure.

Small and Flowering (Understory) Trees. Small and flowering trees grow 15 to 20 feet in height. Their form and rate of flowering can differ substantially if they are growing beneath the canopy of large and intermediate trees, or if they are growing in the open sun. In the open sun their growth is thicker and more round, their flowering more intense.

When their canopies occur above head height, small and flowering trees *imply* intimate space. When these canopies occur at eye level, they *enclose* this space (Figure 5-58). These trees are very effective in small and intimate courtyards, as they provide color and shade without overpowering the space. In such contexts, they are often used as accent materials or focal points (Figure 5-59).

Small and flowering trees are effective at screening mid to low angle sun. They are often used on the southwest sides of buildings, or on the west and northwest sides if augmented by low branching shrub materials (Figure 5-60).

Tall Shrubs. Tall shrubs grow to 15 feet in height. They are shorter and lack the canopy of small trees. Their foliage usually extends close to the ground. They provide a strong sense of enclosure and a high degree of privacy. They are effective screens. Tall shrubs can serve as sculptural elements in a large space. They can also be backdrops against which to display smaller plant material or sculpture (Figure 5-61).

Figure 5-59. Small accent tree to lead the eye.

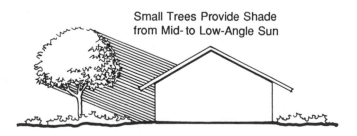

Figure 5-60. Small trees and shade.

Figure 5-61. Tall shrubs as screening/backdrop.

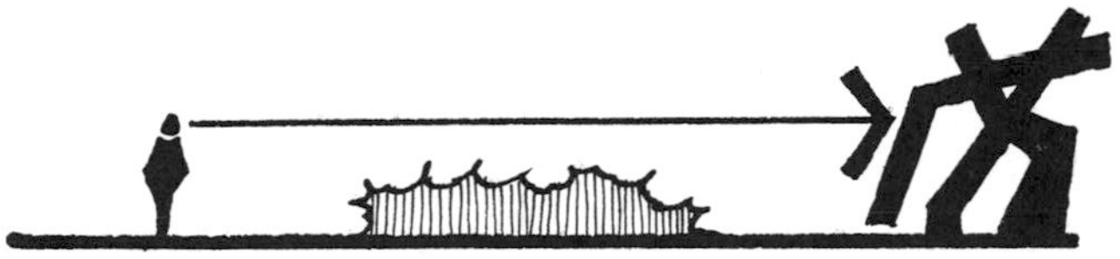

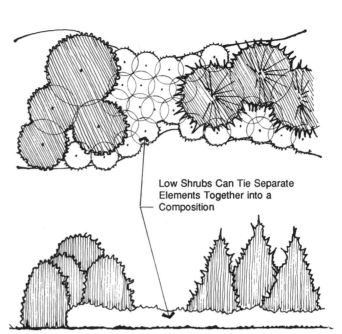

Low Shrubs Can Tie Separate
Elements Together into a
Composition

Figure 5-64. Low shrubs linking plant masses.

Low Shrubs Separate Space
but Do Not Block Vision

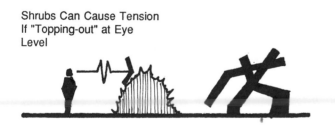

Figure 5-62. Low shrubs and enclosure.

Shrubs Can Cause Tension
If "Topping-out" at Eye
Level

Figure 5-63. Intermediate shrubs at eye level.

Intermediate and Low Shrubs. Intermediate shrubs grow 3 to 6 feet in height, low shrubs 1 to 3 feet. Low and intermediate shrubs define and physically separate spaces without blocking vision. They serve as impediments to pedestrian movement. Low shrubs provide a weaker visual separation (Figure 5-62); intermediate shrubs provide a stronger one.

Intermediate shrubs can become disconcerting if their tops occur at eye level. Tension is created as the observer tries to see over the tops (Figure 5-63). Therefore, it is best to avoid materials that top out in the 4 to 6 foot range, unless these are backed by taller materials.

Low shrubs can effectively link groups of larger plants while allowing vision to penetrate between the groups (Figure 5-64). In so doing, they can effectively unify a composition.

Ground Covers. Ground covers define planted areas. Like small shrubs, they can unify groups of larger plants into one composition. They also imply edges of spaces and create lines that can lead the eye to focal points, building entries or other important parts of a design composition (Figure 5-65). They also can create lines of high visual character and detail as they overlap paving or fine-textured turf.

Ground covers are beneficial in stabilizing slopes and preventing erosion. Slopes steeper than 4:1 (25%) are hard to mow and subject to erosion. On these slopes, ground covers are highly recommended.

Plant Size, Unity, and Variety. A simplified palette, limiting plant materials to canopy trees and ground

Figure 5-65. Ground cover as line.

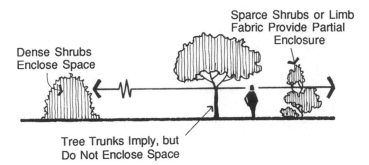

Figure 5-68. Density of edge and degree of enclosure.

Figure 5-66. Unified planting to consolidate disparate elements.

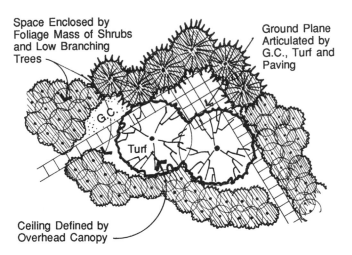

Figure 5-69. Spatial definition.

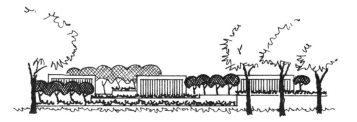

Figure 5-67. Complex planting to add variety to boring compositions.

cover, can be effective in unifying disparate design elements (Figure 5-66). Conversely, a complex multi-tiered planting scheme can provide variety and interest to an otherwise boring sterile architectural composition (Figure 5-67).

Spatial Issues. Spatial issues explored in this section include enclosure, spatial type, depth, enframement,

and the relationship between plant material and landform.

Spatial Enclosure. Enclosure refers to the perceived degree of separation of a space from its surrounding condition. Plant materials that block vision provide enclosure. Those that do not block vision only imply enclosure.

Plant materials at eye level enclose space. The more solid this material, the more strongly the space is enclosed (Figure 5-68). More porous plant masses provide only partial enclosure. Overall spatial definition and enclosure is the net visual effect of the various strata working together, as shown in Figure 5-69.

Spatial Type. Spaces vary by type. In scale, they range from intimate to public, in direction from horizontal to vertical, in enclosure from fully enclosed to open and unarticulated. Figure 5-70 depicts some of these spatial types and degrees of enclosure.

Spatial Depth. Spatial composition is more effective if it incorporates foreground, middle ground, and background. Foreground places the viewer into the space; middle ground usually serves as the subject matter and is displayed in the context of a background.

The skilled designer can use a foreground of plants to frame or enclose the subject matter, and can provide a high degree of contrast (in color, texture, and so on) between the subject and its background (Figure 5-71).

The relationship between foreground and background can be manipulated to accentuate or to mitigate depth. By using coarse-grained plant materials in the foreground and fine-grained ones in the background, the designer can extend the visual depth. Conversely, the use of fine-textured materials in the foreground and coarse-grained ones in the background will foreshorten the space.

Enframement. Plant materials can enframe a view and can, by their shape, enhance the form of the subject matter or focal point of the composition (Figure 5-72).

Plant Material and Landform. Plant material can strengthen or obfuscate landform. Dense plantings along the ridgelines can add visual height to the form, and can increase enclosure (Figure 5-73). Conversely, planting the hollows makes the landform less pronounced. As shown in Figure 5-74, swales that are nec-

Figure 5-71. Depth and composition.

Figure 5-72. Plant material to enframe view.

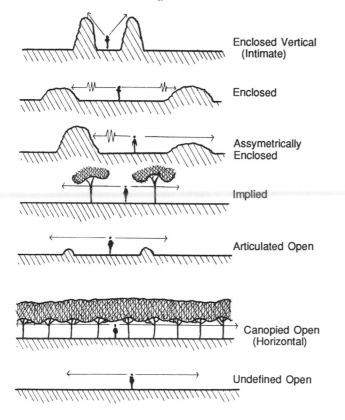

Figure 5-70. Spatial type and degree of enclosure.

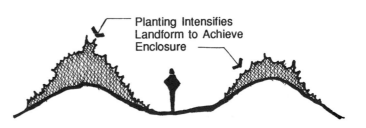

Figure 5-73. Planting to intensify landform.

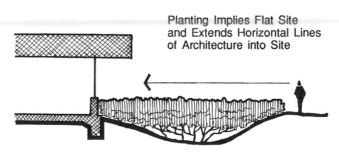

Figure 5-74. Planting to imply flat form.

essary for drainage (around a structure) can be concealed, and the horizontal lines of the building extended into the site by selecting ground covers and shrubs that establish a horizontal plane.

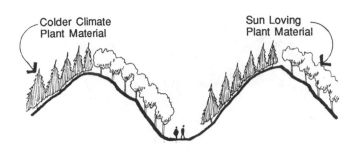

Figure 5-75. Slope-aspect and plant material.

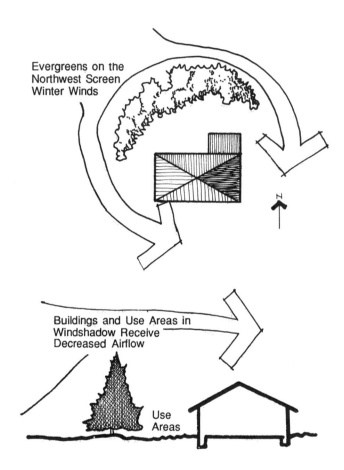

Figure 5-76. Evergreen vegetation and winter airflow.

On reasonably large sites with significant landform, plant materials can be selected to express and even accentuate the effects of slope aspect. For example, south-facing slopes can have soil climates similar to north-facing ones more than two hundred miles away (to the south). Therefore, the plant materials on the two opposing slopes can represent significantly different ecosystems (Figure 5-75). This can provide visual interest and structure to the site, while intensifying the visual and microclimatic differences of aspect.

Other Sensual Issues

In addition to visual issues, the designer is concerned with the smells, sounds, and tactile characteristics of plant materials. These nonvisual senses function to reinforce or mitigate images delivered by the eyes. The splash of color in the spring is made more intense by the aroma that accompanies the flower. As plant material overhangs a path and touches the viewer that passes, awareness of that material is enhanced.

In most cases nonvisual sensory stimuli are secondary in impact to visual ones. However, in certain instances their importance is greatly increased. When designing for the visually impaired, they become crucial.

Physiological comfort is a major sensory issue in planting design. Tree canopies provide protection from the overhead summer sun, and divert the wind. Low-branching trees and shrubs screen low angle sun. They are effective in blocking early morning and, more importantly, late afternoon sun. They also deflect air. If these materials are evergreen, they can be planted to divert winter winds from the northwest and to block the west and northwest late afternoon summer sun (Figure 5-76).

Concrete and other pavings absorb sunshine and reradiate the energy as heat. Plant materials, on the other hand, convert this energy to chemical bonds and do not generate appreciable heat. They also cool the environment through evapotranspiration. For both these reasons, vegetated sites are characterized by cooler summer temperatures than nonvegetated ones (Figure 5-77).

Temporal Aspects

Plants are unique design materials: they are living organisms. They grow, they change in size, and they change their character over time. They change in leaf condition, texture, color, and so on. This section explores some of the relationships between plant material and time including seasonal and successional characteristics and spatial sequence.

Seasonal Character. Based upon their form and seasonal foliage condition, plants are differentiated into three types: deciduous, coniferous evergreen, and broadleaf evergreen. Each type has its own behavior and design potential.

Deciduous Plants. Deciduous plants are the primary plant materials in temperate climates. They can exhibit four different seasonal characters. In the spring, their foliage can be yellow-green, and they can display flower color. Their summer foliage is usually fuller and darker. This foliage can display a splash of fall color before dropping to the ground. Their winter condition can be long and consists of bare branches and trunk texture. Deciduous plants with a short winter condition are referred to as persistent.

Evergreen Conifers. Evergreen conifers are characterized by needlelike leaves that remain throughout the year. Their foliage is usually very dark, and their growth is heavy. They do not generally have colorful flowers. They can appear massive and solemn, conveying a feeling of solidity to a site.

Conifers block views year round and usually provide a high degree of privacy (Figure 5-78). When branching very near the ground, they effectively block the wind. They are, therefore, often planted on the north or northwest sides of structures to exclude cold winter winds from buildings and from site-use areas (Figure 5-76). In this location, they also block the low angle summer afternoon sun.

The designer must be careful that conifers do not block desired winter sun, particularly in the early morning hours.

Broadleaf Evergreens. Broadleaf evergreens look much like deciduous plants, but keep their leaves through-out the year. Their foliage tends to be dark, opaque, and somewhat glassy looking. They usually display vivid spring color.

Most broadleaf evergreens require acid soils; they also do not tolerate wide ranges of temperature. They generally must be protected from winter winds and require at least partial shade in the summer.

Mixed Plantings. Deciduous plants seem dead in the winter; evergreens seem somber and lack seasonal variety. The disadvantages of each can often be overcome, and their opportunities realized by planting a mix of evergreen and deciduous materials (Figure 5-79). This will provide seasonal variety while maintaining some foliage in the winter. The evergreen material should be planted as groupings to avoid a spotty look in the winter condition.

Conifers Provide High Degree of Privacy in Use Areas

Figure 5-78. Conifers and privacy.

Mixed evergreen and deciduous plantings provide year-round life and seasonal variety

Figure 5-79. Mixed evergreen and deciduous plantings.

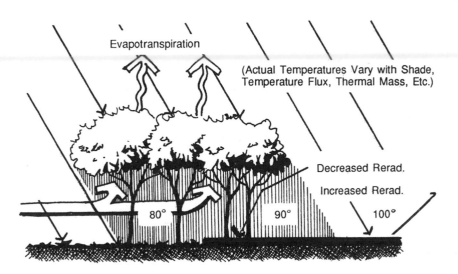
Evapotranspiration

(Actual Temperatures Vary with Shade, Temperature Flux, Thermal Mass, Etc.)

Decreased Rerad.

Increased Rerad.

80° 90° 100°

Figure 5-77. Vegetation and relative summer temperature.

Growth and Succession. Plants' ability to grow and their often high costs are taken into account so that plant materials are usually planted small and allowed to mature. Early successional materials mature quicker, but are shorter lived. Late successional materials are slower growing, but longer lived. It is often desirable, therefore, to plant a mix of early and late successional materials. The early successional materials will provide a mature look quickly and will dominate the composition for the first few years. Over time, the late successional landscape will mature and assert itself as the dominant palette.

Sequential Space. Plant materials can be used to screen views and to create spatial sequences in otherwise undifferentiated space. As one moves through the space, vegetated edges suddenly frame views and then open to expose other spaces and new edges which change their roles as the viewer continues to move.

Plant Material and Movement

We have looked at the temporal aspects of movement whereby the viewer moves and space unfolds over time. This section considers the other type of movement, that is, plant material movement induced by the wind.

Certain plant materials, because of leaf shape or fineness of branching, display leaves that flutter in the lightest breeze. This movement is choreographed on the ground and other surfaces as shadow patterns move. In cold climates, this movement adds life to otherwise dead spaces. In hot climates, it accentuates the sense of airflow, psychologically making one feel more comfortable.

Plants as Environmental Indicators

Plant materials correlate with site conditions. As these conditions change, the plants respond to the changes. Over time, they serve as indicators of site conditions. From plant material the designer can make inferences concerning soil fertility, drainage, available water, erosion and sedimentation, microclimate, and so on.

Early successional materials, with their wide ecological niches give only limited environmental clues (such as the history of site disturbance). Late successional plants, on the other hand, are finely tuned to their environment. They give more specific clues as to site condition.

Plants and Maintenance

Native materials are those that evolved in an area. Ecologically balanced materials, whether native or intro-

duced, bear a synergistic relationship with their environment. These plants require relatively little maintenance.

Plant materials not balanced with their condition require large expenditures of human and fossil fuel energies, water, nutrients, and so forth. These expenditures create the altered habitat required by the plant. Whenever maintenance is a limiting factor (as it usually is), or when resource conservation is an issue, plants not balanced with their environments should be avoided.

Plant Materials and Design Processes

Environmentally responsive site design includes reading the site and responding to conditions. A knowledge of existing plant materials, their relation to environmental condition, and their design potential is essential. This knowledge can contribute to more responsive site design if the landscape designer will:

1. Determine on-site plant materials and their characteristics.
2. Based on these materials, make educated guesses concerning site conditions. Identify redflags (areas of concern). Explore these issues.
3. Analyze existing plant materials in terms of health, ability to tolerate abuse, ability to satisfy program requirements, and so on.
4. Determine plant material that should be saved (giving preference to the middle-aged plant rather than the old and dying specimen).
5. Design for program needs, human needs, and plant needs. When making design decisions, consider microclimatic changes due to design and construction and the resultant impacts to existing and proposed plant materials.

This process, when integrated with other site analysis and design issues, should facilitate responsive decision-making.

CONSTRUCTION MATERIALS AND TECHNOLOGY

Landscape designers also have a myriad of construction materials at their disposal. Each of these materials has its own characteristics, behavior, and design potential. The systems built from these materials are also highly varied. Each system employs some structural concept, utilizes the behavior of specific materials, and helps to determine built form.

Construction materials can be grouped into five general categories: organic materials, inorganic materials used in their natural state, inorganic materials used in a highly modified state, synthetic materials, and composite materials.

Organic Materials

Organic materials are those that come directly from living organisms. Wood is the primary organic building material used in landscape construction. It is used in simple structures, as area and retaining walls, and as a paving material. As a construction material, wood is lightweight, strong, and reasonably durable. In addition, its cellular structure can be impregnated with chemicals to increase weatherability and resistance to insect attack.

For construction purposes, wood is divided into two categories. *Softwoods* come from coniferous evergreen plant materials; *hardwoods* from broadleaf trees (both deciduous and evergreen). Most woods used in exterior construction are softwoods. The construction use of hardwood is generally limited to furniture, finished millwork, and interior situations.

Softwoods

Most lumber for exterior use is softwood. Each species varies as to its availability, hardness, workability, structural behavior, durability, and appearance. Five of the woods more commonly used in exterior construction are cedar, cypress, douglas fir, yellow pine, and redwood.

Cedar. Cedar is a soft, easy to work wood. It is fragrant, and visually pleasing, especially in its rustic weathered state. It is naturally resistant to rot and to warpage. However, it is one of the weakest softwoods and does not hold nails well.

Cypress. Cypress is an excellent wood for use in exterior situations. It is highly resistant to natural decay and to attack by insects. It weathers naturally to a silver grey if left unfinished. It is denser and stronger than cedar, but is still quite workable. It is used in the construction of decks and structures. It is also used for trim work. It is generally available only in 1-inch nominal thicknesses.

Douglas Fir. Douglas fir is one of the strongest softwoods. It is commonly used for its structural performance and is one of the most popular lumber species. However, it has only a moderate resistance to rot, and it does not hold paint well. If used in an exterior situation, it requires the application of a wood preservative. For both these reasons, it is not extensively used in exterior construction.

Southern Yellow Pine. Southern yellow pine is the strongest of the softwoods and holds nails well. When treated with preservatives, it is highly resistant to decay. Though not naturally beautiful, it stains well. On the other hand, it has a high pitch content and must be carefully cured to prevent warpage. Southern yellow pine, impregnated with a wolman salt preservative, is commonly used for exterior structures, decks, and site furniture.

Redwood. Redwood is a strong wood with a natural resistance to rotting and insect attack. It is an attractive wood that requires little or no finishing or preserving It is easy to work, resisting warpage and shrinkage. It is an ideal wood for exterior construction. However, it is a limited and highly valued natural resource that should be protected. It is also expensive and often unavailable.

Hardwoods

Railroad ties, and their recycled use as landscape timbers, is about the only common use of hardwoods in landscape construction.

Inorganic Materials Used in Their Natural State

Inorganic natural materials that are used in substantially the same form as they are found in nature include stone, clay, brick, gravel, and sand.

Stone

Stone is a natural material used extensively in site design. It is used in the construction of landscape structures, area and retaining walls, steps, wall veneers, and pavings. However, because of the costs of shipping, stone materials are usually considered a local resource. On most projects it is usually not economically feasible to ship stone over great distances (from one region to another). Stones vary widely in their behavior, characteristics, and structural properties. The stones most frequently used in site construction are granites, limestones, and sandstones. Marble is also often used.

Granite. Granite is an igneous rock used in various forms. It is a very hard, dense, heavy stone. It is difficult to work but extremely resistant to wear. In the past, small granite blocks called *sets* were used for ship ballast (Figure 5-80). In regions where this ballast was unloaded, these blocks were used extensively for paving.

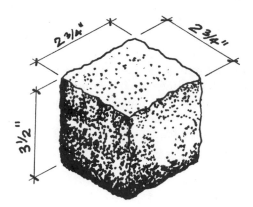

Figure 5-80. Granite sets.

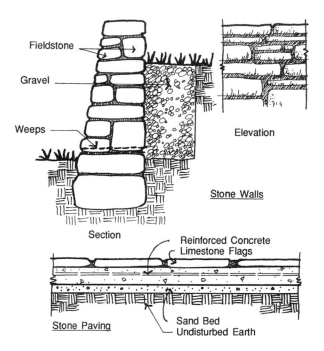

Figure 5-81. Limestone walls and paving.

Granite is also utilized in broken, sawn, and polished forms, and as a veneer. These extremes in finish, and subtle variations between, can be highly controlled for design elegance. As a polished surface, granite achieves a high gloss that is durable and easy to clean.

Limestone. Limestones (and dolomites) are sedimentary rocks ranging in color from white to grey and composed principally of calcium carbonate. They are strong and hard, but are much easier to work than granite. They can be cut, planed, lathed, or worked with hand tools. Limestones vary widely in color and

hardness; many are highly susceptible to chemical decay.

In many parts of the country, limestone appears as independent stones or lenses in the soil called fieldstones. In other areas, it exists as horizontal strata or layers called ledgestones.

Limestone is usually used in somewhat modified forms as paving stones, veneer stones and copings for walls (Figure 5-81). It is used in its natural state to form dry stone walls and as natural landscape rock.

Sandstone. Sandstone is durable and easy to work. It ranges in color from a deep ocher to a deep sienna or amber. Regionally, other colors exist, including brownstones and bluestones. Sandstone is used in landscape construction in much the same manner as limestone. Local availability is the primary determinant of which to use.

Marble. Marble is metamorphosed limestone. It is used as an exterior paving and wall veneer material, usually in a somewhat polished condition. It is a very durable material when used in a dry climate.

Clay

Clay usually comes from aluminous or silicate rocks. It is generally plastic when wet, but hard when dry. Clay construction materials include clay tile pipe, clay tile veneers, and structural clay tile (Figure 5-82).

Clay tile pipe and fittings are generally of two types, solid and perforated. Perforated tile pipe are used to evacuate soil water; solid pipe are used to move water from one location to another. However, as we will see later, clay tile pipe is rapidly being replaced by plastic materials.

Clay tile veneers are usually used as ornamental panels applied to structures or area walls. They can be molded, textured, colored, or painted. Often referred to as terra cotta, this material performs much as burned brick.

Structural clay tiles are modular units, often with a glazed ceramic finish. They can be used as either a veneer or as a load-bearing wall material.

Brick

Brick are small modular building units, composed of nonorganic materials hardened by heat or chemical action. There are three primary types of brick: clay brick (either hard or soft burned), cement brick, and sand-lime brick.

Originally, brick was a modular material based on an 8-inch construction module, as shown in Figure 5-83.

Based on the brick face viewed, either three units or two units or one unit (with mortar joints) formed an 8-inch dimension. These dimensions vary somewhat today. The face of the brick exposed, and its orientation, determine the coursing of the brick to include stretcher, header, rolok, and soldier (Figure 5-84).

The design potentials and limitations of brick accrue to its modular nature. Any size or shape that varies from the module requires the cutting of brick or the molding of special units. Both are quite expensive. On the other hand, bricks lend themselves to the creation of rectilinear form. They can also form radiating or curvilinear patterns if the radius of curvature is adequately large to form these patterns without

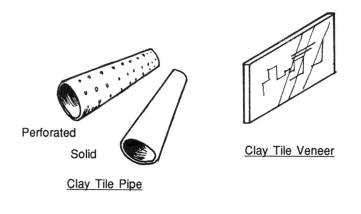

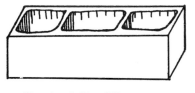

Figure 5-82. Clay construction materials.

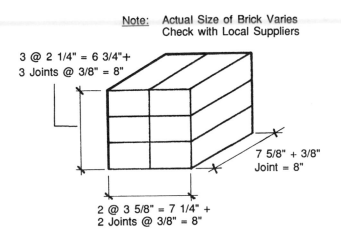

Note: Actual Size of Brick Varies
Check with Local Suppliers

Figure 5-83. Brick as modular unit.

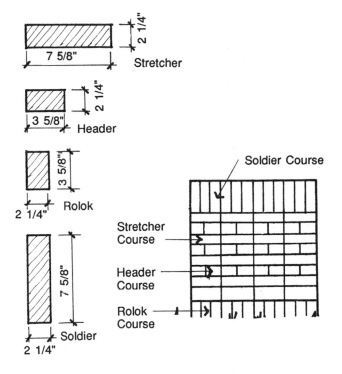

Figure 5-84. Brick coursing.

cutting bricks and without visually objectionable joints.

Despite its restrictions, brick offers many possibilities for creating interesting surface patterns, as shown in Figures 5-85 and 5-86. The most commonly used pattern in both paving and walls is the running bond. It is easy to lay out in construction. As paving, it accentuates one direction (that with continuous lines). Paving bricks are usually oriented with these lines perpendicular to, rather than along, the line of sight. In wall applications, the bond runs horizontally, is easy to lay, and produces a structurally strong veneer with discontinuous vertical joints.

Interlocking pavers are clay masonry units that are shaped to allow the individual units to visually interlock. They are available in a number of patterns, two of which are shown in Figure 5-87.

Clay brick and clay unit pavers are molded from moist clay and then fired in a kiln. Their color and hardness depend upon the clay itself and the firing conditions. Partial firing leaves the clay softer and lighter in color; more complete firing produces darker and harder bricks; extremely high temperatures create burnt, warped and cracked bricks called clinkers. Soft bricks are generally not used in landscape construction, as they do not weather well. Clinkers are very dark in color and difficult to lay and are also seldom used in landscape design. The vast majority of clay brick used in landscape construction are hard

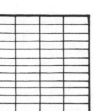

Stacked Bond
(Bricks Laid Flat)

Stacked Bond
(Bricks Laid on Edge)

Running Bond
(Bricks Laid Flat)

Running Bond
(Bricks Laid on Edge)

Herring-Bone
(Bricks Laid Flat)

Herring-Bone
(Bricks Laid on Edge)

Basket Weave
(Bricks Laid Flat)

Basket Weave
(Bricks Laid on Edge)

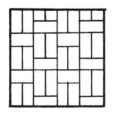

Basket Weave Variation
(Laid Flat)

Basket Weave Variation
(Laid on Edge)

Figure 5-85. Brick paving patterns.

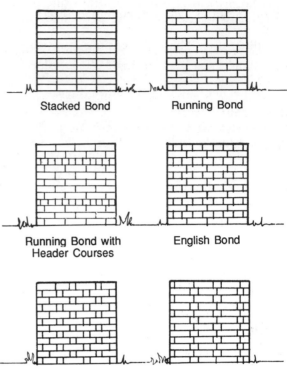

Stacked Bond

Running Bond

Running Bond with
Header Courses

English Bond

Flemish Bond

Flemish Double
Stretcher

Figure 5-86. Brick wall patterns.

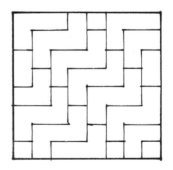

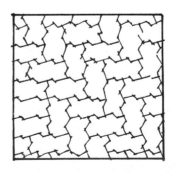

Figure 5-87. Interlocking pavers.

brick. Hard brick is also fractured into fine particles called cinder and used to create paths and running tracks.

Cement brick is used as a veneer and facing for exterior walls when high strength and moisture resistance are critical. Sand-lime brick is a nonclay material used in applications similar to hard brick. It has good fire, frost, and acid resistance. Both cement and sand-lime brick are used in regions where clay is not locally available.

Gravel

Gravel consists of particles of rock, either in an angular crushed form, or as smooth river-washed gravel. When used by itself, gravel has high strength and good drainage characteristics. It is often placed in the bottom of excavations to promote drainage away from other materials (such as wood) that are subject to decay. Gravel is used in conjunction with porous pipe to drain subsoils (french drains).

Because of its strength and good drainage characteristics, gravel is used as a paving subbase. It is also combined with sand and compacted as a building slab subbase. It is also used as the coarse aggregate in concrete.

Pedestrianways and drives are often made of gravel. When so used, the slight shifting of particles and the "crunching" sound created by moving across these surfaces can add to the sensual experience.

Sand

Sand consists of small particles of rock or mineral. It can occur naturally, as in silica beach sand, or can be artificially disintegrated from larger rocks. Bank run sand refers to sand before it is prepared for construction use; screened and washed sand has been prepared for site use.

Sand is used as a fine aggregate for concrete, mortar, and stucco. It is used as a leveling bed to prepare ground surfaces that are to receive rigid pavings and is used to eliminate some of the expansion characteristics of the materials that underlie construction. It is used as a setting bed for flexible modular pavings such as brick, asphalt, or concrete pavers. In this sense, and when it is not underlain by rigid pavement, the surface is free to undulate as the soil expands. This gives a sensuous "hard material rendered soft" feeling. Coarse sand is also a paving material in its own right.

Inorganic Materials Used in a Highly Modified State

Inorganic materials not used in their original state consist primarily of the wide array of metals including aluminum, bronze, copper, iron, steel, and stainless steel.

Aluminum

Aluminum is a lightweight, soft, nonmagnetic metal. It is highly reflective, resists oxidation, and readily conducts heat and electricity. In site design, it is used in four primary ways: as an alloy, as a sheathing material, as a mesh, and as wiring.

As an alloy, aluminum is combined with other materials and used to extrude linear shapes for handrails, siding, trim, and so forth. It is also cast into connectors and supports. As a sheathing, it is usually corrugated for strength, forming very thin lightweight structural sheets. These sheets are used for roofing or siding. Sheets are often perforated or deformed into decorative shapes in lieu of corrugation.

Aluminum mesh is typically used for screens, guards, and fencing. It is available in a variety of sizes and patterns. Aluminum is also extensively used for electrical work.

Bronze

Bronze is an alloy of copper and tin. For site use, it is rolled into sheets, extruded into linear shapes, or forged or cast into more irregular forms. Its two primary uses are as sculpture and as hardware.

As sculpture, bronze can be forged or cast into amorphous shapes. It facilitates the creation of statuary with exquisite detail. It affords a variety of color choices dependent on the amount of tin included in the alloy. Its color is stable over time, but is made more rich by the slight patina that develops on its surface.

Because it is durable and resists oxidation, bronze is also used for the fabrication of rough hardware and accessories such as hinges, plates, bolts, nuts, and anchors.

Copper

Copper is a ductile and malleable reddish-colored metal, which conducts heat and electricity very well. Its outer surface weathers (oxidizes) to a highly visible patina, which resists corrosion (except by acids). Light washes of acid determine the particular visual quality of the patina. Extended exposure to acids in the air can cause rapid corrosion.

Copper is used in site development in three primary forms: wire, tubing, and sheeting. Copper wire is extensively used for electrical work. Copper tubing is used for water supply piping. Even though copper sheeting is expensive, it is a durable, aesthetic, and low-maintenance material used as roofing and is bent into special shapes for flashings, caps, trims, and so on.

Iron

Iron is a metal high in compressive, but low in tensile, strength. It is easily magnetized. It is not resistant to most acids. In site construction, iron is used in its cast form, in its wrought form, and as an alloy in the manufacture of steel.

Cast iron is a product of blast furnaces. It is used as ornamental iron and as piping. Wrought iron is less dense. It is formed by puddling and then hammering or rolling the iron into bars and then rolling the bars into sheets. Wrought iron is used to make pipes and railings.

Steel

Steel is an alloy of iron and carbon. It can be hammered or wrought, rolled, cast, or forged. It can also be welded and riveted, but it cannot be extruded. It is subject to oxidation if not protected by galvanization or by coating with a primer paint. Steel is commonly used as reinforcement, sheet steel, mesh, plate or strip steel, steel bars or tubes, and structural steel. It usually comes in a galvanized sheet, but can be obtained in a self-oxidizing cortan finish.

Steel Reinforcement. Steel reinforcement is embedded in concrete to resist tensile stresses. Its two most common forms are deformed bars or welded wire mesh. Deformed bars are numbered as per their thickness expressed in eighths of an inch (#3 is 3/8 inch in diameter, #6 is 6/8 inch or 3/4 inch, and so on). Welded wire mesh comes in specified mesh size and gauge (6 inches × 6 inches = 16-gauge mesh).

Galvanized Steel. Galvanized steel comes in wire, bar, or sheet form, coated with zinc for protection against corrosion. Galvanized steel culvert piping is corrugated galvanized sheet steel spiraled into a structural shape (Figure 5-88). Galvanized steel is also used for roofing and for siding.

Cortan Steel. Cortan steel is steel that has been treated so as to facilitate its oxidation to a deep rust color. The rich patina is a protective self-curing finish, and scratches and mars will reoxidize. In the process of oxidation, however, runoff will carry the rust color onto adjacent surfaces. Many a bold cortan design statement has been visually spoiled by streaking of adjacent materials. This can be avoided by dealing effectively with runoff and selecting appropriate adjacent materials.

Steel Mesh. Steel mesh includes chain link fencing, and utility and ornamental screening.

Steel Plates and Strips. Steel plates and strips are bent to form roof decking and door and window mullions and frames.

Steel Bars and Tubes. Steel bars and tubes are available in square, rectangular, and round shapes of various sizes and thicknesses. They are used for columns, beams, piles, railings, pipings, and so on.

Structural Steel. Structural Steel includes "I" beams, wide flange beams, "H" columns, "Z" shapes, channels, plates, and so on. From these standard shapes and sizes, structural frames, trusses, space frames, and other structural systems are fabricated. Sophisticated structural steel elements are generally identified by section type and weight per linear foot, angles and plate steel by length, width, and thickness.

Stainless Steel

Stainless steel is an alloy of chromium and steel. It can be drawn, rolled, cast, forged, bent, welded, or riveted. It is used for railings, trims, grilles, screens, and occasionally sheathing.

Synthetic Materials

Synthetic materials are those created by humans. The two most popular synthetics in site development are glass and plastics.

Glass

Glass is a transparent fusion of silica, alkaline flux, and stabilizer into a rigid, noncrystalline mass. An extremely versatile material, it can be formed (while molten) by a number of means. It can be blown into bulbous shapes, flowed into sensuous forms, or cut, flattened, and cooled slowly to reduce its brittleness. It can be drawn by a metal bar from a vat of molten glass and flattened by rollers into a continuous sheet. It can also be floated into a smooth sheet. It can be heat-tempered after forming and can thereby achieve substantial strength. Glass used in exterior conditions should be tempered.

Among the site applications of glass are: sculpture and statuary; rods, bars, and tubes; corrugated glass; faceted and stained glass; float glass; tempered glass; and glass block. Glass can be formed clear or in a wide range of colors.

Sculptured and Statuary Glass. Sculptured and stat-

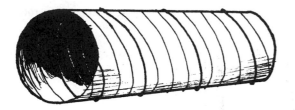

Figure 5-88. Corrugated steel culvert pipe.

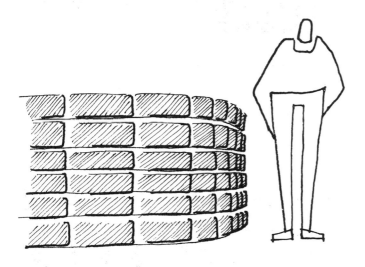

Figure 5-89. Glass block wall.

uary glass can be molded (while hot) into sensuous shapes, or it can be faceted (on cooling) into angular chunks. Its site use should be limited to highly controlled areas because of its susceptibility to vandalism.

Glass Rods, Bars, and Tubes. Glass rods, bars, and tubes can be used as sculpture. They can be used in conjunction with other materials such as wood and metal to develop railing systems. They can encase lamps for exterior lighting. They can enclose neon and other heated gases to provide light of various colors. Corrugated glass can be used for decorative purposes.

Stained and Faceted Glass. Stained and faceted glass are decorative glasses. Stained glass can be pigmented glass, or glass that is painted and fired. The surface of the glass is exposed and pieces are arranged in a design and are then leaded into position. Faceted glass are pieces of pigmented glass that are broken (or faceted) after curing. They are arranged into a design and cast into an epoxy or cement matrix. They can be several inches thick. Stained and faceted glass panels are used as decorative ceilings or as wall panels. Stained glass is sometimes used as floor panels, but can be dangerously slick when wet.

Glass Blocks. Glass blocks are hollow structural glass units, in various modular sizes. They are formed with smooth surfaces, or with a range of surface textures. Glass block is usually laid up with mortar joints (Figure 5-89).

Plastics

Plastics are a diverse group of synthetic materials that can be molded, cast, drawn, or laminated into sculptured forms, sheets, tubes, bars, rods, or films. They exhibit a wide range of structural behaviors, visual expressions, and durability based on their chemical compounds. They can be fabricated in a range of colors and textures.

Plastics have diverse site applications. They are used extensively as preformed site furniture, benches, refuse receptacles, and so on. They are molded into roofing and wall panels, often corrugated and colored. Special high-strength and impact-resistant plastics have been developed and used extensively to protect outdoor light sources. Special fiber-optic plastic rods are being used to transport light onto project sites from concealed sources, and for other unique lighting effects. Finally, corrosion-resistant plastic pipes, both perforated and solid, are rapidly supplanting clay pipe for subsurface drainage systems and for water and wastewater piping.

Composite Materials

Composite construction materials combine two or more materials to create a new one that behaves quite differently from the original materials. Concrete and plywood are two examples.

Concrete

Concrete is a composite consisting of water, portland cement, fine aggregates, and coarse aggregates. The cement is itself a composite of silica, alumina, lime, and other materials and serves to bind together the fine and coarse aggregates. Concrete is a massive material high in compressive strength, but weak in tension. Reinforcing steel is usually added in specific places to resist internal tensile stresses. Concrete with imbedded rebars is a composite referred to as reinforced concrete.

Concrete is formed in a liquid state. In this state, the cement chemically reacts to bind the ingredients together. During this process, the concrete must be contained within the desired shape by some formwork. It must also have its constituent materials retained in their proper locational relationship to achieve desired strengths. Reinforced concrete members can be precast in a plant and assembled at the site, or cast-in-place (with imbedded rebars) on site. For added strength the reinforcing steel can be prestressed while the concrete is curing, or posttensioned after curing.

Precast Concrete Members. Precast concrete members are formed in a concrete plant. These members, with imbedded steel, are then shipped to the site for fabrication. Precasting of concrete eliminates most of the site formwork. This technique is used extensively for bridge beams and similar installations where structural components are highly repetitive and site forming is difficult.

Site Cast (In Situ) Concrete. In most cases, concrete is site cast. In many cases, as with paving, the earth serves to support the concrete, and formwork merely needs to be built at the edges. In this case, site casting is usually the only economically reasonable alternative. Even when the concrete is elevated, economics usually dictate site casting, as the cost of formwork does not normally approach that incurred when shipping precast members.

Site casting of concrete walls and beams can be quite complex. The concrete is usually cast in rectilinear sections. The surfaces that retain the concrete are usually plywood unless the concrete is to be exposed. Concrete to be permanently exposed is called *architectural concrete* and is usually cast against a material that has a special fine-grained, high-density surface (such as steel or plastic).

A grid of steel form ties are installed to retain the sides of the formwork, at a consistent spacing (Figure 5-90). These ties have weakened sections approximately 1 inch from the face of the form, allowing the ties to be snapped and the forms removed after the concrete has cured. Sequentially, the forms are built, then the configuration of reinforcing steel bars are tied and supported in the form. The concrete is poured, vibrated to evenly distribute the aggregate, and allowed to cure. After curing, the forms are snapped free and removed.

If the concrete is meant to be architectural (permanently exposed), the joints of the form must receive great care (such as gasketing or taping) to prevent leakage of water, as such leakage affects the color as well as the hardness of the concrete. Vibration must be done carefully with a high mass vibrator to insure an even visual distribution of aggregates. Finally the holes left when the form ties are broken need to be patched with concrete to match the adjacent areas (this is quite difficult to do). Often, in lieu of patching, the tie pattern will be expressed by planning for enlarged holes that are visually pleasing in

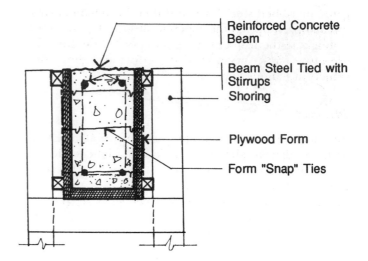

Figure 5-90. Formwork for reinforced concrete beam.

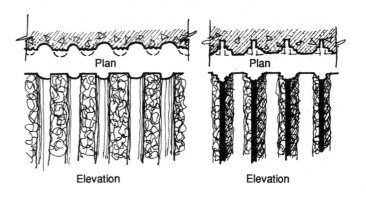

Figure 5-91. Ribbed and hammered concrete finishes.

their arrangement and then plugging these holes with lead shields. The resultant grid pattern of plugs is highly visible and very common in architectural concrete today.

Concrete Finishes. Architectural concrete receives a wide range of surface finishes and textures. When a smooth finish is desired, the semicured concrete is patched as required and then rubbed with a carborundum stone to eliminate irregularities and blemishes. When the aggregate is intended to be exposed, the surface is sandblasted. The wetter the concrete when blasting, and the sharper and coarser the blasting sand, the more pronounced and exposed will be the aggregate. On rare occasions, very coarse aggregates will be hand placed against the forms prior to casting or into the semicured concrete after form removal.

One of the most highly textured concrete finishes is achieved by casting the concrete against a corrugated or ribbed steel form and then bush-hammering (breaking, chipping) the concrete surface (Figure 5-91). Though aesthetically pleasing and bold, these finishes are quite costly, because of the effort and time consumed in hammering.

Plywood

Plywood consists of separate sheets of wood glued together. Adjacent sheets are placed at right angles to each other, greatly increasing its strength. Plywoods are classified by their mastic as interior, exterior, or marine plywoods. The exposed veneers are graded. Plywoods are available with exposed veneers in a wide range of grades and wood species.

Structural Concepts

Built form is an expression of the preceding (and other) materials and the systems by which they are structured. Underlying these systems are some basic issues including external forces, mechanics and statics, internal stresses, elasticity, and the behavior of specific shapes.

External Forces

Site materials are acted on by external forces. These forces include the consistent "dead load" exerted by the building itself and the variable "live loads" exerted by wind, water, furniture, people, automobiles, and so on.

Mechanics and Statics

The science of mechanics is the study of the action of a force upon a mass. Statics addresses the principles of mechanics that keep a mass at rest. Grossly simplified, statics relates to the combination of external forces and the ability of materials to internally resist these forces in such a manner as to preclude motion.

Internal Stresses

The myriad of external forces exert three types of force on building materials: compressive force, tensile force, and torsional force (Figure 5-92). Compressive forces attempt to shorten a member, tensile forces tend to lengthen it, torsional forces tend to twist it.

When these forces are exerted on a member, three types of stresses occur within the material: compressive stresses, tensile stresses, and shear stresses. Compressive stresses are a reaction to compressive forces; tensile stresses resist tensile forces; shear stresses occur as a result of nonaligned forces acting in different directions (Figure 5-93).

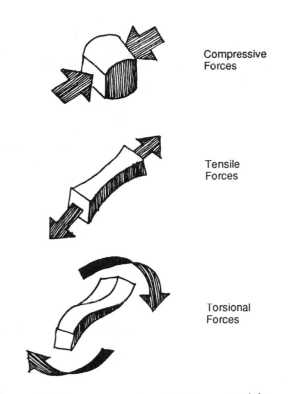

Compressive Forces

Tensile Forces

Torsional Forces

Figure 5-92. Forces exerted on building materials.

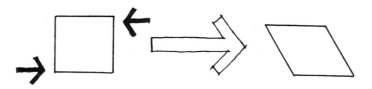

Figure 5-93. Shear stresses.

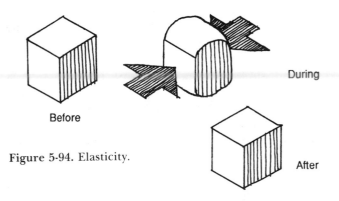

Before

During

After

Figure 5-94. Elasticity.

Elasticity

Elasticity refers to the property of a material that requires a continued external force to change its shape. Conversely, it is the characteristic of that material to return to its original shape after external forces are removed (Figure 5-94).

Behavior of Specific Shapes

In structural design, the triangle is a unique and advantageous shape. It is the strongest and most stable shape, even when its angles (joints) are not rigid. Other polygonal shapes depend upon rigidity of their angles for structural rigidity (Figure 5-95).

The sphere is also a unique and advantageous structural shape. It encloses the maximum amount of space or volume with the minimum amount of surface.

Structural Systems

Materials must be organized and configured so as to create specific shapes while maintaining statics and avoiding material failure. The way these materials are structured, that is, the structural system, translates external forces such as wind, gravity, and so on, into compressive, tensile, and shear stresses within the materials. The specific behavior of the material works with the character of the structural system to determine whether statics is achieved or whether failure occurs.

There are numerous systems for structuring material. These include mass, frame, structural grid, structural slab, folded plate, arch, vault, groined vault, dome, thin shell, truss, space frame, geodesic dome, tensile structure, cable structure, tensegrity, and pneumatic systems.

Mass Structures

Mass structures are those that depend on compressive stresses within the mass to resist the external forces. The most expressive form of mass structure is the tapered mass, shaped as the literal response to the dead weight of the material itself. An example of mass structure supporting only its own weight is a pile of sand (Figure 5-96). The architectural form corollary is the pyramid. When the mass supports an external weight in addition to its own weight, the most expressive form becomes the truncated mass (Figure 5-97).

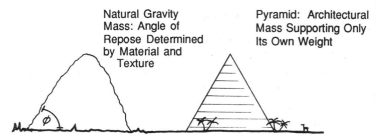

Natural Gravity Mass: Angle of Repose Determined by Material and Texture

Pyramid: Architectural Mass Supporting Only Its Own Weight

Figure 5-96. Mass structures.

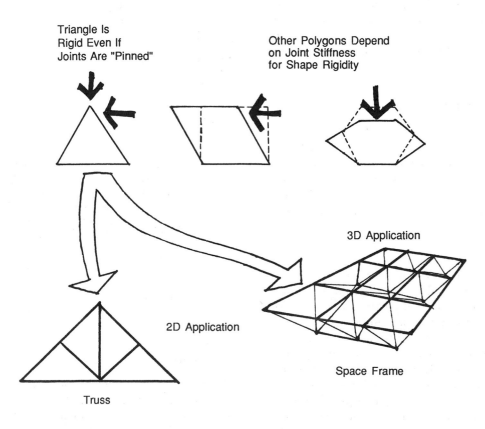

Triangle Is Rigid Even If Joints Are "Pinned"

Other Polygons Depend on Joint Stiffness for Shape Rigidity

3D Application

2D Application

Truss

Space Frame

Figure 5-95. Structural rigidity of triangular shapes.

Openings in mass structures are achieved through corbeling, by post and lintel, or by arch.

Corbeling. Corbeling occurs as upper layers extend beyond those below to close an opening (Figure 5-98). It allows all forces to be translated to compressive stresses and these forces to be transferred to the sides of the opening in a two-dimensional surface. Domes can be corbeled as well.

Post and Lintel. A post and lintel structural system consists of post uprights that support a horizontal beam or lintel (Figure 5-99). The lintel functions as a beam, resisting vertical loads through a combination of compressive, tensile, and shear stresses.

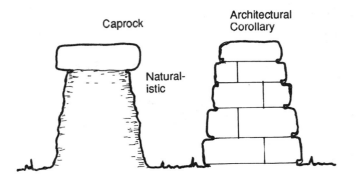

Figure 5-97. Truncated mass structures.

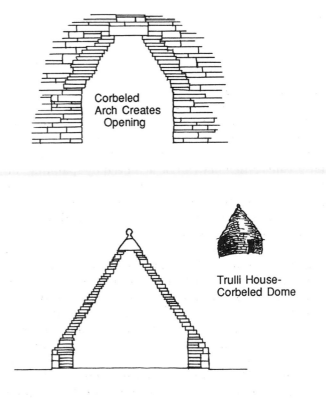

Figure 5-98. Corbeling.

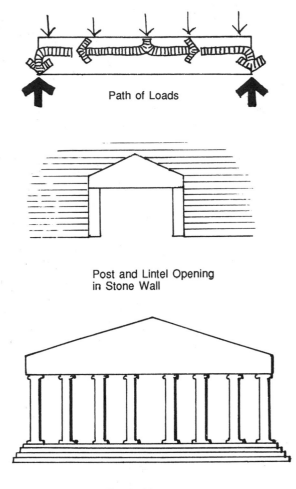

Figure 5-99. Post and lintel construction.

Frame Construction

The post and lintel system, when extended to the third dimension, gives rise to frame construction. There are two basic types of frame constructions: light frame construction, and plank and beam framing.

Light Frame Construction. Most residential structures built today are wood frame structures. They usually set on a concrete slab and often have a veneer of brick, stone, or wood, but the structural system is light wood framing. There are several types of light frame construction, but they all share several characteristics. Floors, ceilings, and roofs are supported by walls (Figure 5-100). Openings in the walls are framed via posts and lintels. Where walls are spaced beyond the reasonable span for joists, the joists bear on beams that are supported by columns.

Most landscape structures are built using a light frame construction technique called platform framing

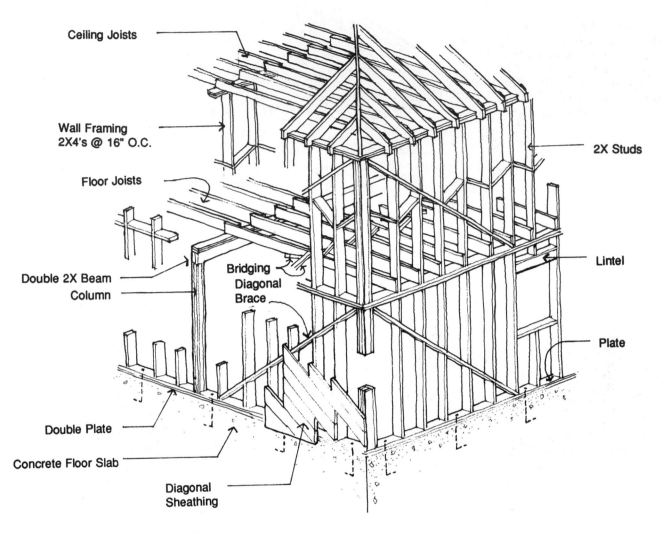

Ceiling Joists

Wall Framing
2X4's @ 16" O.C.

Floor Joists

Double 2X Beam
Column

Bridging
Diagonal
Brace

Double Plate

Concrete Floor Slab

Diagonal
Sheathing

2X Studs

Lintel

Plate

Figure 5-100. Light framing or balloon framing.

(Figure 5-101). Since most wood landscape structures do not have structural walls, platform framing systems for site use usually have four basic structural elements: the floor decking, joists, beams, and columns. The decking bears on joists; the joists transmit these loads to beams. The beams are usually supported by columns or posts. In some cases, the beams are supported by larger horizontal members called girders. In this case, the girders are then supported by columns or posts.

Plank and Beam Framing. Plank and beam framing is more simple than platform framing, because it eliminates the joists (Figure 5-102). The flooring is thicker (a minimum of 3 inches if it spans more than 4 feet). It physically spans from beam to beam and bears directly on them. This system is usually more expensive than platform framing because it requires thicker and better flooring materials. It gives a lighter looking deck with "cleaner" lines than does platform framing, which generally has a more solid, massive quality.

Structural Grids

The simplest system for creating flat horizontal surfaces is the plank and beam system described above. If the flooring material becomes one integral slab, a far greater efficiency can be achieved by spanning the flooring in two directions and allowing it to be supported by a rectilinear grid of beams. This structural grid maximizes its efficiency as the grid cell approaches a square shape.

The structural grid (which must have rigid joints) displays teamwork. If a load acts on one member of the team of beams, the beam deflects, and in so doing, causes the beams around it to deform as well (Figure 5-103). Beams that align with the plane of the force resist it through bending; those not aligned resist through a combination of bending and twisting. Therefore, rigidity of joints in a structural grid is mandatory. This rigidity is easy to achieve with reinforced concrete or welded or bolted steel. It is quite difficult to achieve with wood construction.

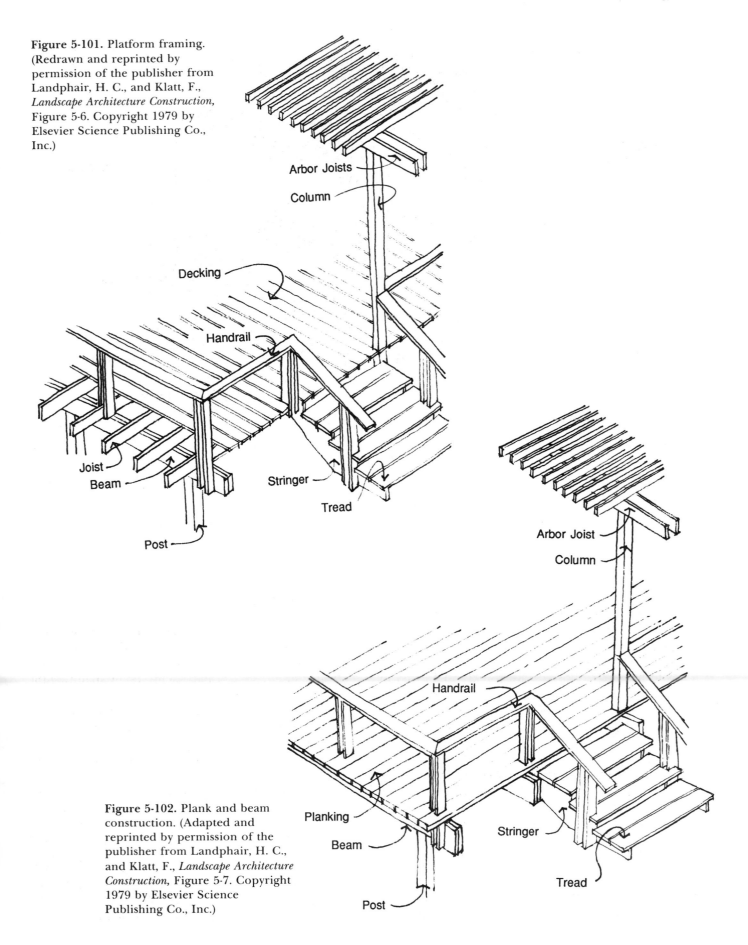

Figure 5-101. Platform framing. (Redrawn and reprinted by permission of the publisher from Landphair, H. C., and Klatt, F., *Landscape Architecture Construction,* Figure 5-6. Copyright 1979 by Elsevier Science Publishing Co., Inc.)

Arbor Joists

Column

Decking

Handrail

Joist

Beam

Stringer

Tread

Post

Arbor Joist

Column

Handrail

Planking

Beam

Stringer

Post

Tread

Figure 5-102. Plank and beam construction. (Adapted and reprinted by permission of the publisher from Landphair, H. C., and Klatt, F., *Landscape Architecture Construction,* Figure 5-7. Copyright 1979 by Elsevier Science Publishing Co., Inc.)

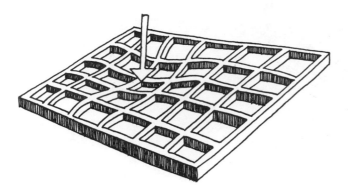

Figure 5-103. Rectangular structural grid.

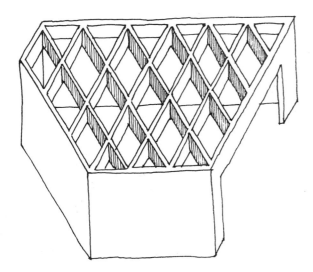

Figure 5-104. Skewed grid.

Figure 5-105. Curved surface grid.

Skewed Grids. When the overall shape does not approximate a square, structural and economic efficiency can sometimes be gained by employing a skewed grid (Figure 5-104).

Curved Surface Grids. The skewed grid can be warped to span very large distances in an efficient manner (Figure 5-105). In the example shown, the structural concept of the arch is combined with the characteristics of skewed grids to increase efficiency.

Structural Slabs

When a slab is loaded, it tends to deform or *dish*. To do so, it not only must bend and twist, but must also stretch. Therefore, for its *thickness*, it supports a reasonably large weight. For example, a slab 1 foot thick might span as far as a structural grid 1½ feet thick.

The strength-to-weight ratio of structural slabs, however, is much lower than that of beamed or grided structures. Therefore, when spans exceed 15 or 20 feet, it is usually more efficient and economical to strengthen the slab with integral beams and to reduce slab thickness. Concrete channels and "double Ts" are precast sections of one-way slabs with integral beams. They create a horizontal plane with a thin shell of concrete that spans between the integral beams (Figure 5-106).

Concrete channels and double Ts are one-way slabs. They span in one direction only. A two-way slab with integral beams is commonly called a waffle slab (Figure 5-107). It is an efficient structure combining the benefits of a slab and a structural grid.

Folded Plates

Folded plates are generally thin slabs of reinforced concrete (Figure 5-108). Their folded shapes are formed prior to casting. Their strength accrues through the geometry of the folds and the increased effective depth of the folded form. Therefore, longer spans can be achieved with less material.

When folded plate structures are loaded, a component of the force becomes lateral thrust, which tends to flatten the folds. The strength of these forms depends to a degree on resisting these forces.

Arches

Arches are two-dimensional compression structures. They are made by carefully forming individual compression members, such as stones, into truncated wedge shapes, and fitting these units together to create curved shapes (Figure 5-109). The uppermost block, the keystone, is weighted by the wall above and

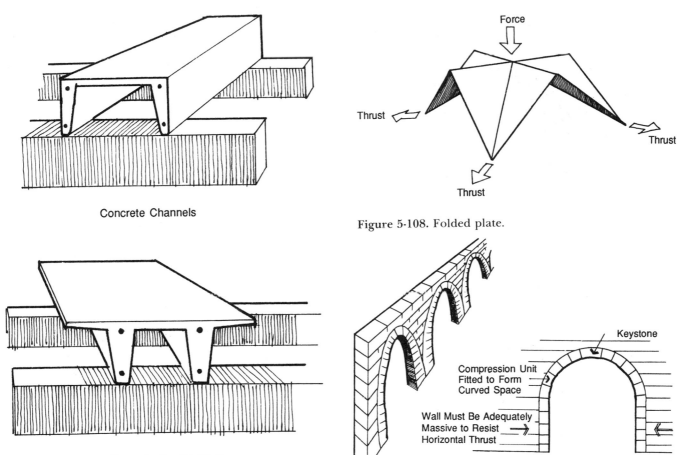

Concrete Channels

Concrete Double Tees

Figure 5-106. Prefabricated one-way slabs with integral beams.

Figure 5-108. Folded plate.

Figure 5-109. Arches.

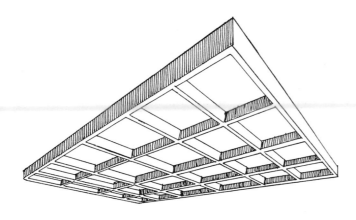

Figure 5-107. Waffle slab.

serves as the wedge, which compresses the arch and provides friction that holds it together.

Arches, developed by the early Romans, allow openings in massive stone walls. They depend on wall massiveness for stability. They curve up from one vertical support and arch gracefully across to the other. A series of these arches converts an otherwise massive wall into a light airy arcade.

Vaults

Vaults are three-dimensional compression structures of arched cross section. Like arches, they are made by carefully forming individual compression members, usually of stone, into truncated wedge shapes, and fitting these together. Keystones run the length along the top of the vault. They compress the vault and provide the friction to hold the individual stones in place.

Vaults transform loads into compressive stresses, but in so doing exert great lateral thrust. To resist this force, the walls must usually be buttressed (thickened), or flying buttresses must be used (Figure 5-110).

Vaults have a very high weight-to-span ratio. They require tremendously massive masonry construction. For both these reasons, vaults are seldom built today.

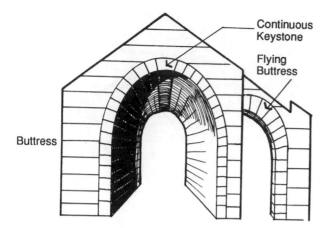

Figure 5-110. Barrell vault.

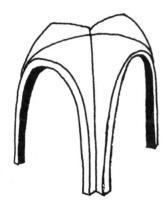

Figure 5-111. Groined vault.

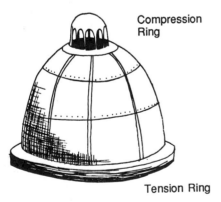

Figure 5-112. Dome.

Groined Vaults. A groin is the line of intersection of two vaulted structures. A groined vault is the form that results when two vaults intersect at right angles (Figure 5-111). When the line of intersection is expressed as two crossing structural diagonal arches, the resulting form is called a ribbed groin vault.

Domes

A dome is a hemispherical roof form that is generated as an arch is rotated about a circular plan (Figure 5-112). Like the arch and the vault, it is a compression structure. A compression ring at the top of the dome serves the same purpose as the keystone in the top of the arch or vault: it compresses and causes friction. A tension ring or large mass is required at the base of the dome to resist outward thrust.

Thin Shells

Thin shells are generally long span structures. They are three-dimensional structures that owe their strength to simultaneous curving in both directions (like an eggshell) (Figure 5-113). The more pronounced the curve, and the closer it approximates a sphere, the stronger and more stable the form.

Curved forms that can be built using straight lines allow forming with conventional lumber. These are especially economical shapes for thin shell construction. Included are hyperbolic paraboloids (saddle shapes) and hyperboloids (Figure 5-114).

Trusses

Trusses are two-dimensional structures composed of triangular shapes (Figure 5-115). They are highly efficient structures spanning great distances and supporting heavy loads with a minimum amount of material. They are often used to support roofs over large areas without intermediate columns.

There are many different truss shapes including the Howe, Flat Howe, Warren, Baltimore, Bowstring, and many more. They all consist of a top chord and a bottom chord separated by intermediate members that triangulate the area between the two chords. The chords and intermediate struts are either in compression or tension and are usually constructed of wood or steel. They can be built of concrete.

Space Frames

Space frames, or double-layer grids, are three-dimensional assemblies consisting of upper and lower grids and intermediate struts (Figure 5-116). The struts subdivide the volume between the grids into tetrahedrals, octahedrals, hexahedrals, or other forms of triangular geometry.

Space frames resist forces through either compressive or tensile stresses. They are usually built from prefabricated systems of struts and connectors. They are extremely efficient, use only small amounts of material, and are capable of spanning great distances.

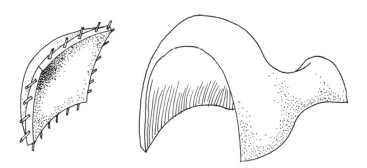

Figure 5-113. Thin shell.

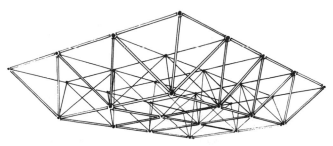

Figure 5-116. Space frame.

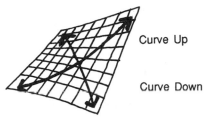

Curve Up

Curve Down

Hyperbolic Paraboloid
(Hyper or Saddle Shape)

Rotational Hyperboloid

Figure 5-114. Thin shells formed by straight lines.

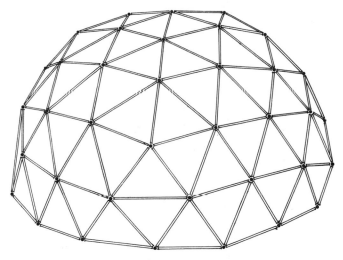

Figure 5-117. Geodesic dome.

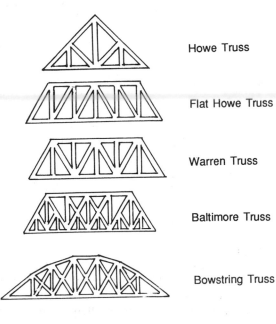

Howe Truss

Flat Howe Truss

Warren Truss

Baltimore Truss

Bowstring Truss

Figure 5-115. Trusses.

Geodesic Domes

Invented by Buckminster Fuller, the geodesic dome is a curved space frame (Figure 5-117). Based on the efficiency of molecular structural systems, the geodesic dome is a triangulated latticework. It combines the structural potential of the dome with that of the space frame to allow the enclosing of enormous areas without internal support. The geodesic dome actually becomes stronger as its scale increases. In fact, Bucky even proposed enclosing Manhattan under a geodesic dome.

The U.S. Pavilion at the Montreal World's Fair was, prior to its destruction by fire, the most famous geodesic dome.

Tensile Structures

Tensile structures consist of tentlike fabric diaphragms stretched over cables, which are themselves stretched over posts (Figure 5-118). The posts serve as compression struts to tension the fabric and cables. The tension must be great to prevent flutter in the fabric (particularly at its edges). Anchor points must resist extreme tensile stresses.

Figure 5-118. Tensile structures.

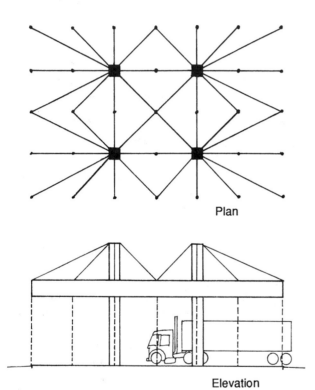

Plan

Elevation

Figure 5-119. Cable structures.

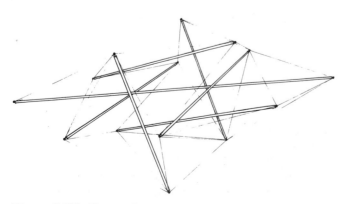

Figure 5-120. Tensegrity structure.

Tensile structures are lightweight and allow disassembly. They are generally open air structures, unless some secondary structure is used to seal the space between the fabric and the ground.

Cable Structures

Cable structures consist of three primary parts: central pylon(s), flat slab, and tension cables (Figure 5-119). The central pylon or pylons transfer stresses to the ground. To do so, they must resist compressive, bending, and torsional forces. The flat slab spans in both directions between suspension points. The tension cables suspend the slab from numerous points and transfer loads to the pylons.

Cable structures have a low weight-to-span ratio. This can be a problem when the wind uplifts the slab, causing flutter. This effect can be minimized by increasing slab weight or by anchoring the slab via cables to the ground. Both of these remedies increase tension stresses on the cables, and compressive, bending, and torsional stresses in the pylon(s).

Tensegrity Structures

Tensegrity structures were invented and patented by Kenneth Snelson (Figure 5-120). They are space frames whose compression members are made of steel or aluminum pipe and whose tension members are steel cable. The structures are usually designed so that no two compression members touch. This results in no continuous lines of compression and compression members that seem to defy gravity as they float in the air.

Tensegrity structures have reinterpreted the utilitarian truss into an expressive three-dimensional art form.

Pneumatic Structures

Pneumatic structures are lightweight, flexible, airtight membranes made of materials such as plastic or teflon. They are supported by differences in air pressure. There are two types: air-inflated and air-supported. Air-inflated structures are double-walled structures. They consist of a series of inflated tubes and act much like a huge low-pressure air mattress. Air-supported structures are single-walled and are supported by increased air pressure on their inner surface (Figure 5-121).

The difference in air pressure required for either type is quite small. A fan can supply the pressure differential if an air lock entrance is employed. The resultant structure is lightweight, transportable, and quick to assemble and disassemble. Its primary drawback, due to its low pressure differential, is instability during windy conditions.

Appropriate Use

This introduction to structures presents an overview of the systems that contribute statics in built form. Each system has its own opportunities and limitations. The same can be said about materials. Each behaves differently; each offers opportunities; each has characteristics that limit its use.

The knowledgeable and responsive designer understands materials and technology and realizes the economics of using appropriate materials and techniques. The sensitive designer does not ask brick to behave like steel. The responsive designer rather capitalizes upon the nature and behavior of brick and explores techniques that are appropriate to brick and that will efficiently, economically, and expressively support the necessary weight, maintain statics, and create meaningful form.

REFERENCES

Booth, Norman. 1983. *Basic Elements of Landscape Architectural Design.* New York: Elsevier Science.

Hanks, Kurt. 1982. *Notes on Architecture: Information Design Series.* Los Altos, CA: William Kaufman.

Landphair, Harlow, and Klatt, Fred. 1979. *Landscape Architecture Construction.* New York: Elsevier.

Landphair, Harlow, and Motloch, John. 1985. *Site Reconnaissance and Engineering: An Introduction for Architects, Landscape Architects and Planners.* New York: Elsevier.

Ramsey, Charles, and Sleeper, Harold. 1988. *Architectural Graphic Standards,* 8th ed. John Ray Hoke, Jr., editor-in-chief. New York: Wiley.

Salvadori, M. G. 1980. *Why Buildings Stand Up: The Strength of Architecture.* New York: Norton.

Schimper, A. F. W. 1903. *Plant Geography upon a Physiological Basis.* Translated by W. R. Fisher, et al. Oxford: Clarendon Press.

SUGGESTED READINGS

Motloch, John. 1985. Site Design for Energy Conservation in Southern Homes. *Yearbook of Landscape Architecture.* New York: Van Nostrand Reinhold.

Untermann, Richard. 1978. *Principles and Practices of Grading, Drainage, and Road Alignment: An Ecologic Approach.* Reston, VA: Reston.

Watson, Donald, and Labs, Kenneth. 1983. *Climatic Design: Energy-Efficient Building Principles and Practices.* New York: McGraw-Hill.

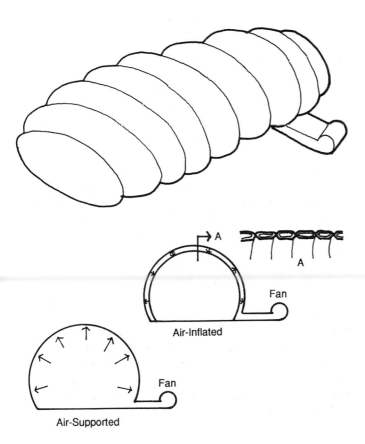

Figure 5-121. Pneumatic structures. (Adapted from *Notes on Architecture,* Hanks, K., p. 17. Crisp Publications, Inc., Los Altos, CA)

6

Sensual Aspects of Perception

Perception is the experience of something by means of our sense organs. It is triggered by stimuli, that is, external physical conditions that activate these organs and, in so doing, awaken latent perceptions in the mind. Stimuli can be understood as physical entities having length, mass, and time. Perceptions, on the other hand, are mental constructs involving both recognition and judgment. Perception is both physiological and psychological, involving the aesthetic experiencing of place. It also includes aspects of human interaction, security, symbolism, social conditioning, and comfort. The sensuous quality of a place is, therefore, the synergism of its physical characteristics and the mind of the viewer.

THE PERCEPTUAL-COGNITIVE PROCESS

Perception-cognition can be understood as a process by which sensual stimuli become mental entities. There are several identifiable steps in this process including pattern observation, form recognition, attribution of meaning to form, loading of emotions onto these meanings, and finally observer reaction to the preceding four steps. For example, in Figure 6-1 we first observe the pattern of the piece. We then recognize the face of the witch and attribute meaning to the image. We attach emotions to these meanings and may react in some way. We may laugh or we may observe our different emotional responses to this fairy-tale image, as compared to the technical images in the preceding chapter.

SIMPLE AND COMPLEX (INTERACTIVE) PERCEPTION

Stimuli are sensory, involving vision, hearing, touch, taste, and smell. Through these senses, we are able to perceive visual form, color, light, texture, audible tone, speech, smell, taste, tactile sensations, haptic form (three-dimensional aspects as perceived by touch), kinesthetic experience (internal perception of body motions), movement, and time. Each of these are simple perceptions. The mind, however, processes information as complex perceptions. The taste of food, for example, is affected by its smell and psychologically by its visual characteristics. For this reason, restaurants avoid displaying food under fluorescent lights, because these lights impart a blue color to the food.

Because our perception of the environment is largely a visual one, the designer must be adept at manipulating visual stimuli to evoke desired perceptions. However, the designer also must be able to reinforce and intensify these visual perceptions by appropriate stimulation of the other senses. Unless the designer does so, the perception will be weak. If sensory stimuli contradict one another, the perception will be chaotic. By effectively using the full sensual palette, the designer can create a strong sense of place.

STIMULI AND MENTAL PATTERNS

Perception is the process whereby mental entities are brought forth when sensory stimuli activate latent in-

Figure 6-1. Perception.

formation in the mind. In order to bring forth desirable content, it is helpful for the landscape designer to understand the form in which this information is stored. The following, from *Lateral Thinking* (1973) by Edward DeBono, is helpful. In this passage, DeBono discusses the brain as a memory surface:

> A landscape is a memory surface. The contours of the surface offer an accumulated memory trace of the water that has fallen on it. The rainfall forms little rivulets that combine into streams and then into rivers. Once the pattern of drainage has been formed then it tends to become ever more permanent since the rain is collected into the drainage channels and tends to make them deeper. It is the rainfall that is doing the sculpting and yet it is the response of the surface to the rainfall that is organizing how the water is doing the sculpting.

According to DeBono, the mind carries on a one-way dialogue with the environment. It does so through the mind's ability to create, store, and later recognize patterns. When stimuli confront the brain, much like the landscape analogy, an existing pattern is accessed. The stimuli becomes a part of the pattern, contributes to it, and brings forth that pattern as the early stages of perception. The mind then attributes meaning, emotion, and response to this pattern.

The pattern brought forth from the mind, the meanings, emotions attributed, and the response evoked in the individual will change substantially with different stimuli. Therefore, as we eliminate or alter the visual stimuli, our perception of place, its scale, size, color, texture, hardness, and so on, will usually change drastically. For this reason, designers will sometimes find it helpful to experience an area with their eyes closed, or from a squatting position at the height that a child would normally view the place. By changing the stimuli being received, the designer becomes more aware of characteristics of the place previously overlooked.

VISUAL AND SPATIAL PERCEPTION

Vision is usually considered the primary sense by which the human being gathers information about the environment. Accordingly, our sensual perception of place is primarily visual; more specifically it is spatial. It is defined by enclosure and made understandable by light. The enclosure that defines exterior places is usually incomplete, the form being completed by the mind's eye based upon implied physical edges, such as changes in grade, overhead canopies, or discontinuous vertical elements such as tree trunks or area walls. Exterior places have dimension, the horizontal usually being much larger than the vertical, and these dimensions are communicated visually via light, color, texture, and detail.

Three-Dimensional Aspects of Perception

Our perception of the world is primarily spatial, and space is three-dimensional. According to Gibson, in *The Perception of the Visual World* (1950), we perceive this three-dimensional reality through perspective as communicated by stimulus variables and their structure and perceived sensory shifts. According to Gibson, cues to the perception of perspective group into four categories: perspective of position, perspective of parallax, perspective independent of position or motion, and perspective as indicated by depth at a contour.

According to Gibson, *perspective of position* includes perspective as communicated by differences in texture, with the scale of the texture decreasing and its density increasing as it recedes to the distance (Figure 6-2). It also includes perspective as implied by size, with decreasing size implying more distant location. *Linear perspective* is that expressed through the conversion of parallel lines to vanishing points (Figure 6-3). Since the Renaissance, linear perspective has been perhaps the most well-known perspective cue to the Western observer. It is also the most well-recognized trick for creating the illusion of three dimensions on a two-dimensional surface. Therefore linear perspective is usually taught in design schools as one of the primary tools for graphic communication.

Perspective of parallax is achieved either by binocular perspective or motion perspective. *Binocular perspective* is the perception of depth because of the separation of the eyes, which results in a different image being perceived by each eye (Figure 6-4). We can perceive this effect by closing and opening first one eye and then the other, while looking at a nearby object, and observing the differing images. We can also close one eye and observe the relative flatness as the eye must rely solely on the other cues described above and below to perceive the third dimension. Binocular perspective is also the phenomenon we use to trick the mind into seeing the third dimension, as we look at stereoscopic pairs of aerial photographs (of the

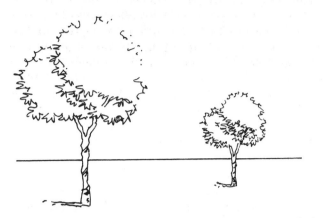

Figure 6-2. Perspective communicated by texture and size.

same area of landscape from two slightly different airplane locations) (Figure 6-5). It is also the means by which three-dimensional movies operate, as each eyepiece displays (via filters) a slightly different view of the same scene, creating the illusion of the third dimension. *Motion perspective* occurs as the perceived rate of movement of an object becomes more rapid as we approach the object. Conversely, objects in the distance that are moving at the same rate as nearby objects will appear to be moving more slowly (Figure 6-6).

According to Gibson, there are cues to *perspective independent of the position or motion of the observer.* Aerial (or *atmospheric*) *perspective* is the perception of depth based on increased haziness and reduced color saturation due to the atmosphere between the viewer and the object viewed. Air quality affects this perception substantially, as dryer and less polluted air is more transparent and makes objects appear closer. *The perspective of blur* occurs as we focus at a certain depth

Figure 6-3. Linear perspective.

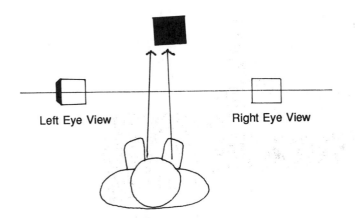

Figure 6-4. Binocular perspective.

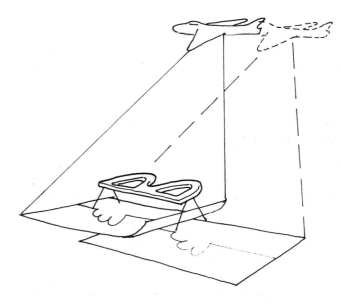

Figure 6-5. Stereo viewing of aerial photographs.

and as objects at other distances from the eye become blurred. The degree of blur relates to the proportional difference in distance from the eye to the object being focused upon and to the other objects being viewed. This effect has been used in a somewhat reverse sense, and to great effect by painters, photographers, and cinematographers as a means of focusing viewer attention upon elements in a composition. Perspective is also implied by relative upward location in a visual field. Since objects that are below our eyes and near to us are perceived lower in the field of vision than more distant ones, such location itself implies nearness. This effect increases as the eye level becomes more elevated from the ground.

Perspective and depth are also implied by the perceived *depth at a contour*. When objects overlap in the visual field, increases in the distance separating these objects results in differences in the perceived texture, bluriness, and rate of motion of the two objects. These differences are cues that help the mind interpret the spatial relationships. Objects with completeness or continuity of outline appear to overlap those with outlines that are interrupted or obscured by other objects. Overlap is especially effective in creating the illusion of three dimensions on a two-dimensional surface. Differences in tonal value, especially the overlap of white and black, imply changes in depth. This is also an effective technique for implying the third dimension on the two-dimensional drawing surface. Typically, the drawing that communicates space effectively will involve some trickery or artist's license, to consciously manipulate values to increase the contrast at spatial overlaps, and thereby intensify the illusion of the third dimension (Figure 6-7).

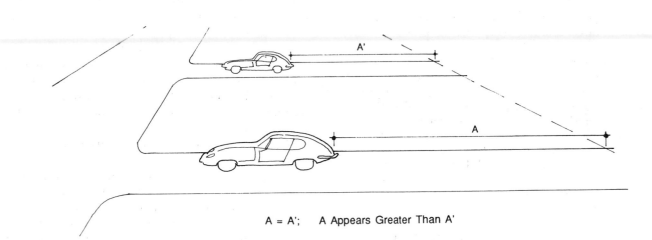

A = A'; A Appears Greater Than A'

Figure 6-6. Distance and perceived velocity.

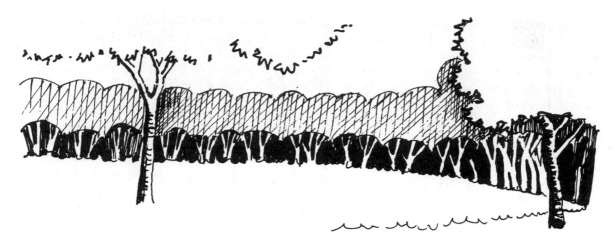

Figure 6-7. Tonal value to increase three-dimensional sense.

Scale

Defined spaces are capable of having strong emotional connotations, based on their perceived size, scale, or proportion. The scale of a space consists of two components: the size of the space in relation to the size of its context, and its size in relation to the observer. Concerning context, downtown Manhattan has a scale perception quite different from the Back Bay of Boston or from the main street of "small town USA." As a large plaza begins to fill with people, it somehow seems less large and overpowering.

In *Site Planning* (1962), Kevin Lynch developed a few tentative guidelines for the size and proportion of comfortable exterior spaces. These were based on observations and related to the characteristics of the human eye and the size of the human being as perceived from various distances. According to Lynch,

> We can detect a man about 4000 feet away, recognize him at 80 feet, see his face clearly at 45 feet, and feel him to be in direct relation to us, whether pleasant or intrusive, at 3–10 feet. Outdoor spaces of the latter dimension seem extremely or intolerably small. Dimensions of 40 feet appear intimate. Up to 80 feet is still an easy human scale. Most of the successful enclosed squares of the past have not exceeded 450 feet in the smaller dimension. . . . an external enclosure is most comfortable when its walls are one-half or one-third as high as the width of the space enclosed, while if the ratio falls below one-fourth, the space ceases to seem enclosed. If the height of walls is greater than the width, then one does not see the skyline or easily judge the wall's height. The space comes to resemble a pit or a trench.

As we design exterior space, we should do so with an awareness of these dimensions, and create space of appropriate scale so as to evoke the desired feelings and facilitate intended behaviors. We should keep in mind that the scale of a space is also dependent upon the manner in which the space is developed. Spatial development is discussed in detail in Chapter 10.

STIMULI, HUMAN INTERACTION, AND SECURITY

Humans, like other animals, occupy and defend territory, psychologically and sometimes physically. These territories relate to human interaction and perceived security. They can be likened to a series of expanding and contracting fields of space. For Americans in social situations, these fields are usually grouped into four categories: intimate, personal, social, and public. The boundaries of these zones are fuzzy, and gradations from close to far occur within each zone. For each field or territory, humans have a situational personality and behave differently as others move from one zone to another. Each field or territory provides stimuli to access specific patterns in the mind, patterns that address interpersonal relationships and socially appropriate behavior. However, in most cases these stimuli operate at a subconscious, experiential level, rather than a conscious, intellectual one. For example, the area within which one can sense the warmth from another human body generally determines intimate territory, and the intimacy of this zone is reinforced by the inability of the eyes to focus at this short distance and the ability to perceive personal fragrances.

The perception of territory and the zones of personal and interpersonal space are not static. The mood of the observer and familiarity with other people affect desired spatial distances. To assert oneself, an individual will aggressively intrude slightly into another's personal space; we also position ourselves closer when visiting with a close friend than when speaking to a stranger. As environmental factors change, so too do territorial envelopes. It is socially acceptable, therefore, to position oneself closer to a stranger in an elevator than in a large scarcely populated room. Low-level lighting brings people closer together, as will a high level of background noise.

Intimate Space (0 to 18 inches)

Within the intimate envelope of space, distorted vision, smells, heat from the other person's body and breath all contribute to the perception of involvement, often intimate, with the other person. Within the inner phase of intimate space (0 to 6 inches) are included activities such as love-making, comforting, and protecting. Within the outer phase (6 to 18 inches), physical contact is usually limited to touching with the hands. At this distance, the voice is usually held to a whisper, and the heat and odor of the other person's breath is usually felt. This distance is usually not appropriate in public situations in middle-class America. However, in certain situations, such as in a crowded elevator or a subway, this zone is used with a revised set of appropriate behaviors, such as very limited movement and avoidance of eye contact and physical contact with the other person.

Personal Space (18 to 48 inches)

The bubble of space, the secure sphere, that a human maintains from others is usually referred to as one's personal space. The inner phase of this envelope (18 to 30 inches) is the close personal zone and is usually reserved for a spouse or very close friend. The outer phase (30 to 48 inches), just outside touching distance, is the normal speaking distance when discussing subjects of personal interest. Different cultures do not share all our territorial rights of personal space and are more willing to share this space in public. Accordingly, many Americans become uncomfortable when a European or Middle Easterner establishes a position uncomfortably close during a social conversation.

Social Space (4 to 12 feet)

The boundary between personal and social space, within a given society, is reasonably consistent. Persons positioned outside this boundary are not expected, nor invited, to make physical contact. To do so requires violation of an established territorial boundary. Conversations that occur at this distance are not intended to be private. The close phase of this territory (4 to 7 feet) is the zone of impersonal business. Persons who work together and persons at social gatherings tend to use this distance. The far phase (7 to 12 feet) is employed to conduct formal business. It is the distance employed as a professional and a client discuss business across a desk. It is also a distance that allows two people to initiate and then disengage conversation without awkwardness. Waiting rooms and other public seating areas usually employ this distance.

Public Distance (12 + feet)

People positioned at the public distance are outside the sphere of involvement. At the inner phase of this public territory (12 to 25 feet), the distance allows time to react or take defensive action if the individual feels threatened. Therefore, few social barriers are established within this zone. In the outer phase of the public zone, the subtle shades of meaning of speech are lost, and there is virtually no interpersonal involvement. The other individual becomes a part of the environment, not an object with whom to interact.

As we design the landscape, we should do so in cognizance of these zones of personal space and locate amenities so that people can position themselves at appropriate distances for their interpersonal relationships and intended behaviors.

Ethological Approach to Behavior

According to Dr. Paul D. MacLean (1973), the human brain consists of three distinct areas. The earliest to evolve, which he referred to as the reptilian brain, mediates behavior that affects survival, such as the "fight or flight syndrome," when encountering danger. It also affects behavior associated with reproduction, territorialism, and our search for food and shelter. Surrounding this reptilian brain is the *limbic system,* which mediates emotions and feelings. Around this is the outer layer of the brain called the *neocortex,* which controls speech, language, and other abstract thought.

In line with this theory of brain structure, many people take an ethological approach to behavior. They contend that a large portion of human behavior can best be accounted for as resonances of dispositions that were acquired in a human's evolutionary past, in relationship with a more primitive environment.

Proxemic and Distemic Space

As we discuss an ethological approach to behavior, we should address the theory of *proxemic and distemic space.* This theory begins with the observation by anthropologists that human society evolved through the banding together of extended families of perhaps a dozen people into tribes of less than a hundred. It was in this context that the human brain evolved. This theory contends that because of sociobiological history humans have a strong tendency to prefer relatively small social groups. This small group social behavior appears to reside in our limbic (feeling) brain, and appears to be the seat of our emotional attachment to familiar persons, places, and things. It limits our ability to have close interpersonal relationships with more than about 100 people. It also makes us feel threatened when unfamiliar people enter our territorial space.

Conversely, the theory of proxemic and distemic space also contends that under the right circumstances the human also has the capacity to transcend this tendency. This ability to abstractly conceptualize large numbers of people and to envision a world community evolved very late in the development of the human brain and resides in the neocortex. According to B. Greenbie (1981), in crowded situations we are able to reform our territorial relationships by extending them into conceptual space. We avoid being overly stressed by interacting personally with a rather small subgroup, and we effectively tune out other subgroups. We establish physical turf, as discussed above, and other conceptual territories such as professional affiliations. We defend these professions as we would physical turf. According to Greenbie, the ability to transcend our small group behavior and to abstractly address large numbers of people "is essential to the full flowering of human personality." It unites us to humanity in the broadest sense.

Edward T. Hall (1966) invented the term *proxemics* to refer to the culturally specific ways in which groups use space, that is, the use of space as an elaboration of culture. Greenbie (1981) used the term to describe "the culturally homogeneous urban and rural villages and city neighborhoods ... as well as certain other types of small group associations in space." In these cases, the spatial behavior of people of the same culture are highly consistent: policing is accomplished by heavy social pressure; there are few interpersonal conflicts; and there is, therefore, little need for behavioral cues in the design of these spaces. Both the social and the physical environment can be extremely complex since they are largely taken for granted because of the high familiarity by all users. These areas are also extremely high in associational meaning (Chapter 16).

Greenbie also discussed, on the other hand, the large portions of major cities that are used by people of many cultural subgroups and that are not the perceptual territory of any one group. These spaces are shared by culturally diverse subgroups with differing values, codes of conduct, myths, symbols, and cognitive attitudes. Because of this diversity, the behavior of one group can be expected to infringe on that of another. Overt behavior must be controlled by explicit behavioral cues, rules, ordinances, and external policing. However, while limits to behavior are established, these limits are generally much broader than in proxemic space. Usually only that behavior that harms other people or their property is forbidden. Greenbie coined the term *distemic* to refer to these spaces. Since these spaces can accommodate large numbers of people, they are often quite spacious. They are usually comfortable if they allow adequate room for individuals to maintain a personal distance as discussed above and if there is a perceived means of egress if they become psychologically distressing. Distemic spaces should be more predictable and legible (Chapter 16) than proxemic ones because users are not strongly familiar with the space and behavior is more varied. Distemic spaces should also be far less complex than proxemic space.

It should also be kept in mind that spaces change over time, as do the users of those spaces (see Chapter 7). A space that functions proxemically at one time of day may embrace a diverse melange of groups at another time. Christopher Alexander's "A City Is Not a Tree" (1965) and Kevin Lynch's *What Time Is This Place?* (1972) both address this issue.

Together, *proxemic and distemic space* function in a complementary manner. In Chapter 16, we will discuss Maslow's "hierarchy of needs," which states that physiological needs (such as security) must be relatively satisfied before more abstract psychological ones become important. Herein it will suffice to contend that *proxemic space* serves as the homeground that satisfies more basic needs and allows us to feel secure. Once this security is achieved, distemic space provides challenge and enrichment. Together, proxemic and distemic space provide the opportunity in the urban landscape to realize the full human potential and to maximize human psychological health.

Greenbie also speaks for the desirability of a rich mosaic of proxemic urban environments, that is, a diversity of neighborhoods that are internally similar. He speaks for the potential of designing distemic spaces adjacent to these diverse proxemic spaces.

Prospect and Refuge

The ethological approach also explains many of our feelings of security or insecurity as we experience the physical and spatial environment. For example, it explains why we are uncomfortable walking in the middle of a large open space (Figure 6-8). Having evolved as an edge species, our ability to survive depended on being able to see our prey and at the same time be concealed from our predators. This involved positioning ourselves and moving slightly within the vegetated edge, rather than being exposed in space (Figure 6-9). It also involved positioning ourselves along escarpments or military crests of hills (Figure 6-10). These locations provided *prospect* for acquiring necessary foodstuffs, and yet *refuge* from predators. Therefore, when the earliest reptilian portion of our brain evolved, it did so with instinctive, precognitive responses based on prospect and refuge.

This is the basis of J. Appleton's *prospect and refuge theory* (1975) of behavior. This theory contends that these reptilian responses are still present today and function much like unconscious filters, presenting the limbic system with a preference for places that afford us prospect and refuge (Figure 6-11).

STIMULI AND SYMBOLIC MEANINGS

Sensory stimuli carry symbolic meanings: vertical elements are inspiring, horizontals are stabilizing; massive elements lend an air of permanence, filigree a sense of nostalgia; angular forms evoke energy and motion, circular forms passivity and restfulness. Certain sounds and smells have symbolic meaning, as do natural materials (such as water, earth, and plants), and architectural elements (such as door, arch, and pediment). Specific places also carry symbolic meaning, varying with culture and with individual experience. The meanings we attribute to physical elements and physical form serve as stimuli to access specific patterns in the mind and evoke emotional responses. Stimuli with special meanings elicit particularly strong or vivid emotional responses. These impart both unique opportunities and constraints for the designer.

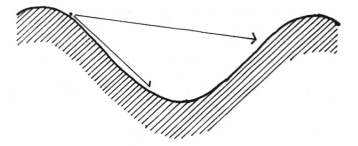

Figure 6-10. Visual prospect.

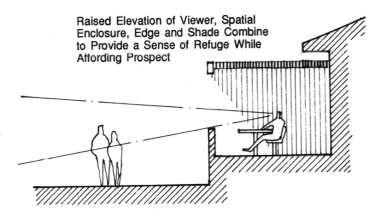

Figure 6-11. Prospect and refuge.

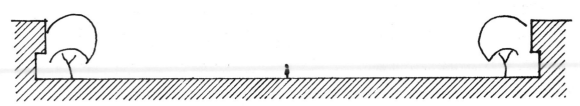

Figure 6-8. Lack of refuge.

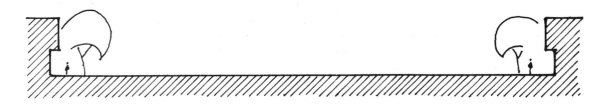

Figure 6-9. Edge refuge.

STIMULI AND SOCIAL CONDITIONING

Acculturation is the process beginning in infancy whereby an individual acquires the culture of society and learns appropriate social behavior and the cultural meanings attributed to specific sensual stimuli. It is on this cultural base that the individual builds a cognitive model of the world.

Each culture perceives differently. Each architectural tradition has its own vocabulary of cues employed by the designer. These cues serve as stimuli to elicit or induce desired behavior by causing the user to perceive the environment in an appropriate manner. However, these cues usually operate at a subconscious level and are seldom fully recognized even by the designer.

Desired behavior, and therefore appropriate design cues, change with each culture. For example, when teaching a group of American students in Italy, the first design project we assigned involved site reconnaissance of a small Tuscan village. Within fifteen minutes, the students had discovered that most of the cues that we employ in the United States to differentiate public spaces from private spaces were unnecessary and therefore absent from the village that had been largely isolated for hundreds of years, and where everyone knew, and was related to, everyone else. As these students discovered, one effective way of becoming aware of one's own subliminal cues is to study and design for a radically different culture.

A number of different cultures exist within any American city. In addition, American landscape architects are doing an increased amount of their work in other, often third world, countries. There are two things that we learned from the 1960s that will serve us well in this context. The first is that the designer must recognize and respond to differing cultural perceptions of personal territory. The second is that the cues that serve as stimuli, and the patterns in the mind that these stimuli access, vary with culture. Designing for other cultures, whether in America or a distant land, requires insight to the consciousness of that culture.

COMFORT-PHYSIOLOGICAL PERCEPTION

Physiological comfort is an absence of physiological stress. It exists in certain ranges of temperature, incoming radiation, humidity, and windspeed that are deemed by an instrument to be pleasant. The instrument that is used to measure comfort is the human body. As long as the internal temperature of the body remains within a desirable temperature range, the perception is one of comfort. When environmental conditions become such that they exceed the range that supports this internal condition, discomfort occurs. As environmental temperatures rise, or as increased activity or fever raise internal temperatures, evaporative cooling (perspiration) on the surface of the skin increases to remove more body heat. Increased airspeed or decreased humidity can operate to reduce the stress induced by rising external temperatures by increasing the benefit of evaporative cooling. Conversely, as ambient temperatures drop, provisions must be made to prevent the escape of heat or to allow more solar radiation to be captured.

One of the primary purposes of shelter is to control the environment so as to improve physiological comfort. Each region has its own combination of seasonal incoming solar radiation (insolation), ambient temperatures, humidity, and windspeed. For each season, winter (the underheated condition) and summer (the overheated condition), the designer must understand environmental conditions and the opportunities that these offer for climate amelioration. For example, the designer should know that in most of Arizona the summers are hot and dry and that there is a low humidity and high temperature swing between day and night (diurnal swing). East Texas is also hot, but the humidity is high and the daily temperature swing is low. The designer should understand these conditions and have a working knowledge of appropriate strategies to improve site comfort. These are discussed at length in *Climatic Design: Energy-Efficient Building Principles and Practices* by Watson and Labs (1983), and more briefly in Landphair and Motloch's *Site Reconnaissance and Engineering* (1985).

DESIGNING APPROPRIATE STIMULI

The task facing the landscape designer is to create desirable, meaningful, and satisfying perceptions. This involves providing for aesthetic experience and a strong sense of place. It includes designing in response to a wide range of human needs, which will be discussed in Chapter 16. The designer must also respond to needs for privacy and interaction, and a sense of security. Design must also convey meaning and be able to affect the observer on an emotional level. Good design also necessitates an understanding of, and response to, cultural influences. It includes providing for basic human physiological comfort. The built environments that result will then be sensually satisfying, meaningful, and pleasant.

REFERENCES

Alexander, Christopher. 1965. A City Is Not A Tree. *Architectural Forum* 122, April (58–62), May (58–62).

Appleton, Jay. 1975. *The Experience of Landscape.* New York: Wiley.

DeBono, Edward. 1973. *Lateral Thinking: Creativity Step by Step.* Harper Colophon Books. New York: Harper & Row.

Gibson, James. 1950. *The Perception of the Visual World.* Boston: Houghton Mifflin.

Greenbie, Barrie. 1981. *Spaces: Dimensions of the Human Landscape.* New Haven: Yale University Press.

Hall, Edward. 1966. *The Hidden Dimension.* Garden City, NY: Doubleday.

Hesselgren, S. 1975. *Man's Perception of Man-Made Environment: An Architectural Theory.* Stroudsburg, PA: Dowden, Hutchinson & Ross.

Landphair, Harlow, and Motloch, John. 1985. *Site Reconnaissance and Engineering: An Introduction for Architects, Landscape Architects and Planners.* New York: Elsevier.

Lynch, Kevin. 1972. *What Time Is This Place?* Cambridge, MA: MIT Press.

Lynch, Kevin. 1962. *Site Planning,* 2nd ed. Cambridge, MA: MIT Press.

MacLean, P. D. The Brain's Generation Gap: Some Human Implications. *Zugon/J. Religion and Science* 8(2):113–127.

Watson, Donald, and Labs, Kenneth. 1983. *Climatic Design: Energy-Efficient Building Principles and Practices.* New York: McGraw-Hill.

SUGGESTED READINGS

Perin, Constance. 1970. *With Man in Mind: An Interdisciplinary Prospectus for Environmental Design.* Cambridge, MA: MIT Press.

Sommer, Robert. 1969. *Personal Space: The Behavioral Basis of Design.* Englewood Cliffs, NJ: Prentice-Hall.

7

Temporal Aspects of Perception

Change is the essence of natural systems as well as cultural systems. In fact, the landscape can be understood as the point-in-time expression of the history of forces that have affected it. This point-in-time expression should be seen as an ephemeral one, as the natural and cultural landscape is constantly evolving. This change or evolution is one of the primary considerations of landscape design.

We also experience the landscape as a sequence of perceptions that are structured in time. As we design, we should keep in mind that our experiencing of place is a temporal phenomenon, that it occurs in the context of preceding observations and in anticipation of subsequent ones. Therefore, the designer's ability to choreograph the temporal aspects of perception is essential to the dynamic experience of place.

According to Webster, *time* is "a continuum which lacks spatial dimensions and in which events succeed one another from past through present to future." It is also the "point or period when something occurs." In keeping with the first definition, we will address time as the continuum of events and will explore the nature of that continuum and its implications to design. We will also address the second definition and will explore physical phenomena as point-in-time expressions of ecological and human forces.

TEMPORAL ASPECTS OF LANDSCAPES

Landscapes are point-in-time expressions of ongoing processes, involving natural and human forces. Landscape form can be seen as a living record of past events. Form as well as landscape material can be un-

derstood as the physical entity from which ongoing ecological, technological, and human forces will sculpt the future landscape. As designers, we should understand the temporal aspects of landscapes, which include landscapes as sequence and landscapes as rhythm.

Landscape as Sequence

Ecological landscapes evolve through a process known as succession. As they change, they do so through sequences that are, to a degree, predictable. Cultural systems also evolve. They change in response to natural systems and their evolution over time, changing technologies, and differences in human populations, attitudes, and perceptions. As landscapes change, they include at any point in time relics of historical forces, expressions of present ones, and the raw materials from which future landscapes will be built.

Landscape as Rhythm

Landscapes change rhythmically. Within daily and seasonal cycles, short-term and long-term sequences, and regular and irregular rhythms, the landscape displays its many moods and characters. These rhythms are perhaps nature's purest statement of system and process, that is, systemic cyclical movements toward some evolving reality. Landscape rhythms include short ones that are diurnal and seasonal. They also include longer cycles, such as those of succession, weather, and climate.

Diurnal Rhythms

Landscapes express a diurnal rhythm, day and night, light and darkness, and this diurnal rhythm greatly affects landscape perception. Visually, the character of light changes throughout the day. In midday, the sun is overhead, shadows are short, the light is harsh, and distances seem shorter. As the sun lowers in the sky, shadows become more prominent. As the sun sinks near the horizon, long exaggerated shadows can contribute a linear and sometimes angular character to the landscape. At dusk and dawn, the landscape begins to flatten spatially and to lose its color, and the viewer becomes more sensitive to nonvisual stimuli, such as landscape smells and sounds. Finally, at night, the landscape is visually recreated. Distances seem greater, vision is directed to the sky above, and our senses of hearing, smell, taste, and touch are heightened.

Seasonal Rhythms

There is a symbolic birth, maturation, aging, and death in the seasonal landscape: spring, summer, fall, and winter. In deciduous and cold landscapes, these four seasons express themselves in a dramatic manner, providing a highly varied seasonal landscape with four distinct personalities. In primarily evergreen landscapes and milder climates, change is less dramatic.

Successional Rhythms

Landscapes undergo successional rhythms including pioneering, establishment, early succession, late succession, perturbance, and reinvasion. These rhythms are somewhat predictable, with a rate of progression related to climate, and the resulting "form" sequences of the landscape are also somewhat predictable, as they visually express the relationship of force, material, and time. These rhythms are also unpredictable, as perturbances can interfere in the process at any time. In this sense, they behave chaotically (along the lines of chaos theory, which contends that reality is ordered by tendencies and probabilities, not by prediction). Humans often function, as in agricultural and urban landscapes, to arrest the process of succession in an early stage, (for a temporary time at least), denying both its linear change over time, and in some cases, its cyclical rhythms.

Weather Cycles

Seasonal rhythms also include the annual cycles of weather. These cycles, in turn, affect the manner in which we design and seasonally use our structures and exterior spaces.

Climate Cycles

The landscape is also characterized by longer and less regularly rhythmic cycles of climate, rainfall, and drought. As climatic conditions change, the spatial character of the environment changes, as does the sense of place. This was quite evocatively expressed in the drought-induced dust bowl of the 1930s. Hopefully, as the greenhouse effect intensifies and our next major drought occurs, our perception of the landscape, human-environment relationships, and landscape design will change dramatically.

TIME-SPACE RELATIONSHIPS

The perception of time and space are inextricably bound, as both time and space are experienced sequentially and concurrently. In fact, time can be seen as the sequential ordering of space as one moves through the landscape. Conversely, the spatial continuum can be seen as a series of experiences organized in time, with spatial relationships communicated by the time it takes to move from one to another. We come to understand space as we change our location over time.

As we move in time and space, our perception is constantly changing. According to Rapoport (1977), as we image the world around us, we seek this perceptual change, that is, we desire to perceive variability. On the other hand, we also seek constancy of schemata, that is, we seek for our mental construct of the world to be reasonably constant. Much of the essence of design concerns the interrelationship of perceptual variation and schematic constancy as we temporally experience the landscape.

CULTURAL ATTITUDES CONCERNING TIME

According to Boulding (1956), there are ten dimensions that affect how we image the world around us. One of these is temporal image, that is, the stream of time, and our place in it. According to Rapoport our understanding of urban organization is primarily the synergism of this temporal image with a spatial image (one's location in space), and a relational image (of the world around us as a system of regularities, that is, our perception of an ordered reality).

Different cultures and groups have different perceptions of time. Some see time in terms of its linear progression; others see time to have a cyclical or rhythmic nature, with past, present, and future linked through successive cycles. Still others focus only on the present and have an instantaneous perception of time. Finally, others concentrate on the future. These goal-oriented people forsake present gratification for the hope of attaining some future goal.

Linear Time

Western cultures have a linear attitude toward time: time moves forward. The past is that which was, the present is, the future will be. These are seen as three different entities. The present is seen as derived from the past and affecting the future, but is distinctly separate from both.

Cyclical Time

Eastern cultures, and many traditional ones, have a cyclical perception of time. This perception sees past, present, and future as inextricably bound by these cycles. This belief is reflected in their cultural values and expressions. These cultures encode their collective consciousness and the interrelatedness of past, present, and future, into their designed environment. The Buddhist and the Hindu, for example, incorporate the lotus into their architecture as timeless symbols of purity, creation, and beauty. Similarly, the pointed arch in Arab architecture symbolizes the Muslim belief that "God is One; and Muhammad is His Prophet." This symbol, which encodes past and future, was a religious symbol long before it became encoded in architecture as the symbol of hands joined in prayer. In these and other cases, architectural symbols reinforce the cultural paradigm, values, and religious beliefs and link past, present, and future.

Instantaneous Time

Many cultures, including the present American one, are dominated by a perception of instantaneous time and instantaneous gratification. For example, in American culture, we want things to happen now, and we want rewards to be immediate. As a culture, we are goal-driven and place a high premium on convenience and the functional aspects of a place. We like the short-order restaurant and the convenience food store, because they are time efficient. Our perception of time results in short-term decision-making, that is, we make decisions that result in maximum gain over the short period. This perception of time does not generally promote long-term efficiency.

The amount of time we perceive to be available to smell the roses affects our perception of landscape and the length of journeys through that landscape. As the time available increases, so does the relative value of environmental exploration and enrichment and the pleasure we receive from landscape perception. Perceiving available time to be great, we leisurely view the landscape, and the trip actually seems shorter. Conversely, when we are rushed, we usually receive less pleasure in experiencing the world around us, and the journey seems extended.

Goal-Oriented Versus Experience-Oriented

Some cultures and individuals focus on the future. These goal-driven people can concentrate on the future goal to the detriment of experiencing the present. Others focus on the present and the richness of experiencing the world around them. They ascribe meaning to the journey, rather than the arrival. This topic was addressed by Pirsig in *Zen and the Art of Motorcycle Maintenance* (1974).

TIME AND PERCEPTION

In considering time and perception, there are several issues. The first concerns the time available to perceive a setting, and to cognize that setting as place. The interrelationship of perception and movement is discussed later in this chapter. The second issue to be considered is generally referred to as the learning curve. As we encounter new settings, environmental learning begins rapidly, and then over time, the rate of processing new landscape information slows. With time, the type of landscape information the viewer focuses on changes. What begins as a relatively preconscious search of overall landscape form and patterns with the intent of increasing understanding, evolves to a conscious search of more detailed and specific information to increase enrichment, depth of meaning, and the mental associations that can be made. This and other issues concerning the types and rate of information processing are discussed at greater length in Chapter 16.

Our mental construct of the world also changes over time. What begins as a street map type of mental construct when we first enter a new portion of the city, may evolve over time to a rich mental construct of districts, special places, landmarks, edges, and relationships. On the other hand, what begins as a relatively large number of routes from one point to another, may evolve into a more selective rating of routes based on the viewer's direction of movement, time available, and the enrichment that the viewer desires along the route.

Finally, the frequency with which we encounter a place affects our attachment to it. The more frequently we experience the place, the less attachment we have to its physical characteristics, and the greater our attachment to the universal concepts that the place implies and the associations it invokes.

TIME AND DISTANCE

Our cognitive map of the world usually consists of a perception of places, relationships, and distances. These distances are often seen and expressed in terms of time. In fact, we usually develop a complex subjective perception of distance based on measured distance, temporal distance, and the pleasure experienced along the trip. Perceived distance is affected by our perception of the time involved; our perception of the time involved is affected by our emotional state as we move, which in turn is affected by the quality of the experience of the landscape. Our perception of distance is also affected by the anticipated difficulty of movement, whether this difficulty is the reduced mobility of the elderly or handicapped person, or is due to congestion, adverse weather, or any number of other causes.

It is important to note that people make their decisions concerning movement through the landscape based on subjective temporal distances, not physically measured ones.

MOVEMENT AND PERCEPTION

Perception of the landscape involves movement, as we experience the landscape as a time-space continuum. As we move, our perspective of the place physically changes. Our perception of the place is also affected by what was previously experienced, and that which is anticipated. For example, entering a grand space via a smaller one can make the grand space seem even more awe-inspiring.

Route Selection

The route that we select to move through a landscape may vary and that variation can radically affect our perception of the landscape. Our selection of routes may vary in a regular rhythmic fashion, as when we select a daytime route for one particular reason, such as its distant view, and a nighttime one for another reason, for example, to experience pools of light flickering on the hillside above. Route selection may also change on a seasonal basis, as when we decide to travel a roadside landscape of azaleas only during their brief period of bloom. Route selection may change over time based on an increasing understanding of the place, and the evolving cognitive maps or mental constructs that emerge. Our perception of the landscape may also change over time as the landscape itself evolves.

Serial Vision

Landscape perception involves *serial vision,* that is, vision as a series of perceptions. In serial vision, and through a series of environmental stimuli, the mind's eye develops a synergistic image of the setting. This image is an organized, three-dimensional understanding of the landscape that places the scene being viewed at any point in time into an overall context. In the mind, this image of setting synergizes with past experience and those anticipated, to produce an image of the complex and evolving place (Chapter 16). Serial vision studies are often conducted as part of design processes, as the designer attempts to foresee the experience of the place. These studies are actually a series of perspective images, viewed very rapidly as sequences that replicate the visual process of movement through the landscape (the animated cartoon is an example of the serial-vision technique). Computer technology is rapidly increasing the designer's ability to integrate serial vision techniques into landscape design. Through computer animation, the landscape designer is now able to draw a series of key images, and the computer will interpolate between these images to animate the design and create the illusion of moving through the designed landscape. The next major leap forward may be to interface these techniques with image-capture and enhancement software, to allow the computer to produce serial design sequences of movement through actual videotaped landscapes, complete with designed changes. As the hardware and software to do so are perfected, and as these techniques are integrated into design processes, they will radically change the manner in which we image place and design landscapes.

Design in a serial sense involves the development of rich story lines (experiential stories organized in time), and the realization of these story lines through effective sensory stimuli, as we move through the landscape. These story lines are experienced as we move along the path through the landscape, and are evoked by the stimuli viewed from that path. These stimuli include events and relationships between events. They include nodes or special places, effective spatial development along the path and at nodes, and the design of effective transitions (Chapter 10).

Landscape Character and Rate of Movement

The rate at which we move through the landscape is affected by its character. In pleasant landscapes, we tend to move more slowly, yet the trip seems to take less time. Conversely, as we move through more boring landscapes, we do so more rapidly while perceiving the trip to be more time consuming.

As landscape complexity increases, we reduce our speed, and as the landscape becomes more simple, we accelerate. The latter is a problem in the design of freeways as the combination of accelerated speeds and lack of adequate stimulation to sustain interest can become a safety concern.

Speed and Perception

Seeing takes time, and we must therefore consider the rate of movement through the landscape and the effect of this rate on perception. For example, it takes the eye something more than a tenth of a second to fix on an object or landscape scene, and unless the eye and the object or scene being viewed are in a relatively fixed relation, the eye does not perceive the view to exist. This can be seen by turning one's head at a moderate speed while attempting to see the landscape, only to discover that unless the eye hesitates briefly along the journey, we fail to perceive any images. The world becomes a blur.

Roadway Design

As we may imagine, fixation time is an important phenomenon in the design of roadways. To the driver moving rapidly through the landscape, the relationship between the eye and the scene is always changing. This change is most rapid with nearby objects, which the driver ceases to see unless the eyes are locked on the object as it moves by. Closely spaced nearby objects (such as vertical bridge railings) literally vanish from view. Moderately distant objects are seen only briefly. The driver or passenger can view only the distant landscape for any appreciable time.

There is a direct relationship between design speed, and the distance at which the eye can focus and still retain an adequately fixed relationship with the scene. Therefore, as design speed increases, the perceptual cone of vision decreases, and the perception of the nearby landscape is greatly reduced. Perception becomes a somewhat detached view of the distant landscape. This change in focal distance also has safety implications. Fixation time combines with the fact that it takes about a second to refocus from dashboard to road view and another three-fourths of a second to

react. Therefore, safe driving at high speed mandates that the driver focus on the distance. These and other issues were presented in a seminal article written by Hamilton and Thurston (1937). In this classic article, Hamilton and Thurston made five propositions concerning the relationship between speed and landscape perception. Some of the temporal aspects of these propositions, and additional comments from Tunnard and Pushkarev (1963) are summarized below:

1. Degree of concentration increases with speed: As speed increases, fixation and reaction time become more important, the number of visual stimuli increases, and the relevancy of information viewed becomes more critical. Vision is focused on the path ahead, and the path directs the eye concerning what to view.
2. Point of concentration recedes with speed: As speed increases, the driver's focusing point becomes more distant. According to Tunnard and Pushkarev, at 25 miles per hour, this distance is 600 feet; at 45 miles per hour, it is 1200 feet; and at 65 miles per hour, it is 2000 feet (see Figure 7-1).
3. Peripheral vision decreases with speed: As the eye concentrates on smaller and more distant detail, the cone of vision decreases. According to Tunnard and Pushkarev, at 25 miles per hour, the horizontal angle of vision is about 100 degrees; at 45 miles per hour, it is about 65 degrees; and at 60

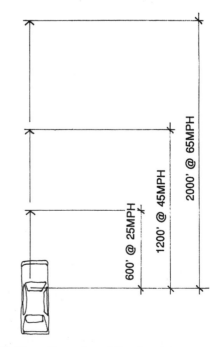

Figure 7-1. Travel speed and focal point.

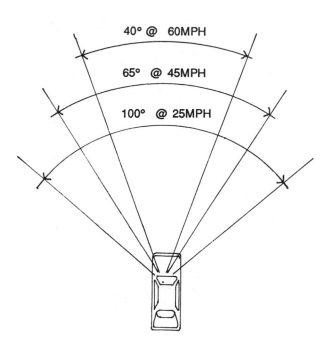

40° @ 60MPH

65° @ 45MPH

100° @ 25MPH

Figure 7-2. Travel speed and peripheral vision.

miles per hour, it is less than 40 degrees, (see Figure 7-2).

4. Foreground detail fades with speed: As speed increases and focus recedes, the clarity of foreground information is lost. According to Tunnard and Pushkarev, at 40 miles per hour, the nearest clear vision is at 80 feet distant; at 50 miles per hour, foreground detail is greatly diminished; and beyond 60 miles per hour, foreground perception is negligible, and only detail beyond 110 feet can be discerned.

5. Spatial perception decreases with speed: As speed increases, vision is directed forward, rather than to the side and the spatial edge. The result is that our perception of space decreases with speed, as does our understanding of the landscape. There are safety considerations to this reduced perception of space, and the reader is directed to Tunnard and Pushkarev for this discussion.

TEMPORAL PARADOX

Time presents a major paradox to the designer. On the one hand, change is the essence of the systems into which we design, yet many of the units with which we build are static. We place static units (buildings, area walls, and so on) into dynamic systems (landscapes). This paradox is especially evident in the differing perception concerning the time-space relationship that has developed between the professions of architecture and landscape architecture. The architect designs almost exclusively with static building ma-

terials and systems. Structural, spatial, mechanical, electrical and plumbing elements, for example, do not evolve. Their growth occurs by the addition of more static units, not by unit growth, regeneration or evolution. On the other hand, many of the landscape architect's materials evolve over time. The landscape is usually installed in an immature state, and the designer watches it mature. The landscape changes, often dramatically, from season to season and modifies its personality in a matter of minutes as the light of day fades into memory. When landscape design responds to site forces and their changing nature, the design becomes an integral part of this living system. When it fails to do so, the same forces work to rid the system of the designed malignancy, and the landscape designer is painfully reminded of change as the essence of natural systems.

In the recent past, the architect has been relatively free to perceive design in a static sense. He has often developed an aesthetic, expressive of the nature of the building systems and the designer's attitudes, perceptions, and theories of aesthetics and design. The architect has often chosen to overlook that buildings have not developed a dialogue with their context and has seen context as secondary in importance. In other cases the architect has only recognized incongruities after the fact and has applied contextual bandages. Unfortunately, some architects, even today, feel the primary role of landscape architecture is to provide these remedial efforts, rather than seeing the landscape architect as an integral member of the design team, knowledgeable about contextual systems and often essential for a successful project, and for protection of public health, safety, and welfare.

The landscape architect has not generally had the luxury of seeing design in a static sense. When modifications to the environment have failed to synergize with context, landscape forces have set about to change, in a negative manner, that which was designed. Over time, the landscape designer's perception of the task at hand, the issues to be considered, and the role of design have evolved to be more systems based. Many landscape architects have grown to place high emphasis on the maintenance of the health and quality of the systems into which landscape projects integrate.

One of the seldom recognized but profound ways that the perceptions of architects and landscape architects often differ is in their attitudes toward the relationships between space and time. In a sense, this difference is similar to that which existed between Renaissance (or better yet baroque) and cubist painters. In the Renaissance view, space was seen from a fixed point (Figure 7-3). The viewer and the subject were fixed in time, and the scene was explained as a single view. Three-dimensional aspects were conveyed via linear perspective. The culture learned to understand the communication of space through perspective, rather than through multiple images that represented movement in space and time. In the cubist approach, the viewer was not fixed in time (or in later phases, the subject was also not fixed, Figure 7-4). Multiple views implied observations occurring at different points in time. These images were superimposed to convey the third dimension. In these expressions, time and a changing relationship of viewer and subject became the essence of three-dimensional communication. Generally, architects of the recent past have approached spatial perception with the bias of Renaissance perception, landscape architects from one more closely aligned with the cubist view. Architects have seen the space as a fixed and rather consistent entity; landscape architects have seen it as one of many events occurring in a continuum of time and space, and more variable and multiexpressional, dependent on changing context, time, sequence, and experience. In both the architectural and the landscape architectural professions, there have, of course, been notable exceptions. Frank Lloyd Wright and Alvar Aalto were architects who placed great significance on visual sequences and the relationship of space and time. Conversely, the Brazilian landscape architect Roberto Burle Marx painted and designed beautiful landscapes to be seen as wholes from special, often external, fixed locations.

Figure 7-4. Communication from multiple points in time. (Marcel Duchamp "Nude Descending a Staircase, No. 2," 1912. Copyright 1990 ARS N.Y./ADAGP)

Figure 7-3. Space communicated from a fixed point. (Pietro Perugino, "The Delivery of The Keys to Saint Peter," 1482, Fresco, Sistine Chapel, Vatican, Rome from *Design Basics,* by David A. Lauer)

DESIGN AS AN EXPRESSION OF TIME

In exploring design as an expression of time, one needs to consider both the short- and the long-term time frame. Design can also address succession, natural rhythms, movement, changes over time, aesthetics, and design process.

Short-Term and Long-Term Decision-Making

Landscape design must address both the present and the future. It must satisfy immediate needs of a client while contributing to the long-term health and sustainability of the landscape and the culture. However, contemporary American culture has a short-term bias. Decisions are usually made to maximize short-term gain. For a number of reasons, including the recent degradation of our landscape and our decreased ability to economically compete in the present condition of resource scarcity, there is a growing awareness of the need to replace our short-term decision-making approach with a more sustainable one. This awareness is changing landscape design processes, as an ever greater percentage of landscape design is shifting from project design to the establishment of planning and design frameworks. In this approach, these frameworks establish the context within which future design decisions, made by many different people over extended periods of time, will occur. This topic is discussed in more detail in Chapter 14.

Landscape Design as Succession

The ability to incorporate change is essential for success in the designed landscape. For example, the designer must be able to create landscapes that will appear pleasing reasonably soon after planting and that will grow into satisfying mature landscapes. This often involves designing with a palette of compatible early and late successional plant materials and planning for the late successional landscape to grow through the early successional one, which has served its function as a reasonably instant landscape. In this manner, the designed landscape becomes an integral part of, and a statement of, landscape succession.

Landscape Design as Rhythm

Landscape design should explore the seasonal aspects of the landscape, and the opportunities and constraints they place on perception. This would include taking advantage of seasonal climatic conditions. It would also involve using plant material effectively for their seasonal behavior, and in so doing to express the unique character of each season, and the unique sense of each place. Designed landscapes can, for instance, include materials and arrangements that create interesting spatial developments and visual statements in all seasons and that change with the season in a rich temporal choreography.

The diurnal aspects of the outdoor environment also provide design opportunities. The landscape designer can create spaces that change their scale, character, and mood dynamically in the short time between day and night. In the evening, darkness can allow the designer to replace the fairly limited effect of daylight with a greater diversity of nighttime light sources and techniques such as downlighting, uplighting, bounce lighting, accent lighting, silhouette lighting, and so on. The change from day to night can also change spatial perception and the relationship between visual and other sensory stimuli. Places designed with this in mind can more fully explore all our senses.

Landscape design can also reflect the time of day the place is used most intensively. For example, Disneyland and New Orleans have both been designed to have a special excitement at night. So too have many amphitheaters and other nighttime arenas. Finally, the diurnal pattern of use affects our mental image of the place; we feel differently about places based on time of use.

Landscape Design as Movement

The exploration and expression of time and the realization of its design potential is one of the most effective means to designing rich sensuous landscapes. By structuring the manner in which one moves through a landscape, and by designing it as a rich evolving sensual experience, the designer maximizes the experience of the landscape. In this manner, the experiences that precede a place, and those that follow, become integral to the experiencing of that place. Good design creates the most opportunistic temporal framework within which to view the event, and uses the event to prepare the observer for experiences that follow. The entire sequence becomes a more effectively designed experience.

Landscape Design and Rate of Change

Landscape design occurs incrementally over time. When ecological or cultural change occurs slowly, the landscape has the opportunity to adjust itself to its changing context, and new gestures can be assimilated into the whole. This fine tuning, which characterizes late successional landscapes as well as many indigenous and vernacular cultural expressions, creates landscapes with a strong sense of place (Chapter 16), and with a high efficiency (Chapter 15). When change is rapid, on the other hand, the landscape does not have this opportunity. In this case, the landscape has a decreased ability for self-organization and self-healing. This becomes an important issue in our heterogeneous, rapidly changing twentieth-century urban landscapes, which are not self-managing. In this condition, the designer must also function as landscape manager. If these cities are to evolve a strong sense, design decisions must occur within the context of management frameworks and implementation structures that will facilitate the evolution of appropriate and meaningful landscapes (Chapter 14).

Time and Aesthetics

In our rapidly changing culture, there is an increasing need to evolve aesthetics that embrace our changing nature, while satisfying our need for stimuli variability, and schematic constancy (Chapters 14 and 16). Design can embrace change and satisfy our need for variety and constancy by developing a taxonomy that incorporates change and by building this taxonomy into a design language or aesthetic. Such a language would embrace both order and spontaneity (Chapter 16) to develop a vocabulary and structure that would communicate place variability within an integrated whole. It would be an evolving language that would embrace the changes that occur over time.

Time and Design Processes

Like design language, design processes must also incorporate time. To do so, they must facilitate the design of temporal networks (the design of events in time) as discussed below. They must facilitate the design of places that respond to needs that change diurnally, weekly, and seasonally. They must also be able to incorporate and respond to ecological and cultural change over time.

DESIGN AS A RESPONSE TO RATE OF MOVEMENT

As we design the landscape, and movement through that landscape, we must do so with an appreciation for the implication of speed. The slower we move, the greater our awareness of the immediate landscape. As speed increases, stimuli increase, and we reduce our cone of vision and our perception of the landscape. As the rate of flow decreases, the cone of vision and head movement increase, and we become more aware of the world around us. The rate of speed at which we move also needs to decrease as landscape complexity increases. Desired complexity decreases as speed increases, and landscape preference depends on the appropriate relationship between landscape complexity and rate of movement. We should also keep in mind that as we design, the character of the space and the nature of the path affect the rate of movement (Chapter 11).

We should also realize that the urban environment is highly complex; and the perception of time is somewhat accelerated. As a result, we can become overstimulated and therefore desensitized to the urban environment and derive less pleasure from it. As designers, we should therefore be particularly sensitive to reducing the complexity of the overall pattern of the urban environment through which we rapidly move and should direct attention to its characteristics that convey the most relevant information and that increase the sense of place and visual satisfaction of the city. On the other hand, we should avoid boredom by communicating richness and spontaneity in the detail viewed as movement slows and as we contemplate a given place. This topic is discussed in more detail in Chapter 16.

DESIGN AS TEMPORAL NETWORKS

To a large degree, design is experienced spatially. Equally important, but seldom considered, is design as the structuring of places over time, which Rapoport (1977) referred to as the development of temporal networks.

Designing landscapes as temporal networks includes the location of facilities so that appropriate groups access these facilities at appropriate times to satisfy their needs while avoiding conflicts with other groups with dissimilar codes of conduct. Temporal networks often include changes in the publicness and privateness of a place and changes in what is perceived as appropriate and inappropriate behavior with time of day or year, and with the specific group that colonizes the space. It is always a pleasant experience to see a design student first become aware that, as Christopher Alexander would say, "the city is not a tree" (1965), and that the designed project is not a single place but rather many different places, changing as one group departs and another establishes territory. Once this synapse is made, the student can understand the profound difference between an alive Italian piazza, effectively networked in time, and a wasteland American urban plaza that becomes vacant and unsafe as employees retire to their bedroom communities.

It should be kept in mind, however, that temporal networks are extremely difficult, if not impossible, to predict. For places to be effectively networked in time, they must embody some degree of open-ended design, allowing many different activities to occur in the space, and allowing the user to modify the place adequately to change its mood. In this manner the space can express the subtle nuances that strike an accord. This point is well presented in William H. Whyte's video entitled "The Street Life Project" (1979), where people are shown to satisfy their need to convert public space and to achieve some sense of home ground, even by such minor symbolic gestures as moving their chair before sitting. These subtleties can seldom be fully predicted, for even the users in many cases cannot be predicted.

Open-ended design also facilitates changes over time. It allows an almost infinite number of temporal sequences to evolve. It also encourages the user of a place to mitigate differences between user and designer perception (Chapter 16) and motivation, and design that does not address user needs.

Design as Social Time and Social Space

A place is perceived in social time and in social space. Groups establish their temporal territories and their spatial territories. As they do so, the degree to which appropriate groups come together in time and space affects the degree of satisfaction they derive from that space, as well as their stress and psychological health. It also determines their level of preference for that place.

DESIGN APPROACHES

There are two basic approaches to designing in response to temporal rhythms. The first is to identify common temporal rhythms and tempos, as well as atypical ones and to design the environments in response to these rhythms. In this case, commonly used areas and systems would be designed as distemic space and be so located as to be accessible by appropriate groups at appropriate times. Less variable spaces could be designed as proxemic home turf.

As the city becomes more heterogeneous, and as it changes rapidly, this approach becomes more problematic. The designer is generally unable to predict the temporal rhythms, or to design in response to them. In this case, the task is to design proxemic and distemic environments that can be modified over time, in response to changing user needs. Design of these places should allow for a maximum amount of user participation to modify the setting over time. It should also promote cultural pluralism, both spatially and temporally. Distemic space should be designed so that various groups can use specific portions of the place at the same time without disrupting other groups with differing norms. It should also accommodate the maximum range of uses over time, and be designed so that use by one group at a specific time does not limit its use by another group at another time. By designing in such a manner, the full range of users can receive maximum pleasure from the place over its temporal cycles of use.

REFERENCES

Alexander, Christopher. 1965. A City Is Not a Tree. *Architectural Forum* 122, April (58–62), (May 58–62).

Boulding, Kenneth. 1956. *The Image: Knowledge in Life and Science.* Ann Arbor: University of Michigan Press.

Hamilton, J. R., and Thurston, Louis L. 1937. *Safe Driving 8: Human Limitations in Automobile Driving.* Garden City, NY: Doubleday, Doran & Company.

Lauer, David. 1979. *Design Basics.* New York: Holt, Rinehart and Winston.

Pirsig, Robert. 1974. *Zen and the Art of Motorcycle Maintenance: An Inquiry into Values.* New York: Morrow.

Rapoport, Amos. 1977. *Human Aspects of Urban Form.* New York: Pergamon Press.

Tunnard, Christopher, and Pushkarev, Boris. 1963. *Man-Made America: Chaos or Control.* New York: Harmony Books.

Whyte, William. 1979. The Street Life Project. Video written and produced by W. H. Whyte, based on *The Social Life of Small Urban Places.* 1979 for NOVA.

SUGGESTED READINGS

Appleyard, Donald, Lynch, Kevin, and Myer, John. 1964. *The View from the Road.* Boston: MIT Press.

Lynch, Kevin. 1972. *What Time Is This Place?* Cambridge, MA: MIT Press.

Parks, Don, and Thrift, Nigel. 1980. *Time, Spaces and Places: A Chronogeographic Perspective.* New York: Wiley.

8

Visual Arts as Ordering Mechanism

To this point, we have spent considerable effort reviewing forces that give meaning to form. We have addressed some of the forces that affect perception and that influence experience. We will now consider visual art as a perceptual attitude and as an ordering mechanism.

In *Basic Design: The Dynamics of Visual Form* (1964), Maurice De Sausmarez stated that

> "Every visual experience is at one and the same time a receiving of fragmentary information, a giving of form to those visual sensations, and the arousing of felt response ... for the artist, what ultimately matters is this quality of feeling which results."

Experience stores images in the mind. The layman and the novice designer are concerned with illustration, that is, with making objects that agree with these stored images. Like laypeople, landscape designers are interested in mental images. However, designers are also concerned with the characteristics of visual perception and the forces inherent in points, lines, forms, colors, and textures. They realize that no art, even the representational, can duplicate reality. Designers understand that the purpose of art is not to duplicate, but rather to synergize images of the real world with the cognitive potential of the mind. This purpose of art is perhaps best described by the marvelous story concerning an artist painting the London Bridge: A fellow looks at the painting and the bridge and says, "I have never seen the London Bridge look like that before." Without looking up, the artist replies, "Yes, but don't you wish you could?" Like the painter, one task of the landscape designer is to effectively manage the physical characteristics of a setting to maximize the visual experience.

Every point, line, form, color, and texture has intrinsic characteristics and forces that it exerts into a context. In combinations, these elements and the manner in which they are organized evoke felt responses in the mind's eye.

Abstraction involves eliminating from consideration some of the attributes of the physical world, concentrating on other aspects, and reconstructing these aspects so as to intensify stimulation of the imagination. In so doing, art becomes symbolic rather than reproductive.

Throughout this topic and the next, we will discuss the manner in which visual elements and their organizations affect perception. Keep in mind that these considerations should be seen as issues, not as rules. It is essential to remember that the disciplined expression, the logical reasoned statement, should not exclude the spontaneous, felt, intuitive gesture. Truly creative acts, whether in art or great scientific discoveries, are almost never achieved by logically reasoned exercises. Rather, they are intuitive leaps. This is why designers work quickly and apparently aimlessly when they design. The spontaneous, unplanned line or shape can trigger the mind to creative insight. A large portion of design is working quickly, generating a lot, being receptive to what flows intuitively, and developing the opportunities that intuition provides.

ELEMENTS AND PRINCIPLES OF VISUAL FORM

Elements of visual form refer to the physical characteristics that can be manipulated to elicit mental responses. Principles refer to the visual relationships between these elements and the perceptual effects they elicit. Design elements include such things as point, line, form, color, and texture. Principles include the organization of elements so as to achieve unity, rhythm, proportion, scale, balance, and so on.

The reader should keep in mind that the following is not intended to deal comprehensively with elements and principles of design. Rather it is meant to introduce vocabulary and to have the reader begin to explore issues.

Visual Elements

Virtually all lists of visual elements include line, form, color, and texture. Others include point. Each of these elements embodies characteristics that the designer can manipulate.

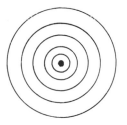

Figure 8-1. Point.

Point

The point is the most primary of elements. It has no length, width, or depth: it is directionless. However it exerts influence. It is felt to have embodied within it, the energy to grow. Therefore it affects the area around itself (Figure 8-1). When placed in a visual field its relation to the field imparts new character and energy to the point. At the center of the field, it seems stable and at rest (actually because of the influence of visual gravity, this point lies slightly above the center of the field) (Figure 8-2). In addition to its growth force, it takes on relationships with the edges and the corners of the field, and these relationships exert force. When the point is moved from this gravitational center, tension occurs and the point becomes unstable.

Points can also be special places in a composition. They can imply intersection; they can generate lines, circles, and spheres (Figure 8-3).

Two points establish a relationship and a shared tension. Each point implies an infinite number of lines, and the line connecting the two points becomes a special line. The segment of that line that occurs between the two points is the most special line in the entire field (Figure 8-4).

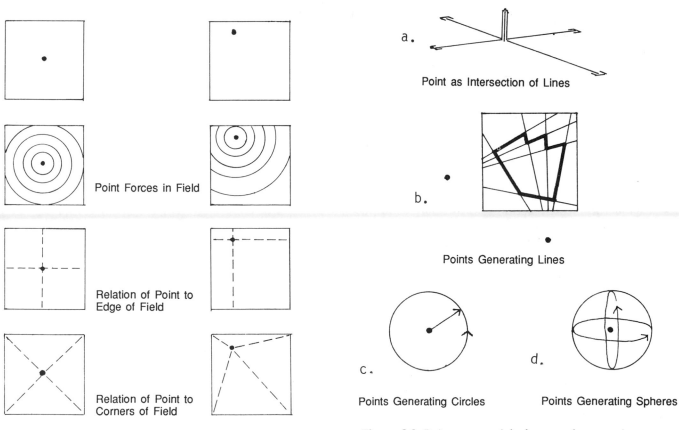

Figure 8-2. Point—relation to visual field.

Figure 8-3. Points as special places and generative influences.

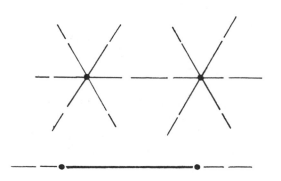

Figure 8-4. Two points generate a line.

Line

A line is a point extended; it is many points related one to another; it is the path of the moving point. Conceptually, it has length and direction, but no width or depth. In actuality, it must have some degree of thickness to be visible. To a degree this width will convey emotion. Thick lines, for example, convey strength; thin lines convey delicacy. The character of the line also implies emotion. Straight lines seem definite and stable, zigzags seem energetic and sometimes schizophrenic, curves seem sensuous.

Line direction affects its energies. The vertical line expresses equilibrium with the major force, gravity. The horizontal line, evocative of the body at rest and the supporting flatness of the ground plane, also implies stability. Together, the two impart a feeling of resolve, all forces in balance. The 90-degree angle they create, the right angle, also takes on the feeling or resolution (Figure 8-5). Lines not oriented horizontally or vertically take on an unresolved feeling. Their forces are unbalanced; they are not at equilibrium; they are visually active and dynamic. They evoke a feeling of tension and of impending change.

Straight lines and right angles also echo techniques of architectural construction. Accordingly, they impart an architectonic quality to form. Straight lines and acute angles impart energy (Figure 8-6). Curved lines, on the other hand, are everywhere in nature, in the arching branch, the meandering stream, the exfoliated rock. The softly sinuous, curving line imparts a feeling of nature, passivity, and resolve.

Line can also imply form or shape. As outline, it communicates form by defining its edge. As contour line, it conveys the surface of form (Figure 8-7).

Parallel lines imply a plane. The closer they are spaced one to another, the stronger this implication (Figure 8-8). A plane has length and width, but no depth.

Planes imply space and mass (Figure 8-9). Architecture usually employs planar surfaces to enclose space.

The vertical plane (wall) usually blocks the vision and encloses space. The overhead plane increases the degree of enclosure.

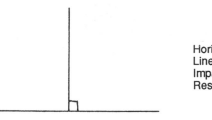

Horizontal and Vertical Lines and 90° Angles Impart Stability and Resolution of Forces

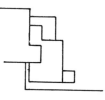

Sloped Lines Impart Motion, Instability and Movement

Figure 8-5. Line direction and stability.

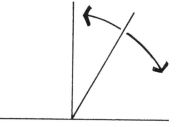

Architectonic Character/ Forces Resolved

Angular Character/ Resolved Feeling

Naturalistic/ Passive Feeling

Figure 8-6. Line character.

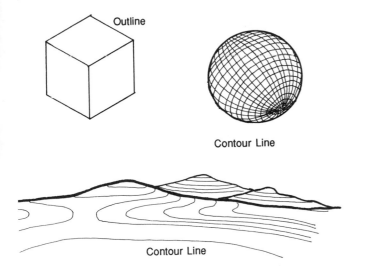

Outline

Contour Line

Contour Line

Figure 8-7. Outline and contour line.

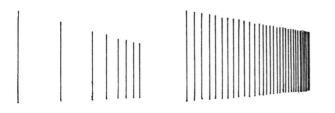

Figure 8-8. Lines imply planes.

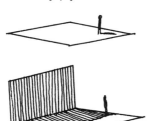

Figure 8-9. Planes imply space.

Form

The outline that delineates the edge of a plane gives it specific shape. In two-dimensional compositions, the shape is referred to as the figure and the field is called the ground (Figure 8-10). Many basic design exercises are concerned with making the relationship of figure and ground more interactive. Usually the figure is seen as the positive shape or generative force, and the ground as the negative shape or the context. However, through these basic design studies, we soon discover that figures themselves can have positive and negative aspects. Where the shape expresses itself as a generative force, we perceive the positive or designed shape.

Ground

Figure

Figure 8-10. Figure/ground.

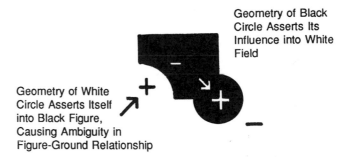

Geometry of Black Circle Asserts Its Influence into White Field

Geometry of White Circle Asserts Itself into Black Figure, Causing Ambiguity in Figure-Ground Relationship

Figure 8-11. Figure/ground ambiguity.

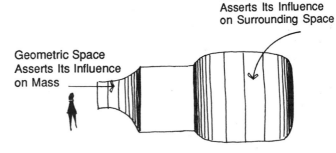

Geometric Mass Asserts Its Influence on Surrounding Space

Geometric Space Asserts Its Influence on Mass

Figure 8-12. Balance of space and mass.

Where the ground takes on this characteristic, it becomes the positive shape (Figure 8-11). The figure becomes the negative or undesigned form and a feeling of figure-ground ambiguity results. Extending this phenomenon, two-dimensional shapes exhibiting a balance of positive and negative forces imply three-dimensional forms that integrate the forces of mass and space (Figure 8-12).

Two-Dimensional Shapes as Spatial Forces. Shapes in a two-dimensional field have three-dimensional implications. They take on spatial characteristics and give spatial meanings to the two-dimensional surface (Figure 8-13). Spatial forces work to separate, by depth, the figure from its ground. When multiple figures come into play, spatial interest can be increased by reversals of figure and ground, relationships of line, and differences in size, value, texture, and color.

Reversals of Figure-Ground. When ambiguity of figure and ground is achieved, the mind becomes dynamically involved with experiencing the forms. As the eye moves across the surface, the mind fluctuates between seeing white figures on black ground, and black figures on white ground (Figure 8-14). The result is a greatly enhanced spatial dynamic and greater visual interest.

Relationships of Line. The length and width of line, its orientation, its location in relation to the picture plane, and its relation to other elements in the composition affect its spatial organization. One of the more important relationships is continuity. Lines of continuity allow the eye to see specific shapes in numerous ways (Figure 8-15). Seen in one way they make one spatial statement. Interpreted in another, the perceived shapes and spatial locations change. By effectively using lines of continuity, the composition takes on multiple meanings; it has an increased power to stimulate the mind and to sustain interest.

Since the Renaissance, we have shown depth through a unique relationship of line called linear perspective. However, in terms of engaging the mind and exploring dynamic spatial relationships, perspective can be counterproductive. It is a mechanical system. It assumes a fixed viewpoint, and it rigidly locks all elements into spatial locations. It sees space as a physical entity, rather than a physical-mental dialogue. It does not consider that the image the eye sees is a serial composition of partial views that change as the eye moves. It rather implies that the eye sees the single unchanging image, that is, the visual trick we call perspective.

The preceding statement does not reduce the value of perspective. To convey images from a fixed point

Figure Recedes: Ground Advances

Figure Advances Ground Recedes

Figure 8-13. Figure/ground and spatial relationships.

Figure 8-14. Figure/ground reversal.

Figure 8-16. Size as spatial force.

Only Eight of the Many Interpretations That the Mind Can Place on Shape A, Because of Lines of Continuity

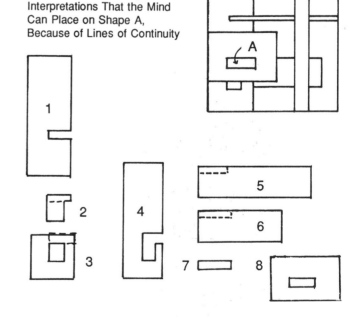

Figure 8-15. Lines of continuity.

in space and time, perspective may be our best visual tool. However, it has decreased relevancy when exploring the illusion of space as a dynamic dialogue between the image and the eye (except perhaps through perspective contradictions, such as those that characterize Escher's work).

Differences in Size. The relative sizes of figures imply locations in space (Figure 8-16). When relative size supports other variables such as line and color, it supports their message. When it contradicts, ambiguity is increased.

Three-Dimensional Form. Our experience of the world around us is spatial. We move through space. Our perception at any given time is that which composes the space we occupy. As we move from one place to another, our perception of the world is a serial spatial experience. Meaningful, exciting serial experiences give strong sense to the experience of place. This sense is usually built by a design vocabulary that evokes the intended sense. It also depends upon effective transitions from one design vocabulary to another.

Design Transitions. When transitions must be made between design vocabularies, such as a shift from formal architectural to sensuous naturalistic form, the most effective place to make these transitions is through the masses (Figure 8-17). For example, a building that separates a high speed highway from a fine-grained residential neighborhood could present two different faces. One face would speak to the forces of the automobile and the scale of the freeway; the other to the fine-grained residential neighborhood. The work of the architect Alvar Aalto often took on this quality.

Design transitions can also be made through vegetative masses. When viewing from the formal side, one sees a regularly spaced alee or bosque of trees; from the less formal side, one sees a varied and rich naturalistic edge (Figure 8-18).

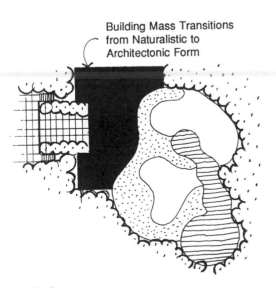

Figure 8-17. Mass as transition between design vocabularies.

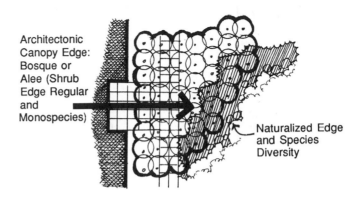

Figure 8-18. Vegetated mass as transition.

Color

Color theory is a complex science, far beyond the scope of this text. For the designer, however, it is essential to remember that color is a property of light, not of objects. Surfaces have no color of their own, only an ability to reflect certain wavelengths of light. As light changes, color changes. Perceived color also changes in relation to surroundings. It changes in its three primary properties: hue (pertaining to the wavelength of light reflected such as red or orange), value (relative lightness or darkness), and intensity (brightness).

Spatial Forces. The sensation of space in a two-dimensional composition can be enhanced through the manipulation of color contrast. This contrast can be achieved in a number of ways including value contrast, hue contrast, temperature contrast, and complementary contrast.

Value Contrast. Every color exhibits a relative lightness or darkness. The more contrast in value existing between adjacent colors, the more they will appear to separate from one another in space. The closer they are in value, the closer they appear in space. In two-dimensional compositions, value contrast can support or mitigate other spatial forces. If reinforcing other spatial forces, it supports the spatial theme; if contradicting other forces, it increases ambiguity (Figure 8-19).

Hue Contrast. Pure saturated hues occur at different tonal values. On a value gradation of 1 (white) to 9 (black), pure yellow has a value of 3, orange a value of 5, green and red are 6, blue 7, and pure violet a value of 8. Adjacent pure hues, therefore, exhibit a value contrast as well as temperature contrast.

Value Used to Imply
Transparency and to
Create Ambiguity

Value Used to Support
Overlap and Obvious
Depth

Figure 8-19. Value as spatial force.

Temperature Contrast. Each color, from hot red-orange to ice blue, has a perceived visual warmness or coolness about it. Due to the slight muscular action in our eyes as we focus on different colors, intense warm colors (red, orange, and yellow) seem to advance; cool colors (blue and green) seem to recede. This muscular activity is also supported by the fact that atmospheric perspective (dust particles in the air) breaks up colored light reflected from far away objects, and makes them appear a cool grey-blue.

When a color is surrounded by other colors, its perceived temperature changes. When surrounded by colors of similar temperature, it becomes more neutral: cool colors feel less cool and warm colors less warm. The colors also appear at about the same depth of space. By surrounding colors with those of contrasting temperatures, the designer will intensify temperature and spatially separate adjacent areas.

Complementary Contrast. For each color, there exists a complement. When the two colors are mixed, they produce a neutral grey-black. When they are juxtaposed, they produce maximum visual vitality in each of the two colors. Complementary contrasts maximize spatial separation.

It should be kept in mind that each of the above variables works interactively with the other spatial forces of color, and with those of figure-ground, line, size, shape, and texture to affect the perceived spatial relationships discussed above.

Texture

Texture refers to the surface characteristic of a shape or object. It unites our senses of sight and touch. Even when we do not touch the surface, visual stimuli

excite the mind to recall sensations of touch. We imagine its feel.

There are two categories of texture: tactile and visual. Tactile texture is that which can be felt by touch. In painting, sand can be mixed with pigment to provide this texture. Collage, the creation of design by gluing bits of colored and textured cloth, paper, or other materials, is a technique of providing tactile texture on the two-dimensional surface. Tactile texture is the beginning of a transition from two-dimensional expression through bas-relief to three-dimensional mass and space.

Visual texture is the manipulation of color and value patterns so as to imply texture on a smooth surface. The impression is a visual one; the texture cannot be felt by touch. Visual texture captures the effect of the dance of light on a textured surface.

In two-dimensional compositions visual texture can imply depth. Rough or coarse visual textures advance, smooth ones recede. As a spatial force, texture can work together with other spatial forces such as figure-ground relationships, differences in size, value or color, or relationships of line.

Design Principles

There is some disagreement among designers as to specific principles of design. We all recognize that organizational principles exist and that these affect the manner in which we perceive compositions. We also generally agree on the principles. We disagree, however, on their placement into categories and the names we place on those categories. With the preceding caveat in mind, we discuss the principles of design to be unity, emphasis or focalization, balance, scale and proportion, rhythm, and simplicity.

Unity

Unity or harmony implies that elements in a composition belong together; they have visual connectedness or relatedness. Unity provides coherence to a composition; it makes it understandable. Designs that lack unity appear to lack order and are often perceived as fragmented.

Providing Unity. A fundamental aspect of compositional unity is that the whole takes precedent over the parts. While each part has meaning, and while there may be a hierarchy of parts, their coming together into an integrated composition is the underlying theme. Unity in a composition can be increased by continuity, by repetition, and by proximity.

Continuity. Continuity refers to the continuation of some element of design. Points, lines, form, color, or texture can continue from one part of the composition to another, and thereby increase unity. In Figure 8-3b, for example, points are understood to provide the continuity between otherwise unrelated lines, that is, points are the generative force of these lines. In Figure 8-15, lines provide continuity between parts of the composition.

Repetition. Visual unity can be increased when some element is repeated in various parts of the composition. Figure 8-19 repeats horizontal and vertical lines, and 90-degree angles; Figures 8-14 and 8-16 repeat shape. Repetition of color is a common means whereby unity is enhanced in a composition.

When we look beyond the subject matter of most successful pieces of art, we see that repetition of design elements such as point, line, form, color, or texture is often the underlying order in the composition.

Proximity. Elements can group together in a composition based on their proximity. Elements that touch or overlap have an increased ability to cluster, as do groups that are distinctly isolated from other elements in the composition (Figure 8-20).

Despite Value and Shape Differences, the Four Central Shapes Unite from Proximity, Overlap, and Isolation from Other Elements

Figure 8-20. Proximity as unifying influence.

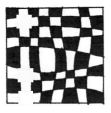

Total Unity/
Lack of Variety

Unity with Variety
Theme with Variation

Figure 8-21. Interplay of unity and variety.

Figure 8-22. Vernacular design.

Providing Variety. While the designer seeks unity, a totally unified composition lacks visual interest (Figure 8-21). The design intent, then, is usually to embrace both poles of the relatedness continuum, that is, unity with variety, theme with variation, order with a healthy hint of spontaneity.

Architectural Issues. *Vernacular architecture* has been characterized as theme with variation. The underlying theme is the order imparted by materials, technology, and place. It expresses itself as a cultural idiom. However, within this order there is room for variation. Each unit, while following the theme, is allowed to vary. The result is a rich fabric called vernacular architecture. It is to this quality of theme with variation that one intuitively responds when experiencing for example, a Greek village (Figure 8-22).

The typical building of the modern architectural tradition was criticized for its lack of variety: it was too unified. On the other hand, the cities that evolved from this tradition were generally too varied. Each building was designed as a piece, but the pieces were not integrated or unified into a meaningful whole. Because of this failure, today's Western city lacks unity as a whole, while also lacking variety within each piece. Currently postmodernism is addressing the blandness of the piece, but as yet has not developed an effective response to the need for the whole to become a meaningful urban fabric. This theme is explored in detail in Chapter 16.

Emphasis or Focalization

The artist can focus attention onto a part, or sequentially to various parts of the composition. Focalization, especially through a hierarchy of points, has a power to engage the mind and increase excitement.

A focal point occurs when one element of the composition differs appreciably from others (Figure 8-23). This difference can be in size, scale, shape, orientation, value, texture, color, or a multitude of other variables. Any element that contrasts the design vocabulary or the continuity of the composition will take on the character of a focal point.

Converging lines also give emphasis to points in a composition. Such radial designs are common in landscape architecture (Figure 8-24).

A point of caution is in order. Applied with restraint, focal points can provide variety in a unified composition. Without this restraint, they can fail to establish the necessary dialogue and can destroy compositional unity.

Balance

Pictorial balance involves the visual resolution of forces. When we view a composition, we intuitively weigh (visually) the composition about its central vertical axis. This weighing process involves a gestaltic response to all the visual elements of the composition. Imbalance, the failure to resolve forces, is a stimulating, yet sometimes disturbing, condition. When an imbalance exists, a feeling of uneasiness pervades the composition. There are two primary types of balance: symmetrical and asymmetrical.

Symmetrical Balance. Our bodies are basically symmetrical. Perhaps this is why the beginning designer attempts to balance compositions as mirror images across a central axis. Symmetrical balance is simple to create and simple to recognize. It is an absolute or perfect balance. It is "balance by sameness" (shape balances shape, color balances color, and so on) (Figure 8-25).

Symmetrical balance is static; it creates a feeling of passive formality. In some cases, symmetrical balance is desirable. It provides a feeling of permanence to government buildings and a sense of stately elegance to mansions. On the other hand, symmetrical compositions are generally dull. They can be excessively predictable. They often lack the power to engage the mind in a dialectic exchange.

Asymmetrical Balance. Asymmetrical balance is achieved by establishing an equal visual weighing through the manipulation of dissimilar variables (Figure 8-26). Color contrast is used to balance size, value to balance hue, and so forth. The aggregate relationship of these variables determines whether balance is achieved. This type of balance, often called informal or occult balance, is much more casual and dynamic then symmetrical balance.

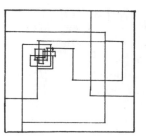

Figure 8-23. Focal point.

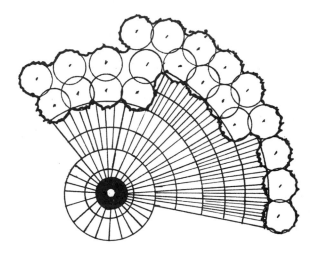

Figure 8-24. Radial design as focal point.

Figure 8-25. Symmetrical balance.

Figure 8-26. Asymmetrical balance.

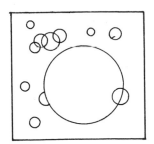

Figure 8-27. Scale as emphasis.

Figure 8-28. Superhuman scale.

Although asymmetrical balance looks less contrived and planned than formal balance, it requires much greater control and greater mastery of design. It explores design as an adjustment based upon interpretation and refinement of condition. On the other hand, symmetry achieves balance through the technique of the mirror image.

Scale and Proportion

Scale and proportion are two ways of interpreting relative size. *Scale* refers to size in relation to the human or some other unit of measure. *Proportion* addresses the size relationship between piece and whole, or between piece and piece. Therefore, a desert vista would be said to have a superhuman scale, but a square shape would be said to have a proportional relationship (side-to-side) of 1:1.

Scale in Two-Dimensional Compositions. Scale in the two-dimensional composition refers to the size of elements in the composition, relative to each other and to the format. Scale can be utilized to give emphasis to an element of the composition (Figure 8-27). It can also be used to communicate the vastness of the field (Figure 8-28).

Scale in the Making of Place. In the physical environment, the size of an object in relation to human size is essential in determining its perceived scale. According to Hans Blumenfeld (1953), there are five kinds of scale. *Intimate human scale* refers to the space within which individual facial expression is recognizable, and

is related to horizontal distances up to 48 feet and vertical ones up to 21 feet. *Human scale* refers to spaces with a maximum horizontal dimension of 72 feet and vertical dimension of 30 feet. *Public human scale* includes public spaces intended for large groups. These spaces rarely exceeded 500 feet in size. *Superhuman scale* refers to monumental space. *Extra-human scale* is not related to the human, but rather to nature. It is the scale of mountains, plains, and pyramids. It is also the scale of recent environmental sculptures such as Christo's "Running Fence" or his "Valley Curtain" (Figure 8.29) or Smithson's "Spiral Jetty." The scale of a piece of art, or of a place, is integrally related to its theme or purpose. Exaggerations of scale, such as the "Valley Curtain" cause us to see the world about us in a unique manner. Superhuman scale causes us to reassess the role of humans in the larger scheme of things; intimate scale to assess the relationship of person to person (Figure 8-30), or the individual to self.

Proportion. Proportion refers to the relative dimensions (length to width to depth) of an element, or the size of a piece in relation to the whole.

Whenever a point is introduced into a format, it divides the format. The proportions of the shapes implied affect our perception. The least dynamic subdi-

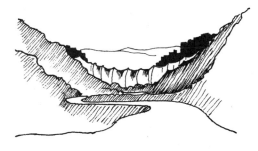

Figure 8-29. Valley curtain by Christo.

Figure 8-30. Intimate scale.

vision is that of equality. Unless desiring to create a static feeling, the designer should avoid breaking a format into equal pieces, (Figure 8-31). The same is true when dividing a line. Most people would agree that an equal division is not the most dynamic one. Beyond this basic agreement, many people contend that there are proportions that are particularly satisfying.

Proportional Systems. Throughout history, designers have searched for proportions that were neither so obvious as to be dull or so instable as to be irritating. Pythagoras believed these ideal proportions to be the underlying order and harmonic structure of the universe, and believed they could be explained by consistent whole number relationships between parts. He developed sets of musical scales based upon the sounds produced by strings which bore a 6:4:3 numerical relationship one to another. Later, during the Renaissance, these harmonic intervals were applied to architectural design.

The *golden section*, also called the golden mean or the golden number, was believed by the early Greeks to be the perfect proportional relationship. They understood the golden section to play an important role in the proportion of the human body; and they proportioned their temples accordingly. The golden section states that the smaller part of a whole is to the larger part, as the larger part is to the sum of the two (Figure 8-32). While many designers today would say that such a system is too rigid for design, it has endured through the centuries. For example, the Parthenon, recognized by many as the most visually satisfying building ever constructed, employed the golden section as an ordering mechanism. This proportional system was also used in the Renaissance, and was the basis of Le Corbusier's *Modular* (1955).

The golden section or the golden spiral can be constructed by extension or by division. As the short side of a golden section is used to generate a square, the remaining rectangle is also a golden section, which can also be so reduced by another square (Figure 8-33); and the resulting geometric progression can be used to expand or subdivide space (Figures 8-34 and 8-35).

Fibonacci Series. Developed during the thirteenth century, the *Fibonacci series* is a set of integers that, as it progresses, approximates the golden section (Figure 8-36). The Fibonácci series occurs repeatedly in plant and animal forms and elsewhere in nature. It predicts the spirals of florets in a daisy flower, the curves of seashells, the spiral of pine cones, and the curve of space. Its consistent recurrence in nature implies that there may be some underlying universal order ex-

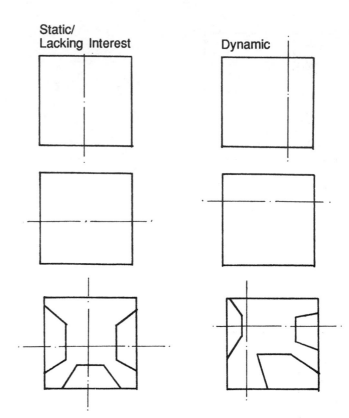

Figure 8-31. Field proportions.

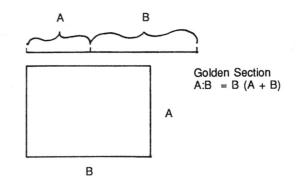

Golden Section
A:B = B (A + B)

Figure 8-32. Golden section.

pressed by the mathematical relationship. This lends validity to its use as an ordering mechanism for design, as this pervasive natural order may well be felt intuitively by the individual.

In the early twentieth century, cubism explored geometry and proportion as ordering mechanisms. Le Corbusier evolved his "Modular" based on the human body and on mathematics, from directions prevalent in cubism.

Whether a perfect proportion exists, or whether ideal relationships order the universe, is yet to be discovered. However, the search for such relationships endures in design.

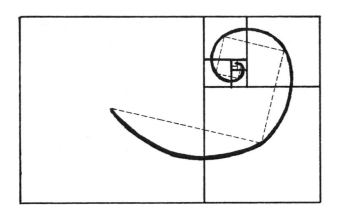

Figure 8-33. Golden spiral. Proportion .618034:1. When the left side is squared, another golden section is created. Each subsequent golden section if reduced by a square to a smaller golden section. This form recurs repeatedly throughout nature.

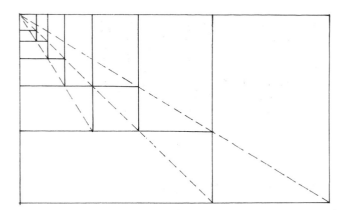

Figure 8-35. Golden section and squares to subdivide and order space. A golden rectangle is one whose sides are proportioned according to the golden section. If a square is a golden rectangle. This can be repeated indefinitely to subdivide the space with a graduation of golden rectangles and squares. All parts are proportional.

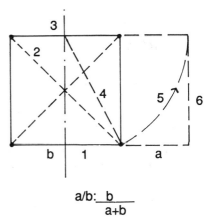

a/b: $\dfrac{b}{a+b}$

1. By Extension

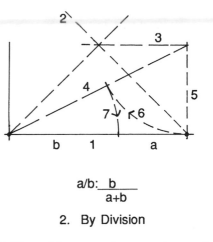

a/b: $\dfrac{b}{a+b}$

2. By Division

Figure 8-34. The golden mean by extension and division.

NUMBER	RATIO	PROPORTION
1	1 : 1	1.00000
2	2 : 1	2.00000
3	3 : 2	1.50000
5	5 : 3	1.66667
8	8 : 5	1.60000
13	13 : 8	1.62500
21	21 : 13	1.61538
34	34 : 21	1.61905
55	55 : 34	1.61765
89	89 : 55	1.61818
144	144 : 89	1.61798
233	233 : 144	1.61806
377	377 : 233	1.61803
610	610 : 377	1.61804
987	987 : 610	1.61803
1597	1597 : 987	1.61803

1.61803398874984948482........

Figure 8-36. Fibonacci series.

Rhythm

Rhythm involves repetition, and unifies a composition through the recurrence of similar items. We associate rhythm in space with those in time, and rhythm therefore links vision to hearing, more specifically to cadence and music. As in music, rhythms can be flowing and connected; this we call legato (Figure 8-37). Conversely, agitated rhythms are referred to as staccato (Figure 8-38).

Rhythm in the visual arts is related to eye movement. The dancing of the eye across repetitive shapes gives a rhythmic feeling. The allusion of rhythm can be created through line, form, color, value, or texture.

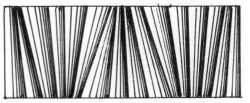

Figure 8-37. Legato rhythm.

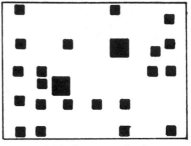

Figure 8-38. Staccato rhythm.

Simplicity

The final principle underlying the visual arts is simplicity, which involves a visual economy of means. It seeks as its goal the communication of maximum meaning with a minimum number of pieces. To achieve this goal each element of the composition must carry meaning; each relationship must be effectively managed.

Though appearing easy to achieve, simplicity might well be the most difficult principle to implement. To engage the mind in a dialogue with the design, to sustain interest, and to do so with an economy of means requires an ability to approach ideal relationships. It is this principle that powers the eternal search for such things as the perfect proportion discussed above.

Design Intent

Many see the intent of art to be the sustaining of interest; its measure of success to be the ability to engage the mind and to elicit response.

Successful art is that which establishes a dialogue with the mind. This dialogue is usually achieved through an incomplete or nonobvious resolution of forces. Conversely, the totally unified composition becomes dull. To sustain interest usually requires at least the hint of spontaneity. This embodiment of chaos is at the heart of intuition. It is the life in art, the mystery and power to engage the mind. The successful designer is one who enjoys spontaneity and is simultaneously able to instill a sense of order or relatedness.

REFERENCES

Blumenfeld, Hans. 1953. Scale in Civic Design. *Town Planning Review.* 24 (1): 35-46.

De Sausmarez, Maurice. 1964. *Basic Design: The Dynamics of Visual Form.* New York: Reinhold.

Le Corbusier, 1955. *The Modular,* 2d ed. London: Faber and Faber.

SUGGESTED READINGS

Ching, Francis. 1979. *Architecture: Form, Space and Order.* New York: Van Nostrand Reinhold.

Harlan, Calvin. 1970. *Vision and Invention: A Course in Art Fundamentals.* Englewood Cliffs, NJ: Prentice-Hall.

Hesselgren, S. 1975. *Man's Perception-of-Man-Made Environment: An Architectural Theory.* Stroudsburg, PA: Dowden, Hutchinson & Ross.

Lauer, David. 1979. *Design Basics.* New York: Holt, Rinehart and Winston.

Pearce, Peter. 1978. *Structure in Nature Is a Strategy for Design.* Cambridge, MA: The MIT Press.

Wong, W. 1988. *Principles of Two-Dimensional Form.* New York: Van Nostrand Reinhold.

9

Geometry as Ordering Mechanism

Perception is the interaction of stimuli and stored images in the mind. Ingrained in the limbic brain is an innate emotional response to forms in nature. There is also an efficiency and sustainability (Chapter 15) in natural form. Therefore, humans intuitively respond positively to natural places. On the other hand, for the past 7000 years, Western culture has embraced euclidean geometry. Stored in our cortical brain is this cultural bias toward rational geometry. In different ways, and with different levels of emotion, we understand and respond to these two different types of geometry, natural and human-made. To better understand the two, we will begin with the more simplified euclidean geometry that has dominated Western literature on geometric order. We will then explore geometry in nature, including inorganic and organic geometric expressions.

EUCLIDEAN GEOMETRY

There are four types of *euclidean geometry:* rectilinear, angular, circular, and combinations of these. To effectively manipulate each of these types, the designer must first understand, and be able to apply, underlying elements and principles of visual art. In addition, each of the four has underlying forces that unite its elements into an integrated form vocabulary. The designer must understand and be able to apply these underlying forces to interrelate elements into a unified composition.

In this section we discuss the forces that generate euclidean form. We also discuss how these forces can be manipulated by the designer to contribute order to geometric compositions. We look at rectilinear, angular, circular, and composite geometric design vocabularies.

Rectilinear Geometry

The forces that generate rectilinear geometry are horizontal and vertical lines and 90-degree angles (Figure 9-1). These are static forces, which speak to resolved gravity, the figure at rest, the horizon, and to angles created by forces in equilibrium.

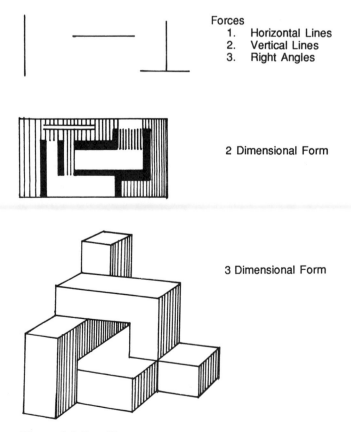

Forces
1. Horizontal Lines
2. Vertical Lines
3. Right Angles

2 Dimensional Form

3 Dimensional Form

Figure 9-1. Rectilinear geometry.

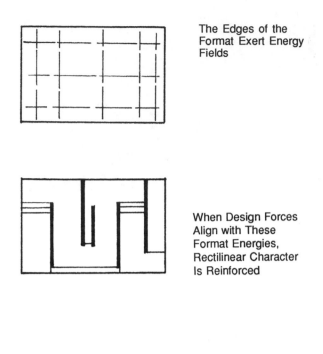

The Edges of the Format Exert Energy Fields

When Design Forces Align with These Format Energies, Rectilinear Character Is Reinforced

When Design Forces Disalign with Format Energies, Some Angular Character-istics Are Imparted to the Composition

Figure 9-2. Format forces in rectilinear compositions.

Because of their underlying forces, rectilinear compositions appear static; they can also be boring. They tolerate a high degree of frivolity while maintaining their continuity. Within their obvious order, they provide many opportunities to manipulate individual elements to achieve variety, dynamic balance, rhythm, and emphasis. They can also do so with little risk of losing their underlying unity, as long as lines remain parallel and perpendicular.

The format or context is quite important when generating rectilinear form. The edges of two-dimensional formats or three-dimensional contexts are often orthogonal. When the rectilinear forces of the design coincide with these edges the static sense of the rectilinear form is reinforced (Figure 9-2). When design forces do not align with format forces, dynamic energies are introduced. Angular relationships between design forms and the format (or environmental) edge impart angular characteristics to the design.

Angular Geometry

The forces that generate angular forms are points, radiating straight lines, and angles (other than 90 degrees). Expanding from points, angular compositions convey dynamic, energetic feelings. Acute angles increase this energy and intensify angularity (Figure 9-3). Obtuse angles control the energy and convey a

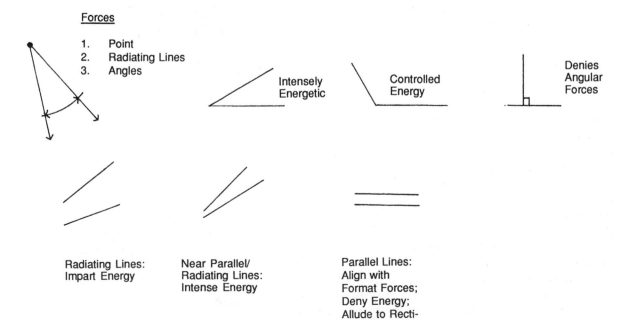

Forces

1. Point
2. Radiating Lines
3. Angles

Intensely Energetic

Controlled Energy

Denies Angular Forces

Radiating Lines: Impart Energy

Near Parallel/ Radiating Lines: Intense Energy

Parallel Lines: Align with Format Forces; Deny Energy; Allude to Recti-linear Compo.

Figure 9-3. Angular forces.

subdued or refined energy. Right (90-degree) angles deny the energy and instead allude to resolved rectilinear form.

Radiating lines convey this energy. Those that approach, but do not become parallel, allude to extremely acute angles. They maximize tensions and intensify angularity. Parallel lines, on the other hand, dissolve this tension. They speak not to radiating energies, but rather to resolved relationships and rectilinear form. Lines that align with format edges also speak to statics and rectilinear form. Those lines that are askew to these edges increase angularity.

Angular compositions are inherently energetic. It is easy to impart excitement to them. It is somewhat more difficult to unify them. Unity can be increased in angular compositions by minimizing the number of points that generate the composition. In this case, the feeling of randomness or unspecified energy will be replaced with a feeling of emanating energies and integration (Figure 9-4). The mind intuitively feels this order.

Angular compositions with obtuse angles or sets of parallel lines relating in a nonrectilinear sense give the feeling of very controlled and highly ordered energies (Figure 9-5).

Circular Geometry

A circle is the trace of a point moving around a stationary point at a fixed dimension. The innate forces of a circle are the center, the arc (and concentric arcs), the radius connecting the moving and the fixed points, and the 90-degree angle where the radius meets the arc (Figure 9-6).

There are a number of special relationships inherent in circular geometry (Figures 9-7 and 9-8). There are also forms caused by interactions that impart a character quite different from the passive, resolved feeling usually associated with circular geometry (Figure 9-9). Slivers of form, for example, can be quite disruptive to otherwise passive circular compositions, but can be used effectively to create energy.

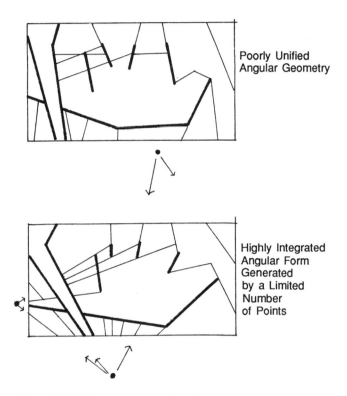

Poorly Unified
Angular Geometry

Highly Integrated
Angular Form
Generated
by a Limited
Number
of Points

Figure 9-4. Points as generative force.

Figure 9-5. Controlled angular geometry.

A Circle Is a Moving Point Traveling about a Fixed Point at a Fixed Distance

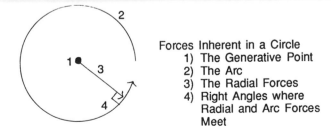

Forces Inherent in a Circle
1) The Generative Point
2) The Arc
3) The Radial Forces
4) Right Angles where Radial and Arc Forces Meet

Figure 9-6. Forces in circular geometry.

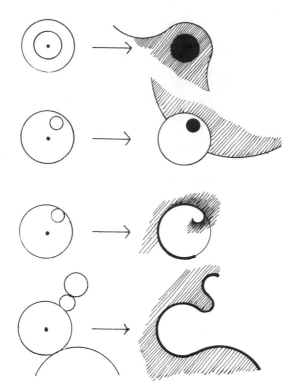

Figure 9-7. Special relationships between circular shapes.

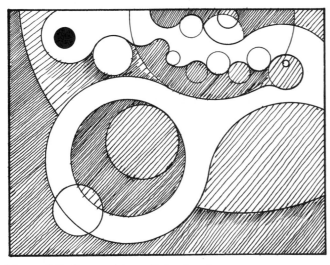

Figure 9-8. Composition of circular shapes.

Figure 9-9. Angular relationships between circular shapes.

Composite Geometry

Composite geometries involve the integration of rectilinear, angular, or circular geometries. As we have seen, each of these three pure geometries has inherent forces. Integrating these geometries involves the development of concurrences between these forces. Where the forces coincide, forms will sit comfortably with both geometries. To explore this concept, we look first at integrations of rectilinear and angular form, then explore rectilinear-circular interactions, circular-angular ones, and finally the composite of all three. We then close this section with some comments concerning alternative manners in which geometries in general can synergize, and the impact of these synergisms.

Rectilinear-Angular Composites

Rectilinear geometry expresses the forces of horizontal and vertical lines, parallel lines, and right (90-degree) angles. Angular form expresses generative points, straight lines, and angles. Therefore, composites that integrate the two geometries would be characterized by generative points, radiating lines, parallel lines, and angles. By employing generative points, lines of continuity, parallel lines, and 90-degree angles in key locations, the designer will be able to visually unite the vocabularies (Figure 9-10).

Rectilinear-Circular Composites

Both rectilinear and circular forms express key points. In rectilinear forms, the corners are special points; in circular forms, the center of curvature has unique generative powers. Both employ 90-degree angles: in the rectangle as axis intersections, in the circle as radii to arc connections. The radial forces of circular forms are straight lines, which are also part of the rectilinear vocabulary of form. At tangential conditions, arcs become straight lines (Figure 9-11).

Composites of rectilinear and circular geometry develop concurrences between these shared forces and conditions. Figure 9-12 shows an overhead view of a

Figure 9-10. Rectilinear–angular composite form.

large building so formed to give dominance to a cubic sculpture by making the art piece the dominant point in its rectilinear-circular composition. Figure 9-13 also employs rectilinear-circular composite geometry.

Angular-Circular Composites

Both angular and circular geometries share special points and radiating lines as generative forces. The two geometries integrate quite easily (Figure 9-14).

Rectilinear-Angular-Circular Composites

Integrating the three geometries involves meshing the three pairs of forces mentioned above. All three geometries have forces generated by points, all three have straight line forces. These shared forces facilitate integration of the three geometries (Figure 9-15).

Integration Strategies

Conceptually, there are various ways in which different geometrical form vocabularies can be integrated. These include gestaltic integration, zoned emphasis, scale interactions, and dialectic interplays of discrete vocabularies.

Gestaltic integration involves a dynamic integration of form so that each perceived shape is an integration of the individual geometries. In this case each piece and the overall composition feels unified (Figure 9-16).

Zoned emphasis organizes the composition by points of emphasis that express separate and relatively pure vocabularies. Transitions occur as composite geometries in the forms between these emphasis areas (Figure 9-17). This approach in landscape architectural design could create, for example, three unique spaces. Each would present a unified singular form

Figure 9-14. Angular–circular composite form.

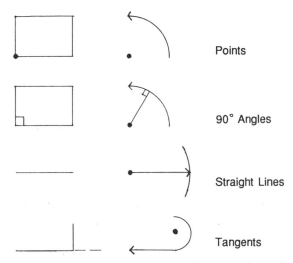

Figure 9-11. Integrating forces in rectilinear and circular composites.

Points

90° Angles

Straight Lines

Tangents

Figure 9-15. Rectilinear–angular–circular composite form. form.

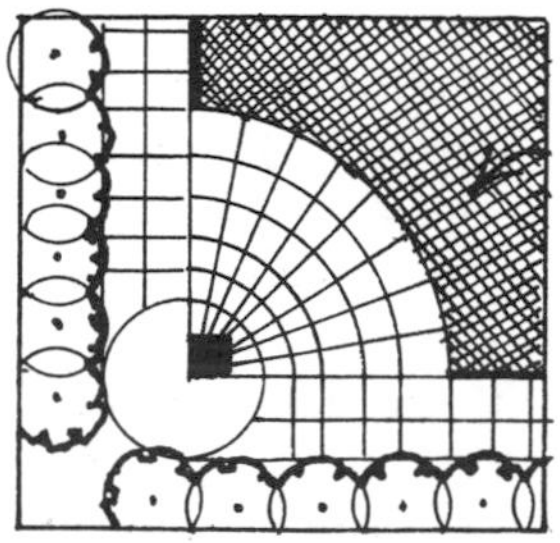

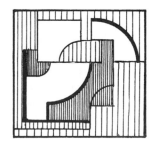

Figure 9-12. Rectilinear–circular composite form.

Figure 9-13. Rectilinear–circular composite form.

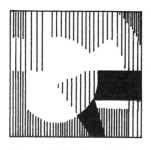

Figure 9-16. Gestaltic integration.

Figure 9-17. Zoned emphasis.

vocabulary and sense of place. The mass separating the spaces would serve as transition zones.

Scale interactions allow one vocabulary to establish itself as the matrix or the pervasive vocabulary of the composition (Figure 9-18). It then introduces another vocabulary, at a radically different scale, to break the pattern of the established vocabulary of form. This is a very dynamic integration, balancing pattern against dominant line. The chance occurrences of form along the path of interference contribute to the dynamic feeling.

Dialectic interplays occur through the coming together of discrete geometrical form vocabularies. When these vocabularies meet, and their intersection is contrived so that relationships satisfy both geometries, a resolved feeling occurs (Figure 9-19). When they meet in a chance encounter, one geometry can become dominant and the other recessive. The recessive geometry gives the illusion of continuing beneath and emerging from the more dominant one, establishing a dialectic interplay between the two geometries (Figure 9-20).

There are innumerable other strategies for integrating different vocabularies of form that grow from euclidean geometry.

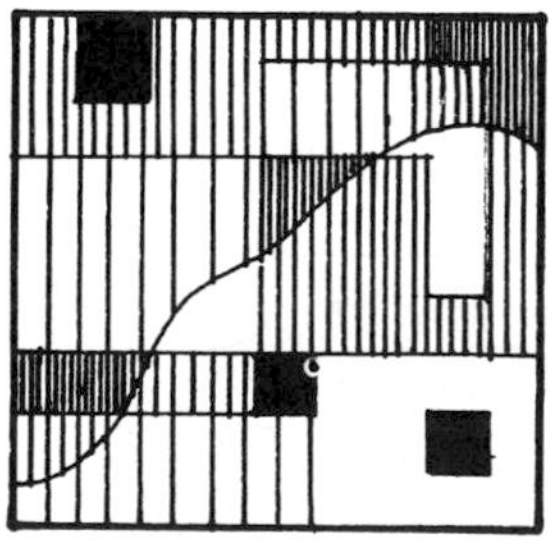

![Figure 9-18 scale interaction diagram]

Figure 9-18. Scale interaction.

Figure 9-19. Resolved interplay.

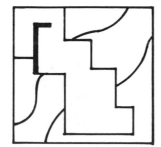

Figure 9-20. Dynamic interplay.

GEOMETRY IN NATURE

A number of people, including R. Buckminster Fuller (1965), Konrad Wachsmann (1961), Georgy Doczi (1981), and Peter Pearce (1978), have studied three-dimensional spatial geometry and geometric relationships in nature and have used natural geometry as a strategy for exploring structural and architectural design. These people have studied efficiency in nature as achieved through the repetitive use of modular systems that facilitate diversity and change through the evolving geometries that result from natural forces. To better understand geometry in nature, therefore, we must investigate these two characteristics. We look first at efficiency networks in nature and then explore the evolving geometric forms of nature. We close with a discussion of the scale independence of nature, and the potential of fractal geometry and the science of chaos to help us better understand natural form and order and to help synergize man and environment.

Efficiency Networks

As Peter Pearce notes in *Structure in Nature Is a Strategy for Design,* many designers have explored efficiency, diversity, and change as the essence of natural systems, focusing on natural expressions. They have studied the geometries produced by the physical and biological processes of nature to understand better the order of the universe and to explore the human role in that order. They have observed that nature seeks to build maximum diversity with a minimum inventory of parts or set of influences, as in the vast number of chemicals built from a small number of basic elements. They have observed that within a given natural or physical process, there are usually a few physical, geometric, or chemical constraints (referred to as rubrics) that determine the form options that can occur. Within these options, diversity and efficiency are achieved as these constraints or form-giving influences operate within the context of environmental variables such as temperature, humidity, air or fluid flow, and pressure. Rubrics can also serve as clues to underlying forces. In *On Growth and Form,* D'Arcy Wentworth Thompson (1963) describes natural expressions as diagrams from which we can deduce the forces that have operated on the rubrics to produce the forms that we observe.

As these people have observed, inorganic natural expressions, as well as organic ones, embrace the conservation of resources as they develop maximum efficiency with minimum elements. They seek to integrate the internal characteristics of an organizational system with external influences, and in so doing to maximize efficiency. For example the snowflake is a geometric expression that uses minimal energy, works with maximum efficiency, and varies in form because of differences in environmental conditions of temperature, humidity, air movement and atmospheric pressure as the flake was forming. In a related manner, the pattern of cracking of a dry creekbed expresses maximum efficiency, as it gives greatest access of all parts of the surface to a pressure-relief crack, while minimizing the total number of cracks. The dendritic pattern that characterizes both inorganic (streams) and organic (tree branches) form also expresses this least-energy maximum-efficiency characteristic.

As stated above, many people have studied rubrics and natural form as a tool for design innovation. For example, Buckminster Fuller's study of the three-dimensional arrangement of polyhedral cells in chemical structures led to his invention of the resource-efficient geodesic dome, an architectural expression of natural structure (Figure 9-21).

In addressing efficient natural networks, we should understand that any surface or volume that separates two regions of space can be created by a combination of polygons. For example, a surface formed by cubes separates two zones of space. However, while the cube is important to architecture, it offers little opportunity for diversity. It is also inefficient in its strength-to-weight ratio. The same can be said about rectilinear geometry in general. So while rectilinear geometry is prevalent in Western architecture, it generally does not occur in natural processes because of its inefficiency and inflexibility.

The triangle is an inherently stable shape. Therefore, we would expect it to occur in nature. It does; and the "network of triangles" is an organizational pattern that recurs throughout nature (Figure 9-22). The most efficient shape that can be organized into triangular networks is the hexagon. The hexagon recurs as an efficient structural pattern in many situations in nature. It occurs as organic crystals form. It also happens as mud dries and surface tension creates an efficient pattern of cracking, with variations to pattern regularity caused by unequal cycles of drying. It is interesting to note that living organisms, however, tend to express pentagonal, not hexagonal, patterns (though the forms of life are not as consistently pentagonal as the forms of crystalline or surface tension structures are hexagonal).

Triangular networks facilitate the closest packing of parts necessary for efficiency; and therefore, we find them throughout nature, from the packing of the bee's hexagonally shaped honeycombs, to soapbubbles, to cellular structures. For example, if seen two-dimensionally, soap bubbles will always meet in threes

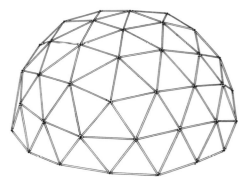

Figure 9-21. Geodesic dome-architectural expression of natural structure.

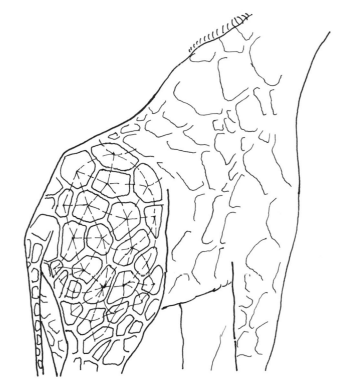

Figure 9-22. Animal skin as a triangular network. (Adapted from Pearce, P., *Structure in Nature Is a Strategy for Design,* Photograph 2.30. Copyright 1978 by Peter Pearce. Published by MIT Press and reprinted by permission.

around the vertex and form an irregular triangular network (Figure 9-23). Seen three-dimensionally, this triangular network will consist of tetrahedrals. Triangular networks are also the basis of the archetypes of truss, folded plate, spaceframe, and geodesic dome.

The sphere is an efficient two-dimensional shape, but if packed three-dimensionally, each sphere is surrounded by twelve other spheres, leaving voids of high surface area, and low-efficiency between the spheres. Extending the spheres to fill these voids results in a polyhedral with twelve equal rhombic faces, called a rhombic polyhedral. This regular efficient three-

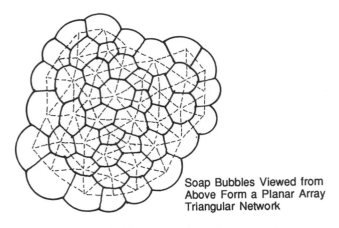

Soap Bubbles Viewed from
Above Form a Planar Array
Triangular Network

Figure 9-23. Soap bubbles as a triangular network.

dimensional form has been translated to create geometrical human-built structural systems that efficiently enclose space. These designed structures range from spaceframes to modular play equipment. In nature, the variation in form necessary to achieve efficiency, while responding to changes in environment, is achieved by combinations of irregular twelve-, fourteen-, fifteen-, and sixteen-sided polyhedrals that approximate the close packing of unequally sized spheres. Transferred to geometric human-built structural systems, these forms can create irregularly shaped architectural membranes and spaceframes, if the available tool-kit of structural connectors (joints) is increased.

The form options that emerge from an exploration of close packing, triangulation, and surface tension in nature are too numerous to address here. The reader is encouraged to explore these options and their application to built structures in *Structure in Nature Is a Strategy for Design,* by Pearce.

Evolving Geometries

Nature is characterized not by fixed geometries, but by evolving ones, that is, geometries that are mathematically accelerating or decelerating. For example, the nautilus shape of a seashell, the meander of a stream, and the spiral of a galaxy are various scale expressions of the evolving geometry of natural form. Geometric progression according to the golden mean is also typical of natural form, an ethological foundation that may explain why many scientific experiments over the last 100 years have shown this proportion to be particularly pleasing. It also may explain why so many of the mathematical models of "ideal" relationships such as the golden section, the Fibonacci series, and the modular are so closely re-

lated to the underlying ratio of 1.618:1 (or conversely 1:0.618).

It is interesting to note the frequency that the Fibonacci numbers appear in nature, such as the number of spirals that occur to form a sunflower floret, or the proportional length of radii (using a consistent rotational angle) of a shell curvature (Figure 9-24). Various shapes of seashells express the Fibonacci series with differences between the tightness of the curve of different shapes, that is, the rate at which the geometry accelerates, accruing to the actual rotational angle between consecutive radii.

According to Doczi, nature expresses itself as an order that "can be seen in certain proportions which appear again and again, and also in the similarly dynamic way all things grow or are made–by a union of complementary opposites." He shows, as an example, how the florets of the daisy grow at the intersection points of two spirals, one running clockwise, the other counter-clockwise (Figure 9-25). As Doczi points out, these spirals are logarithmic, and they retain a constant angle with the radii and are parabolic in form. This pattern of spirals moving in opposite directions occurs frequently in nature. When these opposing forces are balanced and result in natural symmetry, this dynamic symmetry can be seen as a special case of the union of complementary opposites, the Yin and Yang.

T. A. Cook's *The Curves of Life* (1979) and Colman and Coan's *Nature's Harmonic Unity* (1912) address the golden section in nature and art. Cook does so with a focus on diversity, while Colman and Coan place emphasis on unity. Doczi's *The Power of Limits* explores the golden section and other proportional methods and evolving geometries in natural form as expressions of the interrelatedness of unity and diversity that characterizes nature. Similarly, in *On Growth and Form,* Thompson explores the manner in which nature creates forms that are characterized by both similarity and dissimilarity. In Chapter 16, we will explore another expression of the natural interplay between unity and diversity. We will pursue the purported innate human need to perceive this simultaneity of unity and diversity, or of similarity and dissimilarity, as we discuss the interrelatedness of order and spontaneity in placemaking.

Scale Hierarchies and Fractal Geometry

When we consider that the concept of closest packing is independent of size, we would expect natural form to be scale independent, which proves to be the case. For example, as one looks at the dendritic branching of streams, there is an hierarchical branching pattern

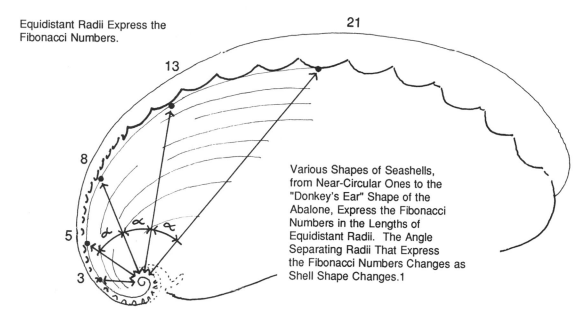

Equidistant Radii Express the Fibonacci Numbers.

21

13

8

5

3

Various Shapes of Seashells, from Near-Circular Ones to the "Donkey's Ear" Shape of the Abalone, Express the Fibonacci Numbers in the Lengths of Equidistant Radii. The Angle Separating Radii That Express the Fibonacci Numbers Changes as Shell Shape Changes.1

Figure 9-24. Seashells express Fibonacci numbers. (From THE POWER OF LIMITS by Gyorgy Doczi, © 1981. Reprinted by arrangement with Shambhala Publications, Inc., 300 Massachusetts Ave., Boston, MA 02115)

The Floret of a Daisy Expresses the Evolving Geometry of Nature. Spirals Move in Opposite Directions. Each Spiral Is Logarithmic; and Each Forms an Equal Angle with Floret Radii.

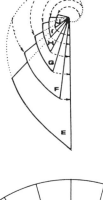

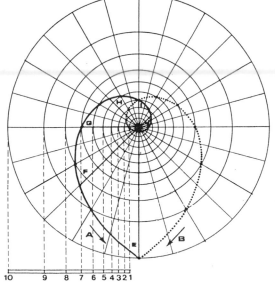

Figure 9-25. Fibonacci numbers in natural form. (From THE POWER OF LIMITS by Gyorgy Doczi, © 1981. Reprinted by arrangement with Shambhala Publications, Inc., 300 Massachusetts Ave., Boston, MA 02115)

consistent in form, frequency, and distribution irrespective of scale.

Fractal geometry grew from the realization that scientific method and euclidean geometry, in their effort to classify and simplify, did not adequately represent the scale independence or complexity of natural forms and systems. Rather, as scale increases, these classical ways of ordering the world reduce complexity to the point that the representations no longer adequately describe reality. In other words, euclidean geometry is unrealistically scale dependent, that is, the apparent texture of the form changes as scale changes.

Benoit Mandelbrot's concept of fractals (1982) addresses this complexity. For example, when geographers began computer mapping coastlines, they found that the lines did not adequately convey the natural form. As they added algorithms to insert additional nodes and make the lines more complex in character, these lines became more natural. To make the lines continue to feel appropriate as the scale was changed, the level of complexity needed to increase so that the apparent complexity was consistent, even though the scale changed. Like natural form, these fractals express a behavior or form irrespective of scale. As scale increases, so too does their detail, so that the apparent texture remains constant. With fractals, there is always more detail than meets the eye.

Whereas euclidean geometry holds distance constant regardless of scale, and the amount of relative detail changes with scale, in fractal geometry distances change with scale, but the apparent texture remains constant. Perhaps the most graphic example of the scale independence of mass and space, for example, is the film and associated book entitled *Powers of Ten* (Morris and Morris, 1982).

Chaos Theory

With euclidean geometry and simplistic mathematical models of form, there is the underlying belief that reality is ordered in some predictive or deterministic manner. There is an understood cause and effect relationship that explains all phenomena, once enough information is known. Therefore, euclidean geometry consists of lines, planes, and masses, ordered into circles and spheres, squares and cubes, triangles and pyramids. But as we saw in the previous section, these fixed, simplistic, pure shapes and forms are of little value in understanding the complexity of natural form. While the efficiency networks and evolving geometries of the previous section better explain some specific forms in nature, they do not allow for its spontaneity and the inability of cause and effect to fully explain natural phenomena or their behavior over time. What was needed was a means for understanding such things as the distributions of zigs and zags of a lightning bolt, or as stated above, the physical length of a coast line that appears to lengthen as the scale of measurement is increased, or the unpredictability of the weather.

Fractals are a part of a new and exciting science of chaos, which offers hope of providing this needed insight. This science presents a new type of mathematical order. As Douglas Hofstadter (1985) said, "It turns out that an eerie type of chaos can lurk just behind the facade of order—and yet, deep inside the chaos lurks an even eerier type of order." According to *chaos theory*, even a few variables can generate a fundamental randomness. More information does not (as a rational science would predict) eliminate the randomness.

Perhaps the best example of the difference between predictive and chaotic behavior is the difference between laminar fluid flow which is even and regular and turbulent flow which is uneven and irregular. This occurs, for example, when a column of cigarette smoke spontaneously breaks into violent swirls.

The science of chaos orders reality not by some euclidean principles applied to form, but rather by underlying processes and continuities of behavior that express themselves at all scales and times. It speaks not to a deterministic order, but to a probabalistic one, what James Gleick (1987) has called an "orderly disorder." It cuts across the traditional barriers of disciplines, from the turbulence of weather to the beat of the human heart, to the three-dimensional form of sand dunes. The science of chaos is highly mathematical yet it offers an explanation of the complex form and behavior of the everyday world. It is a type of science that can bring us closer to understanding the forms that grow from the duality of nature, and the complementarity of opposites, order, and spontaneity. Therefore it is a source of excitement for many designers.

REFERENCES

Colman, Samuel, and Coan, C. Arthur. 1912. *Nature's Harmonic Unity*. New York: Putnam.

Cook, Theodore. 1979. *The Curves of Life*. New York: Dover.

Doczi, Gyorgy. 1981. *The Power of Limits: Proportional Harmonies in Nature, Art and Architecture*. Boulder, CO: Shambhala.

Fuller, R. Buckminster. 1965. Conceptuality of Fundamental Structures. In *Structure in Art and in Science*. Gyorgy Kepes, editor. New York: Braziller.

Gleick, James. 1987. *Chaos: Making a New Science.* New York: Viking Press.

Hofstadter, Douglas. 1985. *Metamagical Themas: Questing for the Essence of Mind and Pattern.* New York: Basic Books.

Mendelbrot, Benoit. 1982. *The Fractal Geometry of Nature.* New York: W.H. Freeman.

Morris, P., and Morris, P. 1982. *Powers of Ten.* New York: Scientific American Books.

Pearce, Peter. 1978. *Structure in Nature Is a Strategy for Design.* Cambridge, MA: MIT Press.

Thompson, D'Arcy. 1963. *On Growth and Form,* Vols. I, II. London: Cambridge University Press.

Wachsmann, Konrad. 1961. *The Turning Point of Building.* New York: Reinhold.

SUGGESTED READINGS

Ching, Francis. 1979. *Architecture: Form, Space and Order.* New York: Van Nostrand Reinhold.

Lauer, David. 1979. *Design Basics.* New York: Holt, Rinehart and Winston.

10

Circulation as Ordering Mechanism

Our experience of the built environment is a temporal-spatial one. We experience space temporally (sequentially), that is, as a succession of perceptions, and from this sequence we develop an understanding of our spatial environment.

This chapter explores circulation as a means of structuring experience and as a generator of form. It begins with the movement of people, looking at pedestrian circulation as movement, material, design consideration, linkage and visual system, spatial experience, and temporal experience. It then explores other types of circulation systems, looking most closely at the system for movement of automobiles (including trucks) and then touching briefly on bus, rail, air, and water transit systems.

PEDESTRIAN CIRCULATION

The design of the pedestrian circulation system involves the simultaneous consideration of many issues. These include the manner in which the pedestrian moves, the surfaces over which people move, and visual, spatial, and temporal concerns.

Circulation as Movement

Our perception of the world is usually formed as we move from place to place. As in any assessment, this perception is not entirely an external one. It is also affected by the character, nature, and speed with which we move.

The character, nature, and speed at which we flow is influenced by the circulation path. Therefore, when designing, we must be able to get on the point of our pencils and understand the manner in which the land-

scape would be displayed as we moved. We also need to understand the forces that affect the manner in which one moves and that affect perception.

Character of Flow

The specific character of movement affects not only our mood as we traverse the landscape, but also the images we receive. As we peruse the line characters shown in Figure 10-1, and imagine moving along these lines of movement, our perceptions of the world would differ based upon the character of flow.

Direct movement imparts a sense of immediacy and purpose; indirect movement of tension or mystery. Fluid movement would allow for efficient travel and would promote a feeling of leisure. Meandering movement would impart a pensive or melancholy feeling. A circuitous route might cause one to stop and linger if there was time, but might be quite distressing if time were short. Energized, angular lines of movement can impart energy and a frenzied, or even schizophrenic feeling.

Nature of Flow

In addition to the character of the line of movement, its nature also affects our perception of place. If we enter by ascending, we focus on the overhead as we look to the sky (Figure 10-2). We struggle to the top, moving slowly, but have a feeling of accomplishment upon arrival.

If we descend into a place, on the other hand, our attention is focused downward. We become very sensitive to the ground surface, paving details, and so-forth. We move with ease, but sometimes at an

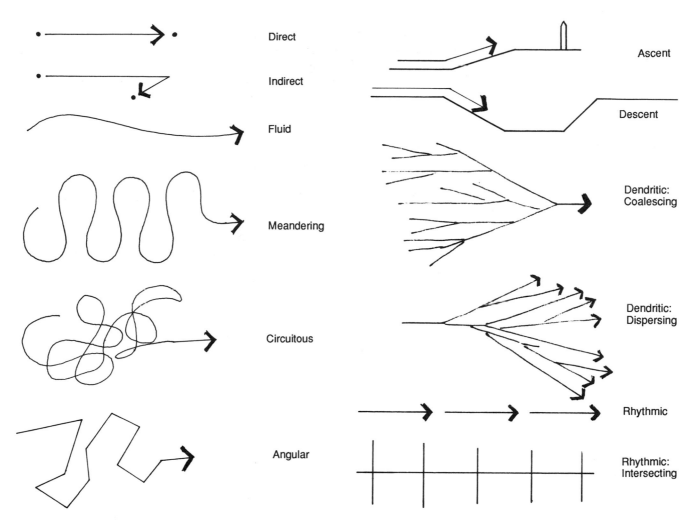

Figure 10-1. Character of flow.

Figure 10-2. Nature of flow.

uncomfortably quick pace. Ease of movement is usually accompanied by a feeling of withdrawal, coupled with the realization that the descent may necessitate a future struggle back to the top.

Dendritic flows allow for intersections in a loosely rhythmic fashion, with few conflicts and a minimum of turbulence. Coalescing flows build to a crescendo; dispersing flows diffuse these energies and can give a feeling of abandonment.

Most flows are rhythmic in nature. For example, when asked to describe their cross-campus journey to class, most students would do so by describing a series of movements to places along the way. As in most journeys, the mental images stored as a result of movement are a rhythmic flow from landmark to landmark, through an otherwise less memorable context.

Intersections impart a rhythmic nature to flow as they change the rate of movement, either through congestion or by inducing one to stop to access alternatives, or to watch the movement of others. Intersec-

tions usually serve as events along the path of movement.

Rate of Flow

Our perception of place changes with the rate at which we move. Moving quickly, we are relatively unaware of details. As we slow, we become more aware of the world around us.

As the path becomes more narrow, we intuitively accelerate and become more goal-oriented and less intimately aware to our context. As it widens, we relax, and become attuned; our senses come alive (Figure 10-3).

Forces That Affect Flow

Appropriate circulation character, nature and rate of flow are determined by many factors operating integratively. The distance to be traveled, the time available, and the innate need for sensual stimuli (enrichment) all affect pedestrian perception and therefore rate of flow. These variables should be effectively manipulated as the circulation system is designed.

If speed or economy is the goal, paths should be direct, reasonably wide, and flat. Impediments to flow (such as intersections) should be minimized. Conversely, if the design intent is sensory enrichment, then an indirect, circuitous or meandering character is more appropriate. In this case, lines of flow should present an evolving, stimulating, and interesting journey through a highly varied environment with rich sensual imagery. Variations of light, materials, tex-

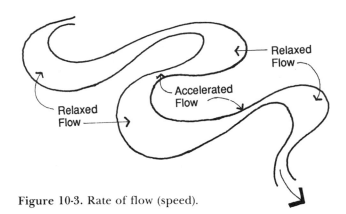

Figure 10-3. Rate of flow (speed).

ture, form, and scale would be appropriate, with this variety structured temporally in response to circulation form as one moves along the path. Usually the design of pedestrian circulation systems includes both alternatives so that the viewer can select the appropriate path based on time availability and desired enrichment.

Human Tendencies

As we design circulation systems and specific elements within these systems, there are certain human tendencies that should be kept in mind. For example, we tend to move toward goals, that is, sensual landmarks. Longer trips are structured as a series of movements to intermediate goals (Figure 10-4). In moving to these goals, we usually travel the easiest route and tend to pursue a particular direction until forced to deviate from it. If time is not short, we seek the most pleasant experience, both physiologically and psychologically. On a hot day, we seek shade, on a cold day, the sun. We also seek variety. We vary our speed as the path changes its width or slope and as the richness and stimulus load of the environment changes. We are enticed by movement, by objects at eye level, by hints of experiences to come, and by breaks in the perceivable pattern.

As animals that evolved in vegetative ecotones, we

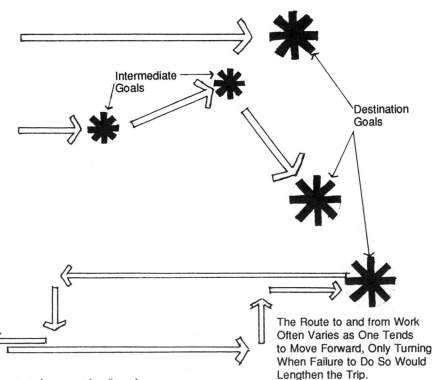

Figure 10-4. Movement as the pursuit of goals.

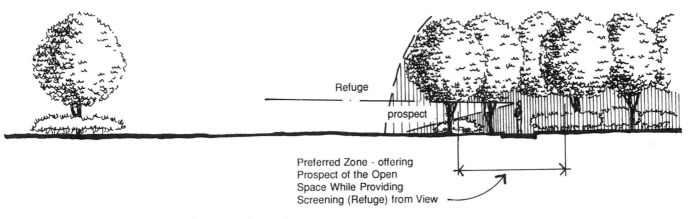

Figure 10-5. Vegetative edge and perceived security.

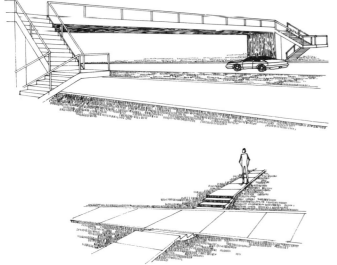

Figure 10-6. Wasted effort.

Figure 10-7. Directional character.

instinctively feel more secure along the edges of spaces. We prefer to move along these edges rather those across large openings (Figure 10-5). In super-human-scaled space, we desire enclosure; yet in overly confined spaces, we desire freedom. We also desire environmental understanding and sensory enrichment.

As we move, we tend to avoid places that are unsafe, disordered, ugly, or uncomfortable. We avoid steep grades and steps up (particularly as we get older). We avoid obviously wasted effort, such as the elevated road crossing (even through it may afford increased safety), or intersections that do not align vertically (Figure 10-6).

We pause or stop as we reach an intermediate goal (such as a landscape feature), when we experience an environmental change (such as a change in paving material), or when we alter direction or gradient. We also feel an urge to stop when movement is restricted, when we come to a decision point or a place with strong identity, personality, or physical or sensual amenities such as a view, a bench, shade on a hot day, or sun on a cold day.

Our movement is influenced by the directional characteristics of the place, by the nature of the circulation path itself, and by visual sequences (Figure 10-7).

Circulation as Material

The palette of materials from which circulation elements may be built is quite large. The appropriateness of any given material is determined by functional and sensual issues and other design considerations. Each of these materials has its own unique characteristics, potential to respond to these design considerations, and constraints that they place on design. The sensitive designer is particularly adept at matching circulation need with appropriate material.

Functional and Sensual Issues

In the design of pedestrian circulation systems, certain pragmatic considerations affect the appropriateness of a surface material for use in a given situation. The type and amount of traffic, weather conditions under which use will occur, surface temperatures, and maintenance considerations are only a few of these pragmatic considerations.

Type of Traffic. The pedestrian moves relatively slowly and in direct contact with the environment. Visual characteristics of the landscape such as line, form, color, texture, rhythm, proportion, balance, scale, and directionality are therefore quite important.

Walking is a relatively nonconstraining type of movement. It places few limits on design. For example, the pedestrian's weight is spread over a reasonably large ground contact (especially those of us with E width shoes), and the human body is capable of negotiating steep grades and abrupt changes in direction. Design of the pedestrian circulation system is, therefore, not a factor of physical limitations of the body, but rather of physical comfort or psychological issues, such as the sensual experience as one moves from place to place. Materials are selected or rejected in part for the way they feel, or for their ability to evoke certain sensations or associations. For example, soil and sod are resilient to the touch and are psychologically relaxing; grass is cool but soggy in rainy weather; concrete can be used in all weather conditions, but is visually and physically hard, hot, reflective, and generally unfriendly. Coarse surface textures can be very uncomfortable as they strain the ankle joints and leg muscles.

When the pedestrian dons a bicycle, speed increases and environmental awareness and scale perception change. Surface textures become even more critical, coarse textures more problematic. Joints, cracks, and misalignments become downright dangerous.

The weight of the passenger and bicycle are distributed over a very small area, especially now that the narrow tire, ten-speed bicycle has become the norm. Bicycleways must therefore be surfaced with a strong, firm, and consistent material with tight joints.

Amount of Traffic. Frequency of use also affects the appropriateness of materials used for circulation elements. While the pedestrian can walk comfortably on lawn surfaces (and in dry weather generally finds the experience refreshing), this surface is able to tolerate only limited use. Under heavy traffic, grass will die and soil will erode. As compared to lawn or ground cover areas, paved surfaces can sustain heavy use.

Therefore, high-traffic circulation elements should be paved.

Weather Conditions. Unpaved surfaces are generally fair-weather ones and will be muddy or impassible in wet periods. On the other hand, paved surfaces maintain their rigidity in various conditions, making them all-weather pathways. They also resist erosion by wind or water. Smooth surfaces tend to be dangerously slick when wet or icy.

Surface Temperature. Lawns and ground covers absorb solar energy and use it through photosynthesis to power life processes. They are also evaporatively cooled by plant evapotranspiration. The air above these surfaces remains cool as do the surfaces themselves.

Wood has a low conductivity. It absorbs and gives off heat very slowly. As such, it is sensed as being at or near skin temperature and is pleasant to walk on in most temperature conditions. On the other hand, brick, stone, concrete, and bituminous concrete absorb and release heat quickly. They are hot in the summer and cold in the winter. In addition, the air above them is often characterized by unpleasant temperature extremes.

Maintenance. Although initially more costly, paved surfaces are usually much easier to maintain than are nonpaved ones. Soil requires raking, ground covers require fertilizing, watering, and weeding. Lawns require these maintenance activities as well as frequent mowing.

Edge Character. Paved surfaces maintain a clean, crisp edge and a more assertive line character than do nonpaved surfaces. Unpaved surfaces, and paved ones where adjacent materials are allowed to encroach, provide a much softer naturalistic edge.

Circulation as Design Consideration

Circulation surfaces can respond to, and communicate, design considerations. These would include concerns for use, form, safety, scale, and directionality.

Use

When the intended use of a surface changes, the difference in use can be communicated by a change in material (Figure 10-8). These changes can occur in response to differing physical needs, or can occur to convey important information, for example, in visually announcing a change in intended use, or level of safety. Material changes can also serve as subliminal cues to induce a desired change in behavior as one moves from one area to another.

Form

The surface, or its material, color, or texture can change to communicate form. For example, the brick and concrete plaza in Figure 10-8 gives distinguishable form, visual significance, and unique sense of place to the brick seating area. Figure 10-9, on the other hand, expresses this area as merely an extension of the plaza form.

Safety

Changes in the circulation material or surface condition can draw attention to physical hazards. As one moves along the brick walk in Figure 10-10, for example, the asphaltic street is perceived as a hazard. The pedestrian is cued to an inherently unsafe condition.

By allowing the walk material to extend into and across the street, the design implies the pedestrian has the right of way and alerts the driver to be especially cautious and to keep a watchful eye for pedestrians (Figure 10-11). The designer must take care, however, not to create a false sense of security for the pedestrian and must be certain that the driver can see and understand the meaning of the material change.

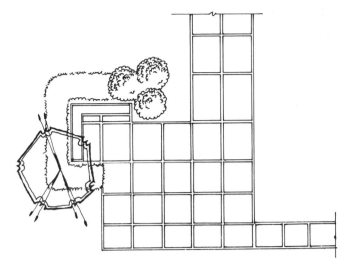

Figure 10-9. Material consistency and change in use.

Figure 10-10. Material as cue to pedestrian.

Figure 10-11. Material as cue to driver.

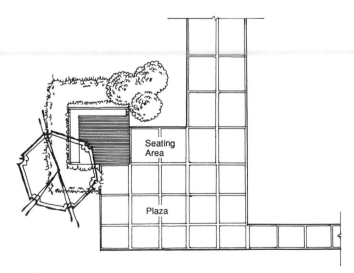

Figure 10-8. Material change to reinforce a change in use.

Scale

The design of circulation elements affects the perceived size of a place. The width of the element implies scale, as does the size of the space at intersections (Figure 10-12). Pedestrian paths 3 to 6 feet in width impart an intimate human scale; those 6 to 15 feet wide, a human scale; those 15 to 40 feet wide, a public human scale. Spaces up to 48 feet in size (which often occur at circulation intersections) support an intimate human scale; those 48 to 72 feet a human scale; those up to 500 feet, a public human scale.

Most ground surface materials (except grass, ground cover, sand-set unit pavers, and asphaltic concrete) require expansion joints to accommodate temperature changes within the material. Rigid pavements also need these joints to accommodate soil expansion without structurally cracking. In a design sense, these joints can be used as lines of continuity to relate pieces of a ground composition, or to relate ground surfaces to adjacent buildings. These relationships will be discussed in detail in Chapter 12.

Expansion joints can also affect the perceived size or scale of a circulation element. When expansion joints are nonexistent or understated, the viewer perceives the size of the entire element. When joints are pronounced, the units formed by expansion joints become the perceived visual size and the paving seems smaller in scale (Figures 10-13 and 10-14).

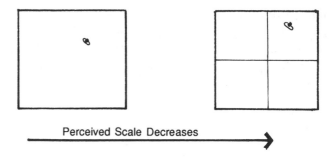

Perceived Scale Decreases

Figure 10-13. Joints and scale perception.

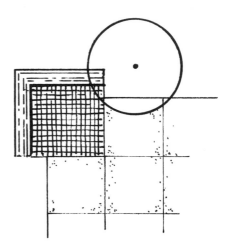

Figure 10-14. Material change and joints for scale modification.

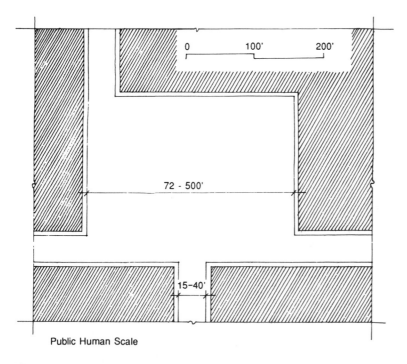

Figure 10-12. Circulation elements and scale.

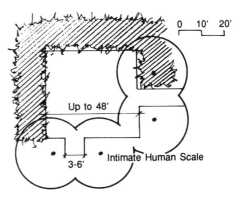

Directionality

Circulation elements usually have a linear character, that is, they imply direction (Figure 10-15). These directional characteristics can be modified by changes in materials and by the joint pattern.

Figure 10-15. Linear nature of circulation elements.

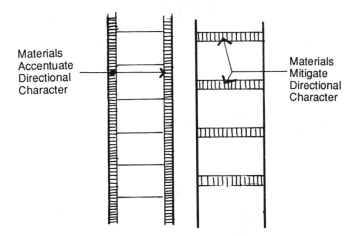

Figure 10-16. Material change to affect directionality.

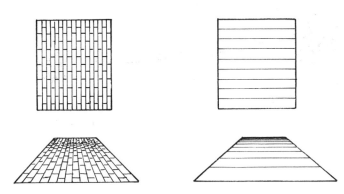

Figure 10-17. Joints and directionality.

Materials. Changes in materials that run the length of the path can strengthen the linear nature of a circulation element and make the path seem narrower and longer. Conversely, changes in material, as bands across the path, can decrease directional character and make the path seem wider and shorter (Figure 10-16).

Joints. Joints within the surface can also affect directional character. Many materials, such as stone or masonry, are modular units, that is, the surface is built by a large number of smaller units. The manner in which these modules are laid, and their jointing pattern, affects directional character (Figure 10-17). Like changes of material, joint patterns that run lengthwise make the walk appear longer and narrower; crosswise patterns make the path appear wider and shorter.

Control joints and expansion joints in pavings (both modular and monolithic) can also be used to either increase or decrease the directional character of circulation elements (Figure 10-18).

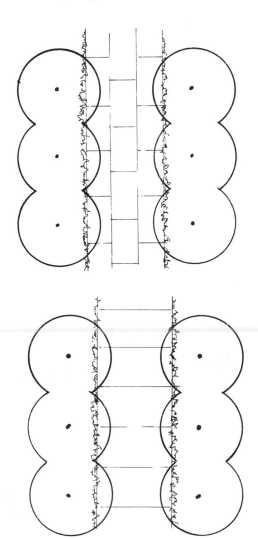

Figure 10-18. Control joints and directionality.

Circulation as Linkage and Visual System

Circulation systems, in their most basic sense, have three components: traffic generators, linear connectors, and events along these connectors (Figure 10-19). The generators serve as goals, which by their presence create a certain number of trips along the connectors. The number of trips and the conditions under which they must function affect the size, material, and design of the connectors. Events occur along the connectors, most commonly in the vicinity of traffic generators, or where connectors cross, that is, intersection points.

The junction of traffic generator and connector is usually considered a special place. Often the connector will expand in response to this place, for example, the plaza at the foot of a church, or at the base of a high-use building (Figure 10-20).

The intersection of circulation connectors also has unique placeness. It is at these places that flows cross and at which people must make decisions. The congestion that results here usually requires greater dimensions. In addition, the chance encounters that occur when pedestrianways cross, makes intersections special places to stop and talk. The path usually responds to these forces as it opens into plazas with benches and other amenities that encourage one to linger (Figure 10-21).

Linkage

In a purely functional sense, circulation paths link generators of traffic. The first step in designing circulation elements usually involves the identification and connection of these traffic generators.

In the earliest stages of designing a circulation system, functional issues such as traffic generators and desired linkages are often communicated via circulation diagrams. These diagrams are usually drawn to show, via line width or numbers, the relative or absolute flow (Figure 10-22).

Visual System

In addition to their functional aspects, circulation elements and the systems they comprise have major form significance. Visually speaking, it is usually desirable that circulation elements read not as unrelated lines, but as an integrated system of form (Figure 10-23). As a system, these lines relate one to another.

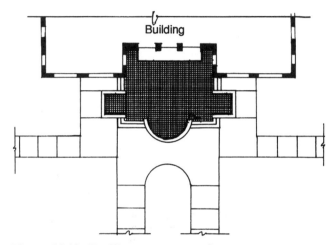

Figure 10-20. Traffic generator as place.

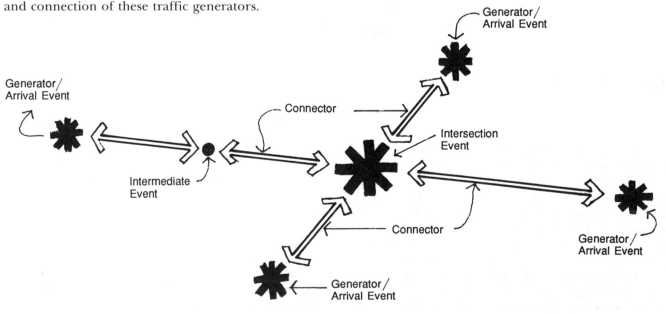

Figure 10-19. Circulation as generator, connector, and event.

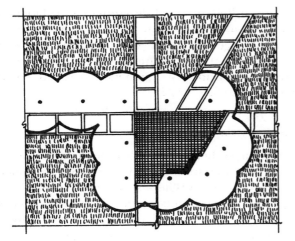

Figure 10-21. Intersection as place.

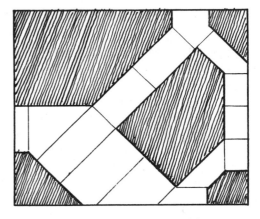

Figure 10-23. Circulation as system of form.

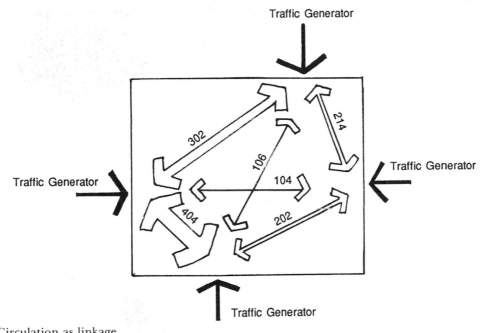

Figure 10-22. Circulation as linkage.

Whereas Figure 10-22 can be seen as a functional diagram of desired linkage, the form shown in Figure 10-23 provides for these connections, requires only minor adjustments to desired travel, and makes a unified form statement. The inexperienced designer often succeeds in diagramming circulation, but tries to apply this diagram literally to the site, usually with little visual meaning or experiential success. The experienced designer interprets the circulation diagram, applying elements and principles of design to create an integrated form that facilitates desired connections while helping to establish the intended character of the place.

Circulation as Spatial Experience

The circulation system does not occur in a visual vacuum. Our visual perception of place is primarily a spatial experience. If circulation form is to have relevancy, and if circulation systems are to be designed so as to maximize the visual experience, they must relate to the spatial composition and character of the site. To do so, circulation form must visually relate to spatial form. It must place the viewer in an appropriate relationship to site spaces and must establish compatible circulation and spatial character. The experience of moving along the circulation system must also or-

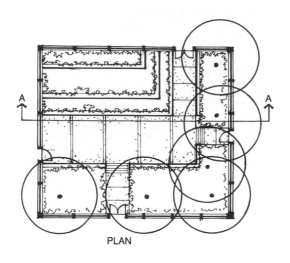

PLAN

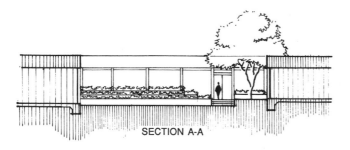

SECTION A-A

Figure 10-24. Circulation and spatial statement.

ganize spatial sequences in a meaningful manner. It must finally address temporal characteristics as one moves across the site. The first two issues will be discussed in the remainder of this section; the third in the next section.

Circulation Form and Spatial Form

If Figure 10-23 were seen as an enclosed courtyard, surrounded by glass walls, and with doors serving as traffic generators, the circulation system would connect and accommodate movement between these doors. It would also present a unified form statement. However, it would do little to reinforce the design statement of "rectangular space within the overall mass." Figure 10-24, on the other hand, provides for necessary linkages and establishes unified form, while supporting the design statement. Movement is only slightly more circuitous, and the circulation form becomes an integral component of an overall spatial intent.

While our visual perception of place is primarily spatial, the manner in which we perceive space is usually determined by the circulation path. It determines where we move, our point of reference, and our relation to the place. It affects also our perceptions of spatial size and character and our sense of security.

When we move through a large open space, as shown in Figure 10-25, we feel dwarfed and insecure.

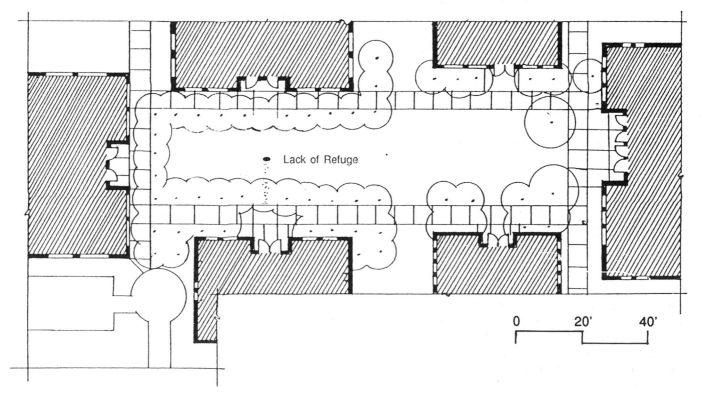

Lack of Refuge

0   20'   40'

Figure 10-25. Insecurity in large open spaces.

Prehistoric man as an edge species, found safety in the vegetated edge and soon discovered that venturing into the open was patently unsafe. The reptilian recesses of our brains that still determine instinctive behavior continue to perceive insecurity in large open spaces. On the other hand, if circulation occurs either near to, or enclosed within, the edge of major spaces, we feel more comfortable (Figure 10-26).

With the above in mind, the relationship between spatial form and circulation system design becomes a powerful one. The designer can impart mystery by concealing space, security by implying refuge from it, or suspense by leaving the viewer exposed within an uncomfortably large space.

Circulation and Spatial Character

The character of the space and that of the circulation system should support a common design theme. In order to do so, both must have compatible form. In addition, circulation form should place one in the appropriate position so as to maximize perception of the spatial character and composition.

Formal spatial compositions imply entering on axis, informal ones an asymmetrical approach. Large-scale spaces are made to feel more expansive by a confined and small-scaled approach; small ones are made more confining by an expansive approach.

Circulation as Temporal Experience

Perception addresses the relatedness of events in space and time, and the individual cognitively responds to sequential stimuli. The circulation system affects our location as we move through the environment, the speed at which we move, and the temporal sequences we perceive. The designer determines the circulation form and spatial form, creating the story line from which perception is built. This story line should include the appropriate cues, inducements, psychological filters, assurances, and placeness to enrich the quality of the experience.

Circulation story lines can include different modes of transportation, such as the story line of pedestrian movement from the corporate office, automobile travel through the urban and suburban roadway system, and automobile and pedestrian movement on site, culminating with arrival inside the house. In an effectively designed story line, the mode of transportation, character of the path, designed mood of the place, and behavior of the user should all be choreographed into a meaningful designed experience.

Most story lines are progressive, that is, they move toward something. In this movement, they may be casual, seemingly unplanned, and informal (Figure 10-27). Conversely, progression can be formal, highly regular, forcefully ordered, and obviously planned

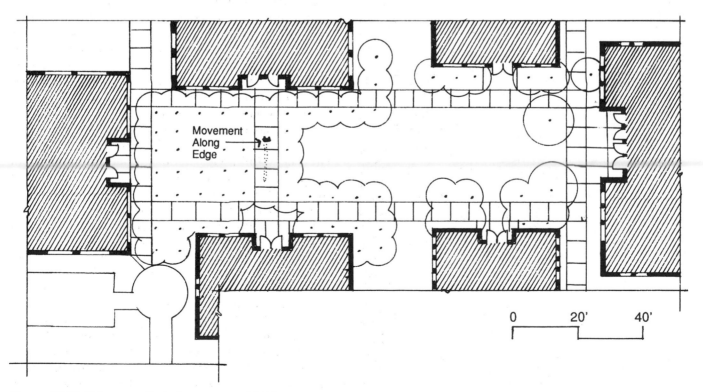

Figure 10-26. Edge security in large open spaces.

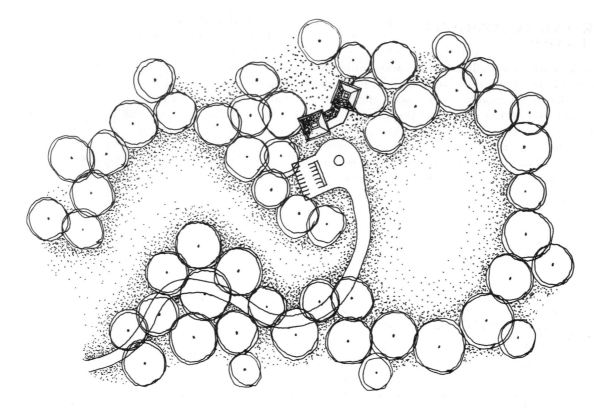

Figure 10-27. Casual storyline.

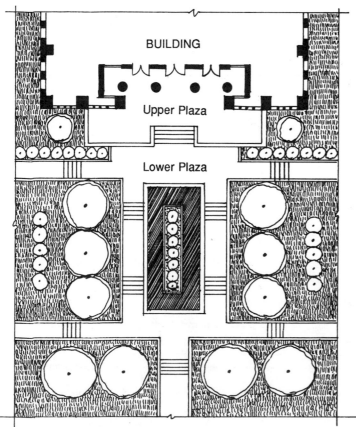

Figure 10-28. Formal storyline.

(Figure 10-28). In either case, the evolving story line is essential to our experience of the place.

Effective dynamic circulation story lines also tend to be rhythmic. They progress toward goals, but as goals are approached or reached, new ones appear. When asked to recall a route frequently traveled, most people describe the route as a story line structured around commonly recognized landmarks, that is, places or events along the path.

The creative designer will consciously create rich story lines and implement them through spatial and circulatory form. Goals and intermediate events will be determined as will their sequence, periodicity, and intensity. Circulation paths will provide access, character, suspense, and transition; events will provide climax and satisfaction and will serve as special places rich with concentrations of meaning.

The sense of entry, appropriate entry sequences, and designed story lines as one approaches and enters a building are design issues common to most site design projects. The entry story line is usually one of the major designed experiences, preparing the viewer emotionally and psychologically for the sense of place and behavior settings of the building. The entry statement as a part of the built site is a major design issue, and effective entry sequences will be discussed in detail in Chapter 12.

TRUCK AND AUTOMOBILE CIRCULATION

As any real estate agent will tell you, automobile access is a major determinant of land use. The location of land in relation to the roadway network, that is, its access, usually determines its market potential.

The road system is also a major determinant of urban form. This system that serves trucks and automobiles must address several often conflicting issues. It must provide access from an almost infinite number of entry points (each residence, office building, or other traffic generator). It must facilitate movement with speeds that will minimize travel times while maintaining safety. It usually also serves as the major system for social contact in residential neighborhoods and provides for storage of the automobile while providing access to pedestrian systems. To satisfy these often conflicting goals, the roadway system is organized hierarchically (Figures 10-29 and 10-30).

As shown in Figure 10-30, a desirable roadway hierarchy separates types and volumes of traffic, design speed and efficiency of flow, and design function.

Each of the roadway types within the hierarchy is

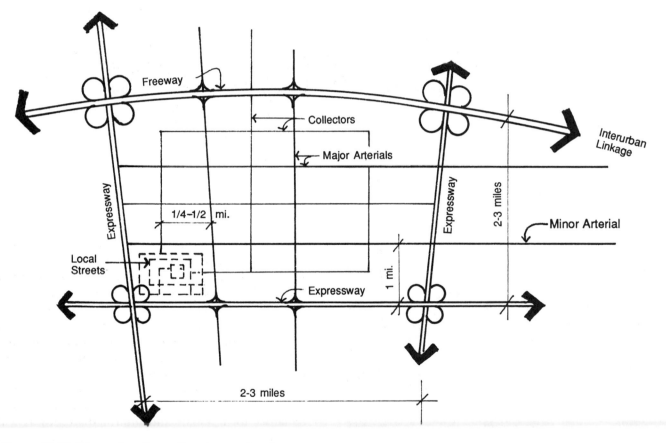

Figure 10-29. Hierarchy of street/roadway network.

Traffic Type	Truck	⟶	Pedestrian
Traffic Volume	High	⟶	Low
Efficiency (Speed)	High	⟶	Low
Function	Social Barrier	⟶	Social Interaction

Street Type	Freeway⟶	Expressway ⟶	Arterial ⟶	Collector ⟶	Sub-Collector ⟶	Local ⟶	Cul-de-sac

Figure 10-30. Roadway hierarchy.

designed to serve specific functions within the urban roadway system. Each is therefore designed uniquely, as shown in Table 10-1 and Figures 10-31 to 10-39.

The remainder of this section first reviews the roadway system and its elements, looking at design considerations, social function, safety, and efficiency. It then explores ecological relationships as a design issue and closes with discussions of automobile storage and vehicular service.

Design Considerations

Automobiles, trucks, and buses are quite heavy and exert concentrated loads. To resist these loads, paving surfaces must be firm and structurally secure in all expected weather conditions.

There are numerous considerations that must be addressed when designing elements within the roadway system. These include the manipulation of hori-

Table 10-1. Roadway hierarchy.

Roadway	Desired Spacing	Design Function	Design Speed	Design Features	Desired R.O.W. Width	Desired Pavement Width	Desired Max. Grade	Comments
Freeway	Varies w/ regional settlement pattern	Provides regional continuity & interurban linkage	60 mph	Limited access; consistent flow; grade separated intersections	200–400'	Varies; 8–60' median; 12 lanes; 8–10' shoulders Figure 10.31	3%	Preferably depressed through urban areas; service roads w/ acceleration & deceleration ramps required for ingress & egress
Expressway	Generally radiate from, or circumferential to, urban center; 2–3 miles spacing desired	Provides urban continuity	50 mph	Only grade separate automobile or pedestrian crossings allowed; parking prohibited	200–300'	Varies 8–30' median; 12 lanes 8–10' shoulders Figure 10.32	4%	Controlled access usually at grade; service roads required with acceleration & deceleration lanes at ingress and egress
Major arterials	1½–2 miles	To link various parts of the urban area; usually forms boundaries of neighborhoods	35–45 mph	Channelized intersections; parking prohibited; access points usually limited to 600' O.C.	120–150'(150–300' to maintain existing vegetated median or to provide reserved bus lane or mass transit)	24' section each side of median; usually 72–84' out-to-out pavem't; wider for existing vegetated median, reserved bus lane, or mass transit Figure 10.33 Figure 10.34	4%	Require planting strips 5–10' wide & 5' detached walks in urban areas; 30' setbacks for bldgs. 60' where buildings back up to street
Minor arterial (secondary road)	¾–1 mile	To provide rapid linkage from collector streets or arterials	35–40 mph	Signals at major intersections; stop signs at minor intersections; access points, usually limited; no parking	80'	Usually 60' consisting of 2–24' roadways (2–12' driving lanes separated by 12' median) Figure 10.35	5%	Require planting strips 5–10' wide & 5' detached walks; frontage not desirable but where it must occur 30' setback for building; 60' where buildings back up to street
Collector street	¼–½ miles	To link residential streets to cross town arterials; to collect neighborhood traffic, Dominant form giver of neighborhood	30 mph	Stop signs at side streets; intersections no closer than 660' O.C.	64'	44' (2–12' traffic lanes & 2–10' parking lanes) Figure 10.36	5%	Require detached 4' walks, preferably with planting strips; all residents fronting onto collector must be rear entry, to avoid backing into traffic

Table 10-1. Roadway hierarchy *(Continued)*

Roadway	Desired Spacing	Design Function	Design Speed	Design Features	Desired R.O.W. Width	Desired Pavement Width	Desired Max. Grade	Comments
Subcollector	At blocks	To provide access to cul-de-sacs and parking courts	30 mph	Nonconductive to through traffic	60′	36′ Figure 10.37	6%	Avoid layout that will encourage through traffic between collectors; require detached 4′ walks preferably w/planting strips
Local street	At blocks	To provide access to residences & cul-de-sacs	25 mph	Nonconductive to through traffic	60′	36′ where parking permitted; 27′ where parking not permitted (20 d. u. maximum) Figure 10.38	6%	Avoid layout that will encourage through traffic between collectors
Cul-de-sacs	At blocks	Access to residence; prohibit all through traffic; maximum protection for pedestrian	20 mph	Street open at only one end; turn around at other	50′ (90′ diameter at turn around)	24–30′ (75′ diameter at turn around) Figure 10.39	5%	Maximum length determined by fire service (usually 500–600′)

Source: Adapted from George Nez, *Standards for New Urban Development—the Denver Background.* Adapted by permission of Urban Land Institute, 625 Indiana Avenue, N.W., Washington, D.C. 20004.

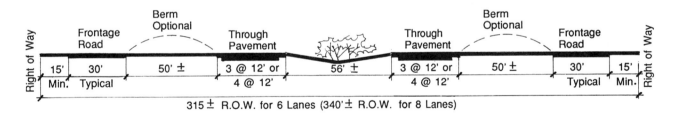

Figure 10-31. Rural freeway cross section (variable). (Adapted from *A Policy on Geometric Design of Highways and Streets,* by the American Association of State Highway and Transportation Officials)

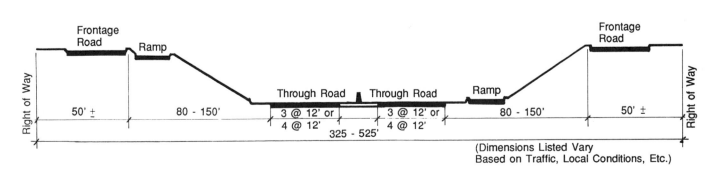

Figure 10-32. "Through town" depressed expressway (highly variable). (Adapted from *A Policy on Geometric Design of Highways and Streets,* by the American Association of State Highway and Transportation Officials))

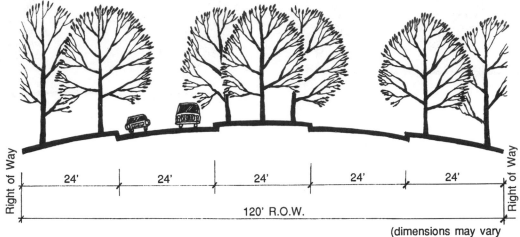

Figure 10-33. Major arterials.

24'   24'   24'   24'   24'

120' R.O.W.

(dimensions may vary with traffic, local conditions, etc.)

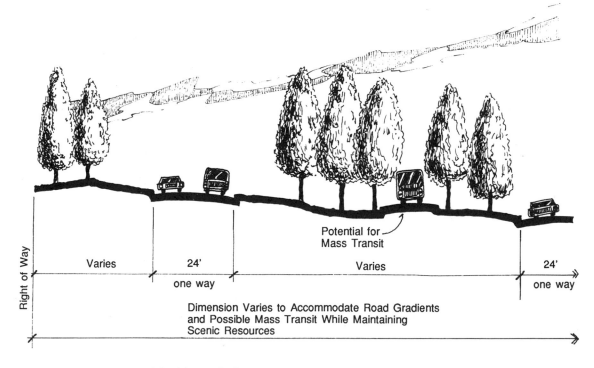

Potential for Mass Transit

Right of Way

Varies   24'
one way

Varies   24'
one way

Dimension Varies to Accommodate Road Gradients and Possible Mass Transit While Maintaining Scenic Resources

Figure 10-34. Typical major arterial with scenic feature and/or mass transit.

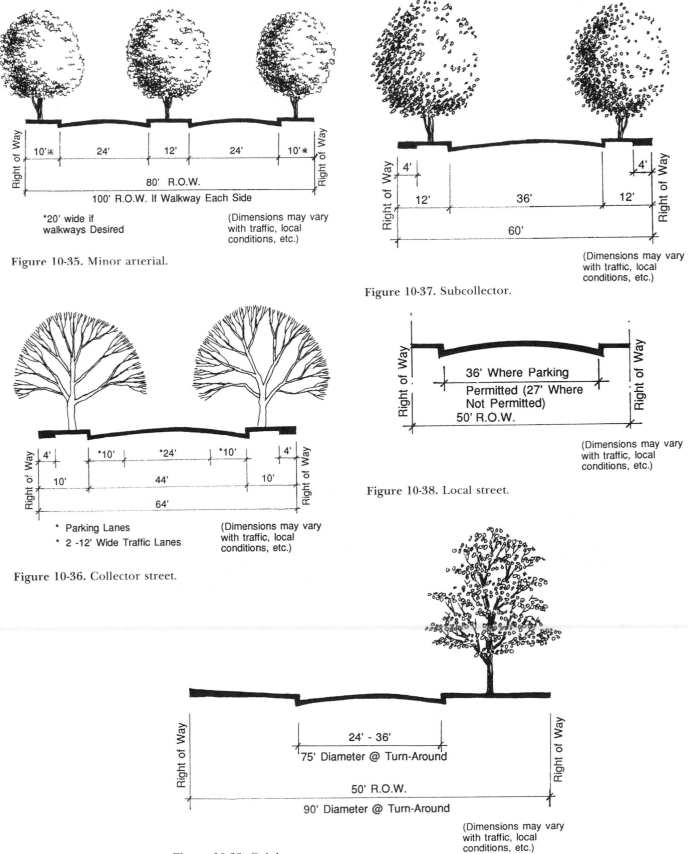

Figure 10-35. Minor arterial.

Right of Way

10'* | 24' | 12' | 24' | 10'*

80' R.O.W.

100' R.O.W. If Walkway Each Side

*20' wide if walkways Desired

(Dimensions may vary with traffic, local conditions, etc.)

Figure 10-37. Subcollector.

Right of Way

4' | 12' | 36' | 12' | 4'

60'

(Dimensions may vary with traffic, local conditions, etc.)

Figure 10-36. Collector street.

Right of Way

4' | *10' | *24' | *10' | 4'

10' | 44' | 10'

64'

* Parking Lanes
* 2 -12' Wide Traffic Lanes

(Dimensions may vary with traffic, local conditions, etc.)

Figure 10-38. Local street.

Right of Way

36' Where Parking Permitted (27' Where Not Permitted)

50' R.O.W.

(Dimensions may vary with traffic, local conditions, etc.)

Figure 10-39. Cul-de-sac.

Right of Way

24' - 36'

75' Diameter @ Turn-Around

50' R.O.W.

90' Diameter @ Turn-Around

(Dimensions may vary with traffic, local conditions, etc.)

zontal and vertical alignment so as to provide adequate sightlines for the speed at which vehicles are intended to travel; the provision of adequate pavement and right-of-way width to accommodate the travel surface, pedestrianways, bicycleways, infrastructure, screening, and other needs; separate roadways (boulevarded sections) at high speed or steep terrain; visual coherence and required sightlines; informational system (signage); visual amenities and scenic resources; response to landform, and necessary regrading; and the design of rich appropriate sensory story lines to be experienced from the roadway.

Social Function

The urban roadway system does much to order our social patterns. In suburbia, for example, it affects our degree of social interaction with our neighbors. The vast majority of our neighborhood acquaintances occur not as a function of physical distance, but as a function of automobile route and travel distance. While we know the neighbors that live along our common approach roadway, we know few of the ones that adjoin our back property lines. The street provides not only the mechanism for contact as we arrive and depart the residence, but also a place for interaction to occur.

Streets perform two distinct social functions. On the one hand, cul-de-sacs and residential streets, with small numbers of slow (and primarily automobile) traffic, function as neighborhood centers. They are the places where most social contact occurs. On the other hand, streets with heavier, faster, and less homogeneous traffic serve as neighborhood boundaries, separating one neighborhood from another. These streets define the edges of urban social units.

Safety

Danger occurs when speeds increase and when differing traffic types and rates of flow interface. For example, the intersection of pedestrian flow and that of high-speed trucks or automobiles is inherently dangerous. An hierarchical organization of streets within the roadway system allows the specialization of streets to increase as their design speed or traffic volume increase, or as the types of traffic become more diverse. It also allows access points to be limited in number along these roadways. By so doing, the number of danger points or interfaces are kept to a minimum, without unduly compromising convenience.

In addressing safety in roadway design, one should realize that design speed, reaction time, and braking distance function together to determine minimum forward sight distances, curve radii, and degree of curvature; maximum gradients; and minimum length of vertical curve for each percent of change in roadway gradient (Table 10-2).

Safety also demands that all habitable structures be accessible in emergency situations. When a single roadway point of entry occurs, the maximum length of the roadway beyond that point is determined by limitations of the fire fighting system. Therefore, in most municipalities, cul-de-sacs are limited to 500 to 600 feet in length, so that all portions of all buildings can be accessed with the standard length fire hose carried on their municipal fire fighting equipment.

Efficiency

The vehicular circulation system consists of traffic generators and destinations linked by a system of roadway connectors. Good design maximizes effi-

Table 10-2. Design speed alignment standards.

Design Speed (mph)	Minimum Forward Site Distance	Curve Radius (ft)	Degree Curve	Maximum Gradient (%)	Minimum Length of Vertical Curve for Each 1% Change in Grade (ft)
20	150			12	10
30	200	260	22	10	20
40	275	477	12	8	35
50	350	819	7	7	70
60	475	1146	5	5	150
70	600	1910	3	4	200

Source: Adapted from Lynch and Hack, *Site Planning,* © 1984 by the Massachusetts Institute of Technology. Published by MIT Press and reprinted by permission.

ciency and safety, while minimizing congestion and travel times.

Efficiency is increased as local traffic is separated from through traffic, as the system is designed so that major high-speed roadways carry a maximum percentage of through-traffic vehicles, and as intersections are minimized on high-speed roads.

Ecological Relationships

Roadways should respond to existing landform and land suitabilities. When the landform becomes steep, roadways should often be boulevarded to minimize the area of cut and fill required (Figure 10-40). Guidelines and standards for roadway planning, design, and construction should also respond to local ecological conditions.

In areas of excessive flatness, drainage requirements and the possibilities of flooding often require greatly expanded rights-of-way. This is especially true when one wishes to maintain indigenous vegetative communities (Figure 10-41).

Automobile Storage

Automobile storage involves transition from the roadway, approach to the parking area (which often includes a building arrival story line, complete with passenger drop-off), automobile parking (usually in a space 9 feet wide x 18 feet long), and access to the pedestrianway.

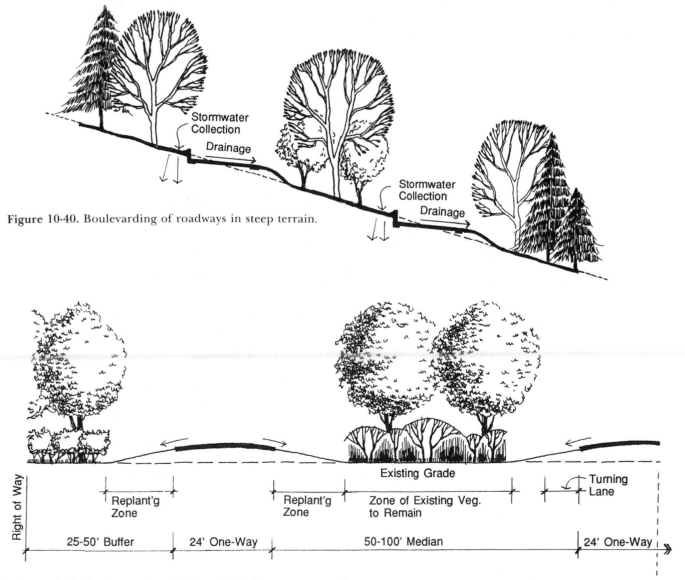

Figure 10-40. Boulevarding of roadways in steep terrain.

Figure 10-41. Roadway at floodplain with indigenous vegetation.

Transition from the Roadway

Transition from the roadway to parking access usually includes the provision of appropriate sightlines, desired turning radii, and in cases of major high-speed roadways, acceleration and deceleration lanes with large entry turning radii. Specific transition requirements for major drives depend upon the design speed of the roadway. In addition, local ordinances usually preclude major site access points within 250 feet of intersections on collectors and limit substantially the number of access points to more major roadways.

Approach to Parking Area

The approaches to parking areas usually include the primary entry story lines, as well as covered (porte-cochere) or uncovered passenger drop-off areas. The effectiveness of these story lines, in large measure, determines how we feel about the project design, and our frame of mind as we enter the building(s).

In the United States, we drive on the right side of the roadway, and passengers generally sit on the right side of the automobile. It is therefore desirable for the vehicle to approach the building from the structure's right side, allowing passenger drop-off on the building front curb in such a manner that the passenger does not have to cross automobile traffic to enter the building. When leaving the building, it is also preferable for the automobile to approach the building from the right, allowing passenger pickup from the building front curb, without walking across the street (Figure 10-42). It is also desirable for passenger drop-off areas to be separated from the through flow of traffic.

Automobile Parking

The automobile storage area consists of two parts: the drive through the storage area, and the parking stalls that this drive accesses (Figure 10-43). If this is kept in mind during design, areas of wasted paving and unnecessary site impact can be avoided.

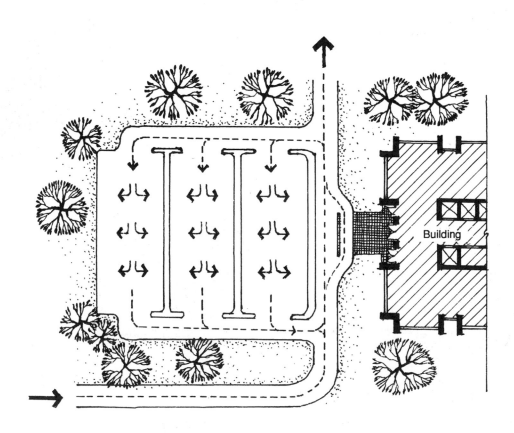

Figure 10-42. Building approach, passenger drop-off, and parking movements.

The width of the drive within parking bays is dependent upon its function (one- or two-way traffic) and, in the case of one-way traffic, the angle at which parking stalls address the access drive (Figure 10-44).

Parking areas should be designed, when possible, as flow through areas (Figure 10-45). A common (though woefully inadequate) alternative, the dead end parking bay, provides parking spaces from which one must drive backwards to exit the parking lot (Figure 10-46). A somewhat improved though still unsatisfactory solution, the "dead head," allows proper exiting from each parking stall, but requires driving backwards to exit the lot, should all the spaces be occupied (Figure 10-47).

Parking for the physically impaired should be located most conveniently to the pedestrian destination point. The automobile storage unit must be enlarged to a 13-foot width to allow for egress from the vehicle and wheelchair movements (Figure 10-48). The parking stall must include a functionally located safe ramp up to the walkway system.

Access to the Pedestrianway

The automobile storage area usually introduces the visitor to the pedestrian experience of the site. As one leaves the automobile, all-weather walking surfaces are highly desirable, but these will generally be used only if they occur in the line of movement to the building entry (Figure 10-49).

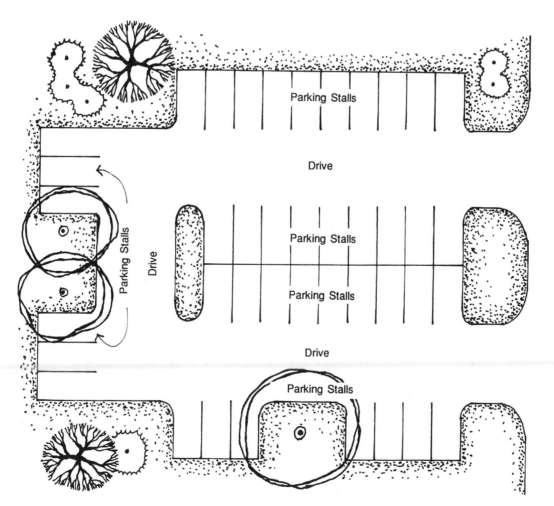

Figure 10-43. Parking as drive and stalls.

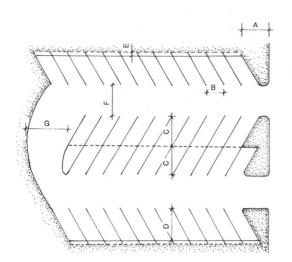

		45°	60°	90°
Offset	A	18'	11'	1'-6"
Car Space	B	12'	10'	8'-7"
Stall Depth	C	16'	18'	18'-6"
Stall Depth	D	18'	19'	19'-0"
Overhang	E	2'	2'-3"	2'-9"
Drive	F	13'	17"-6"	25'-0"
Turn-Around	G	17'	14'	14'-0"

Figure 10-44. Parking drive and stall dimension.

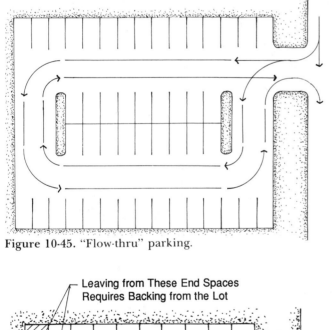

Figure 10-45. "Flow-thru" parking.

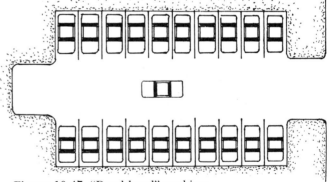

Figure 10-47. "Dead head" parking.

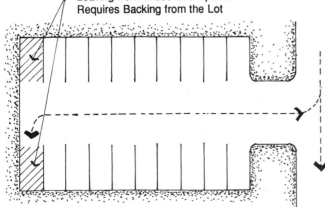

Figure 10-46. "Dead end" parking.

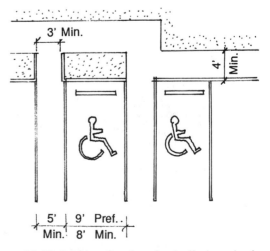

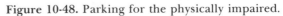

Figure 10-48. Parking for the physically impaired.

Vehicular Service

Most building sites require periodic service by vehicles larger than the automobile. This service is required for the delivery of equipment and furnishings, the collection of solid wastes, and attendance to emergencies including fire.

Service vehicles usually have different site destination points than do automobiles. While the automobile usually arrives at visually prominent image areas, service vehicles are brought to screened service courts. Service vehicles often have much larger turning radii and require greater maneuvering space than automobiles, and these demands differ with the specific service vehicles used. All drives must therefore be designed in response to the performance criteria of specific vehicles that will service the site.

Commercial/Public Areas

On multifamily, commercial, institutional and industrial project sites, service functions, except fire fighting, are usually performed by driving a vehicle on site and placing it adjacent to the building. Access usually includes the service drive and a circulation court that accommodates vehicular turning movements.

The circulation court should be sized to accommodate the most constraining service vehicle anticipated. This court usually consists of two parts: paved loading and unloading areas, and refuse storage area; and pavement for turning movements. Primary movements usually involve forward entry to the service court, backing to the building or refuse area, and forward egress from the court (Figure 10-50). All pavement not required for these movements, for truck

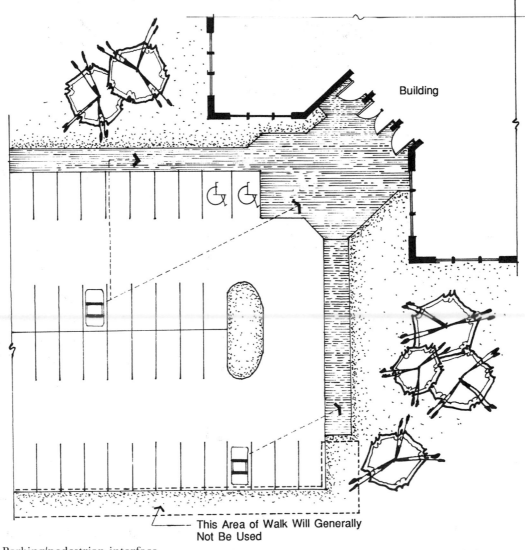

This Area of Walk Will Generally Not Be Used

Figure 10-49. Parking/pedestrian interface.

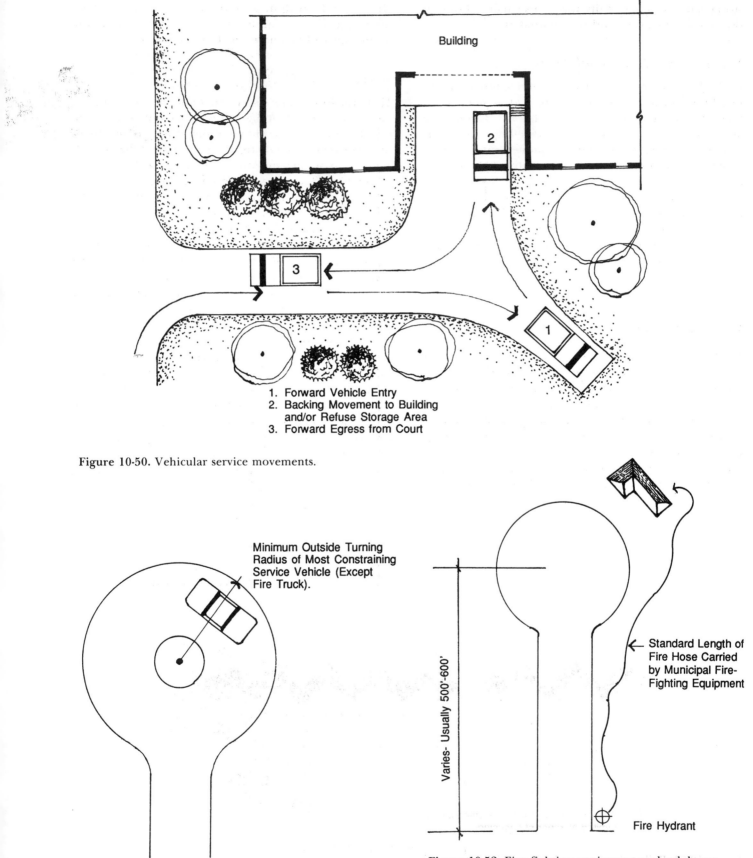

1. Forward Vehicle Entry
2. Backing Movement to Building and/or Refuse Storage Area
3. Forward Egress from Court

Figure 10-50. Vehicular service movements.

Minimum Outside Turning Radius of Most Constraining Service Vehicle (Except Fire Truck).

Varies- Usually 500'-600'

Standard Length of Fire Hose Carried by Municipal Fire-Fighting Equipment

Fire Hydrant

Figure 10-52. Fire fighting equipment and cul-de-sac length.

Figure 10-51. Vehicular service and turn-around diameter.

storage, or for other utility functions (such as housing refuse containers) should be eliminated.

Single Family Residential Areas

In single family residential areas, service functions are usually performed from the curb, and all service vehicles except fire trucks must be able to conveniently access the curb alongside each dwelling. All roads must be designed to facilitate the movement of service vehicles, considering the turning radii of these vehicles, (Figure 10-51).

Firefighting equipment must be able to access a fire hydrant no farther from any part of any building than can be accessed with adequate water pressure (Figure 10-52) from either a fire hydrant or from a fire vehicle if the single entry point is blocked.

BUS TRANSIT

While buses travel on the same streets as automobiles and trucks, they travel along reasonably fixed routes and have fixed points of pedestrian ingress and egress (transit stops). These points can function as major generators of pedestrian traffic and should therefore be seen as nodes in the pedestrian circulation system. In addition, these sites serve as mixing points for buses, automobiles, and pedestrians and can therefore be unsafe. Extreme care should be exercised in designing the pedestrian and roadway systems in these areas and in maintaining visual and spatial relationships that will promote safety.

RAIL TRANSPORT

Rail transportation systems include major terminals that interface with other circulation systems, including those for trucks, buses, automobiles, and pedestrians. They also include fixed land-bound routes, which highly impact urban form.

Rail-bound transportation vehicles, including trains and mass-transit carriers, are major urban form determinates. They are bound by severe gradient and turning radii constraints. Therefore, railroad systems are integrally tied to landform. They usually follow the lines of flattest topography, to the degree that turning radii allow access to these areas. Therefore, in erosional landscapes they tend to follow ridgelines (or secondarily to occur in broad valleys); in uplifted landscapes, they generally occur in continuous valleys or terraced side slopes.

Railroad tracks can be unsafe when they interface with other movement systems, such as those for automobiles or pedestrians. Accordingly, railroad crossings are few in number and highly regulated. Therefore, while railroad tracks serve to link rail terminals, within the city they become urban barriers, forcefully separating land uses and generally breaking the continuity of neighborhoods and minor elements of transportation networks (Figure 10-53).

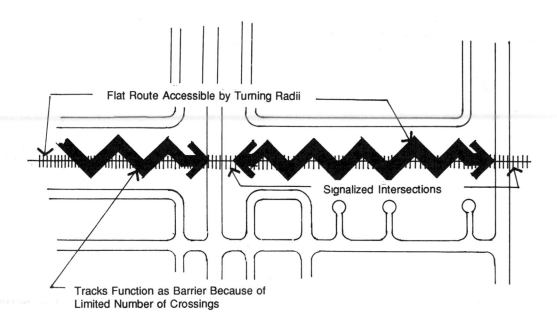

Figure 10-53. Railroad tracks as physical and social barriers.

AIR AND WATER TRANSPORT

Air and water transportation systems are similar to one another in several ways. Each involves land-borne traffic generators (airports and docks) and circulation paths that are removed from the land surface. As definers of urban form, each has terminals that can be major traffic generators. In each case, these terminals must also interface with other transportation systems, including those for trains, trucks, autos, and pedestrians.

The scale and physical character of air and water transportation systems also affects the types of activities that occur in the area of their terminals. They are, therefore, major urban land use and form generators.

REFERENCES

DeChiara, Joseph, and Koppelman, Lee. 1982. *Urban Planning and Design Criteria,* 3d ed. New York: Van Nostrand Reinhold.

Jones, John H. 1961. *The Geometric Design of Modern Highways.* New York: Wiley.

Lynch, Kevin, and Hack, Gary. 1984. *Site Planning,* 3d ed. Cambridge, MA: MIT Press.

A Policy on Geometric Design of Highways and Streets. 1984. Washington, DC: American Association of State Highway and Transportation Officials.

Woods, K. B. 1960. *Highway Engineering Handbook.* New York: McGraw-Hill.

SUGGESTED READINGS

Appleyard, Donald, Lynch, Kevin, and Myer, John. 1964. *The View from the Road.* Cambridge, MA: MIT Press.

Beewer, W. E., and Alter, Charles. 1988. *The Complete Manual of Land Planning and Development.* Englewood Cliffs, NJ: Prentice-Hall.

Brooks, R. Gene. 1988. *Site Planning: Environment, Process, and Development.* Englewood Cliffs, NJ: Prentice-Hall.

DeChiara, Joseph, and Koppleman, Lee. 1978. *Site Design Standards.* New York: McGraw-Hill.

McHarg, Ian. 1969. *Design with Nature.* Garden City, NY: American Museum of Natural History, Natural History Press.

Tunnard, Christopher. 1963. *Man-Made America: Chaos or Control.* New Haven, CT: Yale University Press.

11

Spatial Development

Perception is primarily visual; and visual perception primarily spatial. We experience our world as a sequence of visual stimuli as we move through space. To the degree that the various stimuli we receive within any given space are related, we perceive that space to be coherent. We feel a particular sense of the place, and perceive that place to be comfortable. To the degree that stimuli relate poorly, we perceive the place to be confused and incoherent. We do not feel an intuitive understanding of the place, but rather feel uncomfortable or disoriented.

Spatial development is the manipulation of space, mass, and the characteristics of the designed environment so as to intensify placeness. It involves managing visual perception, the relationships among spaces, and elements and principles of design, using the exterior design palette of landform, water, plant materials, construction materials, and buildings.

SPATIAL PERCEPTION

The design of the built environment presents a major paradox. On the one hand, our culture is object oriented, and our design commissions tend to involve the design of objects: furniture, sculpture, plazas, and buildings. On the other hand, we experience the world spatially. At any given time, our image of reality is most directly influenced by our perception of the three-dimensional volume and the characteristics of its edge and enclosed elements. The edge of our immediate space determines our perception of the world. Our awareness of reality beyond the spatial edge consists only of mental images based on stored experience or imagination.

Relation of Space and Mass

We are encouraged by our culture to perceive objects. Therefore, in basic design terms, the beginning designer intuitively designs identifiable positive shapes (Figure 11-1) and is less concerned with the relationship between these shapes (Figure 11-2). In manipulating three-dimensional form, the designer is usually concerned that the designed mass, including building facades, convey some degree of unity and coherence.

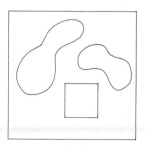

Figure 11-1. Identifiable positive shapes.

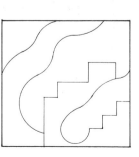

Figure 11-2. Interrelated shapes.

The beginning designer is usually less concerned that portions of the designed mass be as unified or coherent in relation to other masses that are viewed concurrently, and that the spaces formed communicate a unified sense of place.

While the novice designer is usually concerned with the unity of the designed mass, in reality the object is seldom seen in totality. We rarely see at the same time, for example, the opposite sides of a building. While the designer tends to be less concerned with the relationship of the designed object to its context, we almost always perceive specific faces of these designed masses in relation to other objects and their physical context. We usually view a given building facade (or facades) in conjunction with facades of other buildings and in combination with other spatial elements (Figure 11-3). To the degree that the facades relate to one another and to other elements within the space, they establish harmony. The space becomes more integrated, and more coherent. To the degree that elements fail to establish this rapport, the space lacks coherence.

Whereas the novice designer seeks to design meaningful objects, the master artist seeks to create meaningful places. The inexperienced designer designs the mass according to some design attitude or vocabulary of form; the experienced designer explores these attitudes or forms through the integration of mass and space, with an emphasis on spatial development. When transitions between design vocabularies occur, the novice allows these differing expressions to confront one another in space (Figure 11-4). The experienced designer realizes the opportunity to make transitions within the mass, allowing each space to express itself in a unified form vocabulary (Figure 11-5).

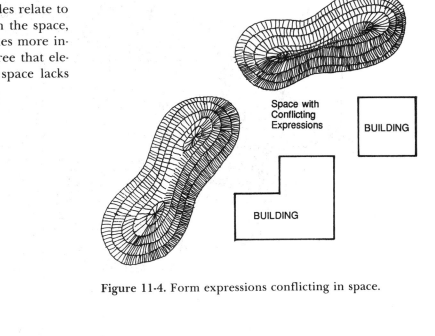

Figure 11-4. Form expressions conflicting in space.

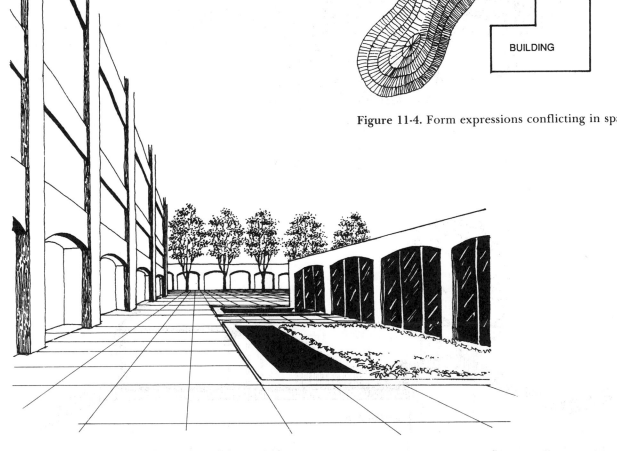

Figure 11-3. Building facades and spatial perception.

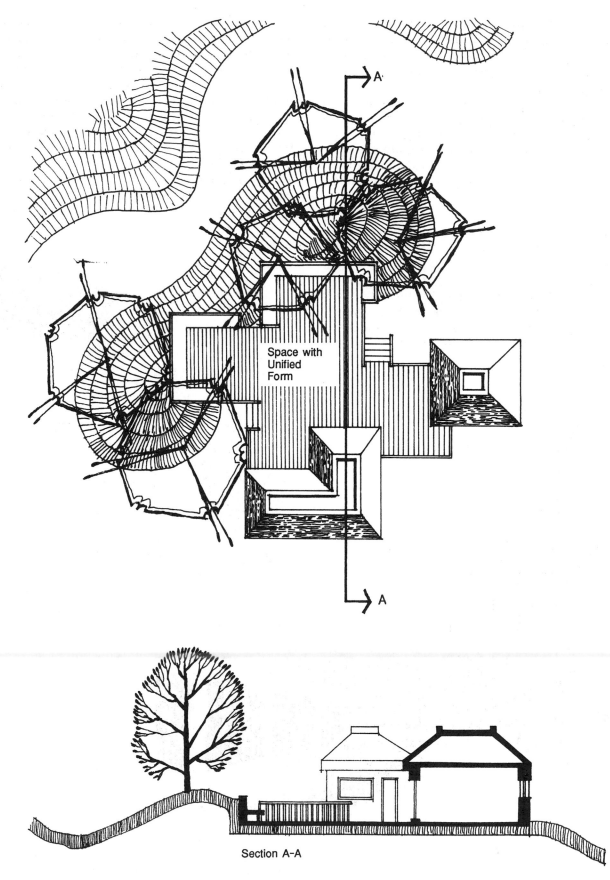

Space with
Unified
Form

Section A-A

Figure 11-5. Space as unified form.

Enclosure and Spatial Perception

Humans are territorial and experience zones or envelopes of space that relate to perceived security. These zones also affect human interaction. For each, the individual has a situational personality and rules of appropriate behavior. These territorial zones have been defined as the zones of intimate space (0–18 inches), personal space (18–48 inches), social space (4–12 feet), and public space (12+ feet).

Spatial Size

Some generalizations can be made about the absolute size of space and the feelings the space evokes when viewed by a stationary or slow-moving person. According to Lynch and Hack, in *Site Planning* (1984), exterior spaces less than 10 feet in dimension seem distressingly small. Outdoor spaces 10 to 40 feet in size seem intimate; those 40 to 80 feet have a human scale. Exterior spaces 80 to 500 feet have a public human scale, and those larger than 500 feet in dimension, a superhuman scale.

There is also a correlation between the size of spaces and perceived territorialism. Generally, the smaller the space, the greater the sense of security, and the more prone the individual is to socially interact. The larger the space, the greater the sense of insecurity, and the less prone the person is to interact. In superhuman-scaled space, the individual usually feels unprotected and sometimes unsafe. As size decreases, the individual perceives increased security and greater psychological comfort. As objects within the space approach or occur at eye level, the viewer is drawn to these objects. The space becomes more human in scale, and humane in its sense.

Degree of Enclosure

In addition to absolute size, our perception of space is affected by its degree of enclosure, which relates to the percentage and character of the edge that is closed and the height of this edge in relation to the angle of vision. According to Lynch and Hack, when the height of a continuous opaque enclosure equals its distance from the viewer, the space is perceived as being fully enclosed (Figure 11-6). If the width-to-height ratio of a space is two to one, the space ceases to seem fully enclosed. At a ratio of three to one, the space seems only minimally enclosed, and at a ratio of four to one, the feeling of enclosure is virtually lost.

Generally speaking, enclosure triggers our instinctive sense for territorialism. As degree of enclosure decreases, we feel more exposed and more unsafe. In intimate space, we feel protected; in expansive space, we feel threatened.

When objects that approach or exceed eye level are introduced, we take refuge near these objects and sense a more human scale. When objects block the vision beyond, they afford great protection and are quite effective in bringing the space to a human scale (Figure 11-7). Planes that extend above eye level create new spatial edge, and provide enclosure. Intersecting planes or interior angles create spatial edge on two sides, and drastically change the perceived size and degree of enclosure. With the sky as the overhead, space is expansive. The introduction of an overhead plane radically changes spatial perception. An overhead enclosed on three sides gives the feeling of being within, and of perusing the landscape from a point of refuge.

Strata and Spatial Enclosure

In addressing enclosure, spatial definition, and character, the location of spatial elements especially their vertical location, is crucial. The implications of vertical location can be best understood by differentiating, and exploring individually, the base plane (and its vertical extensions near to the ground), the overhead plane, and the spatial edge, as shown in Figure 11-8.

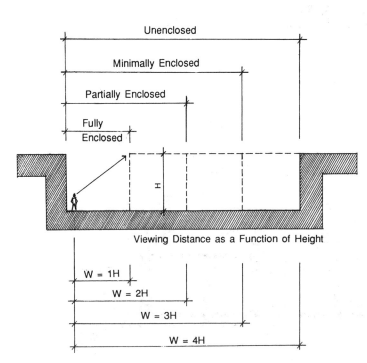

Figure 11-6. Degree of enclosure based on W:H ratio.

Figure 11-7. Degree of enclosure.

Increasing Enclosure

Increasing Sense of Security

Base Plane

The base plane serves as both the functional and spatial floor of the landscape. It is the surface on which we walk and drive; it forms the lowermost spatial limit. It also supports, structurally and biologically, the elements that express themselves spatially in the overhead and the spatial edge.

The base plane is formed initially by environmental processes such as uplift, erosion, and sedimentation; it is often reshaped by people. Its form is usually expressive of these generative forces, local climatic conditions, and the material of which it is made. In addition, the base plane and its materials usually convey information concerning land use, which in turn affects perceived placeness. The sense of place is, therefore, in no small way, affected by the base plane.

As the surface on which we walk, the base plane also influences the route by which we move and experience the landscape. As it structures our movement, it choreographs the story line by which we perceive space, and therefore our perception of place.

As a determinant of spatial story lines, and as the structural and biological support for elements that express themselves spatially in the overhead and edge strata, the organization of the base plane should usually bear a strong pattern relationship to these other spatial strata (Figure 11-9).

Base planes that do not approach eye level may imply or articulate space, but do not physically enclose it. On the other hand, landforms that rise above eye level cease to function as base planes and express themselves rather as spatial edge, and provide enclosure (Figure 11-10).

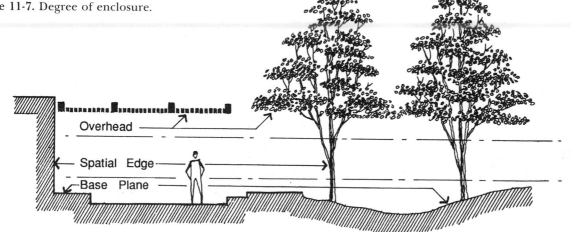

Overhead

Spatial Edge

Base Plane

Figure 11-8. Spatial strata.

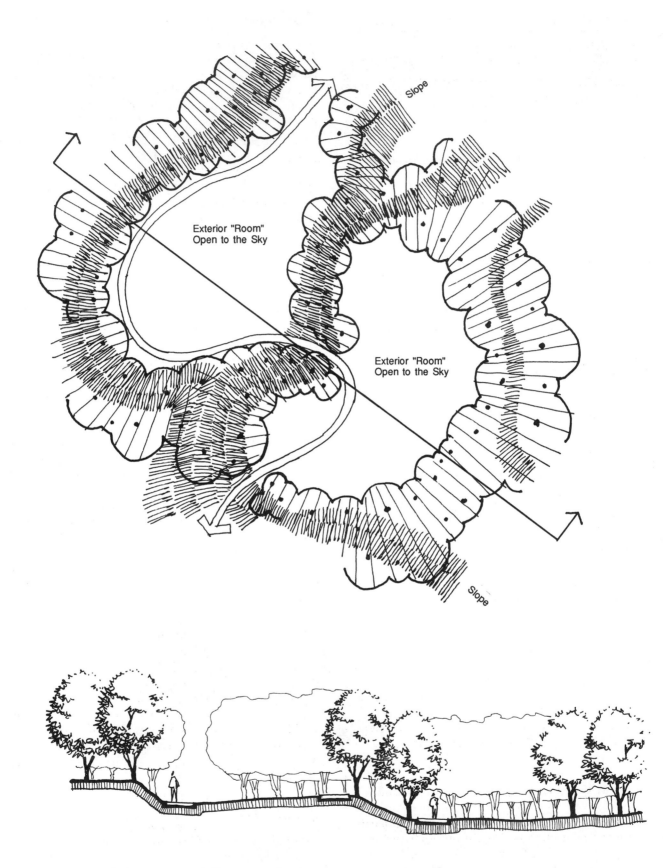

Exterior "Room"
Open to the Sky

Exterior "Room"
Open to the Sky

Slope

Slope

Figure 11-9. Base plane pattern—relation to overhead and edge.

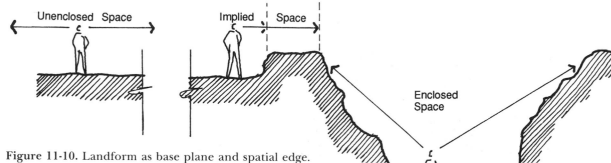

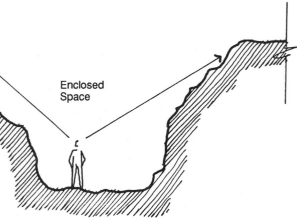

Figure 11-10. Landform as base plane and spatial edge.

Materials. Base plane materials can vary significantly. Each of these materials behaves uniquely under specific use and physical conditions. Each also affects the perceived sense of place in its own inimitable way.

Included in the palette of base plane materials are various types of soil, each with its own characteristic behavior, slope stability, texture, and the like; different plant materials—grasses, ground covers, and shrubs, each possessing its own range of size, texture, color, and so on; water and its power to convey mood; and human-made surface materials such as cinder, brick, concrete, wood, and so on.

Overhead Plane

The overhead plane is the spatial ceiling. It can vary from the ubiquitous sky, blue and expansive by day and sparkling at night, to hard exterior architectural ceilings. It can be as heavy and static as a concrete slab oppressively perched above our heads, or as light and airy as the tracery of locust leaves, fluttering in a gentle breeze.

Functionally and physiologically, the overhead protects us from the elements—the heat of the sun, rain, hail, sleet, and, to a degree, snow. Psychologically, it provides a sense of shelter and protection. It can also provide a unique sense through the character and color it can impart to sunlight, and the shading pattern it can create on walls and the ground plane.

The feeling of "being under" is perceptually unique. It motivates us as children to explore under beds and tables, and later to venture into caves. The overhead plane conveys this feeling, and creates a tremendous sense of enclosure. The dramatic effects of the overhead intensify as the ceiling is brought ever closer to eye level.

Character of Overhead. As anyone who has hidden in a tree to avoid work can tell you, the overhead ceiling is sensed more than seen. It is sensed primarily through movement, shadows it casts on other surfaces, and the changes it effects in the character, quality, and color of light. However, we seldom focus directly on the overhead.

Solid, opaque, and static overheads can be effective in providing shelter from the elements. They can give a feeling of protection and of repose. They reduce the level of light, and if deep can do so dramatically. They can also serve as a surface on which to mount artificial light sources.

Translucent surfaces can provide protection, and can effect changes in the character, quality, and color of light. They can also create a muted pattern on the ground below, as leaves gather on the overhead surface.

Porous overheads, particularly those that move or change over time, can create dramatic effects as light pierces the overhead plane and falls on the base plane or vertical surfaces below. As light penetrates the overhead, it can streak across the space, or can render a dappled mosaic on the ground. The overhead can create an angular, rhythmic shadow pattern as light penetrates a slatted arbor, or a dancing tracery as rays both reflect from and penetrate a moving, fine-textured lacy canopy of foliage. The character of the light, and the shadow pattern, can also vary with season as the sun angle and leaf condition change. A dense summer shading pattern can become a dendritic one in the winter, after deciduous leaves have been lost from the tree canopy above.

As a surface that is sensed more than viewed directly, these feelings of change and movement, and the character of light imparted by the overhead plane, are often quite dramatic and important to spatial perception and sense of place (Chapter 16). In fact this characteristic is often more important than actually viewing the overhead plane.

Spatial Edge

Although relatively small in our cone of vision, the spatial edge near eye level is of critical importance in visual perception. While the overhead and base planes may affect the use, character, and organization of

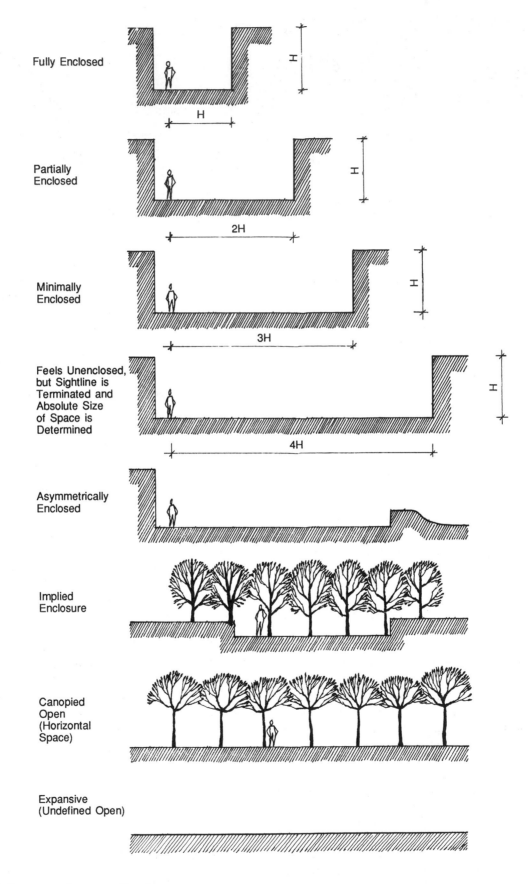

Figure 11-11. Degree and nature of enclosure.

space, and may even imply spatial units, closure of the space at eye level is usually required to provide a true sense of enclosure (Figure 11-11).

Spatial edge is desirable when one seeks privacy. It is also useful in creating suspense or mystery, screening unpleasant views and calling attention (through framing or the like) to desirable ones, defining spatial units, and achieving numerous other spatial intentions. Successful spaces usually have opaque edges that screen out external elements that would otherwise destroy the desired sense of place, and that enframe those views that promote this sense. As such, the spatial edge is important in helping the viewer discover the space in an appropriate manner. Conversely, spaces that are unsuccessful tend to suffer from a poorly defined or improperly formed spatial edge.

The spatial edge encloses space, it terminates the sightline, and it defines the viewshed. The distance from edge to opposite edge determines the absolute size of the space and contributes greatly to its perceived scale (Figure 11-12). The proportion of edge height to viewing distance determines the degree of enclosure.

Sightline Considerations. The horizontal plane at eye level is the line of greatest visual attention. A particularly pleasurable sensation is achieved when visual features are organized in a pleasant relationship to this line of sight. Therefore, pictures to be viewed on a wall are composed in relation to this line. Likewise, a landscape feature viewed at eye level can provide an especially pleasant experience. As natural landform rises above eye level, the "natural-ness" of the landscape increases substantially.

On the other hand, unresolved relationships at eye level are extremely bothersome. Spatial edges that terminate within 12 inches of this line are particularly frustrating, as the viewer receives indecisive visual cues and strains to see beyond this spatial edge (Figure 11-13).

Edge Function. The edge can, and usually does, serve three distinct functions. First, as discussed above, it encloses space. Second, it serves as backdrop to en-

hance the perception of sculptural elements within the space. When serving as backdrop, the edge should not compete for attention, but rather should enhance the features of the element in view. Generally speaking, perception of these sculptural elements is increased and the element enhanced if the edge contrasts the characteristics of the element, in terms of line, form, color, and texture. For example, a smooth sinuous white stone sculpture with subtle surface modulations might best be displayed against a textured deep green foliated mass. Conversely, a lacy wrought-iron sculpture might be displayed to advantage against a smooth white concrete wall. The coarse white peeling bark of a paper birch or an aspen tree might be displayed against a smooth or fine-textured dark background.

The third function of the spatial edge is enframement. A relatively closed edge can build to a crescendo and draw attention to openings that occur. Elements outside the space, enframed by its edge, will visually become part of the edge. In so doing they will become part of the space. Effective enframement can greatly enhance the perceived sense of place (Figure 11-14). Conversely, unintended enframement can incorporate and draw attention to elements that destroy the sense of place (Figure 11-15).

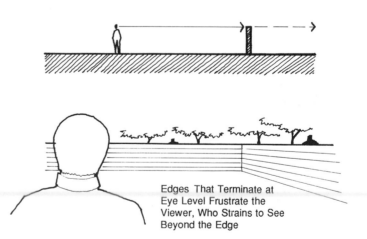

Edges That Terminate at Eye Level Frustrate the Viewer, Who Strains to See Beyond the Edge

Figure 11-13. Edges that terminate at eye level.

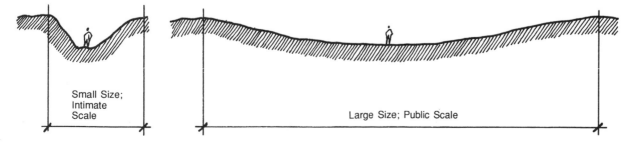

Small Size; Intimate Scale

Large Size; Public Scale

Figure 11-12. Spatial edge, size, and perceived scale.

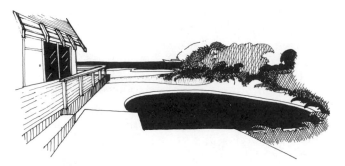

Figure 11-14. Enframement and sense of place.

Figure 11-15. Unintended enframement.

Figure 11-16. Edge as direction.

Edge as Direction. The edge is the most visually apparent spatial stratum. As such, it can effectively lead the eye to special features or to elements of functional importance, such as otherwise hidden building entrances (Figure 11-16). It can also lead the eye to visually important context.

Edge Character

As the most dominant visual stratum, the spatial edge is extremely important in determining spatial character. If edge character relates to the intended use and sense of the place, and if other spatial strata support this character, the various elements of the space will be perceived as relating to one another. The place will

seem coherent, and the user will perceive a resolved quality. This feeling of resolve will establish a rapport within the user, and the space will feel comfortable.

The spatial edge can vary from a rugged cliff face to a smooth polished aluminum or mirrored surface. It can be a dense, hard wall, and convey an architectonic sense (Figure 11-17), or a porous vegetated edge (with dark shadows beyond), implying a deep continuous and mysterious nature (Figure 11-18). The edge can be closed and compressed, approaching a vertical surface (Figure 11-19). It can conversely be layered and can extend over a long distance, as often occurs along the sunlit edge of woodlands, with each successive vegetative layer arching beyond the overlying one to capture a little extra sunlight (Figure 11-20). It may finally be the porous open edge (Figure 11-21), which often occurs on the shaded north side of woodland canopies where little sun is available to power photosynthesis and to support leaf growth.

The edge can be very complex with many layers, incorporating diverse elements at various distances from the viewer. Conversely, it can be reduced to a single material and pure geometric form, displayed at a consistent distance. Each edge condition conveys its own unique character to the space.

Figure 11-17. Architectonic edge.

Figure 11-18. Porous vegetated edge.

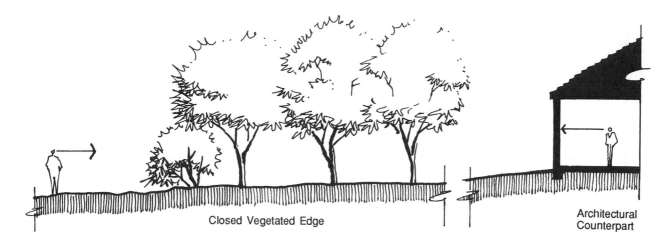

Closed Vegetated Edge

Architectural Counterpart

Figure 11-19. Closed compressed spatial edge.

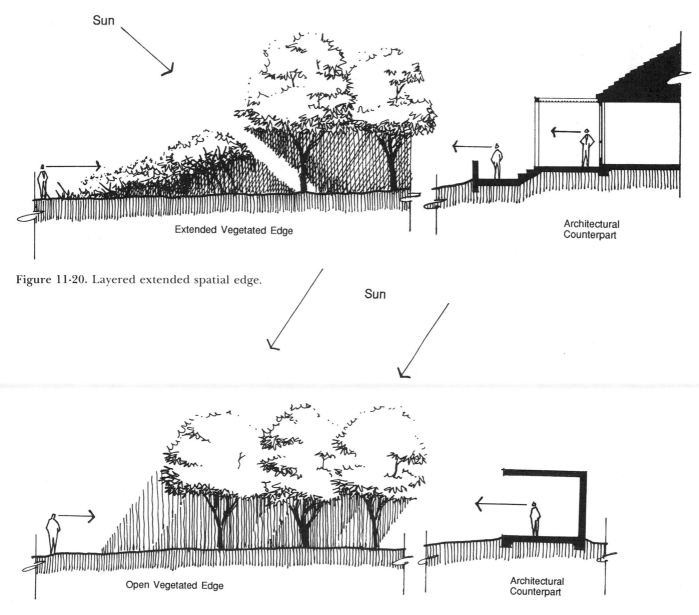

Sun

Extended Vegetated Edge

Architectural Counterpart

Figure 11-20. Layered extended spatial edge.

Sun

Open Vegetated Edge

Architectural Counterpart

Figure 11-21. Porous open edge.

SENSE OF PLACE

All things viewed within a space, including the base plane, overhead plane, spatial edge, enclosed elements, and enframed ones are part of the visual scene, and therefore part of the place.

If the various stimuli relate one to another and support a common theme, then the space has a strong meaningful sense of place. It feels integrated; its elements feel like they belong together. The space can be said to have a high degree of placeness.

To the degree that the elements fail to relate one to another, then the place feels discordant. It is perceived as chaotic and visually incoherent; it feels confused. Such a place can be said to lack placeness, or conversely to be characterized by placelessness.

Common Failures

In designing exterior space and manipulating sense of place, one of the most common shortcomings is the inability to reconcile spatial edge with other strata and with enclosed forms. It is common, for example, to see the designer placing naturalistic base and overhead planes and enclosed elements into a spatial envelope dominated by a hard architectonic edge. Commonly the stated design intent is to create a sense of nature in the urban milieu. However, dominance of the architectonic edge often leads to conflicting stimuli, unintended contradictions, and an inability to evoke the intended sense. Conversely, when designing into a space dominated by an architectonic edge, a more appropriate design concept, and one that can be realized, might be that of "complement through contrast," similar to the Asian Yin-Yang.

There is often an inability to perceive the perceptual importance of the spatial edge, and a lack of concern for the continuity of this edge and its relation to enclosed and enframed elements. The chaotic visual nature of exterior space in American cities today is evidence of this inability.

Issues of Placeness

While the notion of placeness seems simple, it is really a complex, intuitive sense, a mental response operative on several levels. In one sense, it is direct and perceptual—when we see sidewalks crossing a space, we reason the space is used for pedestrian circulation, and this perception affects our interpretation of character and our mental image of the place.

On a second level, sense of place is associational. The place relates, refers, or alludes to our past experience. Its stimuli excite patterns in our mind and bring them forward. These mental patterns are themselves complex and diverse but are based on such things as human-environment perception, cultural values, perception of the individual's social role, past physical and cultural experiences, education, and so on. Our perception of place is a mental response to the patterns that are brought forward. To the degree that the various mental associations support a common notion, a strong placeness emerges.

On a third, and more instinctive level, the mental construct of place is affected by the primordial recesses of our brain. The basic notions of survival, the fight or flight syndrome, and the like radically affect our perception of place. We therefore view spaces within our social "territory" differently from those in an unfamiliar area. The more foreign looking, or the less coherent a place, the more uncomfortable we feel.

Space also conveys individual messages. Based on different experiences, or differing personal ethics or attitudes, we each view the world uniquely. We each impart a somewhat different, though usually related, meaning to a given place.

Spatial Feeling

While individuals may interpret the same space differently, we can make some generalizations concerning characteristics of spaces and the types of responses or feelings they tend to engender. Some of these generalizations are as follows.

Satisfaction. When the various elements of a space relate to one another, the space feels unified or resolved. When its character is also appropriate to its intended use and context, a feeling of satisfaction is evoked.

Pleasure. When a space is not only satisfying but also provides some enrichment for the viewer, it is seen as pleasurable. For example, a unified space is satisfying; one with unity and an intriguing sense of variety is pleasurable.

Relaxation. Physical and psychological comfort, soft-flowing form, cool colors, soft light and sound, familiarity, and the resolution of forces are spatial characteristics that can promote a sense of relaxation.

Frustration. When a space fails to establish meaningful relationships—element to element, element to context, element to user, space to condition, material to use—the viewer may attempt but fails to integrate the data. The space becomes a source of frustration.

Spirituality. Transcending the human experience can contribute to a feeling of spirituality. This can be achieved through scale exaggeration or vertical thrusting to heaven, or the use of basic geometric shapes, pure white color, excessively smooth textures, shafts of light, and other means.

Formality. Relationships that are resolved with a simple obvious order convey formality. Strict adherence to the rules of bilateral symmetry can convey this sense, as can scale exaggeration. However, formal places can run the risk of becoming boring.

Informality. Spaces with an unresolved order, or complex integrative order (such as occult balance) can convey a sense of freedom, and a loose informality. They can also be highly stimulating.

Solemnity. Completely resolved relationships, when combined with dark, receding colors of low saturation, can induce a solemn feeling. They can be introspective and encourage one to reflect.

Contemplation. Simple, high-quality materials and the absence of distracting elements can promote a feeling of contemplation. This feeling is supported by privacy, overt security, soft diffused light, and isolation from outside influences.

Dynamism. Bold angular forms, coarse textures, bright colors, and high contrasts in line, form, color, and texture can convey a dynamic sense. This sense can also be provided by complex organization, multiple spatial foci, movement, and complex or changing patterns of light and shade.

Gaiety and Frivolity. Loose, free-flowing fanciful forms, complex or evolving structural rhythms, and spatial sequences impart a feeling of gaiety. Movement and the playful expression of light, water, and sound also instill this feeling.

Tension. Unresolved forces, including those related to gravity, visual balance, and sound, can induce tension. So too can competition among different points of emphasis, undesirable microclimatic conditions, and physically unsafe or uncomfortable conditions such as glare or strobing light.

Fright. Forced confrontation, physical and mental discomfort, disorientation, excessive complexity, and excessive spatial confinement or expansiveness can convey a sense of danger and instill a feeling of fright. This sense can come from harshness of form or light, aggressive color, unrefined austerity, harsh sounds, or unstable and unsafe conditions.

Pretence. The display of opulence, overstatement, and excessive order can impart a pretentious feeling. This sense can also be created by scale exaggeration and cool colors of high saturation.

Virtually any feeling can be created through the conscious manipulation of space with an awareness of design elements and principles, and the feelings they evoke. Spaces that evoke such strong feelings are said to have a strong sense of place.

Design Appropriateness

In addition to being coherent, the sense of a place must also relate to its intended use. A space can be seen as a setting, with the intention of inducing or supporting certain human behavior. To the degree that this behavior setting promotes its intended use, the space is appropriate and successful. To the degree it fails to encourage intended behavior, it is inappropriate and unsuccessful.

The place must also relate to its physical and cultural context. If it fails to achieve a rapport with its condition, it may be perceived as inappropriate, arbitrary, and capricious.

SPATIAL DEVELOPMENT

As the designer manipulates space and creates a sense of place, numerous issues should be addressed. These include the management of sensory stimuli, the manipulation of each of the spatial strata so as to realize design intent, the design of elements within the space, the relationship of architecture and spatial development, temporal considerations, and the effective use of the land design palette.

Management of Sensory Stimuli

The designer of exterior space must effectively manage sensory stimuli so as to achieve the intended sense of place. This includes the management of visual as well as other sensory information. Elements of visual design including point, line, form, color, and texture must be managed individually and in concert as we develop space so as to create a desired sense of place.

Point

As we develop space, there are special places within the composition that have the potential to concentrate landscape meaning. Space can be developed to convey the importance of, and give special attention to, these points. Accordingly, the placeness of the entire space will be increased, as meaning that is concentrated in these points is thereby conveyed to the space at large.

These special points, where the sense of place, or "genius loci," is focused, can be within the space (Figure 11-22), or can be external points, which, through enframement, become part of the space and intensify its meaning (Figure 11-23).

Line

Lines can lead the eye to discover elements of concentrated meaning in the landscape, as shown in Figures 11-22 and 11-23. They can also give dominance to these elements.

In developing exterior space, the designer can intensify placeness by expressing, as dominant lines, the edges of forms, major changes in depth, and the interface of surfaces of high contrast (in tone, texture, color, and so on) as shown in Figure 11-24. These lines can lead the eye to understand spatial composition better, and to discover points of special meaning. The character of the line as it leads the eye can affect the mental images that are evoked and can instill spatial mood. Groups of lines can also be applied to surfaces and can model the surface, thereby helping the viewer perceive surficial and spatial form, and better understand the place.

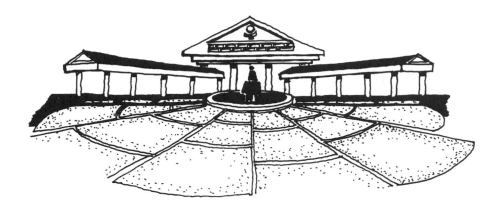

Figure 11-22. Internal point as concentration of meaning.

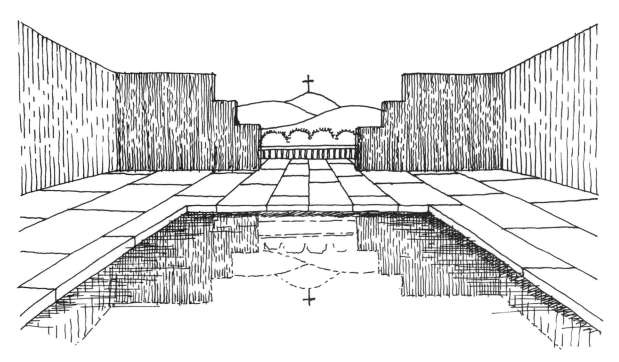

Figure 11-23. Enframed point as concentration of meaning.

To the degree that lines, especially those that are dominant in the composition, work together to support a theme, the design character and sense of place will be enhanced. To the degree that this sense or theme is common to that conveyed by other visual elements, the sense of place will increase.

Figure 11-24. Dominant line and spatial perception.

Form

As we manipulate three-dimensional form, we should resist the cultural bias toward mass dominance. Being aware that our visual experience is primarily spatial, we should focus on spatial development as we manage sense of place. We should consciously manage spatial composition, spatial strata, forms within the spaces, and enframed forms, so as to support a common theme and evoke the desired sense.

As we develop exterior space, we should see experience as a continuum, discovered over time, and should design each space within that continuum so that its form supports the overall design theme, while evoking desired spatial quality and character.

Transitions in form should occur primarily within the masses that separate spaces. Accordingly, as we move from space to space, the sense of place can change; but when viewing any given space, the forms within that space work together to support the spatial theme (Figure 11-25).

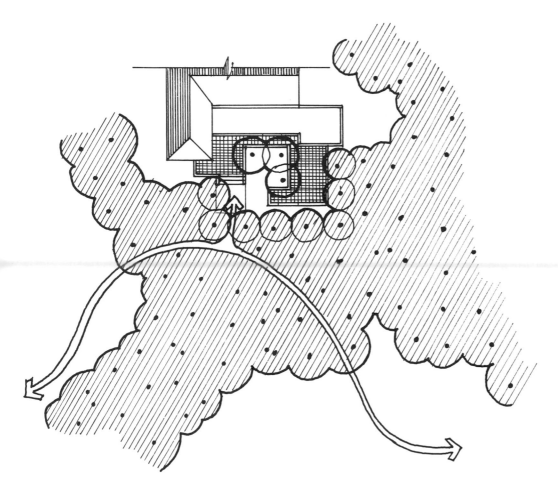

Figure 11-25. Spatial unity.

Color

Color is a property of light. The perception of color is a result of incoming light, modifications to that light, absorptive, reflective, and transmissive characteristics of the surface, relationships to other nearby colors, and characteristics of the eye.

As discussed earlier in this chapter, the overhead plane is important primarily through its effects on light, including light color. To a lesser degree, the base plane, the spatial edge, and enclosed and enframed forms, can affect light color. In addition to affecting the color of the light, each of these spatial elements also selects which frequencies of light to absorb, that is, they possess surface color.

Applications of Color Theory to Spatial Development. As we develop exterior space, we should consciously manipulate color to achieve design intent. We should be sensitive to the diurnal characteristics of light, its different color in the morning, midday, and evening. We should understand the potentials of artificial lighting and nighttime painting with colored light. We should be acutely aware of seasonal variations, not only in light characteristics (due to varying sun angles, relative humidity, and the like), but more important in the seasonal color of landscape elements. The general browning of the winter landscape, with its dormant grasses and lack of tree leaf, the splash of fall color, the breath of life each spring: each offers the site designer unique potentials to intensify placeness.

There are many different approaches to the use of color in spatial development. Many architects feel, for example, that color should be used sparingly in architectural space. As such, the space is neutral, and people, furniture, paintings, and other elements supply color and thereby animate the space. A similar approach can be applied to exterior spatial development, with the added benefit that this neutral backdrop serves as the stageset for displaying diurnal and seasonal color.

A second, somewhat related color theory promotes the use of a dominant color throughout the space. Other colors "play off" this dominant one to create spatial mood and character. Depending on the degree to which they contrast with the dominant hue, other colors can serve as either modulators or as counterpoints; they can reinforce spatial unity or read as spatial focus or accent.

A third approach to the use of color involves the careful management of the relationships of colors throughout the space, to achieve a satisfying gestalt. This technique allows the designer to maximize the relationship between landscape feature and context, as when sculpture is displayed against a spatial edge of contrasting color.

In a fourth view, color can be employed to increase the viewer's awareness of space, and can even create spatial illusion. Certain colors tend to advance in space, others recede. Also, aerial perspective causes the intensity of color to decrease with increasing distance. Therefore, bright intense scarlets will leap toward the viewer, bright yellows will tend to advance, although to a lesser degree, and yellow-greens will advance still less. Conversely, greys and dull lavenders will recede. Hue, saturation, and color temperature can be used to convey the true proportions of a space, by not varying the tendency of colors to advance in either the foreground, middle, or background. By locating advancing colors near the viewer and receding ones in the background, the perceived depth of the space increases. By reversing this strategy—colors that recede in the foreground and ones that advance in the background—the space can be visually compressed. By using similar colors at different distances, the space can be collapsed; by overlapping complementary colors space can be extended.

A fifth approach to spatial development is to use color to allude to the natural color of each of the spatial strata. Many architects feel that having evolved in a less human-manipulated environment, human beings have an intuitive sense that relates to color in the natural environment. A theory growing from this belief sees the desirable development of the base plane in warm earthtones, the ceiling in lighter airy colors, and so on. Buildings that form the spatial edge can be tied to the earth by extending earthtones vertically, they can be tied to the sky by using lighter, cooler colors. This approach to color use could lead to regional biases in color palettes, as the character of light and natural color change with locale.

Mood. Color is effective in evoking feelings, that is, mental responses from the viewer. It has a singularly intense ability to excite, forebode, or soothe. By its mere presence, it can create suspense, anxiety, or frivolity. The ability to manipulate color so as to evoke appropriate feelings and behavior from the viewer is critical to the effective development of exterior space.

Awareness. Spaces, and the elements they contain, have intrinsic meaning. The degree to which that meaning is conveyed is related to the viewer's awareness of the space and its elements. Color can be effective in displaying, modifying, and concealing these elements and their meanings.

Texture

Texture refers to the visual roughness or smoothness of a surface. This perception is a function of the degree of surface variation, the size of perceived pieces, lighting conditions (including sun angle), and viewing context and distance. When seen from a short distance, the perceived texture is that of surface variations. From a longer viewing distance, we lose perception of surface texture and instead perceive the parts as texture. From great distances, textural perception is limited to that implied by overlapping masses (Figure 11-26).

As we develop exterior space, we should manage textures to achieve compositional unity and variety, visual interest, depth perception, and spatial mood. Texture should also support design intent and sense of place.

Textural Classes. Textures are usually classified as either coarse, medium, or fine (Figure 11-27). As we manage these three textural classes, we should keep in mind the following generalizations.

Coarse Texture. Coarse texture is highly visible and tends to feel bold, strong, sure, aggressive, and sometimes rustic or crude. Objects with coarse texture tend to exhibit great variation from light to dark, and usually capture our attention. They are the first elements we notice, and our eyes seem to move from one coarse texture to another within a two- or three-dimensional composition.

Coarse-textured elements tend to create irregular and energetic outlines. They also appear to advance in space. They make spaces seem smaller and can themselves feel overpowering.

Medium Texture. Medium texture tends to be emotionally neutral. Objects of medium texture appear neither aggressive nor timid; they accept but do not demand attention and do not tend to overpower. They exhibit a moderate amount of variation from light to dark, and create relatively smooth outlines. They tend to advance somewhat if viewed in the context of finer textures, to recede if seen within a community of coarser ones.

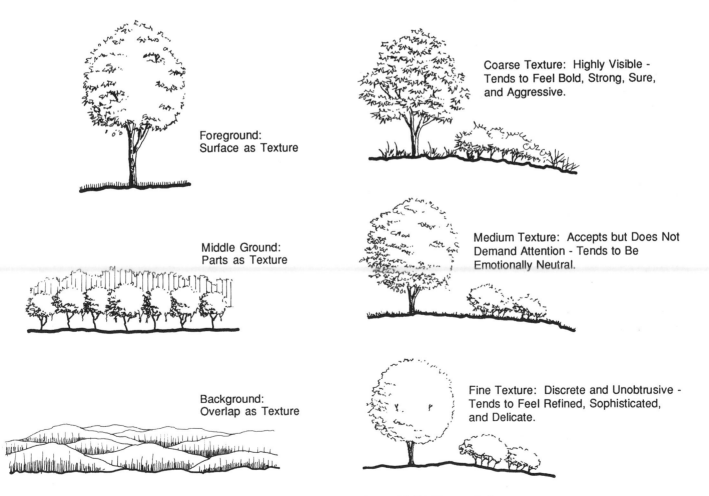

Foreground:
Surface as Texture

Middle Ground:
Parts as Texture

Background:
Overlap as Texture

Coarse Texture: Highly Visible -
Tends to Feel Bold, Strong, Sure,
and Aggressive.

Medium Texture: Accepts but Does Not
Demand Attention - Tends to Be
Emotionally Neutral.

Fine Texture: Discrete and Unobtrusive -
Tends to Feel Refined, Sophisticated,
and Delicate.

Figure 11-26. Viewing distance and perceived texture.

Figure 11-27. Textural classes.

Figure 11-28. Narrow textural range to unify complex space.

Fine Texture. Fine-textured elements consist of small parts, and have fine-grained surface modulations or monolithic form and surface. These elements usually appear refined, sophisticated, or even delicate. They tend to be discrete and are often the last to be discovered in a composition. By their delicacy, refinement, and subtlety, they can however sustain visual interest, particularly when displayed at eye level and viewed from a short distance.

Fine textures tend to create smooth silhouettes and often present a neat, formal appearance. They also tend to recede when used in conjunction with medium or coarse textures.

Texture and Spatial Development. As we develop exterior space, we should take advantage of the characteristics of each textural class, and should employ textural strategies to mitigate the shortcomings of the place and to express and intensify its opportunities.

Characteristics of Textural Classes. Coarse textures tend to attract attention and to advance in space. They can also be overpowering. In spatial development, they can be used in conjunction with other textures to influence perceived depth. They can also be used to make a large space seem smaller.

Being relatively neutral, medium textures can be used extensively in spatial development. Spaces so designed will feel neither aggressive nor timid. Used extensively, they can unify a space and link its components. Medium textures can also be the neutral context within which to view other textures. Objects of medium texture can be seen as subtle features when viewed in the context of one of the other textural classes.

Fine textures can be used for dramatic display of coarsely textured elements, and more subtle presentation of medium-textured ones. They can be used to make small spaces seem larger. In very small spaces, most materials should usually be of a fine texture.

Textural Strategies. When developing exterior space, it is usually desirable to effectively organize a mixture of fine-, medium-, and coarse-textured elements. Spaces so designed tend to exhibit both unity and variety, and feel neither boring nor chaotic.

An effective design strategy bases the actual mix of textural classes in a given space on design intent and desired sense of place, the size of the space, and the degree of unity and variety desired. In an extremely complex space, a relatively narrow range of textures can effectively unify the space (Figure 11-28). Conversely, textural diversity can give life to a boring one (Figure 11-29).

Figure 11-29. Textural diversity to provide visual interest in boring space.

The specific mix of textural classes is usually most crucial in intimately sized spaces, it is less essential as the size of the space and viewing distance increase. Also in small places we are concerned with both surface and form texture. In larger spaces we are less concerned with surface texture and more concerned with the textures implied by pieces of the whole and by overlapping masses.

A second effective textural strategy is the manipulation of textures to affect depth and size perception. To convey the actual depth and size of the space, a relatively consistent textural mix can be used in the foreground, middle, and background. To compress or foreshorten space, fine textures in the foreground and relatively coarse textures in the background are appropriate (Figure 11-30). To extend or lengthen the space, coarse-textured materials in the foreground and successively finer-textured ones as viewing distances increase are in order (Figure 11-31).

Figure 11-30. Texture and foreshortening.

Figure 11-31. Texture and spatial extension.

A third textural strategy involves the manipulation of textures to achieve intended transition. If the design intent is to move smoothly from one sense of place to another, medium textures can be used to go from a space dominated by coarse textures to a finely textured one, or vice versa. Conversely, when the intended transition is forceful, or when the intent is to contrast, surprise, or discover, textural contrast can be maximized at the interface of adjacent spaces.

To be effective, textural strategies should be coordinated with those for color, form, line, and point, to support the sense of place and build a common theme.

Strata and Spatial Development

Base Plane

In developing the base plane several issues must be addressed. These include design intent, planned uses and their relationships, form, sensual experience, appropriateness, the relation between the base plane and architecture, and materials and maintenance issues.

Design Intent. In developing the base plane, the design intent is usually threefold. The designer must create a surface that responds to physical and functional needs. The surface must also maximize the experience of place, and minimize required maintenance.

Planned Uses and Their Relationships. The base plane should be developed with a knowledge of intended uses and the desired relationships among these uses. It should also be organized to support intended physical relationships and use patterns.

Experience of Place. In developing base plane form, certain items need to be addressed. These include sensual experience, design appropriateness, and the relationship between the forms of the base plane and architecture.

Sensual/Temporal Experience. The base plane interrelates functional issues and experiential ones. In determining base plane form, the land uses and linkage issues discussed herein should be provided while maximizing the spatial experience and the visual story that evolves as one moves from place to place.

Appropriateness. Base plane forms should be appropriate on several levels. First, they should relate to regional form. Each physiographic region has certain vocabularies of landform that have evolved in response to, and are compatible with, regional materials and climatic forces. Variations from these vocabularies may not only feel inappropriate, but may also set about negative change that will come back to haunt

the designer. The base plane should be designed to relate to regional form vocabularies. In erosional landscapes, the "buried elephant" look of mounded berms (positive forms) should be avoided. More appropriate (negative form) landforms should be used (Figure 11-32).

On a second level, the form of the base plane should also relate to its more immediate context. This integration of site and contextual form usually results in aesthetic, functional, and maintenance benefits.

On a third level, base plane form must be appropriate to design intent. It must bring forth from the observer the appropriate mental responses to achieve its underlying intent or design concept (Chapter 13). Whether the base plane is expressed as bas-relief or as mass and space; whether it is level, sloped, warped, or terraced, and whether it is "naturalistic" or architectonic, will depend, to large degree, on this underlying design concept.

Base Plane and Architecture. The base plane is the stratum where buildings meet the site. As the two meet, they must do so functionally. Site circulation systems must link to building ones, and building uses must relate to site uses. This is especially true where the building circulation systems open onto the site, and where the site is visually linked to building interior spaces (Chapter 12).

There are numerous other functional relationships between the design of buildings and exterior spatial development. Architectural support systems (structural and infrastructural) must usually be placed under the ground. Some of these systems must facilitate gravity flow through pipes without allowing pipes to ride out of the ground, or to be excessively deep below the surface. These gravity-flow systems, therefore, often impart major constraints to designed landform, the form of specific buildings, and the portions of the site where buildings may reasonably be located. As we manipulate the base plane, we must also interrelate building and site story lines (Chapter 12).

The base plane–building interface is the site of the major form transitions that normally occur on a project site. To a large degree, successful form relationships between buildings and site determine project success. It is therefore essential that these relationships be well designed.

Material and Maintenance Issues. There are numerous material and maintenance issues that should be addressed as the base plane is developed.

Materials. Materials should be appropriate for their intended use, under the various weather conditions that occur. They should also be selected in terms of

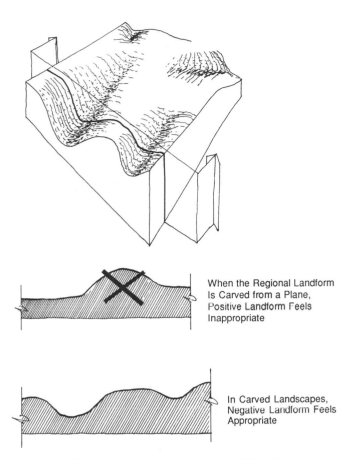

When the Regional Landform Is Carved from a Plane, Positive Landform Feels Inappropriate

In Carved Landscapes, Negative Landform Feels Appropriate

Figure 11-32. Regional appropriateness of landform.

the maintenance they will demand, and the degree of available maintenance.

The base plane consists of circulation elements, as well as elements that do not move people or goods. Circulation elements need to be of proper strength, texture, and weatherability for their intended use—pedestrian, bicycle, automobile, and so on. For those surfaces not serving a circulatory role, sensual characteristics and maintenance are primary issues for consideration.

From a visual sense, there are certain materials that feel appropriate on the base plane. Earth, natural carpets of turf or ground cover, water, rock, concrete, and brick all feel comfortable. Though not so natural in the base plane and presenting maintenance problems and short life because of decay, wood can be used to achieve design intent. Metals are generally short lived when contacting the ground, and usually pose comfort and safety problems. They are therefore usually inappropriate for use on the ground plane.

Maintenance. Materials that require more maintenance than is reasonable to deliver should not be used. Otherwise, sense of place will be destroyed as materials

degrade from inadequate maintenance. All surfaces must also be designed to withstand the anticipated type and volume of traffic.

Gravitational forces subject the base plane to far more wear than the other spatial strata must withstand. In a natural condition, environmental forces that operate under the influence of gravity, over time, establish a form that is in equilibrium to these forces. In manipulating the base plane, variance from these natural forms of equilibrium should be minimized as the amount of deviation tends to correlate with the intensity with which these processes modify that which has been designed.

The dynamic nature of the base plane should also be considered. In most regions of the country, the ground is in movement. Sometimes this movement results from volcanic activities, but more often it is due to expansion and contraction associated with freezing and thawing of soils, or changes in their moisture content. Materials for, and modifications to, the base plane should accommodate soil movements while requiring minimum maintenance. If low-maintenance materials and methods are not used, then materials should be physically separated from this zone of movement to prevent structural and maintenance problems, or the soil should be stabilized.

The base plane should be designed to facilitate the drainage of water (from all areas of the site) to existing drainageways. This requires an understanding of landform manipulation, grading, and drainage. Runoff must also be prevented from entering any structure, even if subsurface drainage systems should become inoperative. Excessive slopes that would increase rates of erosion and sedimentation must also be avoided.

Finally, in addressing base plane materials and maintenance, the site designer must not only address maintenance of the base plane itself, but also that of resources that depend on this stratum. The base plane must be shaped and materials selected so as to create a medium conducive to the establishment and easy maintenance of plant materials. This includes plant materials that function as part of the base plane, and those that comprise other strata, but that obtain nutrients and water from the soil.

The water resource, a limited one that must be managed, is also dependent on the base plane as water must penetrate the ground to access the reservoirs below. When water enters the soil, it becomes available, through capillary action, to plants. It also evaporates to cool near-surface microclimates. The remainder of this water flows downward under the influence of gravity to replenish underground aquifers from which water is extracted for drinking, recreational and industrial use, and other human needs.

In order to maintain the groundwater resource, the base plane must be developed so as to preserve pre-developed rates of water recharge. This can be done through the use of base plane materials (such as soil, turf, ground cover, and porous pavings) that facilitate water infiltration. Land can also be reshaped to drain into retention reservoirs that allow the water to infiltrate and thereby be harvested. Steep slopes, excessive paving, and the placing of water into lined channels, all greatly reduce infiltration and should be avoided.

Overhead Plane

In developing site spaces, the intent and use of the overhead, and its form, material, and maintenance must be considered.

Intent and Use. The overhead plane is usually sensed more than seen. Functionally, it can provide shelter from the rain. By shading, it can reduce incoming solar radiation and can reduce air temperatures by 10 degrees or more; and it can substantially reduce heat loads on buildings.

Beyond these functional issues, the overhead plane exerts unique spatial influences; modifies the amount, quality, character, and color of light; introduces movement; creates dramatic shadows; and possesses the potential to impart a variety of site characters and moods.

The overhead can be designed to add drama, suspense, and character to the site. Dense or solid overheads can be used to create cool, dark, shaded pockets (Figure 11-33). These pockets can be located so as to increase the sensual impact of sunlit exterior spaces. The overhead can also create rich spatial sequences with a range of light characters, to be experienced as one transverses the site.

The overhead can be designed to allow relatively intense light to penetrate holes in a dense canopy and dramatically illuminate elements within the space. It can also break to create rich flowering edge conditions (Figure 11-34). The overhead can be designed to impart energy to otherwise static spaces by introducing spindly trees, lacy foliage, and other overhead features that move in the wind.

Patterns of shade, including dappled, gridded, and

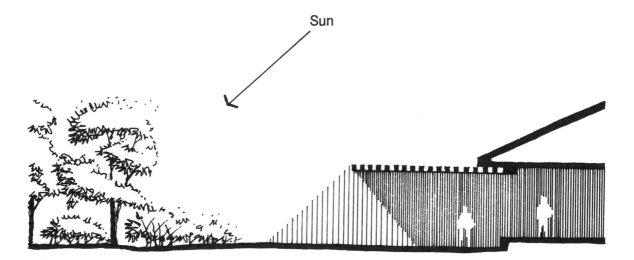

Figure 11-33. Overheads and shading.

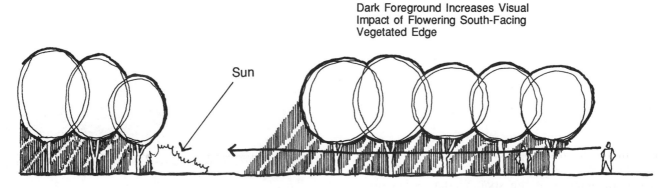

Dark Foreground Increases Visual Impact of Flowering South-Facing Vegetated Edge

Figure 11-34. Openings in canopy to increase drama.

streaked ones can be created by modifying the pattern and porosity of the overhead. In doing so, the shape and orientation of the overhead must be designed in response to sun angle and position of sun by time of day and year. The designer should also be acutely aware of the shadow patterns these overheads will cast on architectural elements and the drama and excitement that can thus be given to a site.

Form Considerations. In developing the overhead plane, the form of the overhead itself, and the form it imparts to the site through the manipulation of light and shadow are of immediate concern. In addition, the changing shadow shapes as plant materials mature over time, and seasonally as deciduous trees and shrubs lose their leaves in the winter, should be considered.

The overhead plane should be artfully formed for microclimatic amelioration. Site designers should also understand the spatial implications as canopies are introduced to improve site comfort or to decrease the costs of providing comfort within buildings. They should know where the overhead plane should be located high to allow breezes to flow beneath and where it should be held closer to the ground.

The height of the overhead should be manipulated to achieve desired mood, lowering it to 8 to 10 feet for intimacy, raising it to 14 to 20 feet for human scale, and elevating it to 20 feet or more to create a monumental feeling.

Material and Maintenance Issues. The range of available materials is large—from light and airy materials such as stretched wires, canvas, and spindly trees that move in the breeze, to rigid penetrated or solid planar surfaces including those made of wood, plastic, metal, concrete, or combinations thereof.

In selecting materials, the amount of movement desired, intended modifications to sunlight, color, shading effects, nighttime effects (including artificial lighting), and so on are of concern. The maintenance required to support the canopy including maintenance of plant materials, and maintenance to resist material weathering and decay, should also be considered.

Vertical Edge

As stated earlier, the vertical edge is the most visually dominant spatial stratum. It determines the size and basic character of the space. It can exclude undesirable elements from the space, and can call attention to special features. As exterior space is developed, effective management of the spatial edge is essential. This management includes response to design intent

and purpose, form considerations, and material and maintenance issues.

Intent and Purpose. The designer should create the spatial edge for design intent and relate the character of the edge to intended spatial mood and character, the characteristics of other strata, intended use, and existing features that are to be incorporated into the space or its edge.

There are numerous purposes that can be served in designing the spatial edge. For example, this edge can encompass, and thereby link elements. It can create enclosure so as to increase privacy or eliminate undesirable visual elements, or it can open to enframe distant elements, and link them to the site.

The edge can be expressed as dominant line to lead the eye through the composition, or to accentuate special elements. It can introduce color, or can create a neutral backdrop against which internal elements can be displayed. It can be designed to develop interest or to buffer or eliminate visual or other sensory distractions.

Occurring low to the horizon, the edge can eliminate late afternoon sun in the overheated summer (Figure 11-35) and can screen undesirable winds in the winter (Figure 11-36).

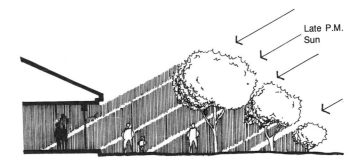

Figure 11-35. Edge as afternoon sunscreen.

Figure 11-36. Edge as windscreen.

Form. The planar form of the edge determines the size and affects the perceived scale and proportion of a space. In addition, the character of the edge can be designed to set the mood of the space. Rectilinear plan forms and vertical edge conditions can impart architectonic characteristics to the landscape (Figure 11-37); sinuous plan forms and layered edge conditions can create the sense of woodland edge (Figure 11-38).

In only a matter of inches, concrete or masonry walls can provide privacy. Effective screening can also be provided by shrubs, although this type of screening usually requires at least 20 feet of depth to achieve privacy (Figure 11-39). A penetrated edge can allow the reduced light levels that occur under a deep canopy beyond to "close" the space visually (Figure 11-40). An edge can be implied with a rhythmic row of tree trunks (Figure 11-41).

Contrast can be maximized at the base plane–edge interface or the overhead–edge intersection, to create dominant line. This line can be used to lead the eye, and its character can contribute mood to the space. The line can direct the eye to breaks in the enclosure, helping the viewer to discover a distant element that imparts a greater sense of place, for example, a distant beach as a framed view for a pool of water.

The edge can be designed to focus energies inward or to direct them outward. The edge can be compressed, penetrated to create impact, or extended to serve as a series of psychological filters.

The edge should be designed in response to existing physical conditions. A brick wall that accidentally impounds water, or an edge of flowering shrub that receives inadequate light to deliver the intended splash of color, will negate design intent.

Materials. The range of materials that can be used to create spatial edge is almost limitless. Clear glass in aluminum frames, stained glass in wood frames, polished marble, painted or weathering steel, concrete, brick, wood, dry-set field stone, and numerous other materials have all been used successfully to create spatial edge. Plant material can also be effective, standing alone or clinging to walls or screens.

Generally speaking, plant material can provide good visual screening, but is relatively ineffective in eliminating unwanted sound. Solid, massive walls, in addition to achieving visual screening, can eliminate or buffer some unwanted sound. Earthform as vertical edge, if at least 12 feet tall, can effectively reduce noise in areas adjacent to the walls (Figure 11-42).

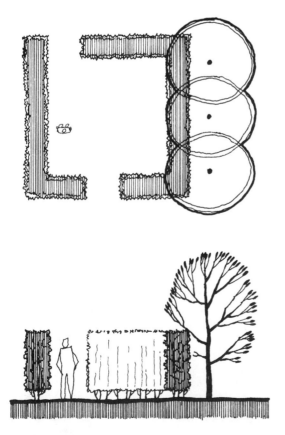

Figure 11-37. Architectonic edge.

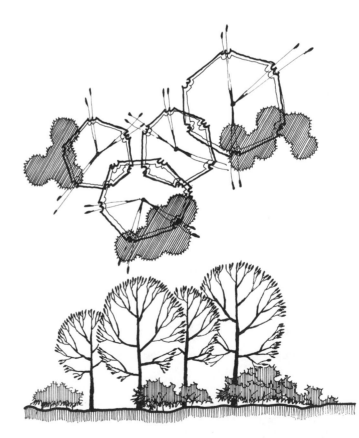

Figure 11-38. Naturalistic edge.

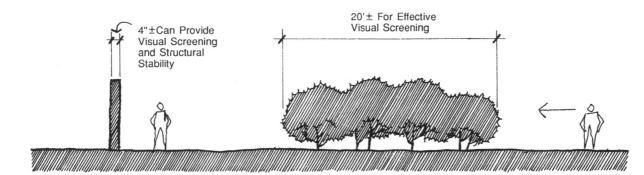

Figure 11-39. Depth of edge.

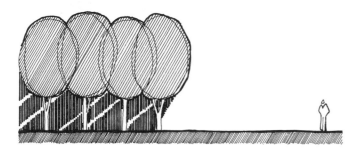

Figure 11-40. Shadowed edge as enclosure.

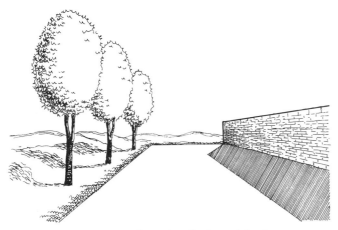

Figure 11-41. Tree trunks as implied spatial edge.

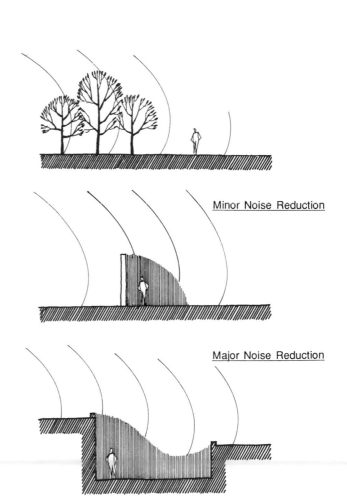

Figure 11-42. Noise attenuation.

Maintenance. Massive walls of stone, masonry or concrete can require relatively low maintenance if placed on rigid foundations. Wood exterior walls are also used extensively but are subject to decay. Vegetated edges can require little maintenance, or can necessitate extensive care, depending on the relationship among the material, soil conditions, available nutrients, available moisture, lighting conditions, microclimate, and other site conditions.

Elements Within the Space

Furniture, sculpture, fountains, equipment, and plant material can all exist as elements within a space. Often these elements express themselves near eye level. At other times, they occur as extensions from the base or overhead planes.

An element in space takes on a sculptural quality. It reads as form, but also interacts with the space, that is, it articulates the space. A dynamic and changing relationship occurs between the element and the space, the element and the spatial edge, and the element and other elements as one moves and changes location in space.

Figure 11-43. Element and space of similar character.

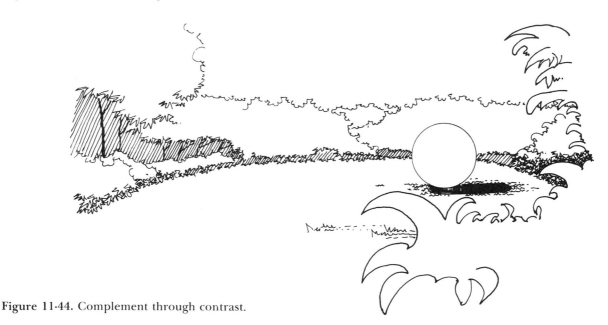

Figure 11-44. Complement through contrast.

Relation to Spatial Character

The character of the element and spatial character should bear a positive relationship. For example, the element and space could be of a similar character (Figure 11-43), or could complement each other through contrast in line, form, color, or texture (Figure 11-44).

By placing a small intricate sculptural element into a simple pure space, we can become more aware of spatial simplicity. Conversely, placing a simple piece of pure geometry into a complex asymmetrical space will make one more aware of the complexity of the space.

Asymmetrical space can be made to feel more dynamic if we focus on a pure element, located off-center in the space (Figures 11-45).

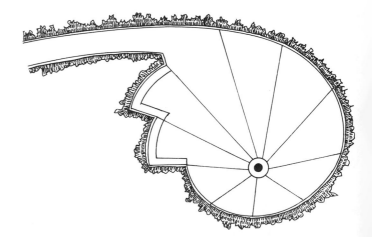

Figure 11-45. Pure element in asymmetrical space.

When the design intent is to display sculpture, the edge can be subdued, giving attention to the element. When the space itself is to be displayed, the element can serve as one of many focal points, or attention can be drawn from the element to the edge by careful manipulation of line, form, color, and texture (Figure 11-46).

When various elements are introduced to a space, the elements interact with one another, and with the spatial edge. Space flows between the objects. As one moves within the space, many varying relationships are expressed and the space takes on increased life. The relationships of element to element and of element to edge are therefore of paramount design importance.

Architecture and Spatial Development

This section begins by discussing the relationship of architecture and spatial development and the role of architects and landscape architects in the design of exterior space. It then addresses the differing spatial implications of singular buildings, and those of building aggregates. It explores architecture as enclosure and as form, including its potential for generating space. It discusses various relationships between architectural mass and spatial development. It addresses architecture as spatial "edge" and explores a range of

moods or character that this edge can instill. It closes with some suggestions that should be kept in mind as architecture is designed to create, and give meaning to, exterior space.

Professional Roles

Architecture satisfies the human need for shelter, while providing appropriate indoor settings to enhance the quality of life. It also modifies the building site. To be effective, architecture must not only address interior spatial needs, but must also provide desired outdoor shelter and enhance the quality of the outdoor experience. It also offers many opportunities to improve site climates.

The building exterior wall has the dual purpose of enclosing interior spaces and defining exterior ones. It should create meaningful spaces, both within and outside the building. Therefore, the building facade is as much an element of site design as it is a building design element.

As the interface between building and site, the building facade must support both the design intent of the architect (who is responsible for design of the building and interior spaces) and the landscape architect (who is often responsible for siting the building and designing exterior space). Ideally, building facades will be designed by the architect sensitive to

Figure 11-46. Edge as link for multiple spatial foci.

Figure 11-47. Individual building as sculpture.

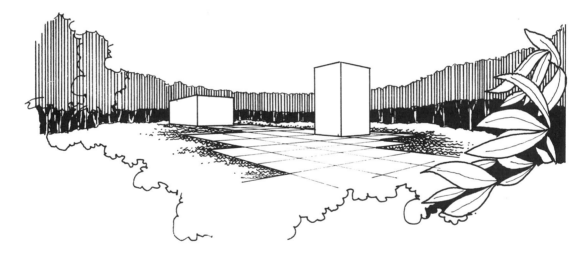

Figure 11-48. Building aggregate as multiple foci.

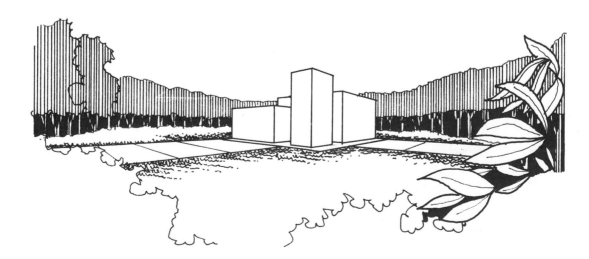

Figure 11-49. Building aggregate as sculptural mass.

site spatial development issues, or according to guidelines established as part of the overall project spatial development theme, mood, and design character.

Individual Buildings Versus Building Aggregates

Singular buildings placed onto a development site tend to be seen as sculpture in space (Figure 11-47). They often serve as the visual focus of the space. In this case, and as dominant element within the space, building character must relate to spatial character. The relationship of the building facade to the spatial edge and other spatial strata must be consciously managed to achieve the designed intent.

The building could be designed to blend with and become an integral part of the site, or to contrast with the site, making the viewer acutely aware of both architectural and building character.

Multiple buildings placed on the site can be located so as to read as numerous foci (Figure 11-48) or as a sculptured mass (Figure 11-49). In addition, the various building facades also read as spatial edge, and by their interaction create exterior space (Figure 11-50).

Architecture as Enclosure

Because they are planar, building facades read as hard spatial edges. The more closed and continuous this edge, the more definite the enclosure. Therefore, the location of building facades and the percentage of the viewshed they fill affect perceived enclosure and the character of space that is created.

Singular buildings are perceived primarily as sculpture; their facades do little to define space. However, when two buildings occur, they usually imply enclosure. When two facades occur at right angles to each other, they imply space (Figure 11-51). This space is asymmetrical in feeling, providing protection on one side and exposure on the other.

When two facades occur parallel to each other, they imply a space with strong directional character. In this manner, parallel building facades direct the eye to the open ends of the space, where emphasis is concentrated. As the facades become longer or closer together, enframement of the views at the ends of the space increases.

When three facades occur at right angles to one another, perceived enclosure increases substantially. The space exhibits a uni-directional character and conveys importance to the view beyond the unenclosed edge.

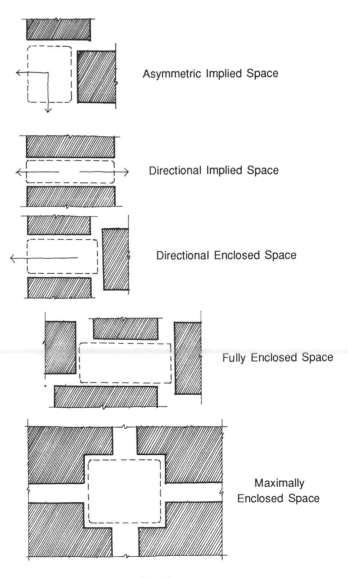

Figure 11-51. Degree of enclosure.

Figure 11-50. Building facades as spatial edge.

The space appears fully enclosed when all four sides are predominantly closed. When building facades close all corners of the space, maximum enclosure occurs.

When exterior spaces adjacent to buildings receive hard architectonic ceilings (concrete, steel, wood, and so on), they are perceived as being within the shroud of the building canopy. They feel like architectural extensions into the site.

Nature of Enclosure. Because they are hard and planar, building facades more forcefully enclose space than do area walls or vegetative enclosure. They can also have a tendency to overpower exterior space.

Because building facades are aggressive, those that are viewed from a distance-to-height ratio less than one to one (D:H < 1:1) generally feel comfortable only if the viewer can relate to architectural detail on the surface of the facade. When surface detail is missing, or the facade is perceived as mass, the viewer usually feels uncomfortable, if viewing from a distance-to-height ratio less than two to one (D:H < 2:1).

Architectural Form

The plan form of the architectural edge affects the perceived degree of enclosure, visual impact, and spatial character.

When breaks in the spatial edge align (Figure 11-52), the perceived degree of enclosure is reduced as one's line of sight (on approach) crosses the space and focuses on the view beyond. Such an axial alignment tends to minimize the impact of the space. Conversely, when breaks in the edge do not align, perceived enclosure is increased as the approach sightline is focused onto the closed edge (Figure 11-53). The viewer is forced to slow and change direction within the space, and is more acutely aware of its character.

The greatest degree of enclosure is felt when the space is fully bounded by building facades or when breaks in the edge display nearby building facades rather than a less architectural edge (Figure 11-54). Such spaces feel like an exterior architectural room. These spaces can be made to feel less severe by the introduction of landscape elements within the space.

When portions of the edge are implied by plant

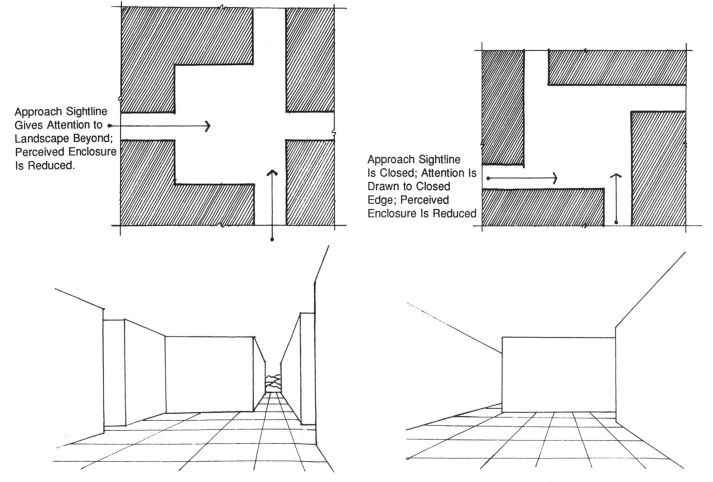

Approach Sightline Gives Attention to Landscape Beyond; Perceived Enclosure Is Reduced.

Approach Sightline Is Closed; Attention Is Drawn to Closed Edge; Perceived Enclosure Is Reduced

Figure 11-52. Aligned approach.

Figure 11-53. Disaligned approach.

materials used in an architectonic manner, the space feels somewhat less enclosed and of a somewhat decreased architectural character than the hard architectural edge (Figure 11-55).

When portions of the edge are implied by plant materials used in a nonarchitectonic manner, the space feels less enclosed still, and much less architectonic (Figure 11-56).

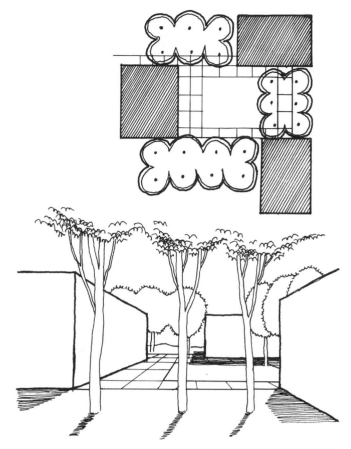

Figure 11-55. Plant material as architectonic edge.

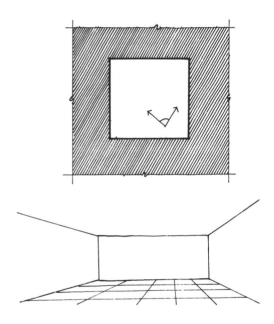

Perceived Enclosure Is Maximized When Facades Are Continuous or When Sightlines Camouflage Breaks in the Architectonic Edge.

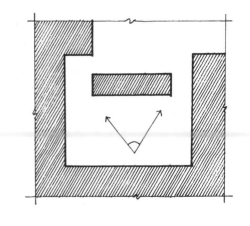

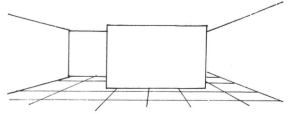

Figure 11-54. Facade continuity and enclosure.

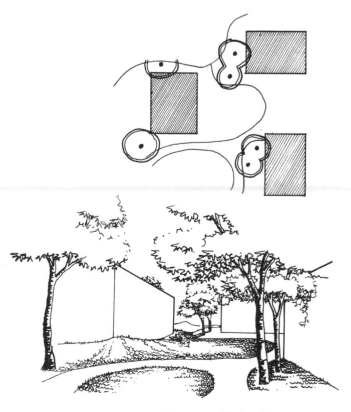

Figure 11-56. Plant material as naturalistic edge.

Relationships Between Mass and Space

When multiple buildings occur on a site, the character of building facades and the relationship among buildings will help determine mass-space relationships.

When individual buildings are rectilinear and when their relationships to one another are not geometrically ordered, exterior space is loosely defined. The buildings are usually perceived as dominant forms, and seen as loosely related pieces of sculpture (Figure 11-57). Conversely, when individual buildings bear geometrically ordered relationships to one another (usually orthogonal), the mind extends the lines of the buildings into the site and more forcefully defines the space.

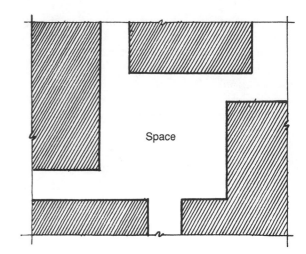

Figure 11-58. Static resolved space.

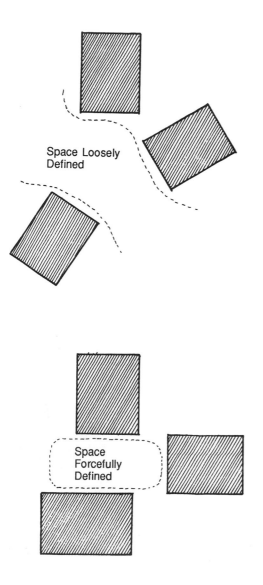

Figure 11-57. Building alignment and spatial definition.

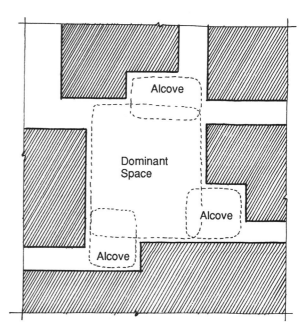

Figure 11-59. Dominant space with alcoves.

Simple Versus Aggregate Space. Buildings can be grouped to form simple space that conveys a static resolved sense (Figure 11-58). They can cluster to provide a dominant space, enriched by a series of spatial alcoves (Figure 11-59). A feeling of arrival and satisfaction is maintained within the major space, while spatial interest is greatly increased by the varied edge condition.

Buildings can also interact to form linear sequences. These directional spatial aggregates can convey a strong sense of movement and energy. The size

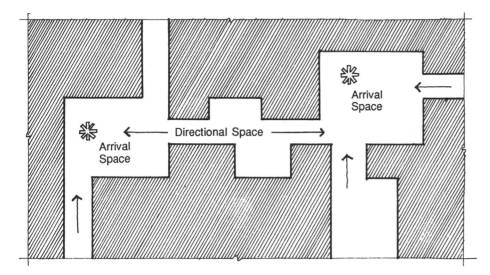

Figure 11-60. Sequential space.

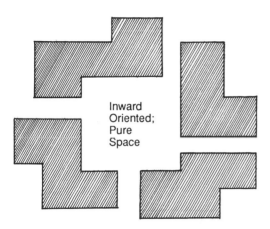

Figure 11-61. Space-dominant built form.

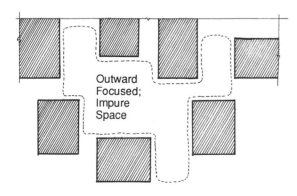

Figure 11-62. Mass-dominant built form.

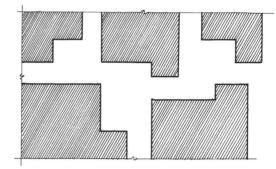

Figure 11-63. Mass-space dynamic interplay.

of individual spaces can be varied to achieve feelings of arrival, goal attainment, and linkage (Figure 11-60). Rich spatial sequences and designed story lines can be realized through these linear spatial aggregates.

Complexity and Emphasis. Complex architectural forms can be used to create simple exterior space (Figure 11-61). The viewer is thus made more aware of the boldness and purity of the inward-oriented exterior space, and this space becomes dominant.

Conversely, simple architectural forms can be used to create complex exterior space (Figure 11-62). The purity of the architectural forms can be "played" against the complexity and dynamic character of the exterior space. The composition tends to be mass dominant.

A balance of complexity between space and mass can be employed to convey a sense of continuity and an integration of mass and space (Figure 11-63). Neither space nor mass will assert dominance in this dynamic interplay.

Edge Character

Like other edges, building facades can enclose space, serve as backdrops, or enframe views. However, they are uniquely variable exterior spatial edges, in that they can also be opaque, reflective, translucent, or transparent.

Opaque architectural facades provide a consistent hard edge to exterior space. Reflective facades impart some of the site characteristics to the architectural edge, and can even camouflage the building. Translucent edges appear opaque when viewed from the light side, but appear to glow when viewed from the dark side.

Transparent building facades express diurnal characteristics. During the day, when viewed from within the building, glazing allows exterior space to become visually part of the building interior. When viewed from the exterior, however, the glazed edge appears closed and hard, sometimes opaque, sometimes reflective.

At night, when viewed from a lighted exterior space, glazing allows the exterior space to penetrate the lighted building. From a darkened exterior space, the facade becomes a three-dimensional illuminated show case. Viewed from within the building at night, interior space is isolated from a darkened site, but incorporates a lighted one into the interior space.

Visual Interest. Building facades are sometimes cold and harsh when massive, inhumanely scaled, lacking in detail or texture, or cold in color temperature (Figure 11-64). However, by varying the roofline, adding detail or texture, extending the edge with arcades or arbors, layering the facades, or employing transparent surfaces or warm colors, facades can be more humane, friendly, and cheerful (Figure 11-65).

Design Direction

Once the design concept underlying the site development is determined (Chapter 13) and programmatic uses are arranged on the site, exterior spaces can be defined, and spatial sequences and story lines can be created. Mass-space relationships can then be determined and the building can be shaped accordingly (and in response to architectural needs). The role and character of specific exterior spaces can be determined, and the architectural facades can be designed to support desired spatial mood and character.

Temporal Considerations

The issues about time that should be considered as exterior space is being developed include change as the essence of natural systems versus the static nature of architecture, diurnal characteristics, and perception as a space-time continuum.

Change in Natural Systems Versus the Static Nature of Architecture

Natural systems are point-in-time expressions of ongoing environmental processes. As such, sites and living organisms are constantly experiencing change. Conversely, architecture consists of relatively static elements. The architectural forms achieved during construction change very little over time, until new construction activities are introduced.

Architectural elements are "complete" when the contractor leaves the project site. The spatial character imparted by architecture (except for diurnal issues already discussed) is reasonably constant over time.

Plant materials, on the other hand, are living organisms. When young, they are very tolerant of abuse, are easy to work with, and are reasonably inexpensive. When mature, they are relatively intolerant of abuse, quite difficult to work with, and quite expensive to move. Plant materials are therefore seldom planted in a mature state. The site designer must understand the spatial characteristics of specific material when planted, and changes to these characteristics as the material achieves maturity and old age. The designer must design exterior space to be satisfying both in a young and a mature state. In fact, the dynamic character of the developed site, maturing as plant materials progress through adolescence, middle age, and senility can be one of the most sensual temporal characteristics of exterior space.

The seasonal characteristics of vegetation also contribute to spatial mood and visual interest. While the architectural spatial components remain static, deciduous plant materials change with the season. Their color changes from spring to summer to fall, and their form, color, and texture change from summer to winter. Their density often evolves from an opaque leafed mass in the summer to a lacy skeleton in the winter. As they change, deciduous plant materials often assume seasonal spatial roles. Material that reads as spatial edge in the summer can become sculptural element within a much larger space in the winter. An overhead vegetative canopy can create dense shade when needed in the summer, and allow light to penetrate in the winter.

Site spatial mood can also change with season. Spaces with edges consisting primarily of architectural surfaces and with deciduous material as sculpture within the spaces can change their basic character, becoming much harsher and more architec-

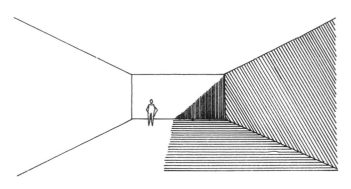

Figure 11-64. Dehumanized architectonic space.

tonic in the winter condition, softer and less dominated by buildings in the summer.

Diurnal Characteristics

Exterior spaces exhibit diurnal variation. Transparent building facades create spatial edges that change their expression (from transparent, to reflective, to opaque) with changing conditions, from day to night.

Exterior spatial character and perceived size and scale also change diurnally. During the day, exterior space is defined and given size by its perceived edge, and can extend to infinity. At night the size of the space is often reduced to the perceived envelope of light.

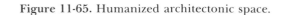

Figure 11-65. Humanized architectonic space.

At night visual emphasis shifts from the spatial edge to the elements being lit. If the edge is continuously lighted, the actual size of the space changes little. More often, specific elements are lit and the perception changes from the daytime one of *continuity of edge* to the nighttime *multiple foci* associated with pools of light and featured elements.

Nighttime spatial perception is also more sensuous than the daytime experience. Surrounded by the dark unknown, colors that are well lighted seem quite intense; and the veil of darkness can instill a mysterious or even foreboding character. On the other hand, artificial lighting effects, including uplighting, downlighting, backlighting, and so on, can create interest, excitement, and even gaiety in the nighttime perception of exterior space.

Space-Time Continuum

Environmental perception is based primarily on serial vision, that is, vision as a series of perceptions. As part of a serial experience, spatial perception and sense of place are affected by the viewer's state of mind and frame of reference. Both are affected by experiences that immediately precede the experience of a place and those that are anticipated.

The perceived size and character of a space are related most closely to the spatial perceptions immediately preceding. A small space can be made to feel more grand by constricting its entrance, a space more bright by entering through a darkened tunnel.

Specific exterior spaces should be consciously designed as part of a spatial sequence or story line that displays each space to its advantage, and that through sequential discovery, unwraps a temporal experience. This experience should be understandable yet stimulating, with elements of continuity and surprise, tension and satisfaction, movement and arrival. Subtle sequences can be developed to filter out one sense of place and accentuate another. Breaks can be introduced to achieve spatial impact.

Speed of Travel. As a temporal experience through a space-time continuum, spatial perception is affected by our rate of movement. As speed increases, spaces seem to reduce in size and our attention is directed forward. As we pause, space seems more expansive and we become more aware of the full circumference and volume of the space. As the mode of travel changes from foot, to bicycle, to automobile, spatial development should also change to address the different perceptions that result.

Spatial perception is affected by observer speed, but the rate of flow is itself a function of spatial development. The proportion, edge character, and rhythmic or linear characteristics of space can be manipulated to affect the rate of flow. Therefore, one interactive temporal issue of spatial design is the simultaneous manipulation of spatial form, rate of flow, and spatial perception so as to maximize the experience as one moves through the landscape.

The Land Design Palette

The land design palette consists of rock and earth, water, and plants. Each offers unique spatial development opportunities.

Rock and Earth

Rock and earth are our environmental base. In a natural condition, they sometimes create spatial edge, as escarpments, cliffs, caves, and mountains. In so doing, they create a sense of mass, and can create space. Only rarely do rocks in nature create ceilings over our heads. However, when they do, they create a powerful sense of being within. Rock and earth materials in an altered state—brick, asphaltic concrete, cinder, concrete, and so on—are used extensively in base plane design, as well as building design.

Rock and earth convey a sense of massiveness and permanence. They can also convey richness of color and surface texture.

In the development of exterior space, rock and earth serve as the static base. They remain constant over time, and lend stability and permanence to exterior space. As elements of the spatial edge, they can serve as a constant backdrop against which other more variable elements can be displayed. They can also be static elements that are displayed within a variable space.

Water

Water is also a primary material of the natural base plane. As a base plane material, it exhibits a range of expressions—as planar form, transparent mass, reflective surface, and moving line. As vertical surface, water occurs naturally as falls, as a thin film that seeps across other surfaces, changing their mood and character, and a fine transparent or frothy spray.

Water offers unique spatial development opportunities. It can be used as a reflective or transparent base material. Its liquidity can be expressed as a clean transparent pool, free of plant and animal life, or it can be part of a diverse ecosystem. It can also structure plant materials by its presence.

As a base plane material, the form of water is dependent on the shape, color, and texture of its container, and the depth and clarity of the water.

As a spatial edge water can stand alone as a front-lit opaque sheet. It can be a backlit, translucent, aerated surface, or a transparent plane.

As an element within space, water has unique power to concentrate meaning, and to intensify spatial mood. As lakes, pools, ponds, or sheets, still water has power to unify a space. As stream or channel, it can be a linear system, linking various spaces into a continuum.

Moving water that pours, trickles, gurgles, seeps, ripples, waves, shoots, drops, or splashes can add energy and excitement. Sprays and mists can substantially cool a space.

Water can be ephemeral, present in one instance, gone the next. It can express spatial rhythm as elements repeat in space, or temporal rhythm, as water appears, swells, retreats, and vanishes, only to reappear and begin the cycle anew.

The power of water is in no small part due to its ability to simultaneously effect sound, light, smell, and touch. By playing with the senses, water has a singularly strong ability to instill spatial character and mood.

Plants

Plant materials include ground covers; low, intermediate, and tall shrubs; small and flowering trees; and intermediate and large trees. Let us briefly review the implications of these materials and other plant materials for spatial development.

Turf, ground covers, herbaceous materials, and low shrubs serve as the vegetated base plane. They blanket the unchanging rock and earth plane with a carpet that is highly variable in line, form, color, and texture. Unlike rock and earth, these plant materials can introduce dramatic seasonal variety to the base plane.

Low shrubs are extensions of the base plane, and physically separate areas and imply spatial edge. However, they generally do not enclose space.

Intermediate and tall shrubs provide a high degree of enclosure and sense of privacy. They are the primary plant material of the vegetated edge. They also serve as backdrop for the display of elements within the space, and can themselves be spatial sculpture.

Small and flowering trees can serve as spatial sculpture and can introduce movement and shade to a space. They are effective when used in small spaces, but tend to get lost in large ones unless they are combined with other elements to create mass. Small and flowering trees can be incorporated into a spatial edge and can increase the visual interest and seasonal variety. They can also be used to screen low-angle sun and create dynamic streaking patterns of shadow in the early morning or late afternoon. As individual specimen, they can create patches of ground shadow. In conjunction with other small trees, they can create a natural thicket or intimately scaled architectonic bosque. In so doing, they can provide a continuous, shadow-producing low canopy.

Large and intermediate trees usually form the vegetated canopy. Their spatial significance is felt primarily through their effects on light and the shadow patterns they introduce to the site. When viewed from great distances, they can enclose space, but when viewed from nearby, they are open at eye level. Their trunks can only imply spatial edge.

Vines are perhaps the most spatially versatile of all plant materials. They can be expressed in either the base, edge, or overhead planes. They can be evergreen and reasonably static over time, or can introduce seasonal character to virtually any surface. Over a reasonably short period of time, they can mature to soften an architectural base, edge, or overhead into a more textured, varied spatial surface. They can hang free and create a highly natural sense, or they can hug building walls, expressing themselves as architectonic planes. They can be effective in quickly and economically changing the mood or character of a space.

REFERENCES

Booth, Norman. 1983. *Basic Elements of Landscape Architectural Design.* New York: Elsevier.

Lynch, Kevin, and Hack, Gary. 1984. *Site Planning*, 3d ed. Cambridge, MA. MIT Press.

Moore, J. E. 1978. *Design for Good Acoustics and Noise Control.* London: Macmillan.

Simonds, John. 1983. *Landscape Architecture: A Manual of Site Planning and Design.* New York: McGraw-Hill.

SUGGESTED READINGS

Alexander, Christopher. 1979. *The Timeless Way of Building.* New York: Oxford University Press.

Laurie, Michael. 1975. *An Introduction to Landscape Architecture.* New York: American Elsevier.

Vitruvius, Pollio. 1960. *Vitruvius: The Ten Books on Architecture.* Morris Hicky Morgan, trans. New York: Dover.

12

Architecture and Site Development

Most site design projects contain buildings—existing and/or planned ones. On the developed site, these buildings can serve as sculpture. They can also, through the shaping of individual buildings, or the arrangement of multiple buildings, cluster to enclose space.

Whether the building serves as sculpture or creates space, the perception of the built landscape is usually a gestalt of building and site. When the building is viewed as sculpture, the site is the context in which it is viewed and appreciated. The site should display the sculpture in its most positive sense. When the building encloses exterior space, site elements become the furniture within an exterior architectural room. In either case, the character of the space and its contents should support and complement each other.

In the highly integrated built site, the gestalt can become an interwoven complex of architecture and site development, with site and architectural elements serving as both sculpture and context, and together building a common theme or sense of place.

SITE DESIGN INTENT

Whether relating through sameness, compatibility, or contrast, architecture and site should be consciously managed to allow mutually supportive relationships to occur. These relationships, referred to as synergisms, occur when both the building designer and the site designer understand the forces that give meaning to architecture and to sites, and when both the architect and the landscape architect respond to these forces in an integrated manner, and combine their efforts in the making of place.

While this entire text promotes an understanding of the forces that give meaning to project sites, this chapter specifically explores the forces that influence

building form and that integrate buildings and sites. It begins by presenting an overview of the morphological influences of architecture. It proceeds to address the differing perceptions and design intent prevalent today in architecture and landscape architecture, and concludes with a discussion of building-site synergisms.

INFLUENCES OF ARCHITECTURAL MORPHOLOGY

The noted architect Michael Graves published a collection of his works (*Michael Graves, Building and Projects*, 1982). In the introduction to this book, he provides an overview of the forces that influence and give meaning to architectural form, as he builds "A Case for Figurative Architecture."

Graves defines the language of architecture to include both "a standard form and a poetic form" of building. Architectural morphology expresses both of these forms in varying degrees. According to Graves:

> The standard form of a building is its common and internal language . . . building in its most basic form, determined by pragmatic, constructional, and technical requirements. In contrast, the poetic form of architecture is responsive to issues external to the building, and incorporates the three dimensional expression of the myths and rituals of society. Poetic forms of architecture are sensitive to the figurative, associative and anthropomorphic attitudes of a culture.

Although not stated in Graves's discussion, the poetic form of building can express the culture's, the client's, or the designer's attitudes, theories and ethics. In so doing, the poetic form of architecture can either reflect the culture, or promote the views of a smaller group, with the intent of changing cultural perceptions.

In the standard form of building, the architect is primarily concerned with the design of the various systems that comprise a building, the integration of these systems to one another, and their interface with larger site and urban systems. In the poetic form of building, the architect addresses symbol, reference, and illusion: the intellectualization and the associational meaning of architecture. The standard form speaks to the physical reality of the building, its poetic form, to a metaphysical reality.

Standard Form of Building

The physical reality of the building is influenced by its support systems, including ones that are circulatory, structural, and mechanical. Together these systems allow for the movement of people while providing structural stability, climate amelioration, distribution of power and water, and collection and removal of waste products from the building. In so doing, they influence building morphology. The standard form of architecture is also influenced by building materials and construction techniques.

Circulation Systems

Circulation can affect building form in several ways. The primary entrance to the building is usually important, both physically and psychologically. Building form usually acknowledges its significance, and the primary entrance often plays a major role in determining overall building form and mass-void relationships (Figure 12-1). The degree to which the architect

wishes to make a statement of entry affects the degree to which the primary entrance influences building morphology. Secondary entrances also play a formative role, although usually to a lesser degree.

Circulation within the building also affects morphology. When vertical elements (stairways, ramps, or elevators) occur along the exterior of the building (or an exterior wall), they usually have a formative effect on building morphology. Stairs and elevators are often expressed as vertical elements (Figure 12-2), and sometimes extend as towers above the roof (to provide roof access or to support building elevators and to house related equipment). Occasionally, as in the Pompidou Center in Paris designed by Richard Rogers and Renzo Piano (Figure 12-3), these circulation elements become the dominant form statement, expressing their importance, and affording dramatic site views.

Horizontal circulation within the building can also affect form. Many buildings, such as airports, motels, office buildings, and so on, achieve efficiency by ar-

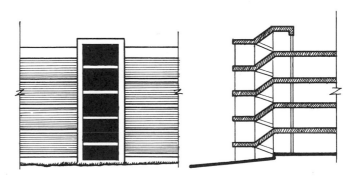

Figure 12-2. Stairs and building form.

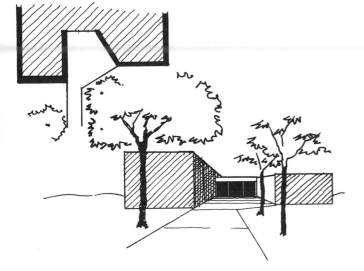

Figure 12-1. Entry and building form.

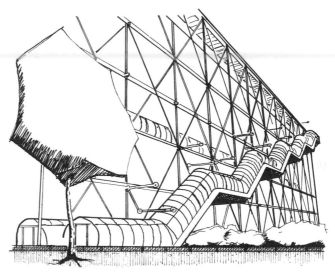

Figure 12-3. Circulation and building form.

ranging similarly sized spaces on either side of a circulation spine. In many cases, circulation areas are glazed to the exterior at the ends of the circulation spine, and therefore this double-loaded corridor promotes a symmetrical organization. Building use spaces read as masses on either side of the void of the corridor (Figure 12-4).

In other cases, to provide light to circulation paths, to open these routes to dramatic site views, or for other reasons, the corridor is pulled to one side of the building. These single-loaded corridors are usually glazed and visually open to the site, and therefore promote asymmetrical building forms (Figure 12-5). As building circulation influences morphology, it also creates opportunities for building-site synergisms.

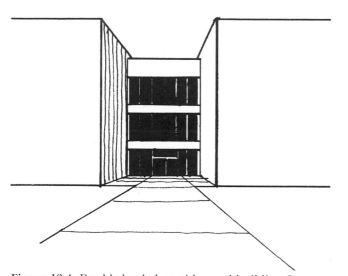

Figure 12-4. Double-loaded corridor and building form.

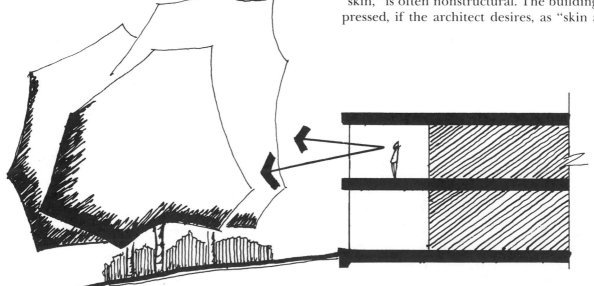

Figure 12-5. Single-loaded corridor and building form.

Structural Systems

The materials and construction techniques by which a building achieves statics are based on underlying structural concepts. Together, these materials and techniques comprise a structural system that normally has a formative influence on building morphology. This influence is usually expressed in two ways: by the size, location, and rhythm of building openings, and by the location and thickness of structural elements.

Building Openings. Most residential buildings and a large percentage of single-story buildings are load-bearing structures. In these structures roof loads are transmitted to the diaphragm of the wall, and transferred by the wall (usually wood frame, masonry, or concrete) to the strengthened edge of the floor slab or to continuous grade beams that contact the earth (Figure 12-6). These structures read as solid masses or as penetrated masses, as in the Cathedral Notre Dame du Haut in Ranchamps, France, by Le Corbusier (Figure 12-7). Large openings that occur must be supported by secondary structural elements such as beams and columns; therefore, openings tend to be small. They are also freed from a regularly spaced repetition, as their location is not determined by a rhythmic structural system (with columns occurring at regular intervals).

Most nonresidential construction, buildings larger than one story in height, buildings employing large open spans, and those that need interior adaptability or flexibility, employ some form of structural grid. These grids usually have rhythmic or repetitive characteristics, for example, columns that occur in a regular or predictable manner. In these structures the exterior wall, functioning primarily as a building "skin," is often nonstructural. The building can be expressed, if the architect desires, as "skin and bones"

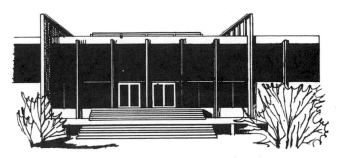

Figure 12-8. Building as structure and skin.

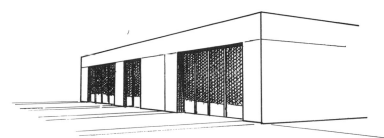

Figure 12-9. Concealed structure and building form.

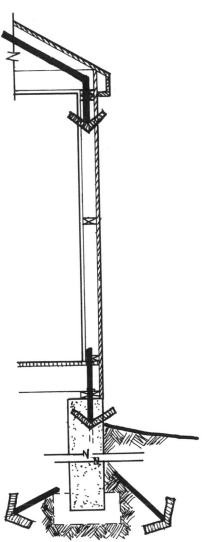

Figure 12-6. Load-bearing exterior walls.

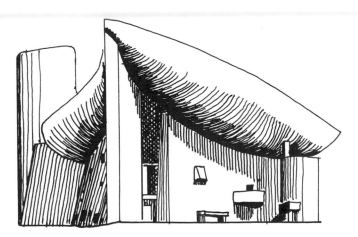

Figure 12-7. Building as penetrated mass.

as in the ITT President's house by Mies Van Der Rohe (Figure 12-8), or the bones can be concealed behind a continuous skin.

When the architect chooses not to express structural elements literally, these elements can still impart major morphological influences. Any departures from the desired column locations are difficult to achieve and costly. Therefore, even when the structural system is concealed, it organizes the mass-void relationships of the building facade in a somewhat regular manner (Figure 12-9).

Structure and Depth. Building elements including floors, walls, and roofs are either load-bearing members of considerable dimension, or are nonstructural "skins" that cover larger structural members. In either case, floors, walls, and roofs are three-dimensional, not two-dimensional forms. Their three-dimensional character is usually apparent, as shown in Figure 12-10.

The strength and rigidity of members subjected to bending stresses (as are most structural elements), are determined by the depth of the member in relation to its bending axis. As spans increase, so too does the required thickness of these members in order to provide the additional strength (Figure 12-11). For each combination of material, structural concept, and span, there is a minimally acceptable thickness of structure. The experienced designer develops a feel for these required thicknesses, often referred to as an intuitive structural sense.

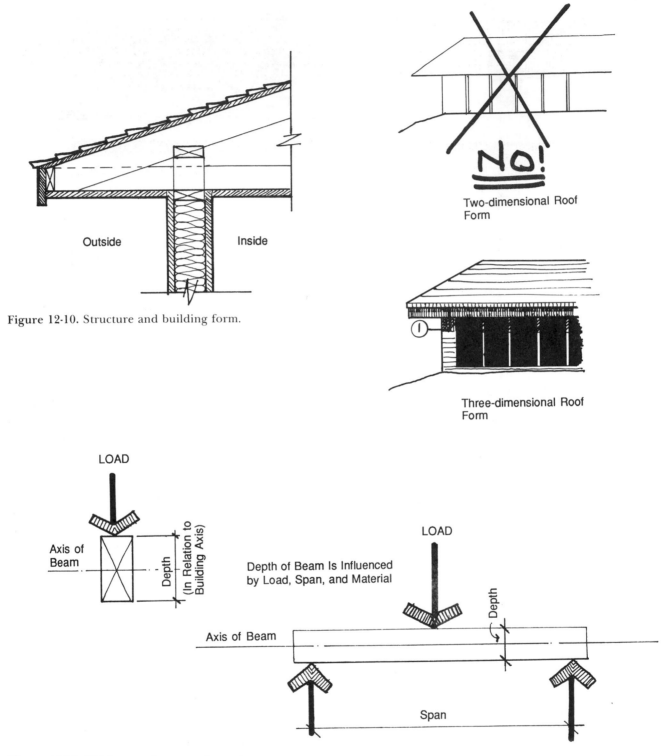

Figure 12-10. Structure and building form.

Two-dimensional Roof Form

Three-dimensional Roof Form

Figure 12-11. Thickness of structural members.

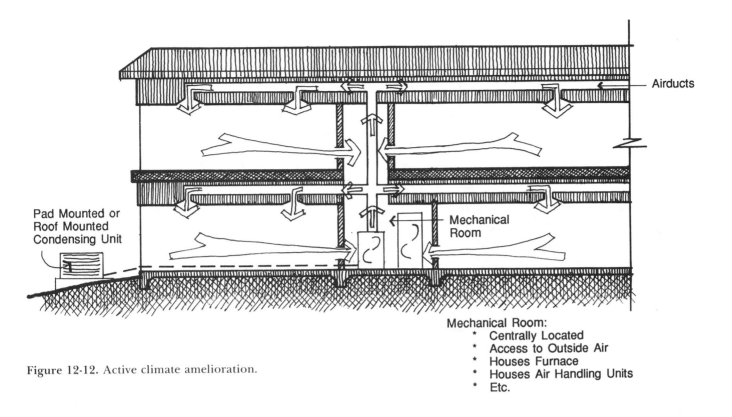

Pad Mounted or Roof Mounted Condensing Unit

Airducts

Mechanical Room

Mechanical Room:
* Centrally Located
* Access to Outside Air
* Houses Furnace
* Houses Air Handling Units
* Etc.

Figure 12-12. Active climate amelioration.

Mechanical Systems

Buildings must include systems for climate amelioration, distribution of power and water, and collection and removal of wastes. These systems each affect built form. Of these mechanical systems, the one for climate amelioration exerts by far the greatest morphological influence.

Climate Amelioration. In discussing building climate amelioration, one must first answer a basic question. Does the building provide comfort actively or through passive means?

Active design strategies for climate amelioration are based on mechanical solutions. When designing active systems, the architect usually isolates the building from site climates, and internally conditions building air. This air is usually heated or cooled in a centrally located mechanical room. From here the conditioned air is forced throughout the building by large fans (air-handling units), which are usually also located in the mechanical room (Figure 12-12).

The amelioration of building climates by active means requires substantially large ducts for the forced distribution of conditioned air, and even larger return air plenums (chases through which air is induced by lower pressure to return to the air-handling units). Often, either the forced air ducts, or more commonly the return air plenums, occur at the exterior of the building. When they do, they can be overtly expressed and can profoundly affect building morphology (Figure 12-13). Even when these plenums are hidden, they are visually solid masses (without windows). These masses affect overall building form, facade rhythm, and other visual characteristics.

Building climates can also be passively conditioned. Passive design strategies provide building comfort through nonmechanical means. Buildings that employ these strategies are, of necessity, finely tuned to site conditions. When buildings are designed to provide comfort passively, morphology varies greatly in different climates. Passive buildings therefore express a high degree of regionalism. In cold climates, buildings are visually open to the sun, and attempt to be-

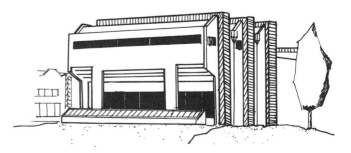

Figure 12-13. Air plenums and building morphology.

come solar heat sinks (Figure 12-14). In hot, humid climates, buildings usually exclude the sun and maximize natural ventilation (Figure 12-15). The litany of regionally appropriate passive design strategies is beyond the scope of this text, but a nice overview is presented in *Climatic Design: Energy-Efficient Building Principles and Practices* (1983), by Donald Watson and Kenneth Labs.

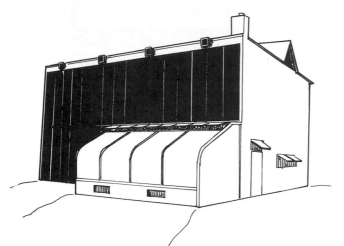

Figure 12-14. Passive design for cold climates. (Don Kelbrough's Trombe Wall House. Adapted from Donald Watson and Kenneth Labs, *Climatic Design*)

Figure 12-15. Passive buildings in hot, arid climates. (Double wind tower system in Kerman, Iran. Adapted from A. Bowen, "Historical Responses to Cooling Needs in Shelter and Settlement," *Passive Cooling Conference Proceedings,* American Solar Energy Society, Miami Beach, Florida, 1981)

Whether building climates are actively or passively conditioned, the site designer should understand the design intent and strategies being employed for climate amelioration. Only then can the site be modified so as to enhance the energy and comfort performance of the building.

Power and Water. The distribution of power (gas or electrical) and water throughout the building involves reasonably small conducts. These are also pressure flow systems. For both reasons, distribution systems usually require relatively small chases that can be located without greatly influencing building morphology.

Sanitary Sewage. The sanitary sewage system exerts a somewhat greater influence on building form. Sewer pipes carry materials that must flow under the influence of gravity; the pipes are also substantially larger than pressure-flow conduits. Therefore, the architect usually takes great care to consolidate uses (such as toilet rooms) that require these services and, in multistory construction, to align them vertically. Both these strategies affect building form, as the chases are almost never glazed, and are often expressed as building masses.

Poetic Form of Building

The poetic form of building addresses symbol, reference, and illusion. It speaks to the art of architecture. As an art form, buildings express the aspirations of a culture, a client, or a designer, and promote myth and ritual.

Never have the poetry of architecture and landscape architecture been farther apart than they are today, and this rift appears to be due in no small part to design education. This section explores the prevalent trends in the poetry of architectural education and in the education of landscape architects in an effort to impart an understanding of the poetry of architecture and landscape architecture, and the issues involved in the synergism of these two expressions of associational meaning.

Design Ethic

The prevalent design ethic in architectural education today is self-expression, that is, architecture as the designer's idea or statement. A primary design goal is maintaining the purity of the design statement. The architect is seen as the dominant force in the design process. This attitude concerning design is one of the most overt expressions of the anthropomorphic tendency of our culture. Nowhere, except perhaps in fine art, is the perception of "human as form-giver" more pronounced than in the self-perception of architect as form-giver.

It is this attitude concerning design (and its contextual and environmental ramifications) that has fueled the recent growth in the profession of landscape architecture, whose ethic embodies the alternative swing of the pendulum. The prevalent design ethic of landscape architecture is stewardship. This ethic promotes landscape design as the management of systems. Whereas the architect embodies the anthropomorphic values of our society, the landscape architect generally embraces the notion of design response. This positions the landscape architect closer to systemic designers, appropriate technologists, and futurists, and to the growing ethic of sustainability.

The landscape architect tends to be a systems thinker and sees design as the artful management of integrated systems, including diverse ones that are cultural, ecological, visual, and so on. Architecture is currently reacting *against* systems thinking, which, having been tried in the 1970s, is now out of vogue. As a systems thinker, the landscape architect interprets design ideas in terms of systems management,

and is often seen by architects as compromising their design ideas. Conversely, the architect is often seen by landscape architects to design without appropriate relation to condition or context.

Perception of Mass and Space

The building is an aggregate of many usable spaces. However as a sculpted entity, it is perceived primarily as mass. The architect tends to be more concerned with the building as a designed mass than with the exterior spaces that this mass creates. This tendency is seldom more clearly perceived than on university campuses. Although the buildings are under common ownership, and this could be managed for their interrelationships and visual integration, effective spatial development, and exciting story lines, most campuses read as a melange of poorly related pieces of architectural sculpture (Figure 12-16). Each building is usually an effective expression of a design concept and form vocabulary. However, each also usually fails to develop a meaningful dialogue with surrounding structures and contributes to the overriding visual chaos. One facade of the building relates well to the

Figure 12-16. Campus as melange of unrelated buildings.

opposite facade (although the two cannot be viewed together), but relates poorly to other building facades, which together define the exterior spaces through which one moves and experiences the campus. The same problem exists in most built environments, and generally characterizes urban spaces.

The landscape architect, whose task centers around providing meaning to the designed landscape, is much more concerned with the visual harmony of exterior spaces created, in large part, by aggregates of buildings, and by building-context synergisms.

Temporal Aspects of Design Poetry

Buildings are static elements. While they may "grow" in increments by the addition of new units, the units themselves are static. Conversely, the landscape architect's roots are in nature, whose essence is change. As an outgrowth of this difference, the poetry of architecture is primarily a static (spatial) one, the landscape architect's poetry is more concerned with space-time continuums and with changes that occur over time: as systems evolve, as spaces change their expression, and as perception of the visual scene evolves as we move through space.

Design Styles-Movements

To establish visual harmony and to communicate more effectively the meaning of architecture and of exterior spaces, the landscape architect must understand the architecture that creates these spaces and the meanings that these buildings impart. For this reason, the landscape architect must be able to understand the design intent of the architect. However, the landscape architect must also establish symbiotic relationships between architecture and site. Therefore, he or she must be able to recognize and address inconsistencies between architectural intent and context when these inconsistencies occur. The landscape architect must also be able to synergize contradictory meanings.

Architectural Movements and Cultural Expression. This section represents an interpretation of recent architectural movements including their intent, successes, and shortcomings. It does not aspire to review history, but only to address the forces that have generated the bulk of the "standing state" of American architecture, and those that influence contemporary architecture. Therefore, it addresses the major movements in post-World War II American architecture.

In addressing the poetry of post-World War II American architecture, it is crucial to realize that throughout this period, architects have not viewed themselves primarily as vehicles for cultural expression, but rather as individuals expressing a view of a better culture. Except for a few "revolutionary" expressions such as *Architecture without Architects* (Rudofsky 1964) and *Learning from Las Vegas* (Robert Venturi et al. 1972), architects have chosen to downplay a large segment of the generative forces of our culture. They have seen these forces as undesirable or irrelevant. Architectural education has rather concentrated on elevating desirable forces to an art form, and on desensitizing the student of architecture to undesirable forces that might compromise the purity of the design statement. As a result, the standing state of American architecture expresses two very different traditions. The first is the intellectualized architectural statement, designed by proponents of the intellectualized movement, the other the cultural expressions of common buildings, designed by architects outside this movement or (for small buildings) by persons other than registered architects. Most American housing falls in the latter category.

The intellectualized architecture is poetry rich. Its advocates see architecture as an art form, and see buildings generated by cultural forces as "buildings, but certainly *not* architecture." Conversely, a growing segment of the public has come to view intellectualized architecture as irrelevant or capricious. They see it as fine art, but not culturally relevant.

The following discussion of style and architectural movements addresses intellectualized architecture, for it is the poetry of these buildings that the landscape designer must understand when working with allied design professionals. It does not address buildings outside the intellectualized movement, or their language, because these buildings are literal expressions of market and other cultural forces. Their meaning does not depend on intellectualization; it is rather conveyed daily through the media and experience. It is, for better or worse, part of our cultural expression.

Modern Architecture. Until the early 1970s the poetry of architecture was dominated by the modern movement. This movement was founded in rationalism. It was an elitist architecture that sought not to express the diversity of our culture, but rather purity of expression. It espoused the use of limited materials and reduced their expression to literal statements such as architecture as machine, form follows function, or skin and bones (Figure 12-8). It attempted to purify society through purity of architecture. As a rational exercise, modern architecture elevated the standard form of the building to its poetic level, that is, the systems of architecture were its language and, to large degree, its meaning. The poetry expressed building systems, including the machine processes that created buildings, as an art form. Cultural forces that did not support this poetry were often left unaddressed.

Of course, post-World War II American culture was not pure. It was characterized by many conflicting forces. It included new feelings of social freedom by black Americans returning from war (a freedom earned by equality on the battlefield), and by women who earned their freedom in wartime factories. Both these feelings conflicted with prewar white chauvinistic perceptions of social structure. By failing to embrace varying forces of our society, modern architecture failed to achieve cultural relevancy. The same forces that generated the turbulent sixties also dealt a blow to modern architecture.

Whether modern architecture died, or merely lost its purity, remains a subject of debate. However, many architects associate the end of modern architecture with the Pruitt-Igoe Housing Project in St. Louis, Missouri. The project had been designed in strict accordance with the poetry of modernism, and had received a design award in 1951 from the American Institute of Architects. Through purity of design, separation of automobile and pedestrian, austerity and cleanliness, it aspired to impart its purity to the behavior of its residents. Unfortunately, it failed to relate to the lifestyle, goals, and aspirations of its residents. Behavior, rather than being purified, was confrontational. On July 15, 1972, after almost twenty years of nearly continuous vandalism, several of its fourteen-story housing units were unceremoniously dynamited by the city.

Postmodern Architecture. About ten years before the death blow demolition of Pruitt-Igoe, the poetry of modern architecture had begun to change. Its purity was being questioned, and a new language was being developed. This new language was not an abrupt break from modernism, but rather an outgrowth, much as eighteenth-century mannerism was an evolution from the High Renaissance. Like mannerism, it was characterized by the removal of the constraints of the preceding period. This new form of architectural poetry appropriately became known as postmodernism, i.e. a break from, yet extension of, the modern movement.

Postmodern architecture can best be understood as a hybrid form of classicism (Figure 12-17). It is imbued with historic reference but open in its expression. As open verse, it seeks to express multiple social influences, and is capable of assimilating diverse materials and technologies. It borrows forms from classicism, but is open in its application of these forms. It also aspires to an open dialogue, that is, to communicate a maximum amount of meaning, but to be an incomplete communication, calling the observer to complete the meaning internally and thereby become a part of the poetry. Above all, postmodern architecture

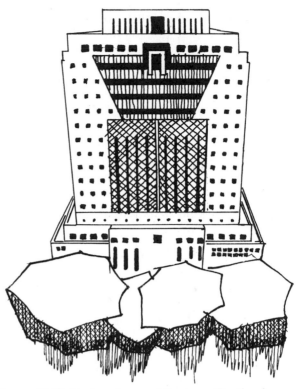

Figure 12-17. Postmodern architecture. (Portland Municipal Building by Michael Graves)

is pluralistic. It promotes individual and highly varied expression and interpretation.

Perhaps the best statement of the intent of postmodern architecture is the explanation given by Charles Jencks in *The Language of Post-Modern Architecture* (1977). According to Jencks, it

> speaks on at least two levels at once: to other architects and a concerned minority who care about specifically architectural meaning, and to the public at large, or the local inhabitants, who care about other issues concerned with comfort, traditional building and a way of life.

The Language of Post-Modern Architecture was, and still remains, perhaps the most insightful book on the subject. However, it was written in the initial stages of the movement and saw postmodernism to be essentially different from, although an extension of, modernism. It also saw postmodern architecture as a bilingual expression, speaking to both the architect and to the public at large.

Most recently, as expressed by the Museum of Modern Art (MOMA) exhibit "Transformations in Modern Architecture" (1981), postmodern architecture has grown to be seen as a continuation of, rather than a revolution against, modernism. This view sees postmodernism to have changed the modern movement substantially, allowing a much broader range of expression and a greater use of metaphor, but not to have broken from the basic tenet of the modern movement. Like the modern movement, postmodern architecture remains elitist. It effectively speaks to the architect (specifically the postmodern architect) and a concerned minority who care about specifically architectural meaning. Despite the early promulgations of bilingualism, postmodern architecture has failed to communicate effectively with the public at large.

Strengths and Weaknesses of Post-World War II Architectural Movements. The strengths of modern architecture were its systems base and its ability to explore systems for design direction. Its failure lay in its reduction of the myriad of overlapping systems and influences to a singular pure statement, and the exclusion of other influences. It failed also because of its perception that architecture should be the formative force (restructuring behavior, culture, environment), rather than a creative response to, and expression of, forces embodied in the place and culture. As Jencks stated in 1977, "The whole question of appropriateness, 'decorum' which every architect from Vitruvius to Lutyens debated, is now rendered obsolete by Mies' universal grammar and universal contempt for place and function."

The strengths of postmodernism are its break from the rigidity of modern architecture, its ability to assimilate, and its desire to communicate both to the intelligentsia and the public at large. Its failure is its abandonment of systemic thinking, its lack of direction, but must of all, its perpetuation and extension of elitism. Like modern architecture, it is reductionist in nature. While it opens its doors to "form interpretations" and new rules of application, and speaks in open verse, it still focuses on form. It usually fails to address the full range of contextual influences in a holistic manner, and sees the design idea as the formative, not the responsive, force. Jencks's criticism of modern architecture as lacking appropriateness is also applicable to postmodern architecture, especially as viewed by the public at large.

As an intellectual exercise and as an art form, postmodernism is stimulating, exciting, and expressive. As a communication of artist to artist, and as art that is provocative, it succeeds. As a cultural statement, it succeeds in expressing the pluralistic and schizophrenic tendencies of our culture. However, it generally fails to develop a rapport with people and place, and usually fails to establish synergisms with its cultural or physical context on a level that can be perceived by other than the architectural intelligentsia. The design idea seldom grows from condition, and where condition and idea clash, condition is discarded as inappropriate. Context may be addressed intellectually in terms of metaphor and allusion, but is not literally addressed in a manner perceived by the general public.

In light of the preceding discussion, and reflecting on more than two decades of postmodern architecture, one can now reassess the movement. It can be seen not as a radical break, but as an extension of modern architecture, with loosened rules, new languages, and greater exploration, and without the direction of modernism. It remains primarily an intellectual, elite communication among architects, or between architects and the minority of people whose primary concern is architecture's visual meaning. While it adds a visual richness through freedom, it also imparts visual chaos to the urban whole, through its lack of contextual relevancy.

BUILT-SITE SYNERGISMS

According to Webster's *New World Dictionary,* synergisms are "cooperative actions of discrete agencies such that the total effect is greater than the sum of the effects taken independently." Synergism occurs as two or more agencies benefit from one another's strengths and apply these strengths to overcome their respective weaknesses. It is dependent on a symbiotic relationship of intimate interaction, and of mutually beneficial association.

Considering that the design of urban environments involves the management of cultural, technological, and ecological systems so as to maximize efficiency and quality of life, certain professional strengths emerge. Contemporary architectural education and the postmodern mindset speak to an ability to concentrate meaning into architecture, and to maximize the efficiency and quality of life within the building or complex of buildings. Conversely, landscape architectural education and the stewardship mindset promotes an ability to integrate pluralistic statements, relate building to building and building to condition, and manage systems. Synergisms occur through cross-fertilization and through creative interaction and interdisciplinary decision-making that combines these strengths.

When built-site synergisms occur, they will exhibit an efficiency of operation within buildings and larger systems, concentration of meaning into the artifacts that architects and landscape architects together place into the landscape, built environments that relate positively to their context, effective communications to both the architectural intelligentsia and the public at large, and visual harmony on the urban as well as project scale.

Above all, built-site synergisms will grow from a common purpose, the realization that the making of place does not consist of designing buildings and sites, but rather the designing of "built sites," that is, places. By common purpose, the efforts of the architect and the landscape architect can be combined to create meaningful places with rich evocative indoor and outdoor environments.

Design Processes

Built-site synergisms occur most often and most strongly when design processes respond to site opportunities and constraints and express an awareness of design potentials throughout their duration.

The design of the built site often begins years before the site is actually built. In the land planning phase of development, land uses and a pattern for development are defined. This development pattern should respond to the patterns of the land (landform, soils and the like) and should apportion uses based on a knowledge of site opportunities and constraints, buildings and site programmatic requirements, and the requirements of structural and infrastructural systems that support these buildings.

Later, when a particular project is identified, the appropriate site and development program must come together so as to realize these site potentials and avoid site constraints, while providing site conditions that support the development program (including buildings and infrastructural systems).

The project site must then be master planned, developing a built-site pattern responsive to site organization and character, and supportive of the development program (including building) needs. As a part of project master planning, structures must be located on the site, and in response to site potentials and problems. Issues to be considered include land and building form relationships (Figure 12-18); site microclimates, the relative comfort of exterior spaces,

and the opportunities and constraints that site climates afford to architecture; and site views in relation to building spaces that desire these views (Figure 12-19).

Once appropriate building locations are identified, structures are designed in response to programmed needs and site conditions, and to take advantage of site opportunities and minimize site problems. They are also designed so as to maximize building performance. The site is modified to improve its ability to serve programmatic needs and to support site ecological and system needs.

Building-Site Systems

As stated earlier, built-site synergisms occur as an integrated system of building and site. To achieve this integration, building and site structural and infra-

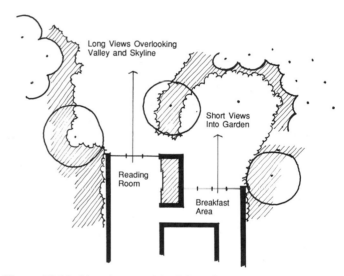

Figure 12-19. Site views and building form.

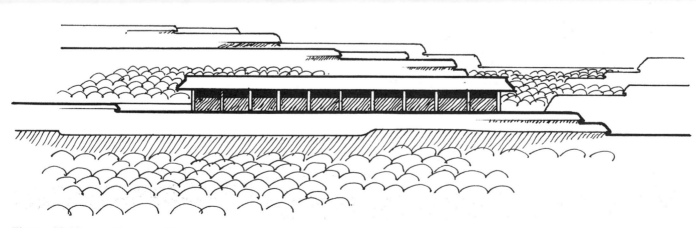

Figure 12-18. Landform and building form.

structural systems must come together in a mutually supportive manner.

Site gravity-flow infrastructural systems such as storm and sanitary sewage must service the building at desirable planar locations, and at acceptable flow elevations, while allowing for gravitational flow within building and site systems. Site pressure-flow systems must service the structure at acceptable planar locations, but are more flexible in the vertical dimension. The building structural system must deliver its loads to the land in such a manner that the building is adequately and consistently supported. Building and site circulation systems must come together for efficient operation, and must create rich perceptual story lines. Finally, the building and site must come together as a visual system, in an appropriate manner to convey the intended relationship between building and site, that is, the appropriate human-environment relationship, and to satisfy the physiological and psychological needs of all users.

Design as Statement of Human-Environment Relationships

The environment and its landscapes are highly variable. In addition, building and site can relate through similarity, compatibility, or contrast. The degree and nature of this relationship can be consciously managed so as to develop the appropriate human-environment relationship. In this manner, when buildings and site synergize, the results are responsive and diverse. In addressing synergisms between building and site, therefore, one must keep in mind that relatedness does not necessitate, and usually precludes, sameness.

When building and site synergize, they may both employ an architectonic vocabulary expressive of the human anthropomorphic nature, as shown in the Kimbell Art Museum, designed by Louis Kahn (Figure 12-20). Building and site may also express themselves as more naturalistic forms, implying an attitude of people in nature, as shown in the Kaufman House by Frank Lloyd Wright (Figure 12-21). They may express themselves as discrete elements, different in character but coming together in a compatible manner, implying humans and nature in coexistence (Figure 12-22).

Figure 12-21. Man in nature.

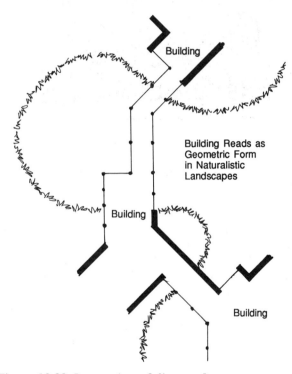

Figure 12-22. Integration of discrete form systems.

Building Reads as Geometric Form in Naturalistic Landscapes

Building

Building

Building

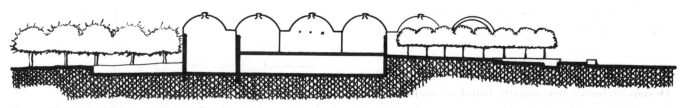

Figure 12-20. Architectonic built form.

Figure 12-23. Complement through contrast.

can be managed independently, along with other elements, or with design principles, so as to create desired building-site relationships.

Point. The landscape has special places, or points. These may be points of visual prominence (Figure 12-24), points with historical meaning (such as the site of the signing of a major treaty), or points that are special for any of a number of other reasons.

These points serve as forces to help organize a composition (in this case the site). These points also imply lines, such as sightlines, and can have visual dominance.

Buildings or other structures can also serve as special points in the landscape, and exert linear influences on that landscape (Figure 12-25). These often occur at intersections of sightlines or other visually prominent locations.

Line. When viewed from a distance, the edges of building masses read as lines. As one approaches a building, these dominant lines on the facade can be

Figure 12-24. Point of visual prominence and historical meaning.

They may even come together in a condition of contrast, as shown in the Douglas House, designed by Richard Meyer (Figure 12-23). Through contrast, the designer can communicate the interplay between the power of building and site. There are, of course, an infinite number of other building-site relationships that can be established, each conveying its own unique message concerning people's relationship to their environment.

Elements and Principles of Design

Building-site visual synergisms occur when design elements and principles are consciously managed so as to achieve the desired degree and type of relationship between building and site. Let us now look at some of the building-site synergisms these design elements and principles can impart.

Design Elements

Design elements are usually listed to include point, line, form, color, and texture. Each of these elements

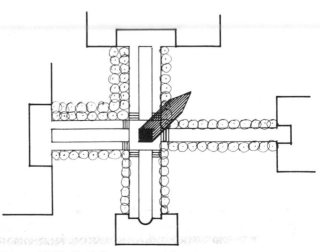

Figure 12-25. Building as special point.

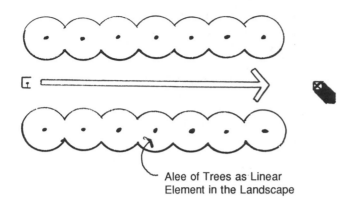

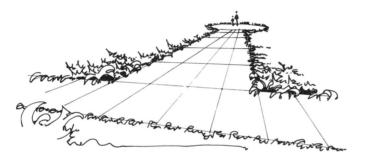

Alee of Trees as Linear
Element in the Landscape

Figure 12-26. Site elements and linear character.

Figure 12-27. Contrasting textures as line.

augmented by other lines, such as window mullions, expansion joints, and so on, to create a hierarchical system.

Sites also have linear characteristics. The alignment of elements (such as trees) imply lines, as do sightlines (Figure 12-26). The edges of forms and interface of materials, colors, textures, and so on also create lines in the landscape (Figure 12-27). As with building facades, expansion joints can introduce linear characteristics to site walls and pavings.

The site designer can choose to allow the lines of the architecture to extend onto the site, implying a continuum of building and site. These lines can extend onto the site in an architectonic manner, implying human assertion into the environment (Figure 12-28). Conversely, the naturalistic lines of the site can exert themselves on the building, implying nature's dominance over people (Figure 12-29). The two systems of line (building system and site system) can meet in a logical manner, but with each maintaining its own character and sense of order (humans in harmony with nature, Figure 12-21), or the two systems can come together without linear transitions. In the latter case (Figure 12-22), the design dynamic can result from the independence and strength of each system, the implied continuity of line through solid forms, and the chance encounter of form that their confrontation creates.

Form. Building and site form can come together in a synergistic manner. The dominant mass-void relationships of a building can extend onto the site (Figure 12-28), or site forms can extend onto (Figure 12-29),

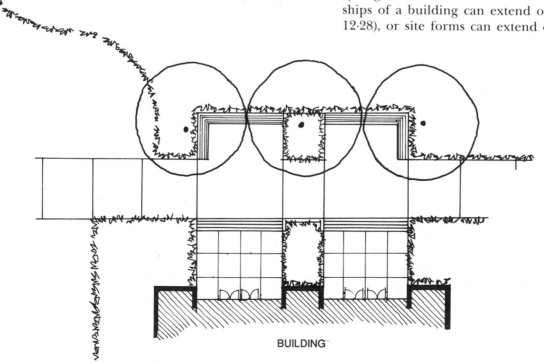

BUILDING

Figure 12-28. Building extension into site.

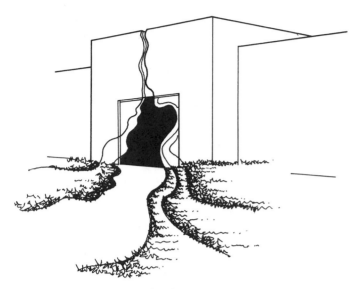

Figure 12-29. Nature's dominance over man.

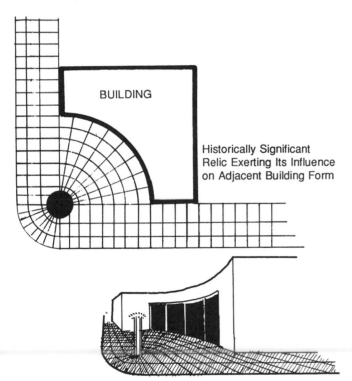

BUILDING

Historically Significant
Relic Exerting Its Influence
on Adjacent Building Form

Figure 12-30. Site as building form generator.

or even penetrate (Figure 12-30), the building. As form extends out from the building in an architectonic sense, the building declares dominance over the site. As the building takes on naturalistic form, nature becomes dominant.

Color and Texture. Building color or texture can be managed so as to establish a sense of place and scale that is in character with the site. This was successfully done in Wright's Kaufman House, shown in Figure 12-21.

Conversely, building color or texture can be contrasted with those of the site. These visual elements, as well as line and form, were successfully contrasted in building and site conditions at Richard Meyer's Douglas House (Figure 12-23).

Design Principles

The design principles listed in Chapter 8 include unity, emphasis or focalization, balance, scale and proportion, rhythm, and simplicity. These principles can be managed independently to create desired building-site relationships. They can also be manipulated in concert with other design principles or elements.

Unity. The architect of recent years has been concerned with architectural form that supports a design theme. Modern architectural themes lean toward unity; postmodern architecture is highly varied. In each movement, buildings explore a degree of unity/variety in support of the building design theme. Neither movement, however, has given adequate concern to the relationship of building and site.

Point, line, form, color, or texture can be consciously managed to unify building and site, as in Taliesen West in Phoenix, Arizona, by Frank Lloyd Wright (Figure 12-31). Conversely, they can be manip-

Figure 12-31. Building-site unity.

ulated to achieve contrast. A pure and simple modern building can be placed into a highly complex and varied natural system, thereby sensitizing the eye not only to the intricate character of the site, but also to the simplicity of the building. On the other hand, the highly complex form of the Brant-Johnson House in Vail, Colorado (Figure 12-32), designed by Robert Venturi, benefits from being viewed in the context of a unified landscape.

Emphasis and Focalization. The degree to which emphasis and focalization are achieved on the built site is a product of the degree to which visual systems are perceived, and breaks in these systems are then established. The breaks are generally seen as foci.

Site form can be emphasized by artful management

of point, line, form, color, and texture so as create dominant site visual systems. The building can then be perceived as a focal point or sculptural feature within this visual system (Figure 12-33). Conversely, site elements can be emphasized by creation of a dominant architectural system, and allowing selected site elements to break this architectural theme as in the garden in Ryoanji, Kyoto (Figure 12-34).

Balance. Site conditions affect the manner in which visual balance is achieved on a project site. For example, the symmetrical balance of the palace and grounds at Versailles by Le Notre seems appropriate in the flat French landscape (Figure 12-35), but formal order seems forced in the Boboli Gardens, in the hills of Tuscany (Figure 12-36).

The manner in which balance is achieved in the

Figure 12-33. Building as sculpture in the landscape.

Figure 12-32. Complex building in unified site.

Earth Wall
Raked Sand
Stone Set in Moss
Tile Pavement
Veranda

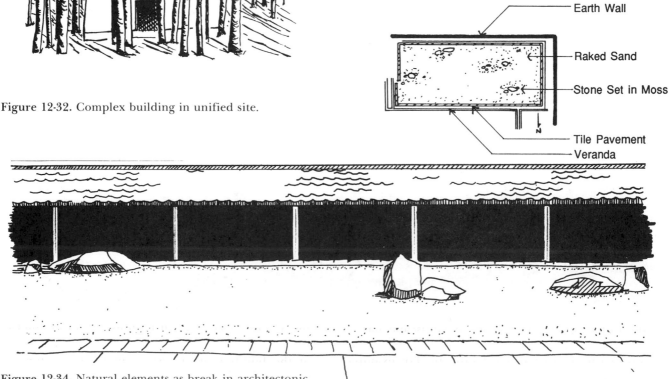

Figure 12-34. Natural elements as break in architectonic system.

Figure 12-35. Formal balance in a flat landscape.

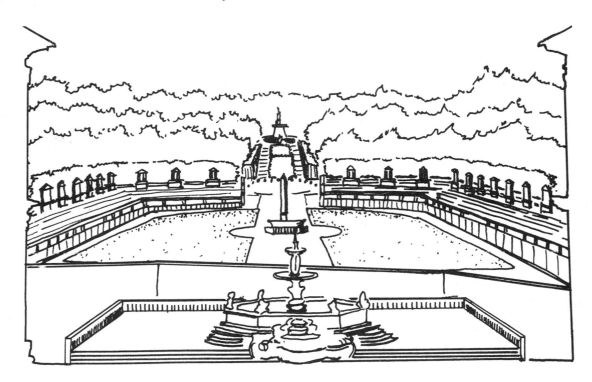

Figure 12-36. Formal balance forced onto a hilly site.

massing of buildings should also relate to site balance. When a formal balance extends from the building, and the site is designed symmetrically, the building and site become unified, and people declare dominion over nature. When a symmetrical building is placed in an informal site, a dynamic interplay between building and site and between people and nature is achieved.

Scale and Proportion. Any given landscape has an intrinsic scale, determined by the environmental processes that have created that landscape. For example, the highly incised eroded landscape of the hill country of central Texas (Figure 12-37), exhibits reasonably small-scaled visual units when compared to those of the visually open West Texas Plains (Figure 12-38).

Building sites also have scale, perhaps that of the landscape, or different, due to development. Usually development reduces the scale of the site by introducing new spatial edge.

Monumentally scaled sites dwarf even large-scaled buildings. Conversely, small-scaled sites can lend monumentality to even small buildings. Fine-grained site development with small-sized units and fine textures at the building-site interface make a structure feel more monumental. Conversely, a site can feel more

Figure 12-37. Small-scaled landscape.

expansive with the introduction of smaller-than-life structures.

Proportion refers to the size relationship between piece and whole, or between piece and piece. Certain rules of proportion appear to govern natural form. These rules have often been applied to buildings as well.

Rhythm. Dominant lines of building facades, as well as building mass-void relationships, often convey a rhythmic character. As discussed in the standard form of building, this rhythm often relates to the repetitive nature of building structural systems, building interior uses, building circulation systems, and materials and their jointing characteristics. Site elements can also be repetitive and rhythmic. Site rhythms can be regular, imparting an architectonic character, such as the alee shown in Figure 12-39. Conversely, they can be irregular, conveying a naturalistic feeling. When site rhythms are regular, the building extends its influence onto the site; irregular site rhythms generally display the building as counterpoint to site (Figure 12-40).

The building can be displayed as monolithic mass in a rhythmic landscape (Figure 12-41). It can conversely appear as rhythmic sculpture in monolithic space (Figure 12-42).

Simplicity. In designing the built site, simplicity is increased as various design forces are integrated. When the building designer and site designer work to achieve a common direction that resolves both site issues and building issues, site and building modifi-

Figure 12-38. Large-scaled "open" landscape.

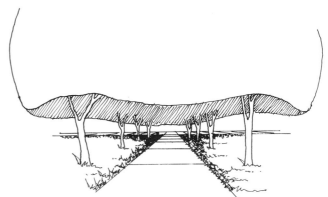

Figure 12-39. Regular site rhythms.

Figure 12-40. Regular architectural rhythm in a loosely structured landscape.

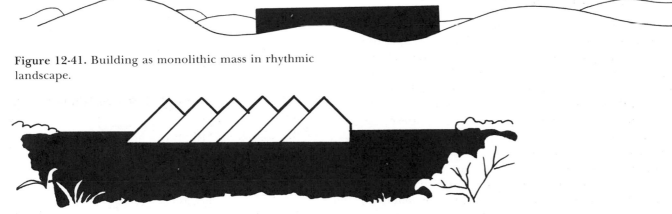

Figure 12-41. Building as monolithic mass in rhythmic landscape.

Figure 12-42. Building as rhythm in monolithic landscape.

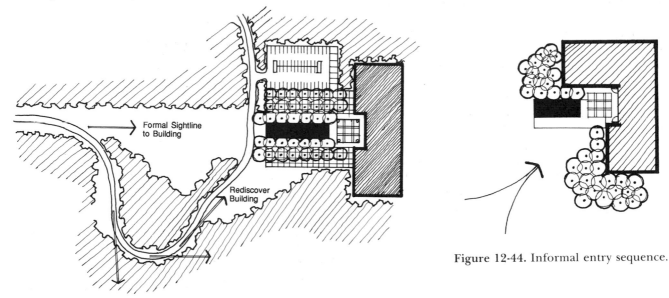

Figure 12-43. Extended entry story line.

Figure 12-44. Informal entry sequence.

cations become part of an integrated system. The natural tendency of the site to evolve is addressed, as is the nature of its architecture. There is little need to compromise design intent to resolve site issues that were not considered.

Entry Statement Synergisms

Primary and secondary entrances to buildings are often major form determinants.

Site access points and on-site vehicle and pedestrian circulation can influence building entry locations and, through these points, affect building morphology. When building form responds to site form and circulation, and site form responds to building form and circulation, and when the site serves to extend or intensify the statement of entry, synergisms occur.

When site and building entries integrate into a meaningful movement system, the sense of entry as procession and as temporal-spatial experience is enhanced. Rich entry sequences or story lines (often quite extended) can occur. The drama of entry can begin, for example, by site design that gives hints of the building or its entry, only to have them become hidden, to be later rediscovered (Figure 12-43). Conversely, site form and circulation can function to conceal building entries, adding impact to their sudden discovery.

Building formality can be intensified by extending its symmetry far into the site, giving one the sense that entry has begun long before arrival at the structure. On the other hand, the informality of an asymmetrical building can be intensified by an "off-axis" approach, as shown in Figure 12-44, or by a circuitous entry procession.

Edge Condition Synergisms

The building can be understood as a visual edge. When viewed from the site, this edge serves to close the exterior space and to function as a wall of the outdoor "room." From within the building, the exterior wall physically separates the building from the site, and defines the limits of the building space.

This built edge condition can be consciously designed to intensify the sense of place and the relationship of building and site. It can be physically open, allowing the site to "penetrate" the building; conversely, it can be physically closed but visually open, with building line, form, color, texture, or materials extending onto the site to dissolve this edge (Figure 12-45). It can also be visually open from within, but appear closed from outside the building (Figure 12-46).

The edge condition can be quite simple or highly complex. The complex edge can occur over large physical dimensions, or can be compressed into a smaller distance. The edge can be extended to serve as a number of design transitions to increase the procession of entry, to provide psychological filters, or to soften the built edge visually. For example, a residence can be more integrated with the site, exterior "rooms" can become extensions of the building, and people can be made to feel that they have left the bustle of urban life behind them long before entering the building. Figure 12-47 is an example of a highly

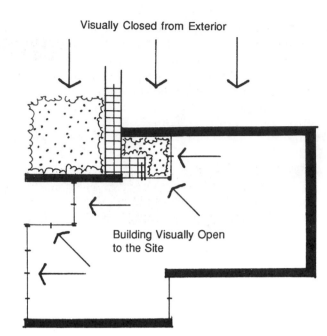

Visually Closed from Exterior

Building Visually Open to the Site

Figure 12-46. The concealed open edge.

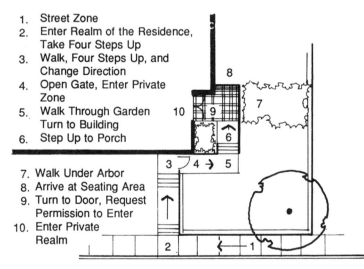

1. Street Zone
2. Enter Realm of the Residence, Take Four Steps Up
3. Walk, Four Steps Up, and Change Direction
4. Open Gate, Enter Private Zone
5. Walk Through Garden Turn to Building
6. Step Up to Porch

7. Walk Under Arbor
8. Arrive at Seating Area
9. Turn to Door, Request Permission to Enter
10. Enter Private Realm

Figure 12-47. The extended edge.

Figure 12-45. The "open" building edge.

extended edge with many psychological filters, occurring over a very small dimension. Through the artful manipulation of the building edge, roof overhang, arbors, area walls, gates, steps, paving, planting, and spatial composition, the building and site function as a multilayered edge, filtering out undesired feelings of urbanness, fusing building and site, and increasing building and site functional relationships and sense of place.

An unlimited range of edge conditions can be designed, each with its unique sense. These edge conditions can intensify spatial development of the site while building the sense of arrival to buildings and maximizing building-site visual relationships. When they achieve all three, built-site synergisms occur.

REFERENCES

Bowen, Arthur. 1981. Historical Response to Cooling Needs in Shelter and Settlement. *International Solar Energy Passive Cooling Conference.* Delaware: American Section of the International Solar Energy Society.

Graves, Michael. 1982. *Michael Graves, Building and Projects.* Karen Vogel Wheeler, Peter Arnell, and Ted Bickford, eds. New York: Rizzoli.

Jencks, Charles. 1977. *The Language of Post-Modern Architecture.* New York: Rizzoli.

Rudofsky, Bernard, 1964. *Architecture Without Architects: A Short Introduction to Non-Pedigreed Architecture.* Garden City, NY: Doubleday.

Transformations in Modern Architecture. 1981. New York: Museum of Modern Art.

Venturi, Robert. 1972. *Learning from Las Vegas.* Cambridge, MA: MIT Press.

Watson, Donald, and Labs, Kenneth. 1983. *Climatic Design: Energy Efficient Building Principles and Practices.* New York: McGraw-Hill.

SUGGESTED READINGS

Booth, Norman, 1983. *Basic Elements of Landscape Architectural Design.* New York: Elsevier Science.

Lynch, Kevin. 1971. *Site Planning,* 2d ed. Cambridge, MA: MIT Press.

Norberg-Schulz, Christian. 1980. *Genius Loci: Towards a Phenomenology of Architecture.* New York: Rizzoli.

———. 1975. *Meaning in Western Architecture.* New York: Praeger.

Tobey, George. 1973. *A History of Landscape Architecture: The Relationship of People to Environment.* New York: American Elsevier.

Vitruvius, Pollio. 1960. *Vitruvius: The Ten Books on Architecture.* Morris Hicky Morgan, trans. New York: Dover.

Part 3

Design Paradigms

13

Design as Creative Problem-Solving

COMMONALITY OF DESIGN PROCESSES

There are as many design processes as there are designers. However, these processes share some common characteristics (Figure 13-1). They all identify some issue to be resolved, or problem to be solved. They all involve the generation of an idea or ideas for resolving the issue or solving the problem. They involve some vehicle for implementing the idea(s). They include evaluation of the implemented idea, which usually leads to a greater understanding of the problem. In rare instances, these characteristics occur consciously as discrete entities. More often, they occur intuitively and without apparent organization.

Design processes are not linear in character nor definite in length. Rather they are cyclical and ongoing. They have no predetermined beginning; the designer may enter by observing a problem, by having an idea, by physically creating something, or by evaluating some given situation. The implied goal is the improvement of some situation; the inevitable result is the realization of new issues to be addressed. Herein lie the frustration and the excitement of design.

Design is, however, goal oriented. Designers seek an end; they desire to devise the better "mousetrap." Therefore, while design is cyclical, it is also progressive. As such, the nature of design might best be seen as similar to the nautilus, the spiral, or the helix. Progressively cyclical, the process cycles but in so doing comes ever closer to some ideal solution or issue resolution (Figure 13-2).

Problem Definition

A classic story concerning problem-solving exists in design education. According to this story, for a number of years tomato growers desired to mechanize

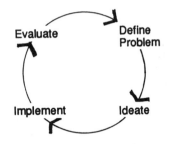

Figure 13-1. Commonality of design process.

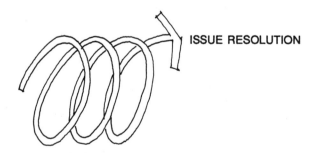

Figure 13-2. Goal-oriented design processes.

their industry. They wanted to harvest their crop with machines, for to do so would revolutionize the industry. However, after several years, no one had been able to design a machine gentle enough to pick ripe tomatoes. Finally, someone asked, "What is the true nature of the problem? Is it to design a machine, or is it to pick tomatoes?" Thus restated, the problem was solved by developing a tougher-skinned tomato. The message of this story is that problems often cannot be solved because they are not understood. The corollary is that most solutions that fail do so not because they fail to solve the defined problem, but rather because the problem was incorrectly defined.

239

Americans traveling in Europe are often frustrated by the Europeans' apparent inability to resolve issues. Europeans, on the other hand, are equally amazed by our premature attempts to solve problems. Our fascination with problem-solving leads us to attempt to resolve issues before we understand their true nature. Under these circumstances, not only do we often fail to solve the problems, we usually create additional ones in the process.

In design situations failures to resolve problems usually result not from the designers' inability to solve problems, but rather from inadequate problem definition. One of the implied goals of design schools is to prepare students to solve future problems that cannot even be predicted today. Therefore, the development of the human skills necessary to define problems is an integral part of educational programs. Problem statements are usually open ended; students are asked to identify the problem, and then to design responses to that problem.

Problem definition is itself a cyclical process. It is usually complex and intuitive. However, it can be understood in a simplified manner, as shown in Figure 13-3. This cyclical process usually begins with some rudimentary understanding of a complex issue. This issue is usually redefined in terms of its subissues or components. The designer then develops a better understanding of these components and their interrelationships. Key components and relationships are usually identified. With this knowledge, the essence of the problem is better understood, and the problem can be better articulated and more effectively solved.

Ideation

To a degree, problem definition is rational, logical, deductive, and pragmatic. Ideation, however, is intuitive. It involves left-handed thought. It is the flash of insight, the spark of creativity.

While ideation occurs in an instant, it often requires a tremendous amount of time to build an understanding of the issues, and for these issues to gestate in the subconscious. Ideation cannot usually be rushed, for incubation is critical. In addition, once the flash of insight occurs, it should be allowed to linger. The creative person usually generates a great number of highly diverse ideas and delays deciding which is really the best. The less effective designer is often not able to tolerate the chaos of allowing ideas to linger. The novice designer judges prematurely, often falls in love with the first idea and generates obvious, unexciting design concepts.

Rich ideation cannot be taught, but is generally shared by all of us. However, in many cases the cerebral pathways to creativity are obstructed by mental road blocks. In *Conceptual Blockbusting* (1979), James Adams addresses techniques for removing these obstructions. The reader should refer back to the list of techniques given in Chapter 3 and should review *Conceptual Blockbusting* for exploratory discussions of these blocks, and techniques for avoiding them.

One of the primary tasks of the design educator and the student of design is the dismantling of conceptual blocks. Restated, this tasks involves the creation of mental environments supportive to rich ideation.

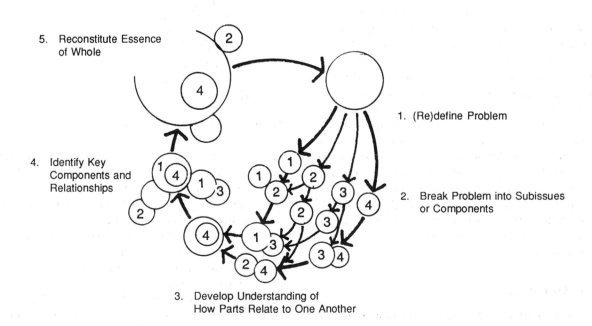

5. Reconstitute Essence of Whole

4. Identify Key Components and Relationships

1. (Re)define Problem

2. Break Problem into Subissues or Components

3. Develop Understanding of How Parts Relate to One Another

Figure 13-3. Problem definition processes.

Implementation

Implementation involves the development and realization of the design idea, and its integration into physical and cultural contexts. In project design, it involves the making of place, and the exciting resolution of systems including ones that are symbolic, visual, spatial, structural, and infrastructural.

Placeness is that set of characteristics that allow a specific location to leave an impression in the mind. In project design, the *making of place* involves idea implementation that imparts these characteristics in the eye of the beholder. Placemaking involves the ability to manage sensual variables and an understanding of the design culture. It involves the creation of *symbolic* landscapes that elicit, in the viewer, strong emotional responses.

Our perception of place is primarily spatial and visual. Implementation of ideas through the effective manipulation of spaces and the integration of designed places into existing *spatial systems* is critical to effective implementation. Likewise, the ability to create visually exciting "special" places within the context of the larger *visual system* (variety within the unified whole) is essential.

Implementation also involves the successful design of structural and infrastructural systems and their integration into larger existing systems. *Structurally* the design must be able to resist gravitational and environmental forces. It must do so while maintaining internal statics. It must also not destroy statics in the larger system. In terms of *infrastructure*, implementation must include the effective and efficient design of subsystems including circulation (transportation), drainage, sewage, electricity and lighting, and telecommunications. It must integrate these into their infrastructural and landscape contexts. Finally, it must do so in a manner that is sustainable without undue investment of energy or resource.

Evaluation

In design processes, evaluation has two primary components. On the one hand, we must evaluate implemented ideas. On the other hand, we must evaluate our definition of problems and the tasks at hand.

Evaluation of the implemented idea occurs on two primary levels. We evaluate the relationship of the developed design to the design idea. This includes evaluation of placeness, visual qualities and the ability of the designed setting to convey desired meanings and evoke intended feelings, spatial development, and structural and infrastructural design. The design is also evaluated as to its effectiveness and efficiency, and its integration with the larger system to which it must relate.

Evaluation of the implemented idea also includes evaluation of the relationship of the developed design to the current understanding of the problem. This is necessary because ideation usually addresses, in a bold and easily understood manner, the nature and essence of the problem, but does not address the large number of detailed issues. Correlation of the implemented idea with the specific issues of the problem can allow the designer to address these issues better.

The second side of evaluation involves critical reassessment of the problem. Usually, through the generation and implementation of ideas, a better understanding of the problem arises. With this greater insight, the designer can reevaluate the problem. Herein lies the true cyclical, helical nature of design processes—reiterations of a cyclical process in pursuit of better understanding and response.

Decision-Making

Cyclical design processes facilitate more effective decision-making. Through multiple cycles, the problem becomes better defined and multiple design responses can be developed (Figure 13-4). These responses can then be weighted and sorted. They can be prioritized and the pros and cons of each solution

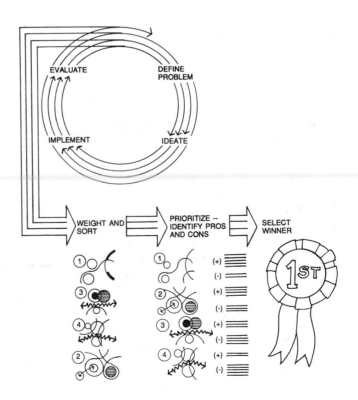

Figure 13-4. Design decision-making.

identified. Finally, the best solution can be determined and pursued. By such a process, the designer can move beyond habitual thought and achieve more effective, responsive design.

DESIGN PROCESSES AND LANDSCAPE ARCHITECTURE

Landscape architectural design progresses in a cyclical manner from an understanding of the landscape and human need, to conceptual responses and specific actions for implementing these through design decision-making. In the process, the basic design model (Figure 13-1) is applied to facilitate different types of landscape decisions (Figure 13-5). This application includes implementation of design and construction, and postoccupancy evaluation of decisions, including their ability to address the problem as defined, and additional insight into the time aspects of the problem.

In the academic experience, most projects usually explore design processes through the schematic design phase. Project design in the classroom setting usually consists of problem definition, concept development, and schematic design (Figure 13-6). Unfortunately, few projects explore the full process, including postoccupancy evaluation of implemented ideas and the resulting problem redefinition. More emphasis on the complete process promotes more knowledgeable and responsive decision-making.

Problem Definition

In contrast with the "creative act," which involves left-handed intuitive thinking, problem definition is analytical. It consists of right-handed thinking, that is, logic and deductive reasoning.

Analysis involves the dissecting of a complex whole, the study of its parts, the identification of new and more meaningful patterns (relationships), and the re-

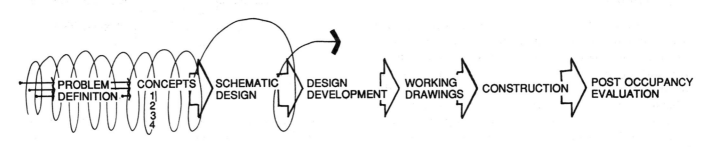

Figure 13-5. Project design processes.

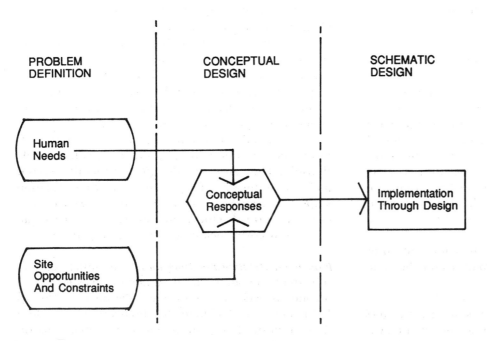

Figure 13-6. Typical design process in "academia."

constitution of these parts into new more meaningful and understandable wholes (Figure 13-3). A problem that commonly occurs is *analysis paralysis,* the failure to see the forest for the trees. Designers often get lost in their data. In order to avoid analysis paralysis, the designer should have a goal in mind, and limit data gathering and analysis to the issues that pursue that goal (or to relevant new goals that emerge). The designer should avoid nonuseful information. Exploring such data wastes time, and it becomes smoke that hides relevant information.

Project design usually entails the provision for human needs within an ecological, cultural, technological, and visual context. Therefore, problem definition usually consists of two major components: the definition of human needs, which is generally referred to as *programming;* and the definition of site structure and function, and the opportunities and constraints these afford, a process called *site analysis.*

Programming

In its most simple form, a program begins as a list of components or elements to be included in a project. In its more comprehensive sense, it is a quantitative and qualitative analysis of behavioral settings (proposed places that promote and support specific behavior), their size, character, and physical characteristics, and the resources to be allocated to them through design. A program does not address site conditions. Rather, it deals with idealized relationships devoid of the limitations of a specific site. It defines the utopian response to human needs. It records the designer's decisions concerning idealized relationships.

Programming Techniques. Programming techniques are highly varied, but usually share some commonalities. They usually begin with a general statement, extend this statement to a list of elements and then proceed to explore relationships among these elements. Initially one-on-one relationships are explored; then these relationships are used to assemble more comprehensive patterns and to reconstitute a better understanding of the whole. These techniques can be seen as another application of the basic problem-definition process, as shown in Figure 13-3.

Programming Tools. The two most commonly used tools for programming are the matrix and the functional relationship diagram.

Matrices. The matrix (Figure 13-7) is an effective tool for identifying and communicating one-on-one relationships. It is usually seen as a two-dimensional chart

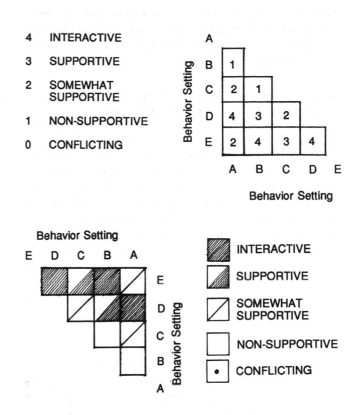

Figure 13-7. One-on-one functional relationships.

organized along two axes. Each axis identifies one set of conditions. Intersections, or grid cells, are addresses at which to identify appropriate one-on-one relationships. These relationships are usually quantified (conveying the desired degree or importance of the relationship) or qualitative (expressing the desired character or type of relationship). The matrix can employ numbers or symbols (dots, half dots, squares, colors, textures, etc.) to communicate these relationships.

Matrices can be used to identify desired relationships of program element (behavioral setting) to program element, proposed element to existing space, element to potential user, proposed element to environmental condition (Figure 13-8), element to economic condition, or any other one-on-one relationship. They allow the designer to identify, record, and communicate a large number of these relationships in a minimum amount of time and space. However, they do *not* achieve the integration of these data so as to discover meaningful aggregate patterns.

Functional Relationship Diagrams. Functional relationship diagrams allow the designer to investigate one-on-one as well as composite relationships (Figure 13-9). They can facilitate the discovery and exploration of desired organizational and spatial relationships, size, general character or shape, environmental

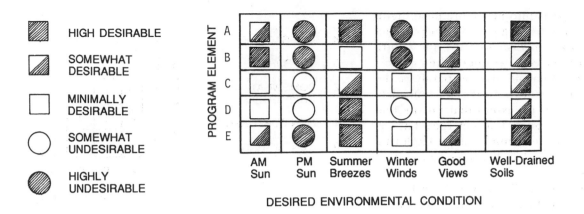

		AM Sun	PM Sun	Summer Breezes	Winter Winds	Good Views	Well-Drained Soils

DESIRED ENVIRONMENTAL CONDITION

Legend:
- HIGH DESIRABLE
- SOMEWHAT DESIRABLE
- MINIMALLY DESIRABLE
- SOMEWHAT UNDESIRABLE
- HIGHLY UNDESIRABLE

Figure 13-8. Desired relationships between program element and environmental condition.

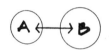

One-on-One Functional Relationships

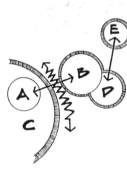

Aggregate or Composite Functional Relationships

Figure 13-9. Functional relationships diagram.

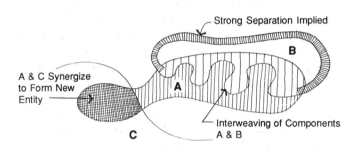

Figure 13-10. "Bubble" shape and implied character.

condition, linkage, separation, or other attributes. They are *not* normally used to address specific shape or actual site conditions.

Specific bubbles in functional relationship diagrams usually denote program elements. The size of the bubble can refer to desired element size or perceived importance. The character of the bubble usually conveys the designer's attitude about the element, its character, internal organization or form potential, relation to context, or other issues (Figure 13-10).

Spatial relationships (proximity) of bubbles combine with edge character, line continuity, line weight, linkage arrows, lines of separation (implying barriers), value, texture, color, and so on to convey desired relationships. These relationships can be identified as physical (access) or sensual (visual, auditory, olfactory), as shown in Figure 13-11.

It is usually desirable for the program analysis to culminate in a summary of the most desirable functional relationships. This summary, communicated in graphic form, is referred to by some designers as the *composite functional relationship diagram*. Others refer to it as the *perfect plan* in recognition of its idealized nature (perfect relationships, as opposed to those actually attainable on any given site). The perfect plan should be organized so as to convey desired relationships among elements, and to communicate desired functional groupings (such as core and ancillary facilities or public and private zones).

The composite functional relationship diagram is an organizational pattern with form implications. It is usually one of the two primary "ideals" against which alternative design concepts are judged, in order to assess their responsiveness to project needs. The other "ideal" against which to compare a design response is the site analysis.

Programming in the broad sense refers to the quantitative and qualitative analysis of behavior settings, their size and characteristics, and the resources to be allocated to them through design. Figure 13-12 shows the culmination of this process for a small but sophisticated residence. It consists of a quantitative list of program elements and their area requirements, and a composite functional relationship diagram (perfect plan) addressing desired organization, and qualitative physical, visual, auditory, olfactory, and tactile relationships. The diagram embodies essential relationships, and as many desired ones as practical. Additional relationships can be explored and conveyed by developing similar (though more detailed) diagrams for project subcomponents. Programming as a process is reviewed graphically in Figure 13-13.

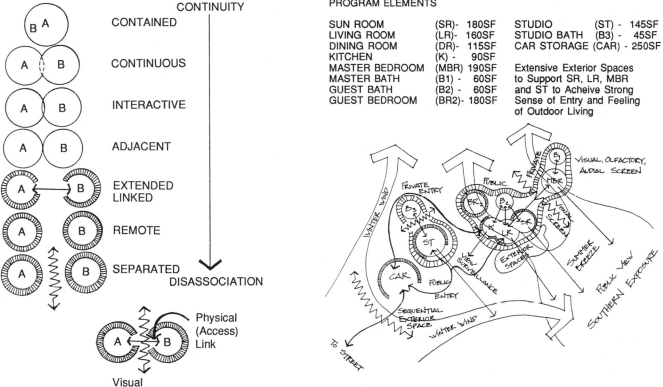

PROGRAM ELEMENTS

SUN ROOM	(SR)-	180SF	STUDIO	(ST) - 145SF
LIVING ROOM	(LR)-	160SF	STUDIO BATH	(B3) - 45SF
DINING ROOM	(DR)-	115SF	CAR STORAGE	(CAR) - 250SF
KITCHEN	(K)-	90SF		
MASTER BEDROOM	(MBR)	190SF		
MASTER BATH	(B1)-	60SF		
GUEST BATH	(B2)-	60SF		
GUEST BEDROOM	(BR2)-	180SF		

Extensive Exterior Spaces to Support SR, LR, MBR and ST to Acheive Strong Sense of Entry and Feeling of Outdoor Living

Figure 13-11. Spatial relationships.

Figure 13-12. Composite functional relationship diagram.

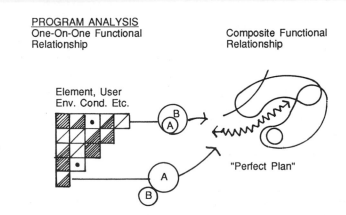

Figure 13-13. Programming process.

Site Analysis

Project sites are integral parts of systems that evolve over time in response to forces of change. As discussed in *Site Reconnaissance and Engineering* (Landphair and Motloch, 1985) the rate at which sites evolve correlates with the degree of imbalance in the system. In an undisturbed condition, sites evolve over time to establish an equilibrium, to function more efficiently and to change more slowly. However, this equilibrium is easily disturbed. Once this built-in stability is disrupted (Figure 13-14), the site begins to change quite rapidly, as site processes work to establish a new equilibrium. To witness this fact, one need only drive through a construction area and witness the soil that has washed over the street as the process of storm runoff establishes a new landform equilibrium. As in most cases, this disequilibrium results in increased maintenance problems and a less sustainable design solution.

To understand a site, the designer must analyze onsite natural and human-made factors, and must also interpret off-site influences. Depending on the scale and complexity of the site, relevant on-site natural factors can include geologic substrate, topography or landform, subsurface and surface water, soils, vegetation and wildlife, microclimate, and spatial and visual considerations. On-site human-made factors can include existing structures, pavements, gravity-flow support systems such as storm and sanitary sewage systems, and pressure-flow systems such as those used to distribute gas, electricity, and telecommunications. Off-site influences include physical elements such as pedestrian circulation, vehicle transportation systems, adjacent land use, visual considerations, and so on. A discussion of site reconnaissance, inventory, and analysis of each of these factors and influences is beyond the scope of this text. The reader is referred to *Site Reconnaissance and Engineering* by Landphair and Motloch, which reviews the subject in depth.

Designers must understand each of the preceding elements, its relationships to other elements, the type of data that must be generated, and the manner in which to interpret these data. They must also consciously avoid, as discussed earlier, analysis paralysis.

In order to understand the project site, the designer must discover and interpret data. Therefore, this phase of the design process consists of two identifiable parts—site inventory and site analysis. Inventory discovers and records data, that is, what exists on or near the site, and where it is located. Site analysis addresses the implication of these data for design.

Site Inventory. Site inventory usually consists of two components, the identification of general site character and the itemization of specific site elements and their various expressions. The identification of general site character can usually be achieved in ten words or fewer, for example, "a dense yaupon-post oak thicket with junipers invading gullies," or "a barren cubic space dominated by dissimilar discordant architecture." Specific site elements and their various expressions are usually arrayed on a base map of the site.

Site Analysis. A good site analysis is contingent on the designer's understanding of the range of forces that determine site conditions. With this knowledge, the designer is able to analyze site data, explore interrelationships of data, discover, through interpretation of this data, the forces that could have produced the site conditions, determine the design implications of site physical conditions and of site forces, identify the most important site conditions (site essence), develop an appropriate development (design) attitude, and define and prioritize site issues to be considered in design.

Communication. Site information is usually conveyed in two different manners—as detailed site analysis information and in summary or essence form. The detailed site analysis, as shown in Figure 13-15, usually includes both inventory and analysis information, and is drawn on the base map of the site. It records, interprets, and serves as a reminder to the designer, of the many different site issues to which the design should respond. It can also communicate this detailed information to the client.

While the site analysis drawing communicates a multitude of detailed information, the site essence statement distills this information and identifies the most important factors for design. The essence statement can be either written or graphic, but is probably best communicated by a combination of the two (Figure 13-16). Together the site analysis and essence com-

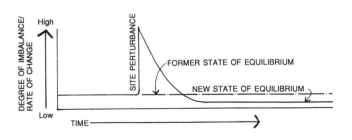

Figure 13-14. Site equilibrium. (Adapted and reprinted by permission of the publisher from Landphair, H. C., and Motloch, J. L., *Site Reconnaissance and Engineering.* Copyright 1985 by Elsevier Science Publishing Co., Inc.)

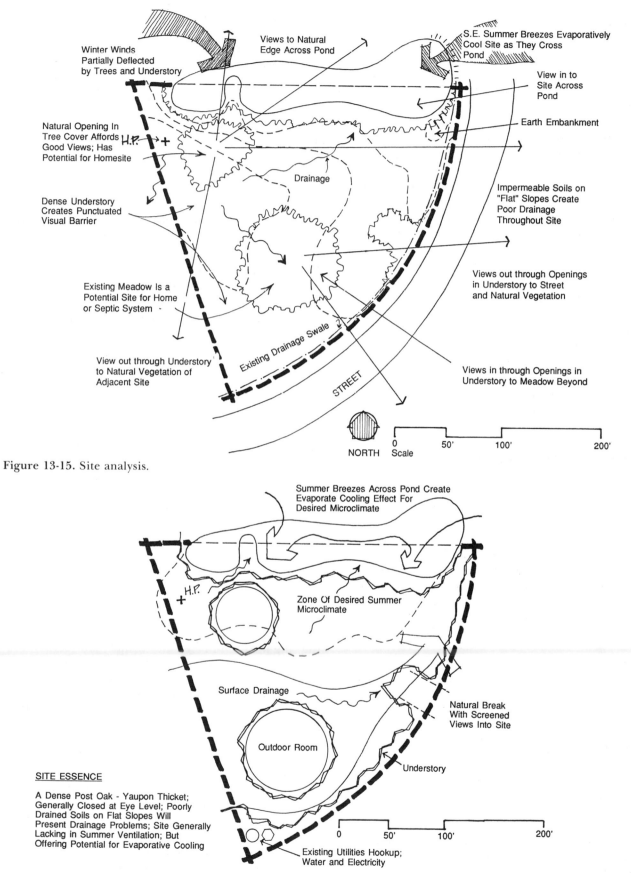

Figure 13-15. Site analysis.

Figure 13-16. Site essence.

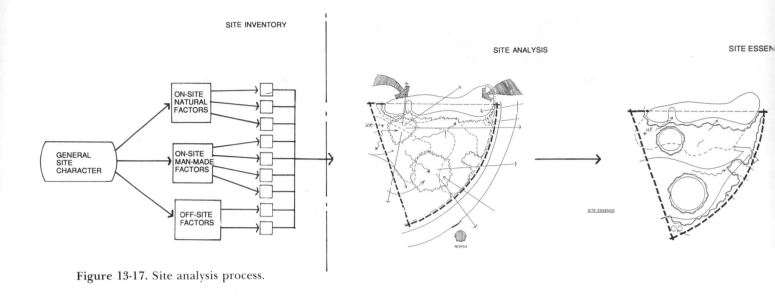

Figure 13-17. Site analysis process.

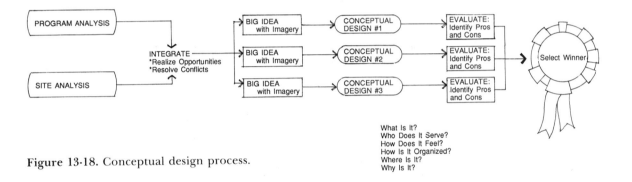

Figure 13-18. Conceptual design process.

munications are the second standard (programming being the first) against which alternative design concepts are judged, in order to assess their responsiveness to project needs. Site analysis is viewed graphically as a process in Figure 13-17.

Design Concept

As stated previously, the development of design concepts is an intuitive process; it involves insight. With this in mind, while strong conceptual design must respond to program and site analyses, it is usually beneficial to delay critical analysis, and rather to begin with an emphasis on intuitive response, and fluency and flexibility in thinking. A number of concepts should be generated quickly. These concepts should differ greatly from one another. After this generative period, the first step in evaluation of these concepts should be the analysis of their range. If the designer has not generated several uniquely different conceptual approaches from substantially different viewpoints, then conceptual design should be extended in

a broader manner. Often three uniquely different viable and exciting concepts are seen as a bare minimum.

The generation of each design concept involves three activities: the integration of the program and site analyses; the generation of a design idea, that is, the "big idea" complete with project imagery; and the organization of program elements and design resources on the project site, or the design concept. Once several concepts are generated, they can each be evaluated, weighted, and sorted, and the design concept to be pursued through schematic design can be selected (Figure 13-18).

Integration of Program and Site Analyses. Conceptual design should be based on the coming together of needs. This entails, as previously stated, both human and site needs. Each offers unique design opportunities and constraints. Realizing opportunities and resolving conflicts between program and site is the beginning of conceptual design.

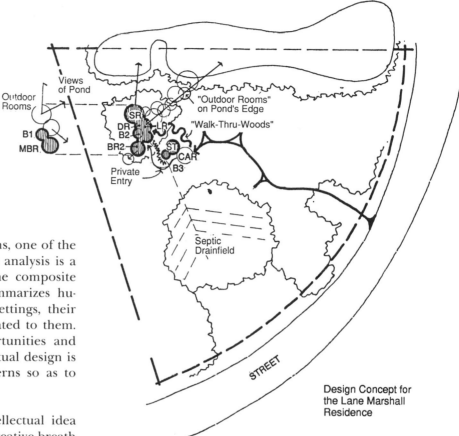

"ON POND'S EDGE"
A Series of Barnlike Rustic Weathered Buildings Set into the Woods, with an Extended "Walk-Through-The-Woods" Entry Sequence, and a Series of "Outdoor Rooms" Adjacent and Perched "On Pond's Edge"

Figure 13-19. Design concept.

As discussed in their respective sections, one of the products of both programming and site analysis is a summary diagram. In programming, the composite functional diagram, or *perfect plan,* summarizes human needs through desired behavior settings, their relationships, and resources to be allocated to them. The site analysis articulates site opportunities and constraints. In its simplest form, conceptual design is the coming together of these two patterns so as to imply design direction and form.

The Big Idea. The big idea is the intellectual idea underlying the design concept. It is the creative breath of the design, the life blood of the solution. It is the proverbial "fire on the mountain." It is also an approach for searching for strong design direction.

The big idea usually involves the coming together of idea, symbol, and sense of place. It can usually be stated in a word or two, e.g. the "Italian Hilltown," the "Greek Village," or the "Outdoor Room." It localizes imagery into a few evocative words and conveys intensified meaning through association. This intensified meaning, in turn, conveys desired project ambience.

The big idea, however, is a gestalt—the idea, project imagery, and organization of project elements occur together. Sometimes this process begins with a word "titillating," "enticing," "alluring," "mysterious," "overt," and so on. At other times, site organization suggests imagery and the big idea is distilled from this imagery. In either case, the big idea is a singular notion, a unifying point of reference. It strengthens the design and it serves as a reference point.

Big ideas are often generated in a brainstorming session. Here ideas are generated and judgments are delayed. After the brainstorming session has been completed, the ideas are explored through imagery and project organization. Usually the best three or four concepts are retained for further exploration, or to show to the client.

While the big idea can usually be stated in only one or two words, the idea can then be extended and the specific associations of the metaphor be made more clear by translating the big idea into a statement of desired project imagery. For example, the big idea of the "Italian Hilltown" could be interpreted as "a sensitive integration of positive and negative form, loosely rectilinear but adjusted in response to influences including topography and circulation ... narrow winding passageways with short viewsheds unfolding as one moves about ... a sense of timeless permanence and unity achieved through consistent use of stone indigenous to the site ... organized *without* the sense of public and private space so typical of the United States."

Design Concept. A design concept consists of all project elements located on the site, design resources applied to the site so as to maximize response to human and site needs, and the realization of the big idea and desired project imagery (Figure 13-19).

As part of the design concept, program elements are located on site so as to maximize their relationship, one to another. Design resources such as screening, solar access, ventilation, views, and the like, are organized according to program and site needs.

Evaluation of Design Concepts. Each design concept is evaluated (functionally) in accordance with the program analysis. The conceptual site development is correlated primarily to the composite functional relationship diagram (perfect plan). One-on-one programmed relationships serve as support data.

Each design concept is also evaluated in light of the site analysis. The concept is judged as to the degree to which it realizes site opportunities and recognizes site constraints. It is also assessed for its sustainability and maintenance implications.

It is helpful if the evaluation of design concepts includes a summary of the pros and cons of each alternative concept. Comparison of these summaries is helpful in weighting, sorting, and prioritizing these concepts.

Selecting the Winner. Selecting the design concept to pursue into schematic design involves the comparison of the functional pros and cons of each alternative concept (in relation to program and site analysis), and evaluating the strength of the big idea, the richness of project imagery, the depth of meaning, and the implications to ecological health and productivity (Chapter 15) and user needs and human physiological and psychological health (Chapter 16). In some cases, one concept will prove to be superior. In others, the concept to be pursued might well be a new "hybrid" one incorporating some of the attributes of two or more concepts. If the latter occurs, the designer should cycle through the conceptual design one last time, distilling the hybrid so that its conceptual strength is not lost.

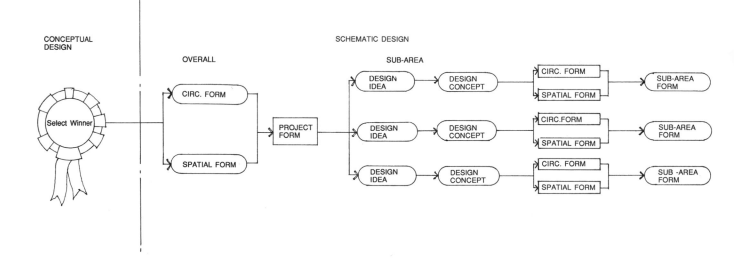

Figure 13-20. Schematic design.

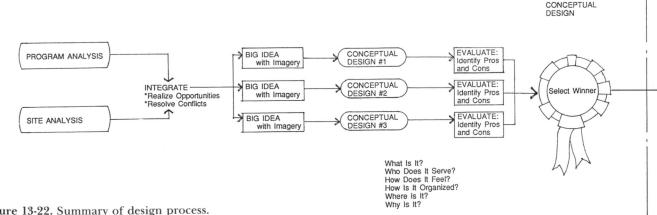

Figure 13-22. Summary of design process.

Schematic Design

Design concepts deal with project organization and design intent, but delay decisions concerning specific materials and form. Schematic design pursues these issues; materials are selected and forms are developed. In schematic design, special emphasis is placed on circulation form and spatial form.

Circulation Form. In determining circulation form, we are concerned with two issues: physical linkages and sensual and temporal aspects of perception. Functionally, we are concerned that circulation systems connect related items, separate items of conflict,

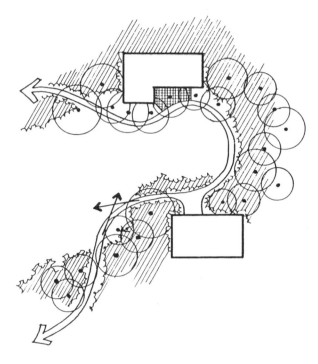

Figure 13-21. Spatial and circulation form.

and facilitate ease and safety of movement. Circulation form grows in large part from these issues.

Circulation form also impacts the sensual and temporal aspects of perception. It determines the vantage point from which we perceive the form of the built project.

Spatial Form. Our perception of the world around us is primarily visual, and more specifically spatial. Therefore, our perception of form in the built project will be primarily a spatial perception.

Project Form. The spatial form of the project and how one moves through and experiences the form are highly interrelated. Project form therefore can be seen as the successful coming together of spatial and circulation form (Figures 13-20 and 13-21). When the two synergize, project form satisfies the functional necessity of conveniently and safely moving people and vehicles from place to place, while enriching the perception of spatial form and the sense and meaning of the place.

Subarea Design. The designer thinks simultaneously at multiple scales. Within the context of, and integrated with, the overall design concept, subareas can express their own ideas, concepts and form (Figure 13-20). These ideas operate and must be integrated within the overall project design, but can provide special places with unique sense and concentrations of meaning within the context of an integrated whole.

Summary of Design Process

The preceding design process is summarized in graphic form in Figure 13-22. This diagram depicts a typical design process when both site and program are known. The process changes somewhat when only a program exists, and the designer's task involves site selection. It also varies when a site is being analyzed to determine appropriate types of development.

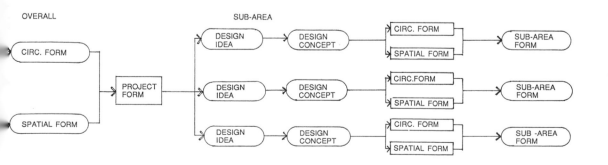

Program-Based Design Processes. Often program needs will be identified long before the site is selected. Under these circumstances, the program analysis can serve to help define criteria for site selection. Once these criteria are determined, alternative sites can be identified. These sites can be inventoried, analyzed, and evaluated in terms of program needs, and the site can then be selected. Once the site has been selected, it can be reviewed to determine its design opportunities and constraints, and its development potential. It can then be integrated with the project program to search for design direction. The revised problem definition phase for program-based design is shown in Figure 13-23.

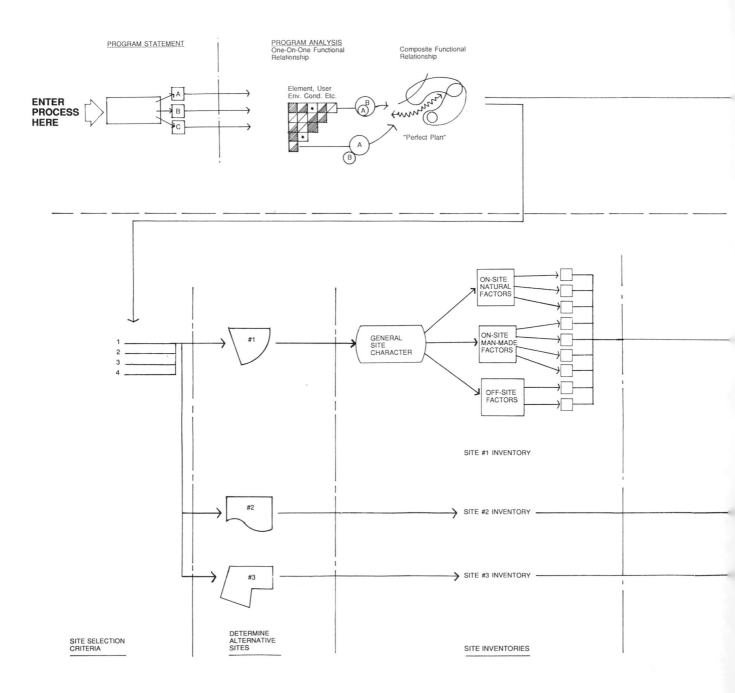

Figure 13-23. Problem definition—program-based design.

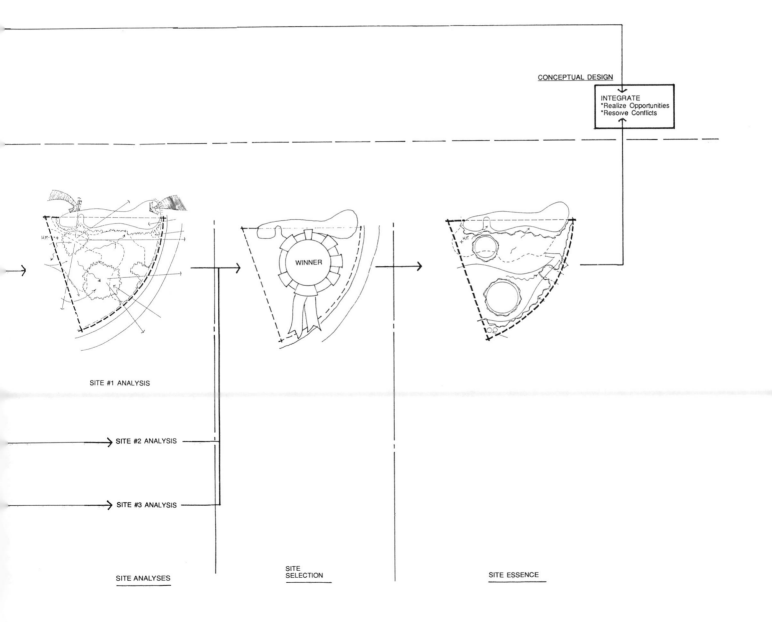

CONCEPTUAL DESIGN

INTEGRATE
*Realize Opportunities
*Resolve Conflicts

SITE #1 ANALYSIS

WINNER

SITE #2 ANALYSIS

SITE #3 ANALYSIS

SITE ANALYSES

SITE
SELECTION

SITE ESSENCE

Site-Based Design Process. Often a site will be analyzed to determine its development potential. Once this potential is determined, alternative programs can be generated and evaluated in terms of site potentials. These programs can be ranked and prioritized and the best program identified. Once the development program is determined, it can be analyzed and integrated with the site analysis to search for design direction in conceptual design. The revised problem definition phase for a site-based design process is shown in Figure 13-24.

"Wiring" Site Design Processes. As the two preceding examples indicate, there is no one process for design. In each case, the process is wired appropriately for the specifics of the project. The ability to "wire" the appropriate process is crucial for good problem-solving and design.

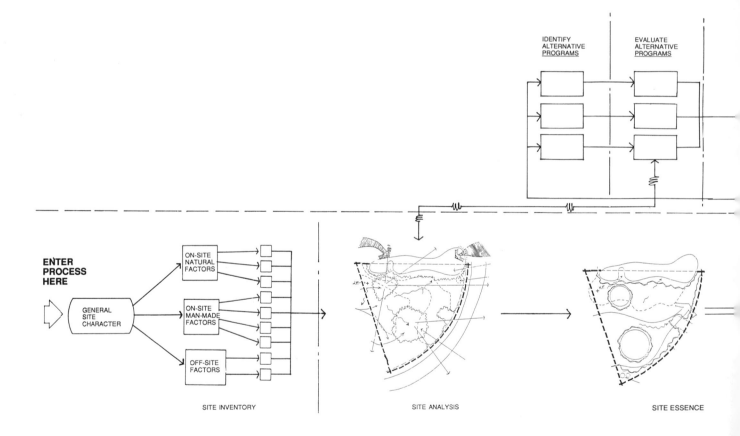

Figure 13-24. Problem definition—site-based design.

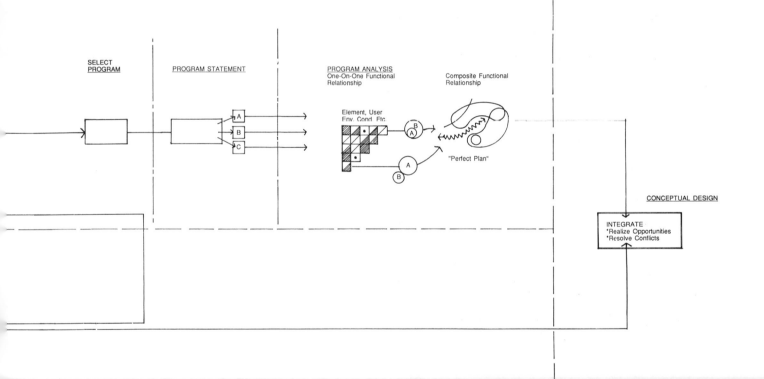

SELECT
PROGRAM

PROGRAM STATEMENT

PROGRAM ANALYSIS
One-On-One Functional
Relationship

Composite Functional
Relationship

Element, User
Env. Cond. Etc.

A
B
C

B
A

A
B

"Perfect Plan"

CONCEPTUAL DESIGN

INTEGRATE
*Realize Opportunities
*Resolve Conflicts

REFERENCES

Adams, James. 1979. *Conceptual Blockbusting: A Guide to Better Ideas*. New York: Norton.

Landphair, Harlow, and Motloch, John. 1985. *Site Reconnaissance and Engineering: An Introduction for Architects, Landscape Architects and Planners*. New York: Elsevier.

SUGGESTED READINGS

Booth, Norman. 1983. *Basic Elements of Landscape Architectural Design*. New York: Elsevier Science.

DeBono, Edward. 1971. *Lateral Thinking for Management: A Handbook of Creativity*. New York: American Management Association.

Hanks, Kurt, Belliston, Larry, and Edwards, David. 1977. *Design Yourself!* Los Altos, CA: William Kaufman.

Koberg, Donald, and Bagnall, James. 1974. *The Universal Traveler: A Soft-Systems Guide to Creativity, Problem-Solving, and the Process of Design*. Los Altos, CA: William Kaufman.

Laurie, Michael. 1986. *An Introduction to Landscape Architecture*. New York: Elsevier.

Lyle, John. 1985. *Design for Human Ecosystems: Landscape, Land Use and Natural Resources*. New York: Van Nostrand Reinhold.

Lynch, Kevin, and Hack, Gary. 1984. *Site Planning,* 3d ed. Cambridge, MA: MIT Press.

Pena, William, with Parshall, Steven, and Kelly, Kevin. 1987. *Problem Seeking: An Architectural Program Primer,* 3d ed. Washington, DC: AIA Press.

Simonds, John. 1983. *Landscape Architecture: A Manual of Site Planning and Design*. New York: McGraw-Hill.

14

Changing Paradigms and Processes

We have discussed Sorokin's *Social and Cultural Dynamics* (1937–41) and the history of civilizations as fluctuations among three value systems, which he referred to as the sensate, the ideational, and the idealistic. For review, the sensate value system, as one polar extreme, contends that matter is reality, and sensory perception is truth and knowledge. The ideational value system, as the other polar extreme, sees reality as lying beyond the material world, in the spiritual one. Its proponents hold that knowledge exists in the inner consciousness, and believe in ideal values, ethics, and truths. Intermediate between these two polar extremes, serving as a transition between them, and expressing itself as a blending of the two is the idealistic value system. Several cultures that embraced the idealistic value system successfully merged materialistic and spiritual truth and beauty in philosophy, art, and science, through a synergism of place, people, and technology. These cultures include the exceptional Golden Age of Greece and the European Renaissance.

As we have discussed, we can understand the present point in human history as one of these rare transition periods. As such, it has a tremendous potential to synergize materialism and spiritualism through truth and beauty. As always in periods of major cultural transition, our present period is characterized by cultural change. However, thanks to our recently and dramatically increased technology, we are changing at an unprecedented rate; and both the speed and degree of this change are unparalleled in history. This has been documented by Toffler in *The Third Wave* (1980), and by Capra in *The Turning Point* (1982). We do not generally understand, however, the degree to which the underlying assumptions (paradigms) and definitions of the environmental design professions are changing, the changing roles of these professions as cultural paradigms shift, and the role that these professions are playing in the cultural change. In this chapter we explore these issues. In so doing, we discuss the range of environmental design professions, including the professions of urban and regional planning, urban design, architecture, and landscape architecture, which together are responsible for designing the contemporary landscape.

PARADIGMS

In the 1930s, a revolution occurred in the field of physics, and the shift in mindset that powered this revolution is today dramatically affecting most other professions. This shift is the movement from a reductive way of seeing the world, which focuses attention on "things," to a relativistic, holistic, and integrative one that focuses attention on relationships (Table 14-1).

This shift in mindset has had a varying effect on the environmental design professions. The most significant changes have included the systems consciousness of a number of planners, architects, and landscape architects (Alexander, 1977; Jacobs, 1989; Mulder, 1986), and the resource management movement that began in the profession of landscape architecture in the 1960s. This movement caused an explosion of consciousness and a major change in the goals and practice in the profession of landscape architecture; and these changes endure today. Other

Table 14-1. Cartesian and holistic paradigms.

	Cartesian Paradigm	Holistic Paradigm
Approach	Reductive	Holistic/integrative
	Mechanistic	Organic/ecological
	Atomistic	Systemic
	Positivist/deterministic	Phenomenological
	Assertive/masculine	Responsive/feminine
Basic Belief in	Value-free science	Value-laden science
	Objectivity	Subjectivity
	Exactness	Tendency
	Absolute	Uncertainty/complementarity
	Mechanical laws	Affinities
	Fundamental laws	Interconnected relationships
	Causal laws	Statistical causality
	Objectivity	Subjectivity
	Specialization	Generalization
	Statics	Intrinsic dynamics
	Truth through logic	Insight through intuition
	Division of:	Oneness of:
	Mind and matter	Mind and matter
	Art and science	Art and science
	Space and time	Space and time
	Divisibility	Indivisible wholes/interrelatedness
	Parts determine wholes	Wholes determine parts
	Independence	Interdependence
Focus on	Things:	Interconnected webs of relationships:
	Measurement	
	Prediction	Observation
	Quantity	Quality
	Analysis	Synthesis
Human-Environment Relations	Human over nature	Harmony with nature
	Exploitation	Management

Source: Adapted from Capra 1982.

major changes heralded by the shift in cultural mind-set were the systems design movement that occurred in architecture in the seventies, but soon vanished, and the sustainable development movement that is currently emerging from seeds planted years ago by the appropriate technology and similar movements. The sustainable development movement is growing in the environmental design professions and at various academic institutions, including the University of Pennsylvania, the University of California at San Louis Obispo, and Texas A&M University.

While some changes in professional mindsets have occurred, however, the mainstream of the environmental design professions have remained entrenched in the reductionist Cartesian mindset. For example, in the contemporary city, planners plan for growth,

designers design specific elements, but in most cases no one designs the complex, interactive whole, that is, no one designs the city as a sustainable, physical, experiential entity. Rather, the city evolves through the accretion of innumerable decisions, made by many people for very different purposes over long periods of time, with little coordination or management of its sustainability or its experiential quality. Yet, it is the sustainability and experiential quality of the whole that affects ecological and human health.

In times past, this spontaneous growth through accretion has often created a dynamic and meaningful human experience. Unfortunately, in the case of the contemporary American city, it usually results in a confusing, incomprehensible, and alienating urban environment.

Existing Environmental Design Paradigms

In *The Turning Point,* Capra discusses the ills of contemporary society as the inevitable result of our tendency to reduce complex issues to more simple terms, and our failure to address interrelationships. Although Capra does not address the design professions per se, the mainstream of these professions have contributed in no small way to these ills; and the path to a more understandable, exciting, and humanely designed environment includes new and more relevant design attitudes, and redefinitions of the ecological and cultural roles of the environmental design professions (Table 14-2).

Capra discusses the transitions to a holistic, integrative, sustainable mindset that were occurring (and that continue to occur) within specific professions. In this discussion, the environmental design professions are conspicuously absent. This is because the mainstream of these professions are entrenched in the Cartesian mindset and are content to perceive their professional task and social value as those of designing elements and pieces (projects) rather than the management of the physical and cultural landscape as integrated systems for increased ecological and human health. We are often quite happy to pursue borrowed aesthetics and borrowed organizational patterns, rather than using ecological, structural, infrastructural, and cultural systems, and an integrative world view, to generate appropriate patterns. We are content to search for direction by pursuing new movements and new styles, rather than embracing the major change in mindset that could allow us to manage the richness of human experience, environmental quality, and quality of life more effectively. We too often search from a reductionist mindset and the egotistical view that the individualized, personalized, visual design statement is somehow more powerful than an holistic, synergistic, and responsive one. We often focus on the elements we design, and the purity of these elements, rather than the effect that the totality of the environment, including its designed and nondesigned components, has on the overall health of the ecological system (sustainability) or the physiological and psychological effect the gestalt has on people. In a Cartesian sense, we often reduce design to a singular issue of form or aesthetic, rather than the integrative synergistic and much more complex one of experience. We frequently design primarily for the client's or project's need, rather than the more difficult task of synergizing these needs with the needs of the larger ecological and human context, and the needs of systems that are ecological, cultural, and infrastructural. We design buildings and sites rather than landscapes. As we design these buildings and sites, we treat them as objects rather than as vehicles

Table 14-2. Responsible and humane design.

Problematic Design Attitudes	Responsible and Humane Design Attitudes
Design of elements	Design of landscapes (including the city as an urban landscape)
Design as individual expression	Design as experience
Design as aesthetic	Design as systems management
Design only as localized problem-solving	Design as concentration of ecological and cultural meaning
Promulgated, borrowed, or imported aesthetics	Evolving context-expressive aesthetics
	Design for ecological and cultural health and well-being

for what Heidegger (1977) referred to as *dwelling,* which "signifies the way we human beings are of the earth." We concentrate on the design of elements or pieces of settings rather than the manner in which these settings interact with the individual's consciousness, the collective consciousness (or shared experiences of the community), or the ecological and cultural contexts into which our designs, through accretion, are being assimilated. We therefore fail to consciously design the experiential phenomenon called place that occurs as the individual perceives and imparts meaning to settings (Figure 14-1). In the process, we degrade the ecological and cultural condition, and thus fail to experience the true significance of dwelling about which both the philosopher Heidegger and the architect Christian Norberg-Schulz (1980) spoke, or to design what the architect Christopher Alexander referred to as the "quality without a name." However, it is at this associational and emotional level that the individual intuitively relates to the designed environment. This is therefore one of the true tests of our social role and value.

As designers in the old mindset, we too often choose to see our task to be the creation of something new that expresses *our* attitudes about people, environment, and design, not the more difficult but equally creative task of integrating various diverse and often contradictory design influences and expressing the

The Place

Mental Construct Affected by
Setting, Previous Experience,
the Individual's Mood, the
Individual's Emotional
Tendencies, Etc.

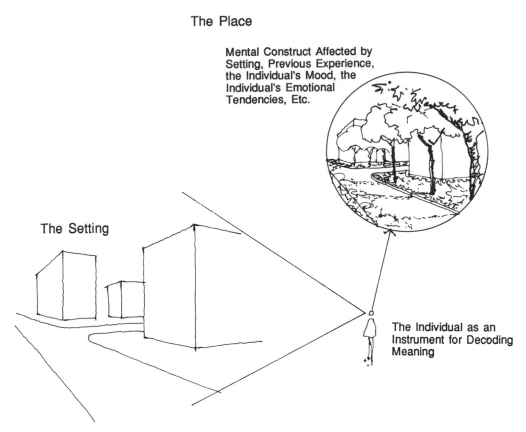

The Setting

The Individual as an
Instrument for Decoding
Meaning

Figure 14-1. Mental construct of place.

forces that drive our culture. We often see our task as the creation of new relationships, not the synergism of old, new, and future ones for the creation of efficient, meaningful, and dynamic places. However, the relevancy of the designed environment is a function of the whole, not the part, and the meaning conveyed (to the user) by the total gestalt of the landscape, not the meaning conveyed (to designers) by the isolated element being designed.

The designer's perception that the "element" is the entity being designed is a false perception. Whereas the designer's intent may be to design the element, he or she is nonetheless designing the gestalt and the element-setting entity, for the element does not exist in a vacuum. It is seen and it functions integrally with its context, and this context changes its perceptual and associational characteristics, and its functional behavior as the designed piece is assimilated and integrated into the whole (Figure 14-2). Furthermore, the landscape changes each time any element within it changes. To be oblivious of the complex interrelatedness of element and context does not eliminate relatedness or interdependency. It merely means that the designer who chooses to remain unaware of this oneness fails to be conscious of the entity that is being designed.

Implications of Current Design Mindsets

To the degree that the designer chooses to remain unaware of the oneness of designed element and context, and therefore to that which is being designed, the resultant landscape is confused and incomprehensible. The intended meaning of the designed project is therefore lost. This is true, of course, unless the intent is only to communicate to other designers who have likewise been educated to focus on the element, or to communicate the schizophrenia that characterizes our culture, by deconstructing the user's ability to cognize place by removing references to known patterns through which people decode, cognize, and ascribe meaning to place. While the first of the preceding intentions—designers communicating to other designers—is a well-established practice in the design professions, the second, called *deconstructivism* is a relatively new and probably short-lived movement. An alternative and preferable design intention would be to develop appropriate and dynamic landscapes through integrative and responsive design, to increase landscape efficiency and productivity, and to communicate the multiplicity of meanings through effective landscape design.

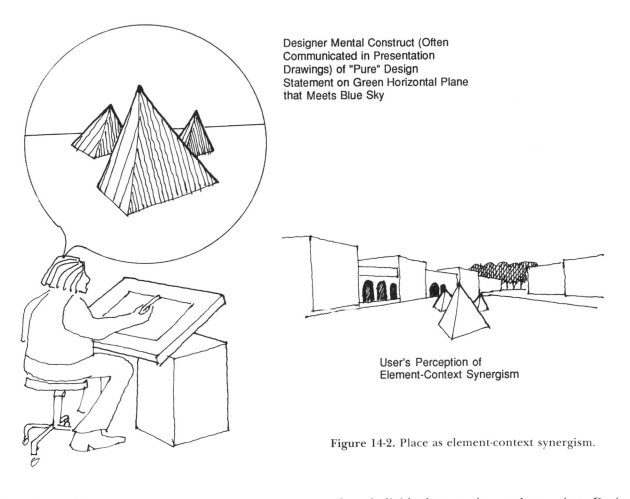

Designer Mental Construct (Often Communicated in Presentation Drawings) of "Pure" Design Statement on Green Horizontal Plane that Meets Blue Sky

User's Perception of Element-Context Synergism

Figure 14-2. Place as element-context synergism.

Design Appropriateness

The appropriateness of designed environments is dependent on the degree to which they sustain and enhance the ecological and cultural environment. To be appropriate, therefore, design must sustain the function and productivity of the system, without undue investment of resource or energy, and without adversely affecting or degrading that system. If design decisions are thus sustainable, the design intent endures over time; if they are not, the design intent is soon lost.

Roots of Our Design Paradigm

To a large degree, our current environmental design paradigm is a continuation of one that had been in effect since World War II. While design movements have changed, the underlying assumptions of most of these movements have been Cartesian and reductionist. There have been notable exceptions, and designers who focused on integration and response, but the mainstream of these movements has been the design of the piece, not the whole; the design of the "project," not the city; and the design of the physical setting, not the mental construct of place that occurs

when individuals experience the setting. Designers have not been adequately concerned with the degree to which the setting is sustainable, or to which it positively addresses the health and productivity of the system of which it is a part. Environmental designers have been concerned primarily with the physical element being designed, not the effect of the environment on the health of the people that experience the city, or the health of the systems being evolved.

Designers have also been overly concerned with the purity of the design statement, rather than the degree to which it is synergized with its context. This is especially true in the profession of architecture, where often in the recent past, "Architecture" and "building" have been seen as two different issues (Wolfe 1981). Architecture (with a capital "A") has been seen as the design of the element in a pure and therefore significant sense. The designing of buildings (with a lower case "b") has been seen as the messier and therefore less meaningful task of integrating complex entities, including the integration of existing networks and systems as influences. Buildings have often been seen (especially by the leaders of major architectural movements) as less pure, more compromised, and therefore not worthy of being called architecture. This view has created an architecture that is elitist and visual, rather than vernacular and experiential. In practice, it has communicated architecture as an exercise in style rather than substance.

Desired Shift in Paradigm

If our designed environments are to be healthy dynamic places in which to live, shifts in mindset are necessary. These shifts will redefine each of the environmental design professions so that they synergize systems that are ecological, structural, infrastructural, and cultural. The redefined goal of design will be ecological and human health and ecological and system sustainability. This requires that we change the specific decisions we make. More importantly, it means that we change our attitudes concerning that about which we make decisions, i.e., that we shift our self-image from that of "project designer" to "system manager through project design." It requires that we change the underlying assumptions within which we make decisions, the mental context within which we design.

Emerging Environmental Design Paradigm

Fortunately, a new environmental design paradigm is emerging. It was born in the 1970s with the systems management movement, but went into remission in differing degrees in the various design professions because the reductionist deterministic mindset interpreted systems design in the narrowest sense. This naive reductive approach allowed singular systems to become deterministic, rather than seeing design as the synergism, in both form and function, of many complex interactive systems, including ones that are ecological, structural, infrastructural, and cultural. Currently, a more holistic systemic approach with a systems management emphasis is being combined with the grass-roots appropriate-technology approach and other similar influences, into an expanded and enlightened paradigm of sustainable development. While a commitment to sustainability has not yet become institutionalized as mainstream, it is growing; and it has the ability to introduce the necessary second-order change in design decision-making. And this change is essential to increased relevance. As the sustainability paradigm becomes mainstream, it will facilitate the redefinition of the environmental design professions into what Eric Jantsch has called "appreciative systems," which realize the person as a "unique device for relating to a reality in whose shaping ... [he or she] is actively and creatively participating" (1975).

As this emerging paradigm shift becomes mainstream, it will result in major redefinitions of the ecological and cultural roles of the environmental design

professions, and redefinitions of what constitutes responsible decision-making within these professions. These redefinitions will focus on wholes, not pieces, and on relationships, not elements. The emphasis will not be on individual elements such as buildings and sites, but rather on *placemaking,* on the mental constructs that occur in the user's mind as he or she experiences the landscape gestalt. It will also be on *sustainability,* the ability of the design decision to sustain or increase the carrying capacity of the system of which it is a part, without additional intervention and without system degradation. The driving force of these new professional definitions will not be design purity or borrowed aesthetics, but rather placeness and sustainability. These professions will embrace the concept of design for health in the broadest sense, including the health of the place as an experiential phenomenon, and the health of the systems that integrate to make places. It will also include the health of the individuals that experience these places. Design for health will include the effective management of systems that are ecological, cultural, and technological, and management of the physiological and psychological health of the individual (Figure 14-3).

Implementing New Design Paradigms

The preceding is easy to say but difficult to achieve because the environmental designer must be able to apply this mindset to real-world decisions in the field, which will include the application of specialized knowledge and its synthesis through project design. To be able to achieve this, designers must avoid the greatest schism that characterizes our culture. They must bridge the rift between art and science. This rift has been growing in the recent past, and now dominates our thinking. It has created immense differences in perception, and has caused major communication difficulties, for example, between planners and designers. As landscape architects have become more systems sensitive, communication has also become more difficult between architects and landscape architects, and the landscape has therefore become more disjointed. For environmental designers to become effective placemakers and effective designers of ecologically and culturally sustainable development, they must become more adept at integrating art with science. They must synergize creative expression with existing and new knowledge through design application, and they must manage the interrelationship between new development and existing physical and human systems.

In the new paradigm, the responsive designer must be able to analyze and synthesize interdisciplinary knowledge into creative design processes that manage

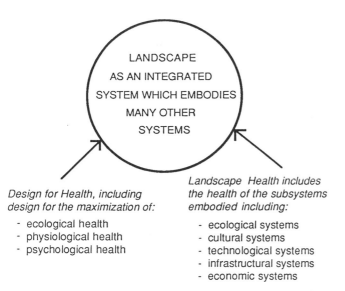

Design for Health, including design for the maximization of:
- ecological health
- physiological health
- psychological health

Landscape Health includes the health of the subsystems embodied including:
- ecological systems
- cultural systems
- technological systems
- infrastructural systems
- economic systems

Figure 14-3. Landscape as system.

ecological, cultural, infrastructural, and economic systems, to maximize human and ecological health and productivity. New and innovative models and design processes for doing so are being evolved. These efforts can lead the environmental design professions, and help us to escape the shackles of our Cartesian mindset, to synergize art and science, and to develop locally, regionally, and globally relevant development patterns, design expressions, and regional aesthetics.

THE EMERGING ROLE OF THE LANDSCAPE DESIGNER

The designed landscape can be what Eric Jantsch has referred to as an appreciative system, can possess what Peter Jacobs referred to as "deeper" meaning, characterized by "integrity, identity, imageability and flexibility"; and can integrate ecology, technology, and culture. However, to do so, new design approaches must emerge. These approaches are necessary because current mainstream ones seldom synergize the diverse perceptions and motivations of our culture with the complexity of our ecological landscape, or integrate specialized interdisciplinary knowledge adequately for design systems to become appreciative. With the evolution of these new approaches, the landscape designer will become the creative manager of settings that maximize the communication of meaning, while enhancing ecological and cultural health and productivity. This person will also be the designer of gestures or symbols in the landscape for the creative management of meaning and human experience, and for the effective synergism of ecological, cultural, technological, and economic systems.

Design Process

The landscape designer will be responsible for the evolution of processes that effectively manage ecological, physiological, and psychological health. Because of the "messy" behavior of complex systems (Beer 1981, Van Gigch 1984), the complexity of landscape systems, and the need to judge project design decisions in the context of larger systems and to be able to assess the degree to which decisions integrate with these systems, the landscape designer must take what is referred to in the field of systems science as a metasystems approach. According to this approach, decisions are made and managed at different levels. At the object level, specific decisions are made. At a broader metalevel, decisions are made concerning the appropriate conditions and processes that will promote appropriate decisions at the object level. The metalevel also determines the range of appropriate decisions that can occur at the object level. In the metasystem approach, landscape designers not only engage in project (object level) design, but also determine the objectives to be achieved by project design and the development controls and design parameters necessary to achieve these objectives (metalevel activities). They develop appropriate models and processes for management and design, and a hierarchical system of management and design decision-making that allows system management issues to determine the design objectives and criteria to be implemented at the project design level by planners, designers, developers, and others. This hierarchical decision-making structure is essential to integrate the diverse decisions made by many people, with differing motives, into integrated systems.

Hierarchical Decision-Making Structures

According to Klir (1981), a hierarchical management structure, differentiated by the range and depth of knowledge at each level, can most effectively manage complex systems. For urban landscape design, one such management structure is a three-tier hierarchy, consisting of the metasystems designer, the systems designer, and the project designer (Figure 14-4). The highest tier integrates physical systems that are generally spatial, with social, fiscal, and political ones that are not usually seen spatially. The metasystems level is essential in integrating these two very different patterns of perception into more holistic place-specific decision-making. The intermediate management tier, the systems designer, manages physical systems and their role in the making of sustainable and meaningful places. The lowest tier, that of project design, includes most of the current project work of the professions of urban design, architecture, and landscape architecture.

In this hierarchy, project-level decisions are made in the context of conceptual frameworks and models created at the systems design level for the management and integration of specific physical systems, within the context of frameworks and models created at the metasystems level for the integration of physical and nonphysical systems. The metasystems designer and the systems designer create paradigms and conceptual frameworks within which project design operates. This hierarchical management structure, of necessity, results in some redefinition of the professional goals and objectives, and the societal roles of the professions of urban design, architecture, and landscape architecture.

In this management hierarchy, the goal of the metasystems designer is the management of the ecological and cultural landscape. To achieve this goal, the primary objective is the synergism of structural, infrastructural, ecological, cultural, visual, and economic systems, for maximum environmental and human health and well-being. In order to promote this objective, landscape designers operating at the metalevel are necessarily systems thinkers. Their primary task is to apply decision-making science and systems science to determine how to make more appropriate decisions about the city and its integrated systems. To do so, they develop a control system of conceptual frameworks, models, and processes within which lower level decision-making occurs.

Performance Measures

In order to implement these management models, some means for evaluating project design performance has to be established. "Health" is one such means discussed above, with health seen in the broad sense to include ecological, and human physiological and psychological health. Some individuals have been working with health-related direct measures of performance. These include John Lyle's work in sustainable development (ecological health, 1985), James Russell and Jacalyn Snodgrass (1987), and R. Bruce Hull's (1990) work in human emotions (psychological health, 1989) and affective response. Others have been working with intermediate qualitative variables; Peter Jacobs's are identity, integrity, imageability, and flexibility; Stephen Kaplan's are understanding and exploration (1987). Still others are searching for quantifiable variables such as this author's order and spontaneity, Joel Schaatz's "energetics" (1974), or Howard Odum's energy flows (1970) and "emergy," or energy memory (1989), which is the amount of energy invested to produce an element. Still others are search-

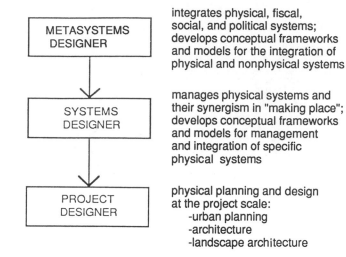

Figure 14-4. Urban landscape management hierarchy.

ing for unifying theories and conceptual frameworks.

The metasystems designer and systems designer must of necessity develop some form of design goals, objectives, and performance criteria against which lower-level decisions can be evaluated. They also promote the integration of lower-level decisions for effective systems and metasystems management.

Implementation

The preceding metasystems, systems, and project design designations, or any other decision evaluation and management structure that occurs, should not imply a separation of decision-making, but rather different scales of emphasis, and breadths of information that are considered in determining the appropriateness of decisions. All three tiers, in fact, can be served by the same individual, at the same time. For example, the systems-sensitive architect or landscape architect can serve simultaneously as the metasystems, systems, and project designer, in a multiple role as project manager and project architect or landscape architect. This is occurring today, as designers that are sensitive to systems management, sustainability, and placemaking are functioning in the capacity of "design facilitators," managing complex interdisciplinary design teams (Mulder), while also serving as project designers. These design facilitators usually employ some method for synergizing client, city planner, urban designer, architect, landscape architect, transportation planner, engineer, market analyst, and so on into a dynamic decision-making team. Roles of team members are only vaguely defined at the project inception, as is the design process itself. Roles, process, tasks, and outcomes evolve over time in response to the expertise and idiosyncracies of the various players, actively engaged in dialogue. This dialectic process has yielded promising results, and has generated projects that are sustainable and evocative, and that have received high professional recognition for design appropriateness, sensitivity, and excellence.

The work of these systems-sensitive individuals and design firms is significant because these efforts are occurring in the real world, and are applications sensitive. Unlike the old Cartesian model, they are "messy" and therefore responsive to the "special nature of reality" (Hatchuel, Agrell, and Van Gigch 1987), which is highly complex and less tractable than bounded rationality. These processes do not proceed in a predetermined manner, but rather evolve in a flexible pluralistic one, sensitive to cross-fertilization. The process is actively dialectic, involving discourse and synergism among a wide range of players. In this manner, problems are defined more holistically, and more appropriate problem-solving models are created. Through cross-fertilization, these interdisciplinary design teams promote the emergence of new ideas (Hatchuel, Agrell, and Van Gigch).

Systems-sensitive design facilitators are usually brought in to manage complex projects that will evolve over long periods of time. These managers function on the metasystems and systems design levels. They manage the innovation that occurs at the project design level by creating conditions that promote creative, responsive, and relevant decision-making at the lower level. They often use processes similar to the intervention-innovation processes developed in the field of management science. In these processes (Figure 14-5), problems are usually identified, existing theories and models are promulgated, and then through dialectic interaction, problems are redefined and new models promulgated. These models usually involve the identification of urban goals and objectives, and the use of these goals and objectives to drive dialectic interaction, to deconstruct established myths, and to establish more appropriate guidelines and standards for the design and evaluation of object-level decisions. Through these modified intervention-innovation processes, the interdisciplinary team develops a hierarchical decision evaluation and control mechanism that can be employed to evaluate and manage specific object-level decisions made by diverse decision-makers operating over extended periods of time. These object-level decisions can be evaluated for their relation to guidelines and standards established by the team, and for the degree to which they contribute to system management, the realization of urban objectives, and the pursuit of urban goals. The goals, objectives, guidelines, and standards are also understood to be flexible, and can be adjusted based on feedback after their application, and in response to changing urban and contextual conditions.

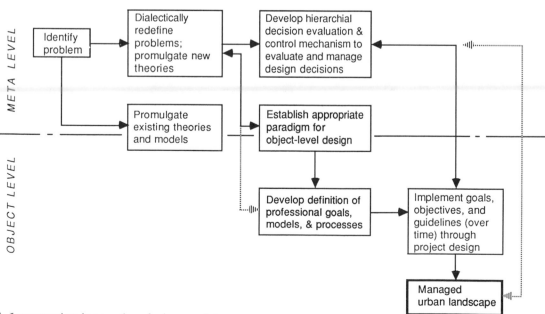

Figure 14-5. Intervention-innovation design model.

REFERENCES

Alexander, Christopher. 1977. *A Pattern Language: Towns, Buildings, Construction.* New York: Oxford University Press.

Beer, Stanford. 1981. *Brain of the Firm,* 2d ed. New York: Wiley.

Capra, Fritjof. 1982. *The Turning Point: Science, Society, and the Rising Culture.* New York: Simon & Schuster.

Hatchuel A., Agrell P., and van Gigch J. P. 1987. Innovation as System Intervention. *Systems Research: The Official Journal of the International Federation for Systems Research* 4 (1).

Heidegger, Martin. 1977. *Basic Writings from Being and Time (1927) to the Task of Thinking (1964).* David Farrell Krell, ed. New York: Harper & Row.

Hull, Bruce. 1990. Mood and Leisure: Causes and Consequences. *Journal of Leisure Research* 22 (2).

Jacobs, Peter. 1989. Cultural Values in the Changing Landscape. Paper read at the First CUBIT International Symposium on Architecture and Culture. College Station, TX: Texas A&M University.

Jantsch, Erich. 1975. *Design for Evolution: Self-Organization and Planning in the Life of Human Systems.* New York: Braziller.

Kaplan, Stephen. 1987. Aesthetic, Affect and Cognition: Environmental Preference from an Evolutionary Perspective. *Environment and Behavior* 19 (1): 3–33.

Klir, George. 1981. Special issue on Reconstructability Analysis. *International J. General Systems* 7 (1): 81–91.

Lyle, John. 1985. *Design for Human Ecosystems: Landscape, Land Use and Natural Resources.* New York: Van Nostrand Reinhold.

Mulder, Chris. 1986. *Master Plan and Management Guidelines for the Songimvelo Natural Resource Area.* Pretoria: Mulder Associates.

Norberg-Schulz, Christian. 1980. *Genius Loci: Towards a Phenomenology of Architecture.* New York: Rizzoli.

Odum, Howard. 1970. *Environment, Power and Society.* New York: Wiley-InterScience.

———. 1989. "Emergy and Evolution." *33rd Annual Meeting of the International Society for the Systems Sciences.* Edinburgh.

Russell, James, and Snodgrass, Jacalyn. 1987. Emotion and the Environment. *Handbook of Environmental Psychology.* Daniel Stokols and Irwin Altman, editors. New York: Wiley.

Schaatz, Joel. 1974. *Energetics and Decision-Making.* Presentation at the Spokane, Washington Expo '74.

Sorokin, Pitirim. 1937–41. *Social and Cultural Dynamics.* Four volumes. New York, Cincinnati: American.

Toffler, Alvin. 1980. *The Third Wave.* New York: Morrow.

Van Gigch, John. 1984. *The Metasystems Paradigm as a New Hierarchical Theory of Organizations.* Annual Meeting of the Society of General Systems Research. New York.

Wolfe, Tom. 1981. *From Bauhaus to Our House.* New York: Farrar, Straus & Giroux.

SUGGESTED READINGS

Churchman, C. West. *Challenge to Reason.* New York: McGraw-Hill.

Rapoport, Amos. 1969. *House Form and Culture.* Englewood Cliffs, NJ: Prentice-Hall.

15

Ecological Health and Sustainability

SYSTEMS THEORY AND LANDSCAPE DESIGN

According to systems theory, there are two types of systems, each with its own corresponding structural type. The first system type is at relative equilibrium, a steady-state condition. It is highly integrated and interactive and changes slowly. This system type, which we call *late successional*, usually develops structures that reinforce the existing conditions and perpetuate, extend, or subtly affect existing relationships, and the status quo. These structures, referred to as equilibrium structures, generally have fine-tuned relationships and few internal conflicts. They change slowly, and when they do, their parts change together interactively. They maintain what is referred to as a *dynamic equilibrium*. While this term appears to be contradictory, it rather expresses the dynamic changing nature of systems (one of the premises of the science of chaos), and the equilibrium condition of all parts adjusted to one another, and changing together.

The second system type is one that is undergoing rapid, profound, and fundamental change. It is inherently unstable and develops structures that maximize both the extent and rate of change. These systems promote the formation of radically new relationships, and are generally characterized by major conflict, contradiction, and severe stress. The structures that usually evolve under these conditions, referred to as *dissipative structures*, dissipate energies by maximizing change and contradiction (Table 15-1).

Landscapes and Architecture

To understand the potential that faces the site designer, we need to understand the distinctions and the interrelatedness of these two types of structure of the

Table 15-1. Systems characteristics, structural type.

Equilibrium Structure	Dissipative Structure
System at equilibrium	System not at equilibrium
System changing slowly	System undergoing profound, rapid change
Functions	
Reinforce existing conditions	Deconstruct existing relationships
Perpetuate status quo	Accelerate change
Characteristics	
Fine-tuned relationships	Lack of stable relationships
High integration	Lack of integration
Few internal conflicts	Many internal conflicts
Slow change	Maximize extent and rate of change
High stability	Inherent instability

landscape and contemporary architecture. On the one hand, the ecological landscape can best be understood as the dynamically changing *equilibrium structure* we have discussed. Through succession, the landscape evolves toward greater organization, integration, diversity, and complexity. Yet, as the science of chaos has shown us, and referring to Douglas Hofstadter (1985) again, "It turns out that an eerie type of chaos can lurk just behind the facade of order—and yet, deep inside the chaos lurks an even eerier type of order." In other words, within this state of dynamic equilibrium, we cannot predict specifically what will happen at a given place and time, but this spontaneity occurs as an expression of some even greater underlying order.

267

Contemporary architecture, on the other hand, is a *dissipative expression* that seeks not to synergize with an existing condition, but rather to make a highly individualized evocative statement (Figure 15-1). Each element makes a new and often different design statement. Each successive design movement appears to relate less to context, until the current expressed intent in some cases is to deconstruct one's learned ability to cognize and ascribe meaning to place. Like the landscape, it is spontaneous. To the degree that it also conveys some greater underlying order, it synergizes and becomes a spontaneous expression integrated with landscape dynamics. To the degree that it fails to express this greater underlying order, it fails to synergize.

One of the primary tasks facing the landscape designer, and one of the most difficult, is to facilitate the synergism of these two differing types of expres-

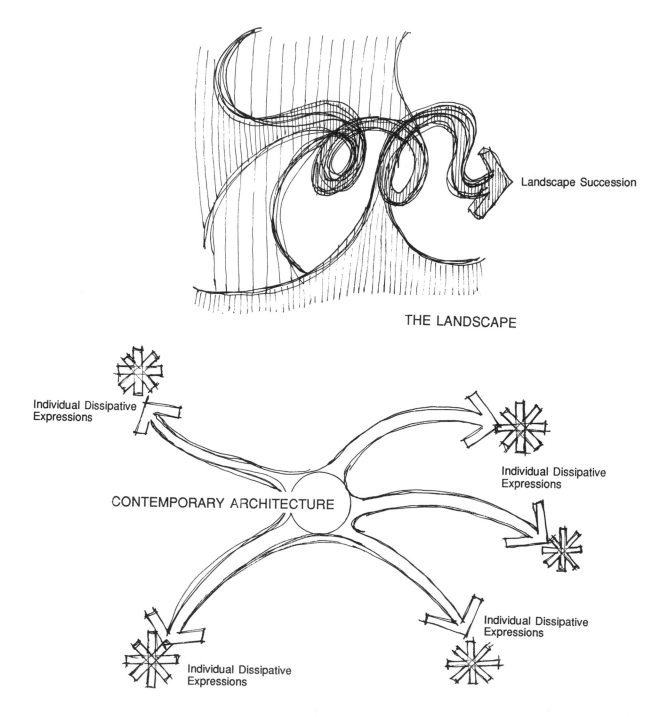

Figure 15-1. Nature of landscape and architecture.

sions. When synergism is achieved, the designed landscape conveys the order and spontaneity that is psychologically satisfying (Chapter 16). It also integrates into the systemic order of the landscape, and promotes long-term efficiency and sustainability.

Landscape Design in the Twenty-First Century

The dynamic, interactive relationship between the landscape and architecture presents unique challenges to the landscape designer. For example, the landscape designer must manage design such that the nature of landscape as dynamic equilibrium structure is maintained, while integrating diverse elements into an efficiently functioning and experientially satisfying system. This problem is made more difficult by our regionally diverse landscapes, and by our heterogeneous and rapidly changing culture and technology. To complicate matters even further, the city is designed by incremental decisions made by many people, with variable intentions, over long periods of time. These decisions are seldom integrated successfully into the system dynamics of the culture *or* the city. Visually speaking, the resulting urban landscape is usually a conglomerate of poorly related expressions—well-designed monuments that form a chaotic milieu. Ecologically, these contradictions and failures in system dynamics create a designed whole that is inefficient and often alienating. Therefore, our designed environments often degrade the health and reduce the productivity of the systems of which they are integral parts. This system breakdown, in turn, usually results in long-term degradation and reduced function of the designed element itself.

System inefficiency, malfunction, and degradation are so pervasive in our culture, that as we approach the twenty-first century, we do so in a crisis situation that is having major negative impacts on the quality of our life and the health of our ecological and cultural systems. There are myriad expressions of this crisis, including environmental degradation, water and energy crises, homelessness, high crime and suicide rates, inadequate health care, and an almost infinite number of other maladies. These crises are all interrelated and are the multifaceted expressions of a single underlying and pervasive inability to sustain the physical and social structures that we create. Our inappropriate paradigm is the underlying cause of these crises and, like the hurricane that spawns a multitude of tornados, it can be understood as the metacrisis that creates the conditions within which these other crises develop, and which thereby drives them (Figure 15-2). Unfortunately, while we must react to the multitude of symptoms that surround us, we should bear

in mind that doing so is only placing "band-aids" on the wounds and not addressing the real crisis. To resolve this problem properly, we must address the metacrisis of our inappropriate paradigm, while simultaneously putting out the brushfires (which must be done in the short term).

The crisis of perception that is responsible for our societal ills is the inevitable result of our short-term thinking, and our propensity to reduce complex realities to their component parts, and then address these parts rather than the integrated whole. We use a Cartesian mindset, a positivist approach and a newtonian scientific method to focus on pieces as we try to understand complexities. We distrust messy approaches that embrace complexity and focus on contextual relationships, but that lack, as the scientists say, "replicability." By focusing on the piece, we make it more difficult to understand and apply ecological, physiological, and psychological interrelatedness to the management and design of systems. In the process, we create ever larger crises, symptoms of the increased system breakdown that occurs because the elements that we design aggregate over time to create systems that are not sustainable.

If the measure of knowledge is understanding the limits of one's knowledge, then perhaps the worst aspect of the crisis in perception is our lack of awareness of the real problem. There is little hope of correcting the ills caused by inappropriate decision-making until a shift in paradigm occurs. However, entrenched in our Cartesian mindset, we continue to perceive that we are designing the piece when, in fact, we are designing the whole, but doing so poorly, by failing to design necessary interrelationships. In our

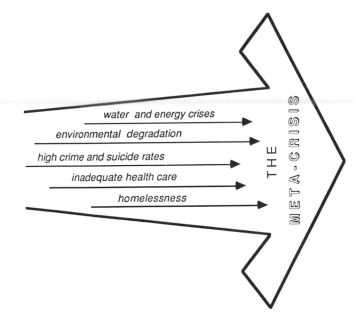

Figure 15-2. Multifaceted expressions of the metacrisis.

naivety, we assume that if we manage the piece, someone else will manage the whole (Schaatz 1974). We fail to realize that through our actions we are unconsciously managing the landscape, doing so poorly, and creating a landscape that is unsustainable except through unnecessary energy consumption and environmental degradation.

If we are to address ecology, culture, and long-term economics adequately, and effectively manage the systems on which our health and ultimately our survival depend, a shift in paradigm must occur. This shift began in physics in the 1930s as a movement away from the mechanistic world view of Descartes and Newton, to a holistic, ecologic, and phenomenological one. Today, this paradigmatic shift is occurring throughout society as more and more people are developing a consciousness that we live in a globally interconnected world in which pieces have meaning primarily through interrelationships. This grass-roots change in public consciousness is being fueled by the exponential rise in number and intensity of expressions of system breakdown and global environmental degradation. It is also being fueled by America's decreased competitiveness in a global economy as we move from a condition of resource abundance to resource paucity. More simply stated, it is becoming more and more difficult to remain unaware of, or insensitive to, the pervasive crises and changing world economics. These crises are driving people to realize that decisions made primarily for short-term gain are not appropriate or sustainable, and that it is essential that we make decisions for long-term function, efficiency, and sustainability. Only by long-term decision-making can we manage the health of ecological, cultural, and economic systems and the health and productivity of the landscape. Long-term decision-making is also essential to remaining economically competitive in the twenty-first century.

SUSTAINABILITY

Since Buckminster Fuller and his "World Game" workshops, we have realized that spaceship earth has a limited carrying capacity (1983). We have also realized that this capacity changes with our decisions concerning the location of human activities, and the manner in which these activities are designed.

If we are to manage the health and productivity of this spaceship, then development must be sustainable—it must sustain or increase the carrying capacity of the system, without system degradation. According to William D. Ruckelshaus (1989), "Sustainable development is the nascent doctrine that economic growth and development must take place, and be maintained over time, within the limits set by ecology in the broadest sense—by the interrelations of human beings and their works, the biosphere and the physical and chemical laws that govern it." If we are to design healthy landscapes, we must therefore manage economic growth and development for its sustainability. As Prime Minister Brundtland, Chair of the World Trade Commission on Environment and Development, said, development must meet "the needs of the present without compromising the ability of future generations to meet their own needs" (1987). Sustainability allows us to provide for present needs, while promoting long-term ecological and physiological health and productivity.

There is a built-in order and efficiency in ecosystems, based on their structure (species populations and their needs), function (interrelationships and energy and mineral flows), and organization (of elements). Sustainability speaks of the necessity for human decisions to integrate into this order, including the structure, function, and organization of human interventions in the landscape.

If human interventions are to be integrated into ecosystem structure, function, and organization, then design processes must embrace both intuitive and rational thinking. The designer must integrate both art and science, while responding to the scale independence expressed by nature, and the fact that decisions made at any scale are reflected at all scales (as we currently witness in the global ozone depletion due to inappropriate local decisions, or conversely massive degradation of local estuarine ecosystems due to oil spills hundreds of miles distant).

The sustainability paradigm is based on an integrated, holistic world view. It takes a systems approach to decision-making, and is the more effective long-term decision-making strategy. It is especially effective in times of limited resource, and has therefore recurred as the dominant decision-making strategy at various times in history, usually during periods of resource paucity.

Sustainability has experienced a recent rebirth with the resource conservation movement of the 1960s. More recently it has evolved beyond the reactive approach of conservation, to the proactive one of managing long term potential. In the earlier reactive resource conservation movement, resource and development were generally seen as adversarial, and the movement sought to conserve resources against the onslaught of development. In the more recent one, this relationship is not seen as adversarial, but rather as synergistic, with development contributing to enhanced quality of life and ecological integrity. The sustainable development paradigm sees ecological, social and economic health and well-being as inextricably interwoven.

Ecosystems

The landscape is more than an aggregate of elements. Therefore, in addressing any of its elements, the designer must be sensitive to the total landscape and its interrelationships as the entity being designed. Individual decisions must be made by measuring their impact on the landscape as an integrated system.

The *ecosystem concept* advanced by A. G. Tansley in 1934 has become the fundamental concept of ecological study, and one of the primary ones of landscape design. According to this concept, the ecosystem can be understood in its most simple form as the interacting assemblage of life forms and their nonliving environment. People are an integral part of most terrestrial ecosystems; and unfortunately human actions are becoming the limiting factor in landscape sustainability, stability, and productivity.

Like most natural phenomena, ecosystems are scale independent, that is, they express themselves in a similar manner regardless of scale; and the behavior and form at one scale reflects itself at other scales. They are also open systems, with energy and material flowing freely across their boundaries. The spatial and scalar openness of ecosystems is of great concern to the landscape designer, as our actions in a given place are affected by, and in turn affect, other landscapes and other scales.

Howard Odum showed us a means for evaluating decisions and activities through the universal unit of measurement of *energetics* or energy flows (1971), and more recently through the measurement of *emergy*, that is, the energy invested to allow decisions or activities to occur. According to Odum, decisions can be evaluated as positive or negative depending on the energy embodied in the decision or the activity, and the benefit to the system derived from that decision. Odum has tracked energy flows through various systems and their components including the amount and quality of energy that enters and leaves that component. Odum has shown how growth-oriented, inefficient, and early successional systems compete most effectively in times of resource plenty; and sustenance-oriented, efficient, late successional ones compete most effectively in times of resource scarcity.

Carrying Capacity

The concept of *carrying capacity* refers to the amount and nature of activity that can be sustained at a given time by ecological and cultural systems, without degradation to these systems over time. Carrying capacity, therefore, can serve as a measure of landscape performance and impact.

Ecological and cultural landscapes are open ecosystems, with material, energy, and human flows across boundaries. When addressing carrying capacity, we must consider both internal and external relationships, and the management and degradation of both the local and extended systems. We must also consider both internal and contextual carrying capacity.

Carrying capacity can be used to (1) identify the base conditions prior to development, (2) predict the anticipated impact of proposed development alternatives, and (3) measure the actual impact of an implemented decision over time. In all three of these cases, it can serve as a measure of sustainability. To be sustainable, development must maintain or improve the carrying capacity and long-term productivity of the immediate system and that of the contextual system, or otherwise contribute in a manner that offsets any adverse local impacts. Positive or negative changes in capacity over time serve as a measure of the effectiveness of management activities. Finally, carrying capacity can be used to identify whether development should occur, which of several approaches to development should occur, appropriate development patterns, limits to development, and criteria for design, and appropriate design decisions for a particular project. It can also be used to evaluate whether a development is performing as predicted, and thereby serve as a tool to evolve development criteria based on actual performance of human-intervention landscapes.

Landscape Ecology

The ecological landscape is a system that evolves to a dynamic equilibrium, and is characterized by increasing order, integration, and complexity. If landscapes are to function efficiently and be sustainable, environmental design decisions must synthesize with the complex order of nature, and integrate natural and human systems (Figure 15-3).

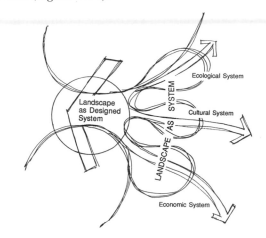

Figure 15-3. Landscape as designed system.

The efficient and appropriate flow of energy and minerals is essential to our survival. To be sustainable, therefore, development must be integrated with the ecology of the landscape, and must be heterogeneous, offering many varied and overlapping niches (Alexander 1965). Second, its function and behavior and its context must be integrated. Third, it must embrace the changing nature of landscape systems. Finally, it must synergize with the complex integrated spatial and scalar organization of landscape systems. By embracing these tenants of landscape ecology, development and ecology can be mutually supportive.

Landscape Management

The 1960s and 1970s witnessed a conflict between preservation and development, and saw the two as fundamentally different. In this text we consider the two as complementary aspects of a single issue, landscape management.

Landscape Preservation

We must preserve our history and ecological roots in the wilderness, for we are an integral part of nature, and without the wilderness we are rootless. However, to preserve the natural environment, we must be sensitive and manage aggressively. To be sustained, even preservation areas must be managed, especially at their edges, with inflows (numbers of people, mineral flows, and so on) strictly monitored. We must also manage landscape diversity.

Landscape Diversity

If our landscapes are to be sustainable over time, we must design for landscape diversity and heterogeneity [Eugene Odum (1971)]. We should design early successional productive ecosystems, and late successional protective ones—different ecological communities of different ages, structure, and function, located for maximum advantage based on landscape carrying capacity and organization. We should manage the landscape for early and late successional natural communities, as well as effective early and late successional human ecosystems.

Behavioral Strategies

If we are to manage our landscapes for sustainability, then human behavior must change as conditions change. A case in point is the rapid growth and advancement of technology and the U.S. economy through the industrial age, allowing us to grow, explore, and more effectively utilize the surplus of resources around us. We have recently moved from a condition of resource surplus to one of resource scarcity. Late successional cultural systems (such as that in Japan) that have long-term development strategies operate more efficiently and therefore have the competitive advantage in this resource-poor condition. Early successional cultural systems (such as the United States) must restructure themselves and change their operational paradigms to function more efficiently and sustainably, if they are to remain competitive.

Land Use

As a first step toward landscape sustainability, Eugene Odum has suggested that all lands be placed into four categories: production areas, where succession is retarded by human intervention to maintain a high level of production; protective areas, where succession is allowed and encouraged so that these areas can produce the stability necessary for sustainability; compromise areas, where both production and protection occur; and urban industry in biologically nonvital areas.

It is imperative that we aggressively manage our environmental resource. This must be done if we are to cease to place our most environmentally destructive industries into our most sensitive ecosystems, a practice that continues to occur at an alarming rate, resulting in the destruction of our estuarine and other highly productive, sensitive, and irreplaceable habitats.

Sustainability

Sustainable development is the intentional planning and design of human ecosystems through the application of ecological understanding, to make conscious, informed decisions concerning conflicts between human and ecosystems needs. It allows us to make the trade-offs that are inherent in design processes, and to gain the ability to integrate creatively and responsively into nature's processes, for ecological and human benefit. By so doing, we can design landscapes that fulfill our human potential while supporting ecosystem needs and the needs of nonhuman communities. As we do so, we need to remember the complexity of nature and in the words of John Lyle, "We have to begin by admitting that our tools are still crude, and we do not know enough to do the job with absolute confidence, recognizing at the same time that we all have to do it anyway" (1985).

According to William Clark (1989), when we manage decision-making for sustainability, we should have three objectives. The first is to be able to control human population growth. The second is to promote economic growth and to distribute the benefits of this growth appropriately to meet basic human needs for the present population and future generations. The third is to refrain from impacting environments beyond the limits of safety, although in many cases we do not yet know those limits. As we create sustainable landscapes, transformation can serve as a measure of our effectiveness. Predevelopment system health and productivity can be established as baselines, and these can be used to predict the impacts of alternative decisions. Changes in health and productivity can be a measure of the actual impacts of implemented projects, and the effectiveness of our management efforts over time.

Sustainability as a World View Implemented Locally

Sustainability is a world view. However, decisions occur locally, and nature is characterized by scale independence and local variability. Therefore, this world view must be implemented locally.

World View

A world view is the individual's view of what constitutes the world, and is the perceived context within which decisions are made. To implement sustainability, we can begin by recommitting ourselves to a world view based on the interdependence of humans and nature. We can base our decisions on long-term economics including the costs of maintaining the designed landscape. We can see the health of any landscape component as integrally linked with the health of all other components, and the health of the whole.

Landscapes function also as open systems, and energy and materials flow freely across boundaries. Therefore, in implementing sustainability, we must manage the immediate systems and the larger systems of which they are part.

Local Implementation

While sustainability is a world view, it must be implemented at a local grass-roots level. Specific development decisions and the processes by which these decisions are made, for example, must grow from the specific conditions and behavior at the location of development. The local system and its behavior must be maintained, and supported. Development patterns that emerge must be integrated with local ecological and cultural ones. The behavior of the development and its ecological and human context must be no less synergized.

While the sustainable development paradigm is easy to describe, it is far more difficult to implement, because of an inadequate understanding of systems dynamics. This difficulty is also due to inadequately developed application methodologies, and a lack of successful sustainable developments "casting shadows on the ground," raising the public level of consciousness, and increasing the social acceptability and fiscal viability of the concept.

In order to implement sustainable development, we must create decision-making and administrative structures that promote the redefinition of design processes. We must develop greater understanding of characteristics that make design sustainable, and of system dynamics and management structures that respond to these dynamics. We must also determine appropriate levels for design performance, and processes that promote appropriate design decisions. These new processes must synergize decisions made at local, regional, and global levels, by innumerable decision-makers with diverse and often divergent perceptions and motivations. We must also convince the design professions to embrace these design processes and tools.

Decision-Making for Sustainability

In contemporary American society, decisions are made by diverse players with differing world views and motivations. The landscape grows incrementally as a result of these decisions. Because of the heterogeneity of decision-makers, our increased technological ability to change the landscape, and accretion, the contemporary landscape is *not* a self-regulating system. If it is to evolve to be environmentally, physiologically, and psychologically healthy, it must be effectively managed.

Decision-Making Levels

Systems theorists tell us that decisions are made and managed at two levels. The first is the object level at which specific decisions are made. The second is the metalevel at which decisions are made concerning the conditions within which object-level decisions are made; and therefore it is the level at which the range of options available at the object level are determined. The implementation of sustainable development will of necessity occur at both these levels. At the object level, design decisions respond to the specifics of the ecological and cultural context. At the metalevel we develop policies, administrative structures, models, and methods that promote object-level synergism of environmental design decisions with systems that are ecological, cultural, and economical.

Natural Response

As we implement sustainability, we must understand that unlike contemporary society, nature is self-organizing, that it functions to increase order and long-term efficiency, and that we can draw on its cues and natural order to increase long-term efficiency and sustainability. Finally, we must embrace the knowledge generated by the sciences to better understand natural processes and natural order, and to make development more responsive to these processes and order, and therefore more sustainable.

Scientific Knowledge

According to Lyle, the scientific ecosystem knowledge available to the designer usually consists of two types. The first is specific data. The second is the principles, concepts, and frameworks by which we develop an understanding of the organization and behavior of ecosystems (such as succession and energy flows). These conceptual frameworks are essential to interrelating and giving meaning to the data, in extrapolating data that we do not have but that we must predict in order to design, and in making decisions concerning the landscape.

STATE OF THE ART

The underlying concept of sustainable development is that the value of any human decision is its contribution to the health and long-term viability and productivity of the ecosystem. The measure of the sustainability is the relationship between its inputs and outputs, and its impacts to carrying capacity.

Sustainability is promoted by a long-term value system and appropriate economic and policy incentives. It is facilitated by locating activities in landscapes most suited for them, prohibiting activities from ecosystems innately unsuited for them, preserving lands particularly suited for critical uses (such as prime agricultural lands), managing lands for the avoidance and mitigation of impacts, and making point-in-time focused decisions based on long-term and holistic cost-benefit analyses. Rather than looking at construction or life-cycle costs of a building (construction, operating, and maintenance costs) as an economic measure, a sustainable development approach suggests that we should look at total costs embodied in the movement from a predevelopment to a developed condition. From an energy standpoint, for example, embodied costs include not only the costs of operating a building, but also the energy involved with constructing the building and the energy consumed in producing the products used to build the project.

Sustainability suggests that we create policy and taxing structures that accurately reflect the total energy embodied in a product or system (for extraction, refinement, production, transport, assembly, and so on) and the embodied resources that a building consumes as we make decisions concerning costs and benefits. Major steps in this direction, for example, could be attained by replacing current policies that subsidize water and energy-wasting industries that generate products that are high in energy and materials costs relative to their value, with alternative policies that provide incentives for decisions that promote sustainable human ecosystems.

Fortunately, the sustainable development movement is rapidly growing and is affecting decision-making. Examples of sustainable behavior abound, as evidenced by the use of natural building materials, a greater appreciation for low water, chemical, and energy using landscapes, and renewable energy technologies. There is a greater perceived urgency in management for clean air and water. Perhaps most important, there is a growing awareness of the need to reuse rather than discard our wastes. This is most evident in the case of our most limiting resource, water. Recently, legislation mandating local reuse of water has burgeoned. There is also an increased awareness of the need to reuse organic and inorganic waste materials. For example, several cities are now processing and recycling their urban sludge as a soil amendment. Following are some of the other current activities toward a sustainable tomorrow that are occurring within the area of landscape design:

Metabolic Planning and Design

The concept of metabolic planning and design (Fisk 1988) begins with local natural resources and develops processes for preparing these raw materials for human use, while building these units into chains (analogous to ecological food chains) that use the outputs (products and wastes) of one metabolic unit as inputs to other units. It should be kept in mind that like natural systems, natural form and fractals, metabolic units are scale independent, that is, they can be cultures, industries, businesses, or households. Each metabolic unit has inputs and outputs. In an efficiently functioning urban system, the input needs of one metabolic unit are served by the outputs (products and wastes) of adjacent units, and inputs and outputs move both spatially and from one scale to another.

In a conceptual sense, metabolic units can be understood as entities that convert renewable and abundant local resources into products, through some conversion processes. These units, and the chains they form, can promote a symbiosis of humans and nature to build a healthier sustainable economy and landscape. For example, coal-fired power plants produce fly ash. According to Fisk, fly ash can be mixed with lime slag to produce a concrete with compressive strengths that have been tested to exceed 12,000 psi. The energy necessary for this process is a fraction of the energy needed to produce portland cement. According to Fisk, concrete produced by this process has been used successfully for building, and he is also developing a method to "foam fly ash using organic, renewable foams to produce a lightweight porous concrete ... for use as a porous paving to increase groundwater replenishment, the lack of which presents a serious condition in many parts of the U.S."

Metabolic planning and design are concerned with individual technologies, and with their ability to form chains and regionally based economies that can help reverse the mindset that focuses on environmental problems rather than on environmental potentials. They are based on a view of sustainability as an economic and ecological management, rather than a conservation, issue.

Metabolic planning and design apply the principles of ecological land use planning to develop a better understanding of the "environment as a matrix of economic potentials of many types in combination with sound environmental principles" (Fisk). According to Fisk, the first step in this effort involves the development of *regional working atlases*, which identify "a series of resources that connect directly with the principal life support needs of the region's population and environment." The resources identified in these regional atlases can serve as a basis for *point resources,* which can be metabolic units or repositories of information or resource (business, research centers, industries, and the like). Metabolic planning and design also involve *network analyses* of the regional economics, and studying the inputs and outputs of metabolic units to determine their impacts on human needs and the potential for developing chains that promote a healthier economy and environment (Fisk).

According to Fisk, metabolic planning and design can be used to organize a community's inputs and outputs, to identify gaps that can be filled by introducing new metabolic units (called *gap businesses* or *gap industries*), and thereby build better economic and environmental chains. At a more expansive level, they identify resources with high economic potential that are not being transformed, because of insufficient knowledge as to how to transform these materials to serve human needs. In this case, the development of key industries will serve as a catalyst to the growth of many secondary and tertiary industries; the new key industries are seen as *trigger industries* (Fisk).

Like fractals, metabolic planning and design are scale independent: they can be applied on any scale. In his work, Fisk has applied metabolic planning and design on four scales—the single unit, the district, the city, and the urban region—and has been able to utilize existing organizations and databases. He has allowed unsatisfied needs on one scale to be transferred to the next scale in the search for inputs, gaps, or trigger industries.

According to Fisk, metabolic planning and design can rely heavily on the *biome system* concept developed by biogeographers. This system of global patterns of flora and fauna, organized into zones of biotic response to similar sets of resources, can serve as an organizational and analytical model. Ecologically based technologies can be developed that correlate human need and support systems with the region's biotic life and physical support system. Various cultures on the face of the earth that share the same biome can be studied to develop a better understanding of the interrelatedness of earth resources (climate, soil, hydrology, biota) and technology (building materials and techniques, water treatment, waste assimilation, food production, and so on), and the alternative technologies available. According to Fisk, the primary database for a particular situation can be the same ecological niche in similar communities of different biogeographical regions within the same global biome. Metabolic planning and design can transfer *equivalent technologies* between different biogeographical regions within the biome, and new *appropriate technologies* intimately connected with the region's metabolic processes can be developed (Fisk).

Design for Human Ecosystems

Another major thrust is the search for a sustainable approach to design is the work and writings of John T. Lyle. In his book *Design for Human Ecosystems,* he explores the concept of development as "man building functioning ecosystems." He focuses on Eugene Odum's third category of landscape management as discussed above, but refers to these areas not as "compromises," but rather as "human ecosystems." He does so *not* in an egocentric manner of humans "creating ecosystems," but rather from the sense that human activities have been modifying ecosystems for twelve thousand years, and that to fulfill our human potential, and to accommodate our growing populations, we must begin to do so more effectively. He acknowledges that the ecosystems we design will be different in structure and function from natural systems, and that they will differ in their stability, productivity, and other characteristics, but he stresses that they will continue to respond to the same natural forces.

Lyle addresses the fact that our previously modified ecosystems have been largely unintentionally developed without an awareness that we were creating these systems. They were also incrementally evolved, usually without an understanding of ecological processes and the interacting systemic character of nature. Finally, they were developed without an ability to predict how these systems would work. He asserts therefore that they usually did not work very well.

In his book, Lyle states that design for human ecosystems should address scale, process, and order. He contends that the designer must recognize that decisions on any scale have impacts on other scales, that the issues of concern change at different scales, and that the designer works in the context of larger systems into which decisions must be integrated. He asserts that the designer must be able to make both intuitive and analytical landscape decisions. These decisions must also synergize with the order of the landscape, including landscape structure, function, and location.

Lyle presents various concepts and techniques for designing sustainable human ecosystems, based on predictions of the consequences of design decisions. He makes decisions based on the structural and functional forms that these decisions introduce into the landscape, a process he refers to as *ecosystematic design*. He sees this as the fourth generation in design processes, the evolutionary result of first instinctive, genetic-based decision-making; then traditional based design where the accumulated knowledge or "collective memory" of the culture shaped its landscape design, and traditional forms were conserved and improved on over time; and then a form-making phase of design, where highly innovative, prescriptive forms were placed into the landscape while seldom achieving an environmental fit. He sees the current phase of which he is a part to be one of

> predictive adaptation [that] uses the skills developed in earlier phases and adds to them our abilities for storing knowledge and for technological manipulation, for reason, insight, and invention, for predicting the behavior of an imagined form in relation to its environment, and for shaping it on that basis.

He sees the process as one of imagining alternatives, and analyzing the behavior of these alternatives. He speaks of the uncertainty that permeates nature (chaos theory), and for checks and balances to prevent catastrophe when this inevitable uncertainty surfaces. He also speaks for the necessity for creative change over time, as the designed system interacts with the environment; and for a continuity of design and management that facilitates this adaptation in the designed landscape.

COMPUTERS AND SUSTAINABILITY

As our understanding of the complexity of reality increases exponentially, so do the tools that we have at our disposal to better understand that order and to predict the impacts of our decisions. The computer now gives us the ability to model human activities and the impacts of alternative decisions, and to model alternative scenarios, assessing their costs and benefits. Sophisticated computer-mapping techniques are being explored as a means to synergize environmental resource, infrastructural, demographic, and economic data to improve decision-making. Work is also being done to link various climate, energy, and mineral flow models to geographical information systems to spatially model the impact of land use and other human decisions in the landscape (1989). We now have the capability to model alternative scenarios and are moving toward the ability to animate the impacts of these decisions to spatially track the flow of energy and minerals through the ecosystem, while analyzing impacts and providing direction to the designer to facilitate knowledge-based decision-making.

REFERENCES

Alexander, Christopher. 1965. A City Is Not a Tree. *Architectural Forum* 122, April (58–62), May (58–62).

Brundtland, 1987. *Our Common Future*. World Trade Commission on Environment and Development. New York: Oxford University Press.

Clark, William. 1989. Managing Planet Earth. *Scientific American* 261 (3):47–54.

Fisk, Pliny. 1988. Regional Planning and Sustainability. Paper read at the Harvard School of Design, Colloquy on Sustainability. Cambridge, MA.

Fuller, R. Buckminster. 1983. *Humans in Universe*. New York: Moutin.

Hofstadter, Douglas. 1985. *Metamagical Themas: Questing for the Essence of Mind and Pattern*. New York: Basic Books.

Lyle, John. 1985. *Design for Human Ecosystems: Landscape, Land Use and Natural Resources*. New York: Van Nostrand Reinhold.

Odum, Eugene. 1971. *Fundamentals of Ecology*, 3d ed. Philadelphia: W. B. Saunders.

Odum, Howard. 1974. Paper read at the Florida Conference on Energy. Gainesville, FL.

Ruckelshaus, William D. 1989. Toward a Sustainable World. *Scientific American* 261 (3):166–174.

Schaatz, Joel. 1974. Energetics and Decision-Making. Presentation at the Spokane, Washington Expo '74.

Steenberghen, Therese, Bruner, Melody, Woodfin, Tom, and Landphair, Harlow. 1989. Linking Water Budget Models and Surface Hydraulics to GIS for Land Planning. GIS/LIS89, ASPRS, Bethesda, MD, 1989.

Tansley, A. G. 1934. Life Form of Plants and Statistical Plant Geography. Christen Raunkin collection of papers. Oxford: Clarendon Press.

SUGGESTED READINGS

Barbier, E. B. 1987. The Concept of Sustainable Economic Development. *Env. Conserv.* 14:101–110.

Bartelmus, Peter. 1986. *Environment and Development.* Boston: Allen & Unwin.

Biswas, Margaret, and Biswas, Asit. 1984. Complementarity Between Environmental and Development Processes. *Env. Conserv.* 11 (1):35–44.

Brown, B. J., Hansen, M. E., Liverman, D. M., Merideth, R. W., Jr. Global Sustainability: Toward Definition. *Env. Man.* 11:713–719.

Caldwell, Lyuten. 1984. Political Aspects of Ecologically Sustainable Development. *Env. Conserv.* 11:299–308.

Capra, Fritjof. 1982. *The Turning Point: Science, Society, and the Rising Culture.* New York: Simon & Schuster.

Costanza, R., and Daley, H. E. 1987. Towards an Ecological Economics. *Ecol. Mod.* 38:1–7.

Fisk, Pliny. 1989. Metabolic Planning and Design: How Healthy Building Could Be the Forerunner of Healthy Businesses, Healthy Cities and a Healthy Environment. Paper read at the Annual Conference of the New England Solar Energy Association and the Quality Building Council.

Jacobs, Peter. 1986. Sustainable Landscapes: Sustainable Societies. *Landscape and Urban Planning* 13:349–358.

Jantsch, Erich. 1975. *Design for Evolution.* New York: Braziller.

Koh, J. 1982. Ecological Design: A Post-Modern Paradigm of Holistic Philosophy and Evolutionary Ethic. *Landscape J.* 1:76–82.

Odum, Eugene. 1971. *Fundamentals of Ecology,* 3d ed. Philadelphia: W.B. Saunders.

Naveh, Z., and Lieberman, A. 1984. *Landscape Ecology.* New York: Springer-Verlag.

Neef, E. 1981. Stages in the Development of Landscape Ecology. *Proceedings Int. Cong. Neth. Soc. Land Ecol.* Veldhoven.

Tisdell, C. A. 1983. An Economist's Critique of the World Conservation Strategy, with Examples from the Australian Experience. *Env. Conserv.* 10:43–51.

16

Psychological Health and Placemaking

Contemporary cities are often characterized by well-designed physical elements (buildings and sites) that aggregate into chaotic, psychologically unhealthy wholes. This is because most decision-makers are designing the city by using a Cartesian design-the-piece paradigm. Many are also capriciously pursuing new styles, rather than focusing on the management of environmental quality and richness of human experience. These people see the task at hand as the design of the project, rather than the phenomenological whole. They often see the project as form or as design statement, not as creative response to condition. They design buildings and sites rather than landscapes, and sometimes they mistakenly define design as form-generation, not experience making. Finally, they concentrate on the design of settings or the elements they contain, rather than the *place* that occurs in the mind as the individual experiences and imparts meaning to the settings they designed.

PLACE PERCEPTION

If we are to design psychologically healthy urban settings rather than confusing alienating ones, we must understand the *individual* as an instrument for decoding information, imparting meaning, and emotionally responding to settings. We must also understand *settings* as physical entities with encoded meaning that are read phenomenally as wholes, rather than as aggregates of pieces. With this knowledge, we can set about to manage the mental construct called place that occurs in the mind (Figure 16-1), and can design places that are psychologically healthy and meaningful. In so doing, we will be managing what Christopher Alexander referred to as that "quality without a name"

Figure 16-1. Place as mental construct.

Figure 16-2. Natural expression.

278

(1977), which evolves over time in natural systems (a process that we call succession, Figure 16-2), and which characterizes vernacular design (Figure 16-3). It is to this quality that the individual intuitively responds on a biological or ethological level, when hiking in the woods, visiting quaint hamlets, or strolling through particularly comfortable neighborhoods in almost any city (Figure 16-4).

Figure 16-3. Vernacular expression.

Place

Place is the mental construct of the temporal-spatial experience that occurs as the individual ascribes meaning to settings, through environmental perception and cognition. It involves what is perceived, and the meanings ascribed through mental associations. Place occurs as the synergism of setting, context, previous experience, and mental (emotional) state. It is a phenomenological concept that depends on the inter-relationship of characteristics, and is perceived through the gestalt of stimuli.

The sensing of place is spatial (Figure 16-5). It is also temporal, that is, it ebbs and flows with user movement, changes in setting (or the manner in which these are displayed), and changes in emotional state (Figure 16-6).

In cognizing place, the individual ascribes two types of meaning. The first, perceptual meaning, depends on the individual's ability to image place, which Kevin Lynch (1960) referred to as the *imageability* of the setting. The second, associational meaning, occurs as the individual relates what is perceived to previous experience, at both the preconscious and the conscious level. Much attention has been given to associational meanings in design texts such as *Meanings in Western*

Figure 16-4. Neighborhood-ness.

Figure 16-5. Spatial perception.

Figure 16-6. Temporal perception.

Architecture (1975) and *Genius Loci: Towards a Phenomenology of Architecture* (1980), wherein Norberg-Schulz defines architecture as "giving meaning concrete presence through the construction of buildings." Far less has been written in the design professions about the perceptual characteristics that allow the user to perceive and be sensitive to these meanings. To develop this understanding, the designer must usually explore literature in the fields of environmental psychology and geography.

Environmental Perception, Affect, and Cognition

Environmental perception is the process by which the individual acquires information through decoding environmental cues; *affect* is the individual's appraisal of a setting; and *cognition* is the process whereby the viewer evaluates, ascribes meaning to, and constructs a mental image of place. According to Kaplan (1987), the individual needs to understand and explore the world, and desires to apply the fruits of this exploration to construct greater understanding and meaning. The individual, however, has a limited ability to process information, and through this processing to ascribe meaning (Worchel and Shebilske, 1986).

Human Needs and Motivation

To be psychologically healthy, designed environments must satisfy basic human needs. According to Maslow, these needs are hierarchical. Biological and physiological needs form the base of this hierarchy, with more complex psychological needs at its apex (1970). According to Maslow, the lower-level biological and physiological needs must be *relatively* satisfied before the psychological ones become significant.

As a result of their basic hierarchical needs, individuals make two types of demands on their environments (Figure 16-7). First, they demand that settings be legible and understandable (Lynch, Kaplan), thereby addressing user needs for safety and security. Second, they demand that settings provide opportunities for involvement, thereby satisfying the individual's need to explore and to motivate oneself to action. If the design satisfies both types of demands, the user will be motivated to seek new information, and to use this information to develop increased levels of understanding and environmental meaning (Wohlwill 1976).

Imageability

Image formation reduces perceived complexity by aggregating parts into some recognizable pattern. In so doing, imaging reduces information load. In addition, once images are formed, they become the pattern to which meanings are ascribed. Mental images and patterns are also stored in the mind, based on past experience. The synergism of environmental stimuli with these stored patterns affect place perception and the formation of images. The task of the landscape designer is to create settings with characteristics that synergize with stored constructs in some positive manner and that facilitate image formation.

Cognition

The ability to cognize place from setting, the *imageability* (Lynch) of the place, is limited by the viewer's ability to process information. In the *Image of the City*, Kevin Lynch identifies five basic elements that con-

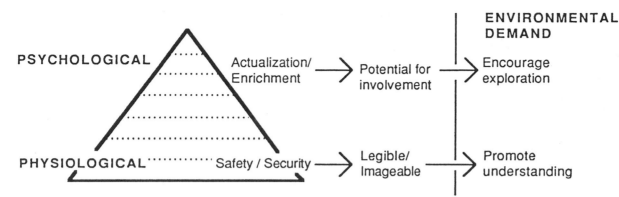

Figure 16-7. Human need and environmental demand.

Figure 16-8. Supersign. Material, proportion, form, capital, base, and so forth combine to form supersign, to which we ascribe meaning concerning purity of form, honesty, nobility, and the like.

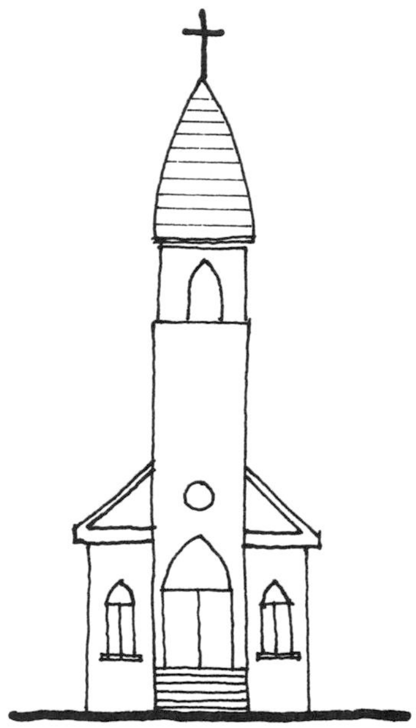

Figure 16-9. Architectural typology.

tribute to the imageability of cities to be "edges, nodes, districts, paths and landmarks." Christopher Alexander, taking a different approach in *A Pattern Language* (1977) and *The Timeless Way of Building* (1979) focuses on the manner in which diverse elements synergize to form patterns and the taxonomies of form that recur as pattern expressions.

As we process visual information, we do so by "chunking" large amounts of stimuli together to form a reduced number of visual units (Miller 1956), thereby reducing perceived complexity and information load (Figure 16-8). We process these chunks deeper as "supersigns," and ascribe meaning to the supersigns as visual symbols that represent, evoke, and

communicate these deeper meanings (Findlay and Fields 1982). In the environmental design professions, we typically refer to designed supersigns as *typologies* (Figure 16-9). The preceding process of chunking, ascribing meaning to supersigns, and identifying typologies allows the viewer to replace large amounts of environmental data with a reduced number of visual units, and by so doing to reduce information load, facilitate information processing, and increase environmental understanding and the individual's ability to ascribe meaning. We should also keep in mind that as we process information, we impose meaning based on experience and patterns that reside in the mind. These mental constructs vary with the individual (constituting the individual's consciousness) and the group (collective consciousness). There are also universal (ethological) characteristics of mental constructs. We should also be sensitive to the fact that as designers, we have somewhat different experiences concerning design and therefore different stored patterns from those of users.

Recent evidence implies that cognition is a two-stage process (Nasar 1987), as shown in Table 16-1, and that the individual's appraisal of a setting is to a large degree precognitive (Zajonc 1980). This precognitive stage, based on a nearly instantaneous response to overall shapes or patterns in the environment, is believed to be rooted in our evolutionary need for rapid appraisal and action for survival and security (Appleton 1975; Kaplan). This need is the basis of Appleton's prospect and refuge theory, which contends that we intuitively prefer places that afford us both prospect over our surroundings and refuge from others (Figure 16-10). It is also the basis of other ethologically based theories of cognition. These theories explain, for example, why most people prefer to walk along the edge of large spaces, rather than be exposed by moving across them. At the precognitive level of perception, chunking and the formation of supersigns are essential, as the user's primary need is for a nearly instantaneous intuitive sense of environmental understanding, which provides a sense of security and satisfies lower-order basic human needs (Figure 16-11).

The second, or cognitive, phase of perception involves the decoding of environmental cues that reside in objects and their relations. In this stage, the user has already established an intuitive understanding of the place, and a sense of security. The user's need for

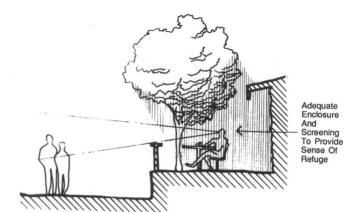

Figure 16-10. Prospect-refuge.

Figure 16-11. Precognitive understanding.

Table 16-1. Two-stage perceptual process.

Precognitive	Cognitive
Nearly instantaneous appraisal and action for survival ↓	Need to sustain interest and discover more information ↓
Satisfies need to understand ↓	Satisfies need to explore ↓
Based on overall shapes and patterns "preferenda" ↓	Based on detail and subtleties ↓
Chunking, supersigns, and typologies are essential ↓	Breaks in the pattern; anomalies are essential ↓
Conveys primarily perceptual meaning	Conveys associational meaning; deeper processing of meaning

understanding, therefore, gives way to a need for enrichment and a desire to explore, discriminate, decode information, attribute associational meaning, and process information more deeply (Figure 16-12).

Relatedness, Order, and Spontaneity

The design of cities is achieved incrementally through the activities of diverse individuals, with differing motivations and resources, operating over long periods of time. The result is usually a highly spontaneous, though often chaotic, urban environment, which is difficult for the user to image and understand, and is therefore alienating.

We propose that design should promote urban imageability, increased understanding, and greater exploration by facilitating the ability to chunk, form symbols, ascribe meaning, and image place. This ability is affected by the degree to which individual elements in a setting, and their characteristics, relate

Figure 16-12. Cognition and exploration.

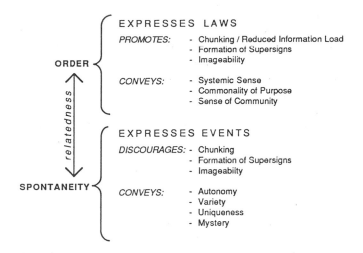

Figure 16-13. Order and spontaneity.

(Ryan 1976). To achieve the objective of psychological health, we can manage this degree by the implementation of appropriate planning and design processes, guidelines and standards. More understandable and stimulating environments will be the result. These will encourage the user to become more sensitized to stimuli, and thereby increase environmental awareness, sensory pleasure, and quality of experience. This, in turn, will result in greater user understanding of the urban environment, which will encourage increased exploration, and the processing of deeper levels of meaning.

Relatedness is the degree to which individual elements in a setting, and their characteristics relate (Ryan); and order and spontaneity can be seen as polar extremes of a relatedness continuum. Together they determine the ability of the individual to relate stimuli, to chunk information and form symbols, to ascribe meaning to these symbols as supersigns, and to image place. Order here is defined as any characteristic that increases the mind's ability to place an individual element or characteristic into a recognizable pattern. Order is increased by redundancy, confirmation, assimilation, and the perception of interaction among elements. Spontaneity, on the other hand, is perceived as a break in the pattern. It is increased by novelty, contradiction, counterpoint, and the perception of an absence of conscious or predetermined relationships.

Together, order and spontaneity determine the degree of visual continuity, and the complexity and information load of a setting (Ulrich 1983, Mehrabian and Russell 1974). They also interrelate to address the individual's simultaneous needs for understanding and exploration. Order increases visual continuity and promotes chunking, the formation of symbols and supersigns, and legibility. It conveys a systemic sense, a commonality of purpose, and a sense of community, while also reducing information load, increasing precognitive understanding, and encouraging involvement. Spontaneity conveys a sense of autonomy, variety, uniqueness, and sometimes mystery while decreasing continuity, discouraging chunking and the formation of symbols and supersigns, and encouraging exploration and the resultant development of deeper meaning (Figure 16-13).

In the precognitive stage, overall patterns that convey order promote understanding and the nearly instantaneous perception of safety and security. In this phase, perception is affected primarily by overall environmental shapes and patterns. Nearly instantaneous understanding is therefore most sensitive to overall design variables such as landscape patterns, vegetative massing, urban form, street rhythms, scale, colors, materials, building height, building proportion, shape, and roof shape. These variables can be highly effective in satisfying the human precognitive, ethological need for environmental understanding.

In the cognitive phase, the user's need for understanding has already been satisfied, and the emphasis shifts to exploration and decoding of associational meaning to develop deeper levels of understanding and meaning. In this phase, smaller-scale variables such as architectural details, street furniture, texture, and landscape detail are more effective in promoting exploration and self-actualization. Subtle variations of stimuli are also very effective.

Stress

According to Mehrabian and Russell (1974), stress is an emotional state characterized by high arousal and low pleasure. It is a response to environmental stimuli, the individual's goals, and his or her ability to adapt to or cope with differences between the two (Baum, Singer, and Baum 1981; Lazarus 1982).

Information overload is a source of environmental stress (Berlyne 1960; Mehrabian and Russell 1974; Wohlwill 1974); and many people feel that the urban environment is pushing the limit of one's ability to cope with, and adapt to, information overload and the resulting cumulative stress (Dubos 1965). This overload of information leads to cognitive fatigue (Singer and Glass 1972), desensitization to setting, and decreased environmental awareness. The result is decreased sensory pleasure and degraded quality of experience.

Recent research leads us to believe that the relevancy of environmental information is extremely critical. It is currently believed that the relevancy of information is even more important than its amount, and that stimuli that do not contribute to our ability to ascribe positive meaning are highly frustrating and stressful (Kaplan 1989).

User and Designer Perceptions, Motivations, and Demands on Settings

One of the greatest difficulties of developing designed environments that promote user understanding and exploration and the conveyance of rich associations and meaning is the differing needs, motivation, and education of the designer and the user, and the resulting differences in perception and cognition between the two. In many cases, the designer places self-expression high as a motive force, has an academic or intellectualized approach to encoding and decoding meaning, and sees the specific design project, rather than the phenomenon of place (synergism of setting and individual), as the entity being designed. The user, on the other hand, is motivated to understand and explore, has a less intellectualized and more intuitive approach to decoding meaning,

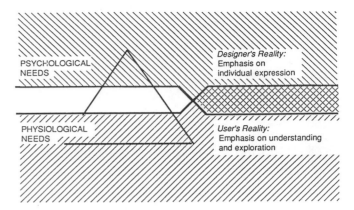

Figure 16-14. User and designer perception.

Figure 16-15. The grand tradition of design.

and perceives and ascribes meaning to the perceptual phenomena of place rather than specific elements or projects (Figure 16-14). Often, the designer's intellectualized vocabularies and processes for decoding architectural and environmental meaning result in a focus on monuments and on what Amos Rapoport (1969) referred to as the grand tradition of design (Figure 16-15), while the user's innate vocabularies and

Figure 16-16. The vernacular tradition of design.

processes maximize the ability to understand and impart meaning to vernacular expressions (Figure 16-16).

Place Preference

According to Hebb's preferred arousal theory (1949), people prefer settings with a desired level of stimulus. Places with an acceptable information load, and settings that allow the individual to affect their information load (open-ended design) by moving furniture, changing colors, or other means, promote personalization and therefore offer opportunities to satisfy user needs for self-actualization. They are perceived to have high placeness, and are highly preferred. Unfortunately, the contemporary American city is characterized by inappropriate information load, close-ended design, and informational irrelevancy. At the level of overall environmental patterns, the overriding chaos frustrates our need to understand, and discourages the approach behavior necessary to explore and appreciate spontaneity. At the detail level, design is overly ordered, bland, and lacking in spontaneity. It fails to provide adequate stimulus to explore and thereby gain greater understanding and deeper meaning. This dual failure occurs because designers overdesign the piece (excessive order), which results in a lack of stimulation at the detail scale, while failing to relate piece to context (excessive spontaneity), which results in chaos at the larger urban pattern scale.

Proxemic and Distemic Space

As we discuss environmental stimuli, information load, and informational relevancy, we should do so in the context of proxemic and distemic space. In proxemic space (the homogeneous neighborhood or the home space), the individual feels safe and secure. Here lies an opportunity to shape the local habitat to satisfy the individual's need for self-expression, especially on the detail scale. As we do so, we must overcome the limitations of standardized construction, and the professional designer's ego, which have functioned in the past to limit the response to the user's need for self-expression.

At the other end of the scale, in heterogeneous distemic space, the user's need shifts to understanding, and a need for simplicity and legibility. According to Greenbie (1981), however, "the larger urban landscape has become a bewildering catchall of discordant elements, without perceptible structure and clear means for orientation for the traveler, as anyone leaving an expressway to enter the typical large city for the first time knows very well." The distemic space of the large city is overly complex, and lacks the necessary cues to facilitate its imaging and legibility by diverse groups of people who are unfamiliar with its spaces and structure. In this case, there is a need for design to be managed for greater understanding.

PLACEMAKING

Placemaking is the cognitive process of perceiving settings, ascribing meaning to these settings, and constructing a mental image of place. *Placeness* refers to the innate ability of a setting to encourage the formation of mental images and to effect major changes in emotional state. *Sense of place* is the mental construct that emerges from these characteristics and their interrelationships. Places with a strong sense, said to have high placeness, are also usually able to be recalled over long periods of time. *Placelessness* refers to the inability of a setting to encourage the formation of vivid images, and to effect major emotional change over long periods of time. Places characterized by placelessness are not usually very memorable.

Amos Rapoport (unpublished paper) has developed a place model that incorporates the perceptual qualities of a setting, cultural traditions, social relations, human activities, and length of residency. In this model, the strength of any given place—its placeness—is related to the degree of interrelatedness among these characteristics. As one establishes relationships and ascribes meaning to a setting, and develops particular emotional and attitudinal responses, the setting becomes place.

The sensing of place is essential to our ability to understand our existence in a holistic manner. Sense of place is also integral to a *sense of community,* which is the mental construct or ambience of a two-way interaction between the place and a group of people. It occurs when a place becomes part of the "collective consciousness" of a group.

Rapoport (1981) also suggests several ways to "make place." These include (1) altering the perceptual characteristics of a setting to make it more noticeably different; (2) using elements and cues that are culturally appropriate; (3) relating elements and cues to known legends, concepts, ideas, or identities of a group; (4) controlling which groups occupy settings, and when they do; and (5) promoting certain behaviors in these settings, and over time associating these behaviors with the setting. Placemaking includes the effective management of the perceptual characteristics of a setting, and its associational meanings. Placemaking employs these five effects to increase the sense of a place.

We now focus on the perceptual characteristics of settings that enhance one's ability to image place and attribute meaning. We leave the more complex and individually variable issue of associational meaning to the excellent texts by Norberg-Schulz and those of other notable authors.

From a perceptual standpoint, placemaking should include the effective management of order and spontaneity for understanding and exploration. In this light, recent research by this author has explored the relatedness expressed by built-environment variables adapted from those identified by Ryan in "The Urban Design of Continuity." These adapted variables included *site characteristics* such as landform, water, and vegetation; *urban pattern* characteristics including structure, form, scale relationships, and circulation; *built-environment conditions* including enclosure, surface character (overhead, vertical, and ground surfaces), spatial development, materials, texture, and color; *architectural characteristics* including building form, height, style, facade character (proportion, rhythm, porosity, directional expression), fenestration (proportion, organization, percentage of wall surface), structural expression, roof shape, details, and expression of change; and *landscape development* including landform modification, introduced water and vegetation, and furnishings. In this recent study, places were observed phenomenologically, and then these specific variables were analyzed for the degree of order and spontaneity they contributed to the setting. The degree to which the variable related visually with other variables was also assessed. Conclusions were drawn concerning the interrelationship of variables in specific cities, and the intercity variability in their expression. This research sought to develop insight concerning relatedness and its effective management for urban placeness (Motloch 1989).

This and other research gives reason to make several conclusions concerning placemaking, order, and spontaneity (Figure 16-17). First, people prefer places that have a simultaneity, balance, and interplay between order and spontaneity; and that tend toward order at the precognitive stage, and spontaneity at the cognitive one. Second, any design variable can contribute order or spontaneity, but certain variables and certain scales are more important in precognition, and others in cognition. This supports the earlier stated belief that certain variables can therefore be more effective in conveying order at the precognitive level without stifling the desire to explore at the cognitive level, and that other variables can more effectively encourage exploration at the cognitive level without creating chaos at the precognitive one. Third, relatedness is phenomenological, and the relatedness expressed by any variable is seen in the context of overall relatedness of the setting and its contents, and in concert with the relatedness conveyed by other variables. Fourth, as the natural environment becomes more overt through dynamic landform, water, or vegetation, a systemic perception of order can be maintained while introducing a highly spontaneous architecture. Conversely, in a more subtle landscape, designed elements must become more systemic, or the setting will likely be incomprehensible. Fifth, when built and natural patterns relate, systemic order and visual continuity increase, allowing greater freedom of detailed expression, while maintaining a strong sense of place. Sixth, designed environments are more preferable when some places function to establish a sense of systemic order (environmental fabric), and others serve as "special places" of concentrated meaning (Norberg-Schulz 1980), and as breaks in this fabric. As concentrations of meaning, and as breaks in the system, these special places can effectively lead the eye to discover their relevant information and special meaning. Order and spontaneity can be managed to maximize the impact of these special places, giving emphasis to expressions that are imbued with special ecological or cultural relevancy and meaning, and thereby increasing the visual satisfaction and pleasure of the built environment. Seventh, the city can be managed for its temporal-spatial richness and diversity, and can provide an ebb and flow of systemic and autonomous expression as one moves. In so doing the designed environment can maximize the communication of meaning, and the dynamic character necessary to provide understanding while encouraging exploration. Finally, existing knowledge of environmental perception and cognition indicates that desired degrees of relatedness can be identified for specific design variables and aggregates of variables, and that these variables can be effectively managed for understanding and exploration of the whole, for

Figure 16-17. Placemaking. Drawing by Ali A. Chowdrury, AIA.

maximum satisfaction of basic human needs, and for a high degree of experiential satisfaction.

Managing Sense of Place

Within the concept of placemaking, psychological health will be a goal of environmental design. Implementing design for psychological health will probably include the effective management of some form of collative variables such as Peter Jacobs's "integrity, identity, imageability and flexibility" (1989) or Stephen Kaplan's "understanding and exploration." To achieve this management, the environmental designer will develop more effective planning and design processes for managing visual continuity, and planning and design guidelines and standards that will achieve the desired degree of relatedness, order, and spontaneity in a given context. These processes, guidelines, and standards will be implemented for effective management of these, or other, collative variables. Designing within the context of these processes, guidelines, and standards, the environmental designer will maxi-

mize the communication of meaning and will increase sensory pleasure and reduce environmental stress. In this manner, the landscape will evolve through the accretion of decisions by many diverse individuals to become a dynamic, rich, diverse, and expressive landscape that will broaden and deepen its meaning.

The sense of place of built environments usually evolves incrementally, through planning and design decisions made by many diverse individuals over extended periods of time. For these environments to be understandable, evocative, meaningful, relevant, and responsive, a shift in design thinking is necessary. This shift will induce the second-order change that is necessary for the institutionalization of health as an urban management goal. Within this new view of design, we can determine appropriate roles and definitions for the environmental planning and design professions, and develop appropriate design frameworks, models, and processes. These will be based on a redefinition of environmental design that will include, as a primary focus, the process of placemaking to maximize the quality of the human experience.

With our current emphasis on project design, the resulting landscape is chaotic, and usually fails to establish a meaningful synergism of context and user. In this condition, the individualized design statement tends to be perceived as just more confusion, and therefore to be inappropriate. In the new phenomenologically sensitive design, however, the individualized design statement can be seen as an urban event displayed as counterpoint to urban fabric. It can be appreciated as a concentration of meaning that will enrich human experience. In this sense, the autonomous expression and the integrative landscape will be synergistic in the making of place.

Developing the sense of a place involves both perceptual and associational characteristics. While the associational aspects are specific to locales and people, perceptual characteristics are somewhat more universally perceived. For that reason, we have limited our discussion to the management of the perceptual characteristics of settings. We have discussed the management of these characteristics in such a manner that users will be encouraged to perceive and impart maximum associational meanings. We have suggested the management of order and spontaneity for their ability to synergize the individualized artistic expression with systemic ones to facilitate the creation, reading, interpretation, and understanding of settings with strong placeness. We have suggested further that the effective management of order and spontaneity, through systemic expressions that interplay with autonomous ones, will communicate more effectively the new organizations that are developing in our current period of dynamic change. It will do so by displaying these new organizations in a coherent, systemic context that facilitates understanding. This is in contrast to the current chaotic urban condition, which fails to communicate effectively, and which desensitizes the viewer, dissuades exploration, conceals meaning, reduces understanding, and decreases sensory pleasure.

By displaying culturally significant expressions in an urban context with appropriate amounts of interrelated information, users will be encouraged to perceive, appraise, and cognize place, and to give appropriate emphasis to the associational meanings that reside in special places. Viewers will become more sensitive to environmental stimuli, and will develop new insight and evolve greater and deeper meaning.

The first step toward achieving greater understanding and deeper meaning in the designed landscape is the development of an understanding of the variables of settings that can be effectively managed, and their relationship to perception, appraisal, and cognition. These variables include building height, proportion, and shape, roof shape, materials, colors, scale, street rhythms, architectural details, street furniture, and landscaping. The second step in increasing understanding is the identification of the desired degrees of relatedness within and among these variables. The third step is the development of specific planning and design guidelines and standards for the effective management of relatedness.

In order to implement these objectives and guidelines, a hierarchical management structure, differentiated by various responsibilities at each level, could be quite effective. The management structure consisting of a three-tiered hierarchy, of the metasystems designer, the systems designer, and the project designer as discussed in Chapter 14 could serve this purpose quite well. In such a structure, the highest tier could identify appropriate meanings and placeness, and coordinate this sense with systems that are spatial, social, fiscal, and political. The intermediate management tier, the systems designer, could manage the visual system (along with others) so as to promote this sense in the making of meaningful places. The lowest tier, that of project design, would implement these management decisions through the project work of the professions of urban design, architecture, and landscape architecture.

A hierarchical management structure and design processes that are responsive to context can promote the generation of evocative places and sustainable landscapes. To do so, these processes will incorporate the problem solving/functional aspects of conventional design processes. They will also embrace the paradigmatic shifts occurring in our society and innovative processes currently being explored. Finally, they will function to synergize the knowledge-bases of diverse professions, through a synergism of planning and design into evocative, sustainable placemaking.

REFERENCES

Alexander, Christopher. 1977. *A Pattern Language: Towns, Buildings, Construction.* New York: Oxford University Press.

———. 1979. *The Timeless Way of Building.* New York: Oxford University Press.

Appleton, Jay. 1975. *The Experience of Landscape.* New York: Wiley.

Baum, Andrew, Singer, Jerome, and Baum, Carlene. 1981. Stress and the Environment. *J. of Soc. Iss.* 37:4–35.

Berlyne, Daniel. 1960. *Conflict, Curiosity and Arousal.* New York: Appleton-Century-Crofts.

Dubos, Rene. 1965. *Man Adapting.* New Haven: Yale University Press.

Findlay, R. A. and Field, K. F. 1982. Functional Roles of Visual Complexity in User Perception of Architecture. P. Bart, A. Chen, and G. Francescato, editors. *13th International Conference of the Environmental Design Research Association.* College Park, MD: EDRA.

Greenbie, Barrie. 1981. *Spaces: Dimensions of the Human Landscape.* New Haven: Yale University Press.

Hebb, D. O. 1949. *The Organization of Behavior.* New York: Wiley.

Jacobs, Peter. 1989. Cultural Values in the Changing Landscape. Paper read at the First CUBIT International Symposium on Architecture and Culture. College Station, TX, Texas A&M University.

Kaplan, Stephen. 1987. Aesthetic, Affect and Cognition: Environmental Preference From an Evolutionary Perspective. *Env. Behav.* 19 (1):3–33.

Lazarus, Richard. 1982. Thoughts on the Relation of Emotion and Cognition. *Am. Psychol.* 37:1019–1024.

Lynch, Kevin. 1960. *Image of the City.* Cambridge, MA: MIT Press.

Maslow, Abraham. 1970. *Motivation and Personality,* 2d ed. New York: Harper & Row.

Mehrabian, Albert, and Russell, James. 1974. *An Approach to Environmental Psychology.* Cambridge, MA: MIT Press.

Miller, G. A. 1956. The Magical Number Seven Plus or Minus Two: Some Limits on our Capacity to Process Information. *Psychol. Rev.* 62:81–97.

Motloch, John. 1989. Placemaking, Order, and Spontaneity. *EDRA20: Annual Conference of the Environmental Design Research Association.* Black Mountain, GA.

Norberg-Schulz, Christian. 1980. *Genius Loci: Towards a Phenomenology of Architecture.* New York: Rizzoli.

Norberg-Schulz, Christian. 1975. *Meaning in Western Architecture.* London and New York: Praeger.

Proshansky, H. M., Ittelson, W. H., and Rivlin, L. G. 1969. *Environmental Psychology.* New York: Holt, Rinehart and Winston.

Rapoport, Amos. 1969. *House Form and Culture.* Englewood Cliffs, NJ: Prentice-Hall.

———. 1981. *The Meaning of the Built Landscape.* Beverly Hills, CA: Sage.

———. 1985. Place, Image and Placemaking. Paper read at the Conference on Placemaking. Melbourne.

Ryan, D. M. 1976. The Urban Design of Continuity. Dissertation in Architecture. Philadelphia: University of Pennsylvania.

Singer, Jerome, and Glass, David. 1972. *Urban Stress: Experiments on Noise and Social Stressors.* New York: Academic Press.

Ulrich, Roger. 1983. Aesthetic and Affective Response to Natural Environment. I. Altman and J. F. Wohlwill, eds. *Hum. Behav. Env.* 6:85–125.

Wohlwill, Joachim. 1976. Environmental Aesthetics: The Environment as a Source of Effect. I. Altman and J. F. Wohlwill, eds. *Hum. Behav. and Env.* (1):37–87.

Worchel, Stephen, and Shebilske, Wayne. 1986. *Psychology, Principles and Applications.* Englewood Cliffs, NJ: Prentice-Hall.

Zajonc, Robert. 1980. Feeling and Thinking: Preferences Need No Inferences. *Am. Psychol.* 35 (2):151–175.

SUGGESTED READINGS

Arnheim, Rudolph. 1977. *The Dynamics of Architectural Form.* Berkeley: University of California Press.

Berlyne, D. E., Craw, M. S., Salapatek, P. H., and Lewis, J. L. 1963. Novelty, Complexity, Incongruity, Extrinsic Motivation and the GSR. *J. Exper. Psychol.* 66: 560–567.

Craik, K. H. 1975. Individual Variations in Landscape Description. *Landscape Assessment: Values, Perspectives and Resources.* E. H. Zube, R. O. Brush, and J. G. Fabos, editors. Stroudsburg, PA: Dowdon, Hutchinson & Ross.

Ittelson, W. 1973. *Environment and Cognition.* New York: Seminar Press.

Jackson, John. 1984 *Discovering the Vernacular Landscape.* New Haven, CT: Yale University Press.

Kaplan, Stephen. Cognitive Maps, Human Needs, and the Designed Environment, W. F. E. Preiser, ed. EDRA4: *Fourth International Conference of the Environmental Design Research Association.* Stroudsburg, PA: Halsted Press.

Meinig, D. W. 1979. *The Interpretation of Ordinary Landscapes.* New York: Oxford University Press.

Motloch, John, and Holloway, John. 1988. *Sense of Place of Italian Cities.* Video. College Station, TX: Texas A&M University.

Nairn, I. 1965. *The American Landscape: A Critical View.* New York: Random House.

Nasar, Jack. 1987. The Affect of Sign Complexity and Coherence on the Perceived Quality of Retail Scenes. *J. Am. Planning Assoc.* 53 (4).

Relph, Edward. 1976. *Place and Placelessness.* London: Pion Press.

Seamon, David, and Mugerauer, Robert, eds. 1985. *Dwelling, Place and Environment: Toward a Phenomenology of Person and World.* Dordrecht, The Netherlands: Martin Nijhoff.

Simonds, John. 1983. *Landscape Architecture: A Manual of Site Planning and Design.* New York: McGraw-Hill.

Smardon, R., Palmer, J., and Fellman, J. 1986. *Foundations for Visual Project Analysis.* New York: Wiley.

Smith, Hadley. 1988. Paper read at Texas A&M University. College Station, TX.

Steele, Fritz. 1981. *Sense of Place.* Boston: CBI.

Tuan, Yi-Fu. 1974. *Topophilia.* Englewood Cliffs, NJ: Prentice-Hall.

Glossary

Abstraction. The process of eliminating from consideration some of the attributes of the physical world, concentrating on other aspects, and reconstructing these aspects so as to intensify imagination.

Acculturation. The process beginning in infancy whereby an individual acquires the culture of society, learns appropriate social behavior, and learns cultural meanings attributed to specific sensual stimuli. It is on this cultural base that the individual builds a cognitive model of the world.

Affect. The individual's appraisal of a setting.

Anthropocentrism. A world view that sees humans as the center of the universe. In this mindset, humans are dominant over nature, and nature exists to serve the needs of people. The environment has value only in its ability to serve; it exists to be exploited for human use and benefit.

Anthropomorphism. A view that sees humans as the primary form giver. Humans determine and give meaning to form.

Appreciative system. A system that realizes man as a "unique device for relating to a reality in whose shaping . . . (he or she) is actively and creatively participating" (Jantsch, 1975).

Appropriateness. The degree to which designed environments sustain and enhance the ecological and cultural environment.

Aquifer. A geological strata that stores and transports groundwater.

Architectonic. In the character of or organized according to the principles of architecture.

Architectural morphology. The form and structure of architecture.

Asymmetrical balance. Balance by establishing an equal visual weighing through the manipulation of dissimilar variables.

Balanced multiple-use ethic. The land ethic espoused by scientific conservationists who believe that certain lands should be used for a variety of purposes but managed so as to conserve them for future generations. The essence of this view is a balance between use and management. Proponents of this view believe that as the level of use and subsequent degradation increase, so too must the level of management to mitigate deleterious effects.

Big Idea. The intellectual idea that underlies a conceptual design.

Biome system. A concept developed by biogeographers. A system of global patterns of flora and fauna, organized into zones of biotic response to similar sets of resources. Serves as an organizational and analytical model that facilitates the transfer of ecologically based technologies that correlate human need and support systems with the region's biotic life and physical support system. Various cultures on the face of the earth that share the same biome can be studied to develop a better understanding of the interrelatedness of earth resources and alternative technologies.

Carrying capacity. The population or amount of activity that can be supported by a given system without that system undergoing degradation.

Cartesian design mindset. Named after the French philosopher René Descartes, this mindset perceives the professional task and societal value of design as that of designing elements and pieces (projects). Usually reduces design to a singular issue of form or aesthetic, rather than the integrative and complex ones of ecological and human health, and human experience.

Cartesian philosophy. Based on the teachings of René Descartes, this philosophy sees reality as based on rational, inductive science, but in a reductive, absolute sense.

Chaos theory. A scientific theory that asserts that a few variables can generate fundamental randomness and that more information does not (as a rational science would predict) eliminate randomness. The science of chaos orders reality not by euclidean principles, but by underlying processes and continuities of behavior that express themselves at all scales and times. Although the science of chaos is mathematical, it explains the complex form and behavior of the everyday world.

Chemical weathering. Occurs primarily as minerals that were formed underground, often under intense heat and pressure, chemically decompose at the earth's surface conditions. The rate of chemical decay depends on climate, tectonics, rock composition, and time. It often accelerates in the chemically enriched urban environment. Chemical weathering dominates in humid climates.

Cognition. The process whereby the viewer evaluates, ascribes meaning to, and constructs a mental image of place. Recent evidence implies cognition to be a two-phased process consisting of precognition (based on a near-instantaneous response to overall patterns) and a cognitive phase (deeper processing of information).

Comfort (physiological). The absence of physiological stress. The sensation that results from a preferred combination of temperature, radiant energy, humidity, and windspeed.

Communalism. A world view that focuses on social interrelatedness and perceived obligations between the individual and others within a society. This view gives the collective community body great power in determining what types of individual behavior and decision-making are appropriate. Individuals are psychologically fused with others in the culture: there is a social consciousness. Individual health and well-being are perceived as inextricably linked with the health and well-being of others and the health and wellness of the society. This view promotes community expressions, as the collective consciousness of the landscape takes precedent over individual expressions.

Consumptive tradition. A cultural tradition characterized by exploitive approaches to farming, ranching, timber and mineral extraction, and manufacturing. It has focused attention on the use of non renewable resources and on maximum short-term gain. It has paid little attention to long-term system health or sustainability.

Contour interval. The vertical dimension of separation (usually consistent) of consecutive contour lines on a contour plan.

Contour line. Lines of equal elevation. Consecutive contour lines on a plan usually have a consistent vertical separation.

Cultural perception. The world view that provides the philosophical underpinnings of a culture and that influences basic attitudes concerning the meaning of mankind, man-nature relations, social interaction, economics, and time.

Cyclical time. The perception that past, present, and future are inextricably bound by temporal cycles. This belief is usually reflected in cultural values and expressions, including landscape design expressions that integrate past, present, and future.

Design ethic. The set of moral principles or values that guide the designer's actions.

Design goal. A desired result from a planning or design activity. Generally not quantifiable.

Design guideline. Directions to be pursued through design, which promote the realization of some design objective.

Design objective. A specific desired result that is measurable and achievable. Intended to lead toward the satisfaction of design goals.

Design paradigms. World views held by the designer. These views affect design decisions, and thereby the character, function, and sustainability of the designed landscape.

Design standard. Specific quantity, quality, or condition necessary to address a design guideline and promote attainment of a design objective.

Detention structures. Physical structures that collect stormwater (usually development-generated) and detain it, metering outflow from the reservoir, usually at the predevelopment rate of runoff. Detention structures allow the total amount of runoff, but not its rate, to increase as development occurs.

Dissipative structures. Structures that often occur in systems that are undergoing rapid, profound, and fundamental change. These systems promote the formation of radically new relationships and are characterized by conflict, contradiction, and stress. The dissipative structures that form function to maximize both the extent and rate of change and to dissipate energies by maximizing change and contradiction.

Distemic space. Spaces shared by culturally diverse subgroups with differing values, codes of conduct, myths, symbols, and cognitive attitudes. The behavior of one group can be expected to infringe upon that of another. Overt behavior must be controlled by explicit behavioral cues, rules, ordinances, and external policing. Usually only behavior that harms other people or their property is forbidden.

Diurnal rhythms. The rhythm of day and night (light and darkness) that greatly affects landscape perception and design.

Drainage pattern. The pattern of surface flow of water within a watershed.

Dwelling. A term used by Heidegger that "signifies the way we human beings are of the earth." The associational and emotional level at which the individual intuitively relates to the designed environment.

Early successional. In the early stages of a predictable sequence of change.

Early successional cultural systems. Cultural systems that adopt short-term effectiveness as their competitive strategy. These systems tend to be successful in periods of resource abundance, because they use the surplus to grow rapidly. This is the basic strategy (in nature) of early successional ecosystems.

Eastern world view. A dynamic world view based on continuums and complementarities. In this view, reality is not absolute. All manifestations of reality are generated by the dynamic interplay of opposing forces, such as the Yin and the Yang. There is a oneness with context that leads to experiencing life as an on going dialogue, a desire to maximize environmental quality, and a long-term value system.

Ecological ethic. A land ethic that seeks to balance human needs and those of other life forms, with the central intent being the maintenance of the carrying capacity of the system.

Ecological forces. Natural forces that group themselves into three categories: geological (tectonic, hydrologic, glacial, wind and weathering) processes; soil-forming processes; and biological processes. These processes interact to form an ecological system, that is, an ecosystem. Change is the essence of these systems. Through the process called succession, ecological forces, operating through time, evolve our rich and varied landscapes.

Ecological system. The structure and function of the non living (abiotic) and living (biotic) components of an area. Within the system, parts relate holistically. Ecosystems evolve over time toward greater order, complexity, and stability, and efficient utilization of energy.

Ecosystem concept. Advanced by A. G. Tansley in 1935. The fundamental concept of ecological study, and one of the underlying concepts of landscape design. According to this concept, an ecosystem is the interacting assemblage of life forms and their non living environment.

Ecosystematic design. A design ethic (Lyle 1983) based on predictions of the consequences of design decisions. According to this ethic, decisions are based on the structural and functional forms that these decisions introduce into the landscape.

Ecotones. The interfaces of two or more ecological zones, generally highly valued as wildlife habitat and animal movement zones.

Economic ethic. An ethic that sees land as an economic resource. Seeks to make land resources available for use and is often operative when the level of technology is low and the environment is harsh. Predominates in technologically advanced societies that perceive the human role to be dominion over the earth or that perceive resource to be that which provides short-term economic gain.

Elasticity. The property of a material that requires a continued external force to change its shape. Conversely, the characteristic of the material to return to its original shape after an external force is removed.

Elements of visual form. Visual characteristics which can be manipulated to elicit mental responses.

Enclosure. The perceived degree of separation of a space from its surrounding condition.

Energy. The capacity to do work.

Entropy. The universal tendency toward disorder.

Environmental perception. The process by which the individual acquires information through decoding environmental cues.

Equilibrium structures. Structures (usually occurring in systems that are in a state of equilibrium) that function to reinforce the existing conditions and perpetuate, extend, or subtly evolve existing relationships, and the status quo. These structures generally have fine-tuned relationships and few internal conflicts. They change slowly, and their parts change together interactively. They function to maintain a dynamic equilibrium.

Ethological approach. Contends that a large portion of human behavior can best be accounted for as resonances of dispositions that were acquired in human's evolutionary past, in relationships with a more primitive environment.

Euclidean geometry. Geometry that is mathematically static. Includes rectilinear, angular, and circular geometries, and their three-dimensional counterparts.

Evolving geometries. Geometries that are mathematically accelerating or decelerating. Natural form is characterized by evolving geometries.

Fibonacci series. A set of integers, developed during the thirteenth century, that as it progresses, approximates the golden section. Occurs repeatedly in plant and animal forms and elsewhere in nature.

Formative influences. Entities that impart order, and give form and meaning to the landscape. The character of the built landscape, its form, material, scale, texture, and spirit are responses to these form-giving influences.

Fractal geometry. Benoit Mandelbrot's concept grew from the realization that scientific method and euclidean geometry, in their effort to classify and simplify, did not adequately represent the scale independence or complexity of natural forms and systems. In fractal geometry, the level of complexity increases as the scale increases, so that apparent complexity remains consistent. Occurring in nature, fractals express a behavior or form irrespective of scale. Fractals are part of the new science of chaos.

Geological processes. Processes by which rocks are formed, differentiated, eroded, and deposited to be reformed again into rocks. They involve tectonic forces (the forces powered from within the earth due to radioactive decay) and erosional and weathering forces.

Golden section. A proportional relationship whereby the smaller part of a whole is to the larger part, as the larger part is to the whole. Believed by early Greeks to be the perfect proportional relationship and to play an important role in the proportion of the human body. The Greeks proportioned their temples according to this relationship.

Grading. Modifications to existing landform. Grading is performed to achieve drainage, to cause water to flow away from buildings or site use areas, to create desired visual effects, and for a wide range of other reasons.

Grand tradition of design. The subconsciously conceived, professionally designed component of the total landscape, including its monumental and overt buildings. The stock in trade of the professional designer, who seeks to communicate the uniqueness of man. The high art that is generally taught in schools of design. It is based on an anthropomorphic mindset.

Gravity-flow systems. Systems which operate under the influence of gravity and which are dependent on landform for their function. The form of these systems, including those for storm and sanitary sewerage, is tied directly to topography.

Groined vault. The structural form that results when two vaults intersect at a right (90°) angle.

Groundwater. Water below the surface of the land, between particles and in fractures, moving slowly downhill under the influence of gravity, where permeability allows.

Habitat. The set of environmental conditions that affect the life of plants and animals. The type of place where an organism usually lives.

Hachures. Lines drawn parallel to the lines of steepest slope, connecting consecutive lines of elevation. Perhaps the most visually powerful manner of communicating landform in the two-dimensional plan drawing.

Hardwood. Wood that comes from broad leaf trees, both deciduous and evergreen.

Holistic design. Design that synergizes various physical and cultural influences. Integrative design.

Holistic mindset. Perceives the professional task and societal value of design to be the management of the physical and cultural landscape as integrated systems for increased ecological and human health.

Human ecosystems. A concept (Lyle 1985) that sees development as "man building functioning ecosystems."

Human needs. According to Maslow, a hierarchical set of needs, with biological and physiological needs at the base, and more complex psychological needs at its apex (1970). Lower-level biological and physiological needs must be relatively satisfied before psychological ones become significant. As a result, individuals demand that settings first be legible and understandable (addressing user needs for safety and security), and thereafter that they provide opportunities for involvement (satisfying the need to explore and motivate).

Hydrologic cycle. The movement of water from the ocean to the atmosphere, through rain, across the surface as runoff, through the land as soil water, and through aquifers as groundwater, and back to the sea.

Hydrologic forces. Forces exerted by the movement of water.

Idealistic value system. Sees reality both materially and spiritually. Periods of history characterized by this view, including the Golden Age of Greece and the Renaissance are often unique periods of truth and beauty that achieve a synergism of philosophy, art, and science with place, people, and technology.

Ideational value system. Sees reality as lying beyond the material world, in the spiritual one. Contends that knowledge exists in the inner consciousness; and espouses ideal values, ethics, and truths. This value system expresses itself in Western societies through the Judeo-Christian concept of God, and Platonic ideals, and in Eastern cultures through Taoism, Zen Buddhism, and Hindu beliefs.

Imageability. The ability of a place to form vivid mental images.

Individualism. A world view that sees the individual as self-providing and minimizes communal obligations. The individual has the right to make any decisions that do not limit the rights of others. The health and well-being of the individual is a personal obligation, and the health and well-being of each individual is seen apart from that of others. This view promotes individualistic, overt expressions and (when occurring in a heterogeneous, rapidly changing culture) a visually complex cultural landscape.

Infiltration. The movement of surface water into the ground.

Infrastructure. Systems introduced in industrial and post-industrial societies so that ecological systems can better serve concentrations of people. Includes systems for the movement of people, power, stormwater and wastewater, and information.

Insolation. Incoming solar radiation.

Instantaneous time. View dominated by the present, and instantaneous gratification. Largely the view of American culture, this perception results in short-term decision-making, that is, opting for decisions that maximize gain over a short time period. This perception does not generally promote long-term efficiency.

Land. The solid part of the surface of the earth.

Land ethics. Individual (or cultural) attitudes concerning the relationship of man and environment that lead to perceptions concerning resource. As attitudes change so too do perceptions of resource.

Landform. The three-dimensional relief of the surface of the earth.

Landscape. Point-in-time expressions of ongoing ecological, technological, and cultural processes. An inclusive term, embracing both wilderness and urbanness. Wilderness is natural landscape, suburbia is suburban landscape, and the inner city is urban landscape.

Landscape architecture. A profession whose societal role is the synergism of art and science for the management, planning, and design of the physical and cultural landscape, including its vestal wilderness and its growing urbanness.

Landscape design. The creation of evocative, meaningful, and sustainable landscapes. The conscious process of managing, planning, and physically changing the landscape.

Landscape ecology. A world view that sees elements of the landscape interwoven into a complex interactive whole, consisting of many overlapping niches. In this view, the whole and all of its parts are integrated in function and behavior and are integrated with their context. All parts and the whole are changing in a dynamic equilibrium, and man is but one of these many parts.

Late successional. In the later stages of an evolutionary sequence.

Late successional cultural systems. Cultures that embrace a long-term strategy and that place their emphasis on maintaining the long-term health and productivity of the system. In times of resource scarcity, these cultures have been very successful.

Linear time. The perception of time as moving forward. The past is "that which was"; the present "is"; the future "will be." Seen as three different entities. Present is seen to be derived from the past and affecting the future, but distinctly separate from both.

Long-term thinking. Sees the longer time period as relevant, and selects for behavior that maximizes long-term effectiveness. Places a portion of energies back into the system to sustain it and maximize its carrying capacity over time.

Macroclimate. Climate at the regional scale.

Mechanical weathering. Includes the physical breakage of rocks by wind, water, glaciers, temperature changes, and plant growth. Dominates in dry climates of extreme temperatures.

Mechanics. The science of the study of the action of a force on a mass.

Metabolic planning and design. A concept (Fisk, 1988) that begins with local natural resources and develops processes for preparing these raw materials for human use, while building them into chains (analogous to ecological food chains) that use the outputs (products and wastes) of one metabolic unit as inputs to other units.

Metacrisis. The underlying cause of numerous interrelated crises. The prevasive imbalance which creates a large number of crises indicative of a system breakdown.

Metasystems approach. Hierarchically different levels of decision-making. Specific decisions are made at an object level (project design). Decisions concerning the conditions and processes that promote appropriate object level decisions are made at the metalevel. The metalevel also determines the appropriate range for object level decisions.

Metasystem level of design. The level of design decision-making that functions to integrate physical systems that are generally seen spatially with social, fiscal, and political ones that are not usually seen spatially. Essential in integrating different systems into more holistic place specific decision-making.

Metasystem management. Managing the decision-making environment within which planning and design occurs.

Microclimate. The climate at a specific location. Site-scale climate.

Military crest. An imaginary line that generally parallels (but lies somewhat below) a ridgeline or promontory. Occurs along the upper slopes at a break in slope, is less visible from the distance, and affords good views into the valley. Offers both prospect and refuge. Historically the place where troops would survey the valley without being silhouetted from afar.

Mitigation. To lessen the impact of development, as in the recovery or dedication of land, necessary to compensate for loss of habitat.

Modern architecture. The dominant trend in world architecture in the 1960s and early 1970s. Included a strong desire to avoid subjective meanings and to reduce design to a single (usually functional) statement. In the late 1970s and in the 1980s, designers (especially architects) reacted strongly against modernism, because of its tendencies to reduce meaning to functional terms, and to take its shapes from disciplines such as machine technology, and its inability to develop a coherent visual language.

Naturalistic. Utilizing the evolving lines and forms of nature.

Negative land forms. Land forms generated by, and expressive of, forces that are external to the mass. Includes land forms generated by erosional forces (wind, rain, and ice flows) and weathering forces (physical and chemical decay).

Negentropy *(negative entropy)*. The tendency of biological systems to increase order, organization, complexity, and efficiency, and to therefore increase the amount of energy stored for later re-use.

Newtonian science. A reductive positivist, rational science that seeks to develop understanding of simple pieces and to use that knowledge to build a better understanding of complex wholes. Based on the scientific method of inquiry.

Order. A condition or characteristic that increases the mind's ability to place an individual element or characteristic into a recognizable pattern. Order is increased by confirmation, redundancy, assimilation, and perceived interaction among elements or characteristics.

Pattern recognition. The ability to read the landscape as a pattern, and as cues to the forces that generated that pattern and the character of its elements.

Percentage method. The definition of slope steepness as a percentage, determined by dividing the difference in vertical elevation by the horizontal distance, and then converting this decimal to a percentage.

Perception. The process whereby mental entities are brought forth when sensory stimuli activate latent information in the mind.

Perception-cognition. A process by which sensual stimuli become mental entities.

Photosynthesis. The process whereby plants containing chlorophyll capture solar energy and concentrate a portion of this energy into chemical bonds, making it available to more advanced life forms. Photosynthesis is the crucial first step in the food chain, cycling nutrients through ecosystems and using solar energy to achieve work.

Place. The mental construct of the temporal-spatial experience that occurs as the individual ascribes meaning to settings, through environmental perception and cognition. It involves the setting being perceived, and the meanings being ascribed through mental associations. Place occurs as the synergism of setting, context, previous experience, and mental (emotional) state. It is a phenomenological effect that depends on the interrelationship of the gestalt of stimuli. It is also temporal, that is, it ebbs and flows with user movement, changes in setting (or the manner in which they are displayed), and changes in emotional state.

Placemaking. In a cognitive sense, the process of perceiving settings, ascribing meaning to these settings, and constructing mental images of place. In a design sense, the design of places for the mental constructs that occur in the mind as one experiences the landscape gestalt. Effective placemaking facilitates the design of positive, healthy places.

Placelessness. The inability of a setting to form vivid mental images, and to effect major changes in emotional state over long periods of time. Places characterized by placelessness are not usually very memorable.

Placeness. The innate ability of a setting to form mental images, to affect major changes in emotional state, and to be remembered over extended periods of time.

Plant strata. The various horizontal layers that comprise a plant community, including canopy tree, understory tree, shrub, and ground cover.

Poetic form of architecture. Term coined by architect Michael Graves that addresses form as the embodiment of the myths and rituals of society into three-dimensional forms. Responsive to the figurative, associative, and anthropomorphic attitudes of a culture.

Positive landforms. Landforms generated by and expressive of forces from within the mass.

Positivism. World view that reduces complex entities to their simplest elemental parts and studies those parts to develop an understanding of the whole. Assumes that the sum of the parts does in fact constitute the whole. Reduces complexity and restructures the world in a manner that is more controllable, predictable, and replicable. The rational view of reality upon which newtonian science is built, and the dominant mechanistic view around which present Western culture is structured.

Postmodernism. A 1970s and 1980s reaction against the modern movement, postmodernism has largely abandoned problem-solving as a design approach. Embraces the concepts of design languages, typologies of form, and meanings.

Preservation ethic. A land ethic that promotes the maintenance of land in an undisturbed state. Land serves as a living ecological laboratory with uses limited to non destructive ones. Preserves land for future generations. Harvesting of many natural resources does not occur within this ethic, which is seen by members of the economic ethic as being wasteful of resources.

Pressure-flow systems. Systems in which flow is induced by an external force other than gravity. The form of these systems, including electricity, natural gas, and communication and transportation, is freed from the constraints of topography, except for constraints imposed by gravity-flow systems that may accompany these systems.

Primitive. An approach to design whereby the individual builds structure and infrastructure. Architectural and cultural landscape expressions are extremely consistent, as the cultures tend to be homogeneous and tradition oriented. Over time, forms are subtly adjusted to satisfy cultural, physical, and maintenance needs; and the culture develops an expressive tradition that integrates place, culture, and form.

Principles of visual form. Visual relationships between elements. The perceptual effects they elicited by these relationships.

Profile. Two-dimensional drawing showing the vertical configuration of both the existing and proposed form, in an overlain fashion.

Programming. The definition and analysis of human needs.

Project level of design. The design of the particular building, site, or environmental gesture. Includes most of the current project work of the professions of urban design, architecture, and landscape architecture.

Proportion. Size relationship between piece and piece or between piece and whole.

Prospect and refuge theory. Contends that people have a preference for places that afford the prospect of being able to view the landscape, while simultaneously affording refuge from being seen.

Proxemics. The culturally specific ways in which groups use space, that is, the use of space as an elaboration of culture.

Proxemic space. The homeground space occupied by a homogeneous group with a highly consistent spatial behavior. Policing is accomplished by heavy social pressure; there are few interpersonal conflicts and little need for behavioral cues. Both the social and the physical environment can be extremely complex because they are largely taken for granted because of high familiarity by all users. These areas are usually high in associational meaning.

Reductionism. The tendency to reduce complex data or phenomena to simple terms. Simplification.

Ratio method. The definition of slope steepness as a ratio of horizontal dimension to vertical elevation difference (3:1, 2:1, 1:1). By convention, the second number is the vertical difference, reduced to a factor of 1.

Regional landform. The vocabulary of landform that characterizes a particular region.

Regional landscapes. Regionally differing sets of landscape expressions that holistically respond to a multiplicity of influences.

Relatedness. The degree to which individual elements in a setting, and their characteristics, relate.

Retention structures. Landscape structures that collect storm runoff and store it until it can infiltrate and thereby be retained permanently on site.

Ribbed groin vault. A groined vault where the line of intersection of the two vaults is expressed as two crossing structural diagonal arches.

Ridgeline. Topographic high that divides the landscape into two separate drainage areas called watersheds.

Rubrics. A few physical, geometric, or chemical constraints that usually determine the form options that can occur within a given natural or physical process. Diversity and efficiency are achieved as forms respond to the constraints imposed by these influences, operating within the context of environmental variables such as temperature, humidity, air or fluid flow, and pressure.

Scale. Size in relation to the human or some other unit of measure. The scale of a space consists of two components: its size in relation to the size of its context, and its size in relation to the observer(s).

Seasonal rhythm. The rhythm of symbolic birth, maturation, aging, and death in the seasonal landscape: spring, summer, fall, and winter. In deciduous and cold landscapes, these four seasons express themselves in a dramatic manner, providing a highly varied landscape with four distinct seasonal personalities. In evergreen landscapes and milder climates, change is less dramatic.

Second-order change. Change in the conditions within which decisions are made.

Section. Two-dimensional drawing showing the vertical configuration of either the existing or proposed form.

Semiotics. The science of language and logic. Concerned with the creation of a vocabulary of symbols and the use of these symbols to communicate meaning.

Sensate value system. Contends that matter is reality, sensory perception is truth and knowledge, and that any spiritual phenomenon is merely an expression of a material reality.

Sense of community. The mental construct or ambience of a two-way interaction between a place and a group of people. Occurs when a place becomes part of the collective consciousness of a group.

Sense of place. The mental construct that emerges from characteristics of a setting, their interrelationships, and the associations they evoke. Places with a strong sense, said to have high placeness, are also usually able to be recalled over long periods of time.

Serial vision. Vision as a series of perceptions. The experience of the landscape as a sequence of perceptions, structured in time.

Settings. Physical entities with encoded meaning that are read phenomenally as wholes, rather than as aggregates of pieces. Particular locations, designed or non designed, that are experienced by people.

Short-term thinking. Sees the relevant time period as the near one and makes decisions that maximize short-term benefits. Short-term thinking exploits resources for immediate benefit.

Slope. The amount of incline of a surface, quantified according to two systems. The ratio method of slope description defines slope steepness as a ratio of horizontal distance to vertical elevation difference (3:1, 2:1, 1:1, etc.). The percentage method describes slope as a percentage, determined by dividing the difference in vertical elevation by the horizontal distance and then converting this decimal to a percentage.

Slope aspect or slope orientation. The slope and direction of the land surface. Combines with the vertical angle and planar direction of the sun to determine the relative amount of solar radiation incident upon the ground surface at any given time.

Softwood. Wood that comes from coniferous evergreen plant materials.

Soil-forming processes. The processes by which soil is formed. Consists of mechanical and chemical weathering, and abiotic (non living) and biotic (living) activities.

Spontaneity. A condition perceived as a break in the pattern. Spontaneity is increased by novelty, contradiction, and the absence of perceived conscious or predetermined relationships.

Standard form of building. The common and internal language of a building, determined by practical and constructional requirements.

Statics. A branch of mechanics that deals with the relation of forces that keep a mass at rest or equilibrium.

Stewardship tradition. An ecologically sensitive cultural tradition that focuses attention on the use of renewable resources and the long-term health and sustainability of the landscape.

Story line. The evolving sensory experience of the landscape. Spatial sequence and serial vision are major components of the story.

Stress. An emotional state characterized by high arousal and low pleasure. A response to environmental stimuli, individual goals, and one's ability to adapt to, or cope with, differences between the two.

Succession. The natural tendency of biological systems to change over time in response to available energy and resources. The organizational sequence through which natural systems evolve over time toward greater order, complexity, and stability, and toward a more efficient utilization of the energy resource.

Successional rhythms. The long-term landscape rhythms of succession, including pioneering, establishment, early succession, late succession, perturbance, and reinvasion. Somewhat predictable, with a rate of progression related to climate.

Sustainable development. Development ethic that sees the value of any human decision to be its contribution to ecosystem health and long-term viability and productivity. Promotes long-term value systems, economics, and policy incentives. Locates activities in landscapes most suited for them; prohibits activities from ecosystems innately unsuited for them; preserves lands particularly suited for critical uses (such as prime agricultural lands); and manages lands for the avoidance and mitigation of impacts. Makes point-in-time decisions based on long-term effects and holistic cost-benefit analyses.

Sustainability. The ability of a landscape or a planning or design decision to sustain the carrying capacity of the system of which it is a part, without additional intervention and without resource depletion or system degradation.

Symmetrical balance. Balance of compositions as mirror images across a central axis.

Synergism. "Cooperative actions of discrete agencies such that the total effect is greater than the sum of the effects taken independently" (Webster's *New World Dictionary*). Assumes that two or more agencies benefit from each other's strengths and apply these strengths to overcome their respective weaknesses. Dependent upon a symbiotic relationship of intimate interaction, and on mutually beneficial association.

Systems level of design. The level of decision-making that functions to manage physical systems and their integration for sustainable and meaningful places.

Taxonomy (of form). The systematic ordering of form into group types.

Tectonic forces. Forces powered from within the earth, that function to move the geological plates of the earth, and in so doing to create regions of tectonic activity. In some of these regions, the earth's crust is being destroyed; in others it is being twisted, contorted or broken; in still others new crust is being created.

Temporal networks. Design as the structuring of human experience over time.

Temporal rhythms. Cyclical landscape changes on either a regular or irregular basis.

Topoclimate. Climate as affected by landform.

Topography. (landform). The three-dimensional relief of the surface of the earth.

Triangular networks. Organizational patterns that facilitate the closest packing of parts necessary for efficiency. Occur throughout nature, from the packing of hexagonally shaped honeycombs, to soap bubbles, and cellular structures.

Typology (of form). Study of form based upon its type or idealistic morphology.

Vernacular. "The direct and unselfconscious translation into physical form of a culture, its needs and values, as well as the desires, dreams and passions of a people ... the 'ideal' environment of a people expressed in buildings and settlements, with no designer, artist, or architect with an axe to grind." (Rapoport, 1969). Architecture that is built by tradesmen, in concert with the resident, so that the dweller is an integral part of the formative process. Form, model, materials, and construction do not change from one building to another. Rather the model is adjusted in response to family requirements, site, microclimate, and so forth.

Viewshed. The expanse that can be viewed from a given location.

Watershed. All the land surface that sheds its water to a given discharge point. Since the area of a watershed is all the area that drains to a given point in a drainageway, and water quantity and quality is an important environmental variable to manage, the watershed is often the most reasonable and effective landscape management unit.

Weathering. The primary mechanism of erosion, consisting of mechanical weathering or decay, and chemical weathering.

Western view. A world view of fixed absolutes. The health of a human is generally seen apart from the health of the environment. Often results in a goal-oriented attitude and a short-term value system.

Wetland. Land surface that is inundated or saturated by surface or groundwater at a frequency and duration necessary to support a prevalence of vegetation adapted for life in saturated soil conditions.

Index